COMPUTER GRAPHICS PROGRAMMING IN OPENGL WITH JAVA

SECOND EDITION

Computer Graphics Programming in OpenGL with Java

Second Edition

V. Scott Gordon, PhD
California State University, Sacramento

John Clevenger, PhD
California State University, Sacramento

Mercury Learning and Information
Dulles, Virginia
Boston, Massachusetts
New Delhi

Publisher: David Pallai

MERCURY LEARNING AND INFORMATION
22841 Quicksilver Drive
Dulles, VA 20166
info@merclearning.com
www.merclearning.com
(800) 232-0223

V. Scott Gordon & John Clevenger.
Computer Graphics Programming in OpenGL with Java, Second Edition
ISBN: 978-1-683922-19-3

Library of Congress Control Number: 2018949984

181920321   Printed on acid-free paper in the United States of America.

Contents

Preface

This book is designed primarily as a textbook for a typical computer science undergraduate course in OpenGL 3D graphics programming. However, we have also endeavored to create a text that could be used to teach oneself, without an accompanying course. With both of those aims in mind, we have tried to explain things as clearly and simply as we can. Every programming example is stripped down and simplified as much as possible, but still complete so that the reader may run them all as presented.

One of the things that we hope is unique about this book is that we have strived to make it accessible to a beginner—that is, someone new to 3D graphics programming. While there is by no means a lack of information available on the topic—quite the contrary—many students are initially overwhelmed. This text is our attempt to write the book we wish we had had when we were starting out, with step-by-step explanations of the basics, progressing in an organized manner up through advanced topics. We considered titling the book *Shader Programming Made Easy*; however, we don't think that there really is any way of making shader programming "easy." We hope that we have come close.

This book teaches OpenGL programming in *Java*, using *JOGL*—a Java "wrapper" for OpenGL's native C calls [JO16]. There are several advantages to learning graphics programming in Java rather than in C:

- It is more convenient for students at schools that conduct most of their curriculum in Java.
- Java's I/O, window, and event handling are arguably cleaner than in C.
- Java's excellent support for object-oriented design patterns can foster good design.
- JOGL includes some very nice tools, such as for loading textures, animation loops, etc.

It is worth mentioning that there do exist other Java bindings for OpenGL. One that has become very popular is Lightweight Java Game Library, or **LWJGL** [LW16]. Like JOGL, **LWJGL** also offers bindings for OpenAL and OpenCL. This textbook focuses only on JOGL.

Another thing that makes this book unique is that it has a "sister" textbook: *Computer Graphics Programming in OpenGL with C++*. The two books are organized in lockstep, with the same chapter and section numbers and topics, figures, exercises, and theoretical descriptions. Wherever possible, the code is organized similarly. Of course, the use of Java versus C++ leads to considerable programming differences. Still, we believe that we have provided virtually identical learning paths, even allowing a student to choose either option within a single classroom.

An important point of clarification is that there exist both different *versions* of OpenGL (briefly discussed later) and different *variants* of OpenGL. For example, in addition to "standard OpenGL" (sometimes called "desktop OpenGL"), there exists a variant called "OpenGL ES" which is tailored for development of *embedded systems* (hence the "ES"). "Embedded systems" include devices such as mobile phones, game consoles, automobiles, and industrial control systems. OpenGL ES is mostly a subset of standard OpenGL, eliminating a large number of operations that are typically not needed for embedded systems. OpenGL ES also adds some additional functionality, typically application-specific operations for particular target environments. The JOGL suite of Java bindings includes interfaces for different versions of OpenGL ES, although we do not use them in this book.

Yet another variant of OpenGL is called "WebGL." Based on OpenGL ES, WebGL is designed to support the use of OpenGL in web browsers. WebGL allows an application to use JavaScript[1] to invoke OpenGL ES operations, which makes it easy to embed OpenGL graphics into standard HTML (web) documents. Most modern web browsers support WebGL, including Apple Safari, Google Chrome, Microsoft Internet Explorer, Mozilla Firefox, and Opera. Since web programming is outside the scope of this book, we will not cover any WebGL specifics. Note however that because WebGL is based on OpenGL ES, which in turn is based on standard OpenGL, much of what *is* covered in this book can be transferred directly to learning about these OpenGL variants.

The very topic of 3D graphics lends itself to impressive, even beautiful images. Indeed, many popular textbooks on the topic are filled with breathtaking scenes, and it is enticing to leaf through their galleries. While we acknowledge the motivational utility

---

[1] JavaScript is a scripting language that can be used to embed code in webpages. It has strong similarities to Java, but also many important differences.

of such examples, our aim is to teach, not to impress. The images in this book are simply the outputs of the example programs, and since this is an introductory text, the resulting scenes are unlikely to impress an expert. However, the techniques presented do constitute the foundational elements for producing today's stunning 3D effects.

We also haven't tried to create an OpenGL or JOGL "reference." Our coverage of OpenGL and JOGL represents only a tiny fraction of their capabilities. Rather, our aim is to use OpenGL and JOGL as vehicles for teaching the fundamentals of modern shader-based 3D graphics programming, and provide the reader with a sufficiently deep understanding for further study. If along the way this text helps to expand awareness of JOGL and other related technologies, that would be nice too.

What's New in This Edition

The biggest change we have made in this second edition is switching math libraries. In the first edition, we used a math library called "graphicslib3D" which we had built ourselves to support an advanced graphics course at California State University Sacramento. Since then, a new Java-based math library called "JOML" has emerged that offers many advantages over graphicslib3D. First, JOML was developed with speed in mind, and using it enables us to more effectively introduce performance-related topics. Second, JOML is becoming an extremely popular math library among JOGL users, and therefore learning it is a valuable skill. Finally, JOML is an open source project with an active developer community, and as such is likely to enjoy better long-term support than graphicslib3D.

The switch to JOML affects virtually every program in the book, although in most cases the changes are small. Readers who have used our previous edition will find that their existing code may not work without updating the code (and the library) to JOML. We hope that any minor inconvenience will be offset by improved performance and the benefits of standardization to a more widely used library.

As we did for graphicslib3D in our previous edition, we have included the latest version of JOML on the companion disc distributed with this book. However, readers are encouraged to seek out and utilize the newest version of JOML as it is being continually updated. For this reason, our installation instructions describe how to obtain the latest version of JOML from the Internet.

There are some new sections in the book that we hope readers will find exciting. As alluded to above, we have added a section on *coding for performance*. We also added a section on generating *soft shadows* that we promised in the instructor notes for our previous edition. The techniques for soft shadows also help with reducing jagged-edge shadow artifacts, and so users are likely to use them frequently, even when soft shadows aren't necessary. We also added a new section in Chapter 13 (on geometry), showing how to generate hair or fur by using a geometry shader to change primitive types.

Almost immediately after our first edition was released, we were asked how to run the programs on a Macintosh. After getting all of our examples running on a Mac, we published the steps on our website. That information has become an additional appendix in this edition. In fact, for this edition, we have moved all installation details into appendices.

We also added an appendix on using NVIDIA's *Nsight* graphics debugger. The first time we saw this tool we were blown away and desperately wanted to include it in our book. Nsight was developed for use with C++, but after some experimentation—and some much appreciated help from NVIDIA—we were able to get it to work with Java/JOGL. We are delighted to include it in this second edition.

We have made numerous corrections and—we hope—improvements. The chapter on skyboxes is largely rewritten, for example. Throughout the book, much of the code has been restructured, such as by moving commonly reused functions into a separate utility module. We also went through the entire book and spruced up the quality and resolution of the figures.

Intended Audience

This book is targeted at students of computer science. This could mean undergraduates pursuing a BS degree, but it could also mean anyone who studies computer science. As such, we are assuming that the reader has at least a solid background in object-oriented programming, at the level of someone who is, say, a computer science major at the junior or senior level.

There are also some specific things that we use in this book but don't cover because we assume the reader already has sufficient background, including the following:

- Java and its Abstract Window Toolkit (AWT) or Swing library, especially for GUI-building
- Java configuration details, such as manipulating the CLASSPATH
- event-driven programming
- basic matrix algebra and trigonometry
- awareness of color models, such as RGB, RGBA, etc.

The audience for this new second edition is also hoped to be expanded by the release of its "sister" textbook, *Computer Graphics Programming in OpenGL with C++*. In particular, we envision the possibility of a learning environment where students are free to utilize either Java or C++ *in the same classroom*, selecting one or the other book. The two texts cover the material sufficiently in lockstep that we believe conducting a course in this manner should be possible.

How to Use This Book

This book is designed to be read from front to back. That is, material in later chapters frequently relies on information learned in earlier chapters. So it probably won't work to jump back and forth in the chapters; rather, work your way forward through the material.

This book is intended mostly as a practical, hands-on guide. While there is plenty of theoretical material included, the reader should treat this text as a sort of "workbook," in which you learn basic concepts by actually programming them yourself. We have provided code for all of the examples, but to really learn the concepts you will want to "play" with those examples—extend them to build your own 3D scenes.

At the end of each chapter are a few problems to solve. Some are very simple, involving merely making simple modifications to the provided code. The problems that are marked "*(PROJECT)*," however, are expected to take some time to solve and require writing a significant amount of code, or combining techniques from various examples. There are also a few marked "*(RESEARCH)*" that encourage independent study because this textbook doesn't provide sufficient detail to solve them.

OpenGL calls, whether made in C or in Java through JOGL, often involve long lists of parameters. While writing this book, the authors debated whether or not to, in each case, describe all of the parameters. We decided that at the very beginning we would describe every detail. But as the topics progress, we decided to avoid getting bogged down in every piece of minutiae in the OpenGL calls (and there are *many*), for fear of the reader losing sight of the big picture. For this reason, it is essential when working through the examples to have ready access to reference material for Java, OpenGL, and JOGL.

For this, there are a number of excellent reference sources that we recommend using in conjunction with this book. The *javadocs* for Java and JOGL are *absolutely essential*, and can be accessed online or downloaded. The reader should bookmark them for easy access in a browser, and *expect to access them continuously* for looking up items such as parameter and constructor details. Use the following URLs for the Java and JOGL javadocs:

https://docs.oracle.com/javase/8/docs/api/
https://jogamp.org/deployment/webstart/javadoc/jogl/javadoc

Many of the entries in the JOGL javadoc are simply pointers to the corresponding entry in the OpenGL documentation:

https://www.opengl.org/sdk/docs/man/

Our examples utilize a mathematics library called JOML. This is a Java library that also has its own set of javadocs. After installing JOML (described in the appendices), the reader should locate the accompanying javadoc link and bookmark it. At press time, the current link is

https://joml-ci.github.io/JOML/apidocs/

There are many other books on 3D graphics programming that we recommend reading in parallel with this book (such as for solving the "research" problems), including the following five that we often refer to:

- (Sellers et al.) *OpenGL SuperBible* [SW15]
- (Kessenich et al.) *OpenGL Programming Guide* [KS16] (the "red book")
- (Wolff) *OpenGL 4 Shading Language Cookbook* [WO13]
- (Angel and Shreiner) *Interactive Computer Graphics* [AS14]
- (Luna) *Introduction to 3D Game Programming with DirectX 12* [LU16]

Companion Files

This book is accompanied by a companion disc that contains the following items:

- All of the Java/OpenGL programs and related utility class files and GLSL shader code presented in the book, along with batch files for compiling and running them
- The models and texture files used in the various programs and examples
- The cubemap and skydome image files used to make the skies and horizons
- Normal maps and height maps for lighting and surface detail effects
- All of the figures in the book, as image files
- The JOML mathematics library (version 1.9.11)

Readers who have purchased the electronic version of this book may obtain these files by contacting the publisher at info@merclearning.com.

Instructor Ancillaries

Instructors in a college or university setting are encouraged to obtain the *instructor ancillary package* that is available for this book, which contains the following additional items:

- A complete set of PowerPoint slides covering all topics in the book
- Solutions to most of the exercises at the ends of the chapters, including code where applicable
- Sample syllabus for a course based on the book
- Additional hints for presenting the material, chapter-by-chapter

This instructor ancillary package is available by contacting the publisher at info@ merclearning.com.

Acknowledgments

Early drafts of this book (prior to the first edition) were used in the CSc-155 (Advanced Computer Graphics Programming) course at CSU Sacramento, and benefited from many student corrections and comments (and in some cases, code). The authors would like to particularly thank Mitchell Brannan, Tiffany Chiapuzio-Wong, Samson Chua, Anthony Doan, Kian Faroughi, Cody Jackson, John Johnston, Zeeshan Khaliq, Raymond Rivera, Oscar Solorzano, Darren Takemoto, Jon Tinney, James Womack, and Victor Zepeda for their suggestions.

Feedback started coming in almost immediately after the first edition was published. We were especially excited to hear from instructors who adopted the book for their courses and shared their experiences. Dr. Mauricio Papa from the University of Tulsa traded several useful emails with us. Sean McCrory prepared a wonderfully detailed set of corrections to a couple of our lighting (Chapter 7) and Perlin noise (Chapter 14) implementations. We also heard from many students at various institutions, and their questions helped us to assess strengths and weaknesses in our book.

A sort of "acid test" for our book came in the fall of 2017, when our colleague Dr. Pinar Muyan-Ozcelik used the first edition while teaching our CSc-155 course for her first time. This gave us an opportunity to assess whether our book achieved its goal as a "teach yourself" resource. The course went well, and along the way Dr. Muyan-Ozcelik kept a running log of questions and corrections for each chapter, which led to many improvements in this second edition.

Kai Burjack, lead developer of the JOML math library, has been extraordinarily generous with his time and assistance as we migrated from graphicslib3D to JOML. He reviewed key segments of our book and gave us insight into some important aspects of JOML. He also helped guide us in using JOML correctly.

We are extremely grateful for the ongoing assistance provided to us by Julien Gouesse, engine support maintainer at JogAmp. Mr. Gouesse has provided technical information on JOGL textures, cube maps, buffer handling, proper loading of shader source files, and a variety of other topics. His help has led to significant improvements in our text.

Jay Turberville of Studio 522 Productions in Scottsdale (Arizona) built the dolphin model shown on the cover and used throughout this book. Our students love it. Studio 522 Productions does incredibly high-quality 3D animation and video production, as well as custom 3D modeling. We were thrilled that Mr. Turberville kindly offered to build such a wonderful model just for these books.

We wish to thank a few other artists and researchers who were gracious enough to allow us to utilize their models and textures. James Hastings-Trew of Planet Pixel Emporium provided many of the planetary surface textures. Paul Bourke allowed us to use his wonderful star field. Dr. Marc Levoy of Stanford University granted us permission to use the famous "Stanford Dragon" model. Paul Baker's bump-mapping tutorial formed the basis of the "torus" model we used in many examples. We also thank Mercury Learning for allowing us to use some of the textures from *Introduction to 3D Game Programming with DirectX 12* [LU16].

Dr. Danny Kopec connected us with Mercury Learning and introduced us to its publisher, David Pallai. Dr. Kopec's textbook, *Artificial Intelligence in the 21st Century,* inspired us to consider Mercury, and our telephone conversations with him were extremely informative. We were deeply saddened by Dr. Kopec's untimely passing, and regret that he didn't have the chance to see our book come to fruition.

Finally, we wish to thank David Pallai and Jennifer Blaney of Mercury Learning for their continued enthusiasm for this project and for guiding us through the textbook publishing process.

Errata

If you find any errors in our book, please let us know! Despite our best efforts, this book certainly contains mistakes. We will do our best to post corrections as soon as errors are reported to us. Shortly after the publication of the first edition, we established a webpage for collecting errata and posting corrections—the same webpage will continue to be used for the second edition:

http://athena.ecs.csus.edu/~gordonvs/errata.html

The publisher, Mercury Learning, also maintains a link to our errata page. So if the URL for our errata page should ever change, check the Mercury Learning website for the latest link.

About the Authors

Dr. V. Scott Gordon has been a professor in the California State University system for over twenty years, and currently teaches advanced graphics and game engineering courses at CSU Sacramento. He has authored or coauthored over thirty publications in a variety of areas, including artificial intelligence, neural networks, evolutionary computation, software engineering, video and strategy game programming, and computer science education. Dr. Gordon obtained his PhD at Colorado State University. He is also a jazz drummer and a competitive table tennis player.

Dr. John Clevenger has over forty years of experience teaching a wide variety of courses, including advanced graphics, game architecture, operating systems, VLSI chip design, system simulation, and other topics. He is the developer of several software frameworks and tools for teaching graphics and game architecture, including the graphicslib3D library used in the first edition of this textbook. He is the technical director of the ACM International Collegiate Programming Contest, and oversees the ongoing development of PC^2, the most widely used programming contest support system in the world. Dr. Clevenger obtained his PhD at the University of California, Davis. He is also a performing jazz musician and spends summer vacations in his mountain cabin.

References

[AS14] E. Angel and D. Shreiner, *Interactive Computer Graphics: A Top-Down Approach with WebGL*, 7th ed. (Pearson, 2014).

[JO16] JogAmp, accessed July 2016, http://jogamp.org/

[KS16] J. Kessenich, G. Sellers, and D. Shreiner, *OpenGL Programming Guide: The Official Guide to Learning OpenGL, Version 4.5 with SPIR-V*, 9th ed. (Addison-Wesley, 2016).

[LU16] F. Luna, *Introduction to 3D Game Programming with DirectX 12*, 2nd ed. (Mercury Learning, 2016).

[LW16] Lightweight Java Game Library (LWJGL), accessed July 2016, https://www.lwjgl.org/

[SW15] G. Sellers, R. Wright Jr., and N. Haemel, *OpenGL SuperBible: Comprehensive Tutorial and Reference*, 7th ed. (Addison-Wesley, 2015).

[WO13] D. Wolff, *OpenGL Shading Language Cookbook*, 2nd ed. (Packt Publishing, 2013).

GETTING STARTED

Graphics programming has a reputation for being among the most challenging computer science topics to learn. These days, graphics programming is *shader based*—that is, some of the program is written in a standard language such as Java or C++ for running on the CPU and some is written in a special-purpose *shader* language for running directly on the graphics card (GPU). Shader programming has a steep learning curve, so that even drawing something simple requires a convoluted set of steps to pass graphics data down a "pipeline." Modern graphics cards are able to process this data in *parallel*, and so the graphics programmer must understand the parallel architecture of the GPU, even when drawing simple shapes.

The payoff, however, is extraordinary power. The blossoming of stunning virtual reality in videogames and increasingly realistic effects in Hollywood movies can be greatly attributed to advances in shader programming. If reading this book is your entrée into 3D graphics, you are taking on a personal challenge that will reward you not only with pretty pictures but with a level of control over your machine that you never imagined was possible. Welcome to the exciting world of computer graphics programming!

1.1 LANGUAGES AND LIBRARIES

Modern graphics programming is done using a *graphics library.* That is, the programmer writes code which invokes functions in a predefined library (or set of libraries) that provide support for lower-level graphical operations. There are many graphics libraries in use today, but the most common library for platform-independent graphics programming is called *OpenGL (Open Graphics Library).* This book describes how to use OpenGL for 3D graphics programming in Java.

Using OpenGL with Java requires configuring several libraries. In this section, we describe which libraries are needed, some common options for each, and the option(s) that we will use throughout the book. Details on how to install and configure these libraries for your specific platform can be found in the appendices.

Running the programs in this book requires the following languages and libraries:

- Java
- OpenGL / GLSL
- JOGL
- JOML

It is likely that the reader will need to do a few preparatory steps to ensure that each of these are installed and properly accessible on his or her system. In the following subsections we briefly describe each of them; see the appendices for details on how to install and/or configure them for use.

1.1.1 Java

Java was developed at Sun Microsystems in the early 1990s, and the first stable release of a development kit (JDK) occurred in 1995. In 2010, Oracle Corporation acquired Sun and has maintained Java since that time [OR16]. This book assumes at least Java version 8, which was released in 2014.

1.1.2 OpenGL / GLSL

Version 1.0 of OpenGL appeared in 1992 as an "open" alternative to vendor-specific application programming interfaces (APIs) for computer graphics. Its specification and development was managed and controlled by the *OpenGL Architecture Review Board (ARB)*, a then newly formed group of industry participants. In 2006 the ARB transferred control of the OpenGL specification to the *Khronos Group*, a nonprofit consortium which manages not only the OpenGL specification but a wide variety of other open industry standards.

Since its beginning OpenGL has been revised and extended regularly. In 2004, version 2.0 introduced the OpenGL Shading Language (GLSL), allowing "shader programs" to be installed and run directly in graphics pipeline stages.

In 2009, version 3.1 removed a large number of features that had been deprecated, to enforce the use of shader programming as opposed to earlier approaches (referred to as "immediate mode").[1] Among the more recent features, version 4.0 (in 2010) added a *tessellation* stage to the programmable pipeline.

This textbook assumes that the user is using a machine with a graphics card that supports at least version 4.3 of OpenGL. If you are not sure which version of OpenGL your GPU supports, there are free applications available on the web that can be used to find out. One such application is GLView, by a company named "realtech VR" [GV16].

1.1.3 JOGL

JOGL is a set of OpenGL *bindings* (sometimes called a *"wrapper"*) which provides a mechanism for invoking C-based OpenGL functions from Java code. JOGL first appeared in 2003, published on the website Java.net. Since 2010 it has been an independent open source project, part of a suite of Java bindings maintained by *JogAmp* [JO16], an online community of developers. JogAmp also maintains JOAL and JOCL, bindings for OpenAL and OpenCL, respectively. As new versions of OpenGL and/or Java are released, new versions of JOGL are developed to support continued compatibility. JogAmp also maintains a short online user's guide that includes valuable guidelines for installing and using JOGL efficiently and effectively [JU16]. This book assumes at least version 2.3 of JOGL.

1.1.4 JOML

3D graphics programming makes heavy use of vector and matrix algebra. For this reason, use of OpenGL is greatly facilitated by an accompanying function library or class package to support common mathematical tasks. For example, the popular *OpenGL SuperBible* [SW15] utilizes a C library called "vmath"; in this book, we use a Java library called Java OpenGL Math Library, or JOML.

JOML provides classes and basic math functions related to graphics concepts, such as *vector*, *matrix*, and *quaternion*. It also contains a variety of utility classes for creating and using common 3D graphics structures, such as a stack for building

---

[1] Despite this, many graphics card manufacturers (notably NVIDIA) continue to support deprecated functionality.

hierarchical structures, perspective and look-at matrices, and a few basic shapes such as a rectangle and a sphere.

JOML was conceived in mid-2015 by Richard Greenlees and is an open source project currently being developed and maintained by Kai Burjack, who took over the project shortly after its inception. While it is relatively new, it has enjoyed wide-spread adoption because of its high-performance characteristics. JOML is specifi-cally designed to maximize performance in an OpenGL render loop (animation).

The previous edition of this book utilized our own in-house Java mathematics library called graphicslib3D. We hope that users of our earlier edition appreciate the better support and performance of JOML.

■1.2■ INSTALLATION AND CONFIGURATION

While developing the second edition of this book, we decided to include platform-specific details for the Macintosh (which were omitted from the first edition). We then wrestled with the best approach for including the platform-specific configuration information necessary to run the example programs. Configuring a system for using OpenGL on a Mac is somewhat more complicated than the equiv-alent configuration for the Windows PC. Ultimately, we opted to separate installa-tion and configuration information into individual platform-specific appendices. We hope that this will provide each reader with a single relevant place to look for information regarding his or her specific system, while at the same time avoiding bogging down the rest of the text with platform-specific details which may not be relevant to every reader. In this edition, we provide detailed configuration instruc-tions for Microsoft Windows in Appendix A and for the Macintosh in Appendix B.

References

[GV16] GLView, realtech-vr, accessed July 2016, http://www.realtech-vr.com/glview/

[JO16] JogAmp, accessed July 2016, http://jogamp.org/

[JU16] *JOGL Users Guide*, accessed July 2016, https://jogamp.org/jogl/doc/userguide/

[OR16] Java Software, Oracle Corp., accessed July 2016, https://www.oracle.com/java/index.html

[SW15] G. Sellers, R. Wright Jr., and N. Haemel, *OpenGL SuperBible: Comprehensive Tutorial and Reference*, 7th ed. (Addison-Wesley, 2015).

CHAPTER 2

THE OPENGL GRAPHICS PIPELINE

OpenGL (Open Graphics Library) is a multiplatform 2D and 3D graphics API that incorporates both hardware and software. Using OpenGL requires a graphics card (GPU) that supports a sufficiently up-to-date version of OpenGL (as described in Chapter 1).

On the hardware side, OpenGL provides a multistage *graphics pipeline* that is partially programmable using a language called **GLSL** (OpenGL Shading Language).

On the software side, OpenGL's API is written in C, and thus the calls are directly compatible with C and C++. However, stable language *bindings* (or "wrappers") are available for more than a dozen other popular languages (Java, Perl, Python, Visual Basic, Delphi, Haskell, Lisp, Ruby, etc.) with virtually equivalent performance. This textbook uses the popular Java wrapper **JOGL** (Java OpenGL). When using JOGL, the programmer writes a Java program that runs on the CPU (more specifically, on the Java Virtual Machine, or JVM) and includes JOGL (and thus, OpenGL) calls. We will refer to a Java program that contains JOGL calls as a *Java/JOGL application*. One important task of a Java/JOGL application is to install the programmer's GLSL code onto the GPU.

An overview of a JOGL-based graphics application is shown in Figure 2.1, with the software components highlighted in pink.

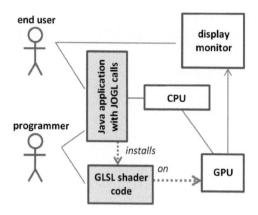

Figure 2.1
Overview of a JOGL-based graphics application.

Some of the code we will write will be in Java, with JOGL calls, and some will be written in GLSL. Our Java/JOGL application will work together with our GLSL modules and the hardware to create our 3D graphics output. Once our application is complete, the end user will interact with the Java application.

GLSL is an example of a *shader language*. Shader languages are intended to run on a GPU in the context of a graphics pipeline. There are other shader languages, such as HLSL, which works with Microsoft's 3D framework *DirectX*. GLSL is the specific shader language that is compatible with OpenGL, and thus we will write shader code in GLSL, in addition to our Java/JOGL application code.

For the rest of this chapter, we will take a brief "tour" of the OpenGL pipeline. The reader is not expected to understand every detail thoroughly, but just to get a feel for how the stages work together.

▮2.1▮ THE OPENGL PIPELINE

Modern 3D graphics programming utilizes a *pipeline*, in which the process of converting a 3D scene to a 2D image is broken down into a series of steps. OpenGL and DirectX both utilize similar pipelines.

A simplified overview of the OpenGL graphics pipeline is shown in Figure 2.2 (not every stage is shown, just the major ones we will study). The Java/JOGL application sends graphics data into the vertex shader, processing proceeds through the pipeline, and pixels emerge for display on the monitor.

The stages shaded in blue (vertex, tessellation, geometry, and fragment) are *programmable* in GLSL. It is one of the responsibilities of the Java/JOGL application to load GLSL programs into these shader stages, as follows:

1. It uses Java to obtain the GLSL shader code, either from text files or hardcoded as strings.

2. It then creates OpenGL shader objects, and loads the GLSL shader code into them.

3. Finally, it uses OpenGL commands to compile and link objects and install them on the GPU.

In practice, it is usually necessary to provide GLSL code for at least the *vertex* and *fragment* stages, whereas the tessellation and geometry stages are optional. Let's walk through the entire process and see what takes place at each step.

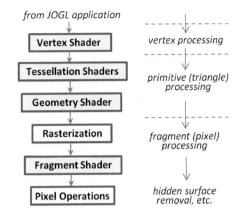

Figure 2.2
Overview of the OpenGL pipeline.

2.1.1 ■ Java/JOGL Application

The bulk of our graphics application is written in Java. Depending on the purpose of the program, it may interact with the end user using standard Java libraries such as AWT or Swing. For tasks related to 3D rendering, it uses the JOGL library. Other windowing libraries exist that interface with JOGL, such as SWT and NEWT, that have some performance advantages; in this book, however, we use AWT and Swing because of the likelihood the reader already has familiarity with them.

JOGL includes a class called GLCanvas that is compatible with the standard Java JFrame, and on which we can draw 3D scenes. As already mentioned, JOGL also gives us commands for installing GLSL programs onto the programmable shader stages and compiling them. Finally, JOGL uses *buffers* for sending 3D models and other related graphics data down the pipeline.

Before we try writing shaders, let's write a simple Java/JOGL application that instantiates a GLCanvas and sets its background color. Doing that won't require any shaders at all! The code is shown in Program 2.1. It extends JFrame and instantiates a GLCanvas, adding it to the JFrame. It also implements GLEventListener, required to utilize OpenGL—this necessitates implementing some methods, specifically display(), init(), reshape(), and dispose(). The display() method is where we place code that draws to the GLCanvas. In this example, we use the glClearColor() command to specify the color value to be applied when clearing the background—in this case

(1,0,0,1), corresponding to the RGB values of the color red, plus a "1" for the opacity component. We then use the OpenGL call glClear(GL_COLOR_BUFFER_BIT) to actually fill the color buffer with that color.

Program 2.1 First Java/JOGL Application

```
import javax.swing.*;
import static com.jogamp.opengl.GL4.*;
import com.jogamp.opengl.*;
import com.jogamp.opengl.awt.GLCanvas;

public class Code extends JFrame implements GLEventListener
{   private GLCanvas myCanvas;

    public Code()
    {   setTitle("Chapter2 - program1");
        setSize(600, 400);
        setLocation(200, 200);
        myCanvas = new GLCanvas();
        myCanvas.addGLEventListener(this);
        this.add(myCanvas);
        this.setVisible(true);
    }

    public void display(GLAutoDrawable drawable)
    {   GL4 gl = (GL4) GLContext.getCurrentGL();
        gl.glClearColor(1.0f, 0.0f, 0.0f, 1.0f);
        gl.glClear(GL_COLOR_BUFFER_BIT);
    }

    public static void main(String[ ] args)
    {   new Code();
    }

    public void init(GLAutoDrawable drawable) { }
    public void reshape(GLAutoDrawable drawable, int x, int y, int width, int height) { }
    public void dispose(GLAutoDrawable drawable) { }
}
```

When running a Java/JOGL application (such as Program 2.1) on a Microsoft Windows machine, it is advisable to add a command-line option to disable the use of Direct3D acceleration, such as

```
java -Dsun.java2d.d3d=false Code
```

The mechanism by which these functions are deployed is as follows: When a GLCanvas is made "visible" (by our calling "setVisible(true)" on the JFrame that contains it), it initializes OpenGL, which in turn creates a "GL4" object that our application can use for making OpenGL function calls. OpenGL then does a "callback," calling init(), and passes it a "drawable" object

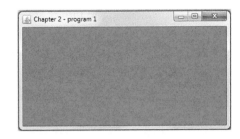

Figure 2.3
Output of Program 2.1.

(in this case the drawable object is the GLCanvas, although that isn't obvious from the code). In this particular example, init() doesn't do anything—in most applications it is where we would read in GLSL code, load 3D models, and so on. OpenGL (actually, JOGL) next calls display(), also sending it the drawable object. It is typical to immediately obtain the GL4 object and put it in a variable called "gl" (actually, GL4 is an interface—in practice we don't need to know the actual GL object class).

Later we will see that if we want our scene to be animated, our Java/JOGL application will need to tell JOGL to make additional calls to display().

Now is an appropriate time to take a closer look at JOGL calls in Program 2.1. Consider this one:

gl.glClear(GL_COLOR_BUFFER_BIT);

Since JOGL is a Java binding for OpenGL, that means that calls to JOGL in turn generate calls to OpenGL's library of C functions. In this case, the C function being called, as described in the OpenGL reference documentation (available on the web at https://www.opengl.org/sdk/docs) is:

void glClear(GLbitfield mask);

The first thing to notice is that the name of the JOGL function is the same as that of the original OpenGL C function, except it is preceded by "gl."—which is the name of the GL4 object. The period "." after the "gl" is significant because "gl" is the object on which we are invoking the OpenGL function.

To reiterate, GL4 is a Java interface to the OpenGL functions. We can obtain it in one of two ways: (a) by calling drawable.getGL(), utilizing the "GLAutoDrawable" object provided automatically when the various GLEventListener functions are invoked (called back) by OpenGL, or (b) by calling GLContext.getCurrentGL() as done in Program 2.1. Obtaining the current GL4 object is important because, in general, any OpenGL function described in the OpenGL documentation can be called from JOGL by preceding it with the name of the appropriate GL4 object (such as "gl." here).

The parameter references a "GLbitfield" called "GL_COLOR_BUFFER_BIT"; OpenGL has many predefined constants (some of them are called *enums*), and this one references the *color buffer* that contains the pixels as they are rendered. OpenGL has several color buffers, and this command clears all of them—that is, it fills them with a predefined color called the "clear color." Note that "clear" in this context doesn't mean "a color that is clear"; rather, it refers to the color that is applied when a color buffer is reset (cleared).

Immediately before the call to glClear() is the call to glClearColor(). Again, this specifies the value placed in the elements of a color buffer when it is cleared. Here we have specified (1,0,0,1), which corresponds to the RGBA color *red*. If a "clear color" isn't specified, the default value is black.

Finally, besides display() and init(), we also must implement reshape() and dispose(). The reshape() function is called when a GLCanvas is resized, and dispose() is called when the application exits. In Program 2.1 we left them both empty.

2.1.2 Vertex and Fragment Shaders

Our first JOGL program didn't actually draw anything—it simply filled the color buffer with a single color. To actually draw something, we need to include a *vertex shader* and a *fragment shader*.

You may be surprised to learn that OpenGL is capable of drawing only a few kinds of very simple things, such as *points*, *lines*, or *triangles*. These simple things are called *primitives*, and for this reason, most 3D models are made up of lots and lots of primitives, usually triangles.

Primitives are made up of *vertices*—for example, a triangle consists of three vertices. The vertices can come from a variety of sources—they can be read from files and then loaded into buffers by the Java/JOGL application, or they can be hardcoded in the Java code or even in the GLSL code.

Before any of this can happen, the Java/JOGL application must compile and link appropriate GLSL vertex and fragment shader programs, and then load them into the pipeline. We will see the commands for doing this shortly.

The application also is responsible for telling OpenGL to construct triangles. We do this by using JOGL to call the following OpenGL function:

glDrawArrays(GLenum mode, Glint first, GLsizei count);

The mode is the type of primitive—for triangles we use GL_TRIANGLES. The parameter "first" indicates which vertex to start with (generally vertex number 0, the first one), and count specifies the total number of vertices to be drawn.

When glDrawArrays() is called, the GLSL code in the pipeline starts executing. Let's now add some GLSL code to that pipeline.

Regardless of where they originate, all of the vertices pass through the vertex shader. They do so *one-by-one*; that is, the shader is executed *once per vertex*. For a large and complex model with a lot of vertices, the vertex shader may execute hundreds, thousands, or even millions of times, often in parallel.

Let's write a simple program with only one vertex, hardcoded in the vertex shader. That's not enough to draw a triangle, but it is enough to draw a point. For it to display, we also need to provide a *fragment shader*. For simplicity we will declare the two shader programs as arrays of strings.

Program 2.2 Shaders, Drawing a POINT

```
(.....imports as before)
public class Code extends JFrame implements GLEventListener
{   private int renderingProgram;  ⎫
    private int vao[ ] = new int[1];  ⎬ new declarations
                                       ⎭
    public Code() { (.....constructor as before) }
    public void display(GLAutoDrawable drawable)
    {   GL4 gl = (GL4) GLContext.getCurrentGL();
        gl.glUseProgram(renderingProgram);
        gl.glDrawArrays(GL_POINTS, 0, 1);
    }

    public void init(GLAutoDrawable drawable)
    {   GL4 gl = (GL4) GLContext.getCurrentGL();
        renderingProgram = createShaderProgram();
```

```
    gl.glGenVertexArrays(vao.length, vao, 0);
    gl.glBindVertexArray(vao[0]);
}
private int createShaderProgram()
{   GL4 gl = (GL4) GLContext.getCurrentGL();

    String vshaderSource[ ] =
    {   "#version 430     \n",
        "void main(void) \n",
        "{  gl_Position = vec4(0.0, 0.0, 0.0, 1.0); }  \n",
    };
    String fshaderSource[ ] =
    {   "#version 430     \n",
        "out vec4 color;   \n",
        "void main(void) \n",
        "{  color = vec4(0.0, 0.0, 1.0, 1.0);  }  \n",
    };
    int vShader = gl.glCreateShader(GL_VERTEX_SHADER);
    gl.glShaderSource(vShader, 3, vshaderSource, null, 0);  // 3 is the count of lines of source code
    gl.glCompileShader(vShader);

    int fShader=gl.glCreateShader(GL_FRAGMENT_SHADER);
    gl.glShaderSource(fShader, 4, fshaderSource, null, 0);  // 4 is the count of lines of source code
    gl.glCompileShader(fShader);

    int vfProgram = gl.glCreateProgram();
    gl.glAttachShader(vfProgram, vShader);
    gl.glAttachShader(vfProgram, fShader);
    gl.glLinkProgram(vfProgram);

    gl.glDeleteShader(vShader);
    gl.glDeleteShader(fShader);
    return vfProgram;
}
... main(), reshape(), and dispose() as before
```

Figure 2.4
Output of Program 2.2.

The program appears to have output a blank canvas. But close examination reveals a tiny blue dot in the center of the window (assuming that this printed page is of sufficient resolution). The default size of a point in OpenGL is one pixel.

There are many important details in Program 2.2 (color-coded in the program, for convenience) for us to discuss. First, note that init() is no longer empty—it now calls another function named "createShaderProgram()" (that we wrote). This function starts by declaring two shaders as arrays of strings called vshaderSource and fshaderSource. It then calls glCreateShader(), which generates the desired type of shader (note the predefined value GL_VERTEX_SHADER, and then later GL_FRAGMENT_SHADER). OpenGL creates the shader object (initially empty), and returns an integer ID that is an index for referencing it later—the code stores this ID in the variable vShader (and fShader). It then calls glShaderSource(), which loads the GLSL code from the string array into the empty shader object. glShaderSource() has five parameters: (a) the shader object in which to store the shader, (b) the number of strings in the shader source code, (c) the array of strings containing the source code, and two additional parameters we aren't using (they will be explained later, in the supplementary chapter notes). Note also that the two commented lines of code in the blue section, highlighting the parameter values 3 and 4, refer to the number of lines of code in each shader (the \n's delineate each line in the shader source code). The shaders are then each compiled using glCompileShader().

The application then creates a *program* object named vfprogram and saves the integer ID that points to it. An OpenGL "program" object contains a series of compiled shaders, and here we see the commands glCreateProgram() to create the program object, glAttachShader() to attach each of the shaders to it, and then glLinkProgram() to request that the GLSL compiler ensure that they are compatible.

After init() finishes, display() is called automatically (recall this is also a JOGL callback). One of the first things that display() does is call glUseProgram(), which loads the program containing the two compiled shaders into the OpenGL pipeline stages (onto the GPU!). Note that glUseProgram() *doesn't run the shaders*; it just loads them onto the hardware.

As we will see later in Chapter 4, ordinarily at this point the Java/JOGL program would prepare the vertices of the model being drawn for sending down the pipeline. But not in this case, because for our first shader program we simply hardcoded a single vertex in the vertex shader. Therefore in this example the display() function next proceeds to the glDrawArrays() call, which initiates pipeline processing. The primitive type is GL_POINTS, and there is just one point to display.

Now let's look at the shaders themselves, shown in green earlier (and duplicated ahead). As we saw, they have been declared in the Java/JOGL program as arrays of strings. This is a clumsy way to code, but it is sufficient in this very simple case. The vertex shader is:

```
#version 430
void main(void)
{   gl_Position = vec4(0.0,  0.0,  0.0,  1.0); }
```

The first line indicates the OpenGL version, in this case 4.30. There follows a "main" function (as we will see, GLSL is somewhat Java-like in syntax). The primary purpose of any vertex shader is to send a vertex down the pipeline (which, as mentioned before, it does for every vertex). The built-in variable gl_Position is used to set a vertex's coordinate position in 3D space and is sent to the next stage in the pipeline. The GLSL datatype vec4 is used to hold a 4-tuple, suitable for such coordinates, with the associated four values representing X, Y, Z, and a fourth value set here to 1.0 (we will learn the purpose of this fourth value in Chapter 3). In this case, the vertex is hardcoded to the origin location (0,0,0).

The vertices move through the pipeline to the *rasterizer*, where they are transformed into pixel locations (or more accurately, *fragments*—described later). Eventually, these pixels (fragments) reach the fragment shader:

```
#version 430
out vec4 color;
void main(void)
{   color = vec4(0.0,  0.0,  1.0,  1.0); }
```

The purpose of any fragment shader is to set the RGB color of a pixel to be displayed. In this case the specified output color (0, 0, 1) is blue (the fourth value 1.0 specifies the level of opacity). Note the "out" tag indicating that the variable color is an output. (It wasn't necessary to specify an "out" tag for gl_Position in the vertex shader, because gl_Position is a predefined output variable.)

There is one detail in the code that we haven't discussed, in the last two lines in the init() function (shown in red). They probably appear a bit cryptic. As we will see in Chapter 4, when sets of data are prepared for sending down the pipeline, they are organized into *buffers*. Those buffers are in turn organized into *Vertex Array Objects* (VAOs). In our example, we hardcoded a single point in the vertex shader, so we didn't need any buffers. However, OpenGL still requires at least one VAO to be created whenever shaders are being used, even if the application isn't using any buffers. So the two lines create the required VAO.

Finally, there is the issue of how the *vertex* that came out of the vertex shader became a *pixel* in the fragment shader. Recall from Figure 2.2 that between vertex processing and pixel processing is the *rasterization* stage. It is there that primitives (such as points or triangles) are converted into sets of pixels. The default size of an OpenGL "point" is one pixel, so that is why our single point was rendered as a single pixel.

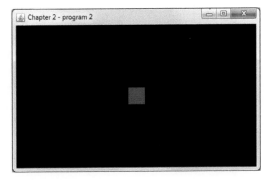

Figure 2.5
Changing glPointSize.

Let's add the following command in display(), right before the glDrawArrays() call:

gl.glPointSize(30.0f);

Now, when the rasterizer receives the vertex from the vertex shader, it will set pixel color values that form a point having a size of 30 pixels. The resulting output is shown in Figure 2.5.

Let's now continue examining the remainder of the OpenGL pipeline.

2.1.3 Tessellation

We cover tessellation in Chapter 12. The programmable tessellation stage is one of the most recent additions to OpenGL (in version 4.0). It provides a *tessellator* that can generate a large number of triangles, typically as a grid, and also some tools to manipulate those triangles in a variety of ways. For example, the programmer might manipulate a tessellated grid of triangles as shown in Figure 2.6.

Tessellation is useful when a lot of vertices are needed on what is otherwise a simple shape, such as on a square area or curved surface. It is also very useful for generating complex terrain, as we will see later. In such instances, it is sometimes much more efficient to have the tessellator in the GPU generate the triangle mesh in hardware, rather than doing it in Java.

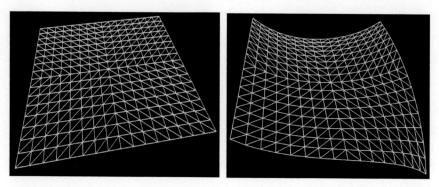

Figure 2.6
Grid produced by tessellator.

2.1.4 Geometry Shader

We cover the geometry shader stage in Chapter 13. Whereas the *vertex shader* gives the programmer the ability to manipulate one *vertex* at a time (i.e., "per-vertex" processing), and the *fragment shader* (as we will see) allows manipulating one *pixel* at a time ("per-fragment" processing), the *geometry shader* provides the capability to manipulate one *primitive* at a time—"per-primitive" processing.

Recalling that the most common primitive is the *triangle*, by the time we have reached the geometry stage, the pipeline must have completed grouping the vertices into triangles (a process called *primitive assembly*). The geometry shader then makes all three vertices in each triangle accessible to the programmer simultaneously.

There are a number of uses for per-primitive processing. The primitives could be altered, such as by stretching or shrinking them. Some of the primitives could be deleted, thus putting "holes" in the object being rendered—this is one way of turning a simple model into a more complex one.

The geometry shader also provides a mechanism for generating additional primitives. Here, too, this opens the door to many possibilities for turning simple models into more complex ones.

An interesting use for the geometry shader is adding surface texture such as bumps or scales—even "hair" or "fur"—to an object. Consider for example, the simple torus shown in Figure 2.7 (we will see how to generate this later in the book). The surface of this torus is built out of many hundreds of triangles. If at each triangle, we use a geometry shader to add additional triangles that face outward, we get the result shown in Figure 2.8. This "scaly torus" would be computationally expensive to try and model from scratch in the Java/JOGL application side.

Figure 2.7
Torus model.

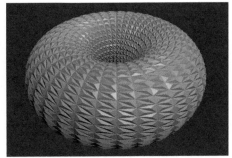

Figure 2.8
Torus modified in geometry shader.

It might seem redundant to provide a per-primitive shader stage, when the tessellation stage(s) give the programmer access to *all* of the vertices in an entire model simultaneously. The difference is that tessellation only offers this capability in very limited circumstances—specifically when the model is a grid of triangles generated by the tessellator. It does not provide such simultaneous access to all the vertices of, say, an arbitrary model being sent in from Java through a buffer.

Rasterization

Ultimately, our 3D world of vertices, triangles, colors, and so on needs to be displayed on a 2D monitor. That 2D monitor screen is made up of a *raster*—a rectangular array of pixels.

When a 3D object is *rasterized*, OpenGL converts the primitives in the object (usually triangles) into *fragments*. A fragment holds the information associated with a pixel. Rasterization determines the locations of pixels that need to be drawn in order to produce the triangle specified by its three vertices.

Rasterization starts by interpolating, pairwise, between the three vertices of the triangle. There are some options for doing this interpolation; for now it is sufficient to consider simple linear interpolation as shown in Figure 2.9. The original three vertices are shown in red.

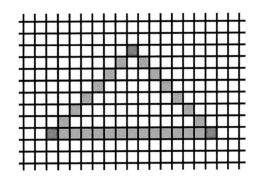

Figure 2.9
Rasterization (step 1).

If rasterization were to stop here, the resulting image would appear as wireframe. This is an option in OpenGL, by adding the following command in the display() function, before the call to glDrawArrays():

gl.glPolygonMode(GL_FRONT_AND_BACK, GL_LINE);

If the torus shown previously in Section 2.1.4 is rendered with the addition of this line of code, it appears as shown in Figure 2.10.

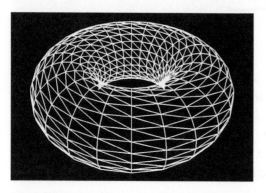

Figure 2.10
Torus with wireframe rendering.

If we didn't insert the preceding line of code (or if GL_FILL had been specified instead of GL_LINE), interpolation would continue along raster lines and fill the interior of the triangle, as shown in Figure 2.11. When applied to the torus, this results in the fully rasterized or "solid" torus shown in Figure 2.12 (on the left). Note that in this case the overall shape and curvature of the torus is not evident—that is because we haven't included any texturing or lighting techniques, so it appears "flat." At the right, the same "flat" torus is shown with the wireframe rendering superimposed. The torus shown earlier in Figure 2.7 included lighting effects, and thus revealed the shape of the torus much more clearly. We will study lighting in Chapter 7.

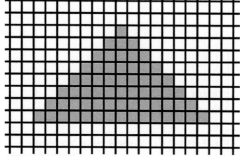

Figure 2.11
Fully rasterized triangle.

As we will see in later chapters, the rasterizer can interpolate more than just pixels. *Any* variable that is output by the vertex shader and input by the fragment shader will be interpolated based on the corresponding pixel position. We will use this capability to generate smooth color gradations, realistic lighting, and many more effects.

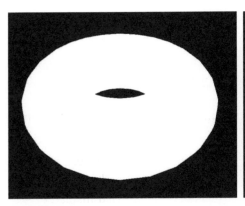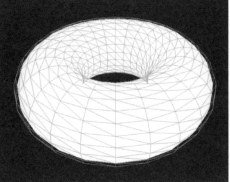

Figure 2.12
Torus with fully rasterized primitives (left) and with wireframe grid superimposed (right).

2.1.6 Fragment Shader

As mentioned earlier, the purpose of the fragment shader is to assign colors to the rasterized pixels. We have already seen an example of a fragment shader in Program 2.2. There the fragment shader simply hardcoded its output to a specific value, so every generated pixel had the same color. However, GLSL affords us virtually limitless creativity to calculate colors in other ways.

One simple example would be to base the output color of a pixel on its location. Recall that in the vertex shader, the outgoing coordinates of a vertex are specified using the predefined variable gl_Position. In the fragment shader, there is a similar variable available to the programmer for accessing the coordinates of an incoming *fragment*, called gl_FragCoord. We can modify the fragment shader from Program 2.2 so that it uses gl_FragCoord (in this case referencing its x component using the GLSL *field selector* notation) to set each pixel's color based on its location, as shown here:

```
#version 430
out vec4 color;
void main(void)
{   if (gl_FragCoord.x < 200) color = vec4(1.0, 0.0, 0.0, 1.0); else color = vec4(0.0, 0.0, 1.0, 1.0);
}
```

Assuming that we increase the GL_PointSize as we did at the end of Section 2.1.2, the pixel colors will now vary across the rendered point—red where the x coordinates are less than 200, and blue otherwise, as seen in Figure 2.13.

Figure 2.13
Fragment shader color variation.

2.1.7 Pixel Operations

As objects in our scene are drawn in the display() function using the glDrawArrays() command, we usually expect objects in front to block our view of objects behind them. This also extends to the objects themselves, wherein we expect to see the front of an object, but generally not the back.

To achieve this, we need *hidden surface removal*, or *HSR*. OpenGL can perform a variety of HSR operations, depending on the effect we want in our scene. And even though this phase is not programmable, it is extremely important that we understand how it works. Not only will we need to configure it properly; we will later need to carefully manipulate it when we add shadows to our scene.

Hidden surface removal is accomplished by OpenGL through the cleverly coordinated use of two buffers: the *color buffer* (which we have discussed previously) and the *depth buffer* (sometimes called the *Z-buffer*). Both of these buffers are the same size as the raster—that is, there is an entry in each buffer for every pixel on the screen.

As various objects are drawn in a scene, pixel colors are generated by the fragment shader. The pixel colors are placed in the color buffer—it is the color buffer that is ultimately written to the screen. When multiple objects occupy some of the same pixels in the color buffer, a determination must be made as to which pixel color(s) are retained, based on which object is nearest the viewer.

Hidden surface removal is done as follows:

- Before a scene is rendered, the depth buffer is filled with values representing maximum depth.
- As a pixel color is output by the fragment shader, its distance from the viewer is calculated.
- If the computed distance is *less than* the distance stored in the depth buffer (for that pixel), then (a) the pixel color replaces the color in the

color buffer, and (b) the distance replaces the value in the depth buffer. Otherwise, the pixel is discarded.

This procedure is called the *Z-buffer algorithm*, as expressed in Figure 2.14.

```
Color [ ] [ ] colorBuf = new Color [pixelRows][pixelCols];
double [ ] [ ] depthBuf = new double [pixelRows][pixelCols];
for (each row and column)    // initialize color and depth buffers
{    colorBuf [row][col] = backgroundColor;
     depthBuf [row][col] = far away;
}

for (each shape)      // update buffers when new pixel is closer
{    for (each pixel in the shape)
     {    if (depth at pixel < depthBuf value)
          {    depthBuf [pixel.row][pixel.col] = depth at pixel;
               colorBuf [pixel.row][pixel.col] = color at pixel;
}    }    }
return colorBuf;
```

Figure 2.14
Z-buffer algorithm.

2.2 ■ DETECTING OPENGL AND GLSL ERRORS

The workflow for compiling and running GLSL code differs from standard coding, in that *GLSL compilation happens at Java runtime*. Another complication is that GLSL code doesn't run on the CPU (it runs on the GPU), so *the operating system cannot always catch OpenGL runtime errors*. This makes debugging difficult, because it is often hard to detect if a shader failed, and why.

Program 2.3 (which follows) presents some modules for catching and displaying GLSL errors. They make use of the error string lookup tool gluErrorString() from the "GLU" library [GL16], as well as OpenGL functions glGetShaderiv() and glGetProgramiv(), which are used to provide information about compiled GLSL shaders and programs. Accompanying them is the createShaderProgram() function from the previous Program 2.2, but with the error-detecting calls added.

Program 2.3 contains the following three utilities:

- **checkOpenGLError**—checks the OpenGL error flag for the occurrence of an OpenGL error
- **printShaderLog**—displays the contents of OpenGL's log when GLSL compilation has failed
- **printProgramLog**—displays the contents of OpenGL's log when GLSL linking has failed

The first, checkOpenGLError(), is useful for detecting both GLSL compilation errors and OpenGL runtime errors, so it is highly recommended for use throughout a Java/JOGL application during development. For example, in the prior example (Program 2.2), the calls to glCompileShader() and glLinkProgram() could easily be augmented with the code shown in Program 2.3 to ensure that any typos or other compile errors would be caught and their cause reported. Calls to checkOpenGLError() could be added after runtime OpenGL calls, such as immediately after the call to glDrawArrays().

Another reason that it is important to use these tools is that *a GLSL error does not cause the JOGL program to stop.* So unless the programmer takes steps to catch errors at the point that they happen, debugging will be very difficult.

Program 2.3 Modules to Catch GLSL Errors

```
. . . .
import com.jogamp.opengl.glu.GLU;
. . . .

private void printShaderLog(int shader)
{   GL4 gl = (GL4) GLContext.getCurrentGL();
    int[ ] len = new int[1];
    int[ ] chWrittn = new int[1];
    byte[ ] log = null;

    // determine the length of the shader compilation log
    gl.glGetShaderiv(shader, GL_INFO_LOG_LENGTH, len, 0);
    if (len[0] > 0)
    {   log = new byte[len[0]];
        gl.glGetShaderInfoLog(shader, len[0], chWrittn, 0, log, 0);
        System.out.println("Shader Info Log: ");
        for (int i = 0; i < log.length; i++)
        {   System.out.print((char) log[i]);
} } }
```

```
void printProgramLog(int prog)
{   GL4 gl = (GL4) GLContext.getCurrentGL();
    int[ ] len = new int[1];
    int[ ] chWrittn = new int[1];
    byte[ ] log = null;

    // determine the length of the program linking log
    gl.glGetProgramiv(prog,GL_INFO_LOG_LENGTH,len, 0);
    if (len[0] > 0)
    {   log = new byte[len[0]];
        gl.glGetProgramInfoLog(prog, len[0], chWrittn, 0,log, 0);
        System.out.println("Program Info Log: ");
        for (int i = 0; i < log.length; i++)
        {   System.out.print((char) log[i]);
}   }   }

boolean checkOpenGLError()
{   GL4 gl = (GL4) GLContext.getCurrentGL();
    boolean foundError = false;
    GLU glu = new GLU();
    int glErr = gl.glGetError();
    while (glErr != GL_NO_ERROR)
    {   System.err.println("glError: " + glu.gluErrorString(glErr));
        foundError = true;
        glErr = gl.glGetError();
    }
    return foundError;
}
```

Example of checking for OpenGL errors:

```
private int createShaderProgram()
{   GL4 gl = (GL4) GLContext.getCurrentGL();
    // arrays to collect GLSL compilation status values.
    // note: one-element arrays are used because the associated JOGL calls require arrays.
    int[ ] vertCompiled = new int[1];
    int[ ] fragCompiled = new int[1];
    int[ ] linked = new int[1];

    . . . .
    // catch errors while compiling shaders

    gl.glCompileShader(vShader);
    checkOpenGLError();
    gl.glGetShaderiv(vShader, GL_COMPILE_STATUS, vertCompiled, 0);
```

```
if (vertCompiled[0] != 1)
{   System.out.println("vertex compilation failed.");
    printShaderLog(vShader);
}

gl.glCompileShader(fShader);
checkOpenGLError();
gl.glGetShaderiv(fShader, GL_COMPILE_STATUS, fragCompiled, 0);
if (fragCompiled[0] != 1)
{   System.out.println("fragment compilation failed.");
    printShaderLog(fShader);
}

if ((vertCompiled[0] != 1) || (fragCompiled[0] != 1))
{   System.out.println("\nCompilation error; return-flags:");
    System.out.println(" vertCompiled = " + vertCompiled[0] + " ;  fragCompiled = " + fragCompiled[0]);
}
. . . .
// catch errors while linking shaders
gl.glLinkProgram(vfprogram);
checkOpenGLError();
gl.glGetProgramiv(vfprogram, GL_LINK_STATUS, linked,0);
if (linked[0] != 1)
{   System.out.println("linking failed.");
    printProgramLog(vfprogram);
}
. . . .
}
```

Another set of tools that can help in tracking down the source of OpenGL and GLSL errors is JOGL's *composable pipeline* mechanism. There is a rich set of capabilities available in the DebugGL and TraceGL JOGL classes, which provide debugging and tracing support, respectively. One way of utilizing these capabilities in simple cases is to add one or both of the following command line options:

```
-Djogl.debug.DebugGL
-Djogl.debug.TraceGL
```

For example, the application can be run with both capabilities enabled as follows:

```
java -Dsun.java2d.d3d=false -Djogl.debug.DebugGL -Djogl.debug.TraceGL Code
```

Enabling debugging causes glGetError() to be invoked at each OpenGL call. Although any error messages generated tend to not be as informative as is the case when retrieving the error codes as shown in Program 2.3, it can be a quick way of narrowing down the likely location where an error has occurred.

Enabling tracing causes a line of output on the command window to be displayed for each OpenGL call executed—including those called directly by the application, and others invoked by JOGL. For example, a trace for Program 2.2 produces the following output, which reflects the order of calls in a typical run:

```
glFinish()
glCreateShader(<int> 0x8B31) = 1
glShaderSource(<int> 0x1, <int> 0x3, <[Ljava.lang.String;>, <java.nio.IntBuffer> null)
glCompileShader(<int> 0x1)
glCreateShader(<int> 0x8B30) = 2
glShaderSource(<int> 0x2, <int> 0x4, <[Ljava.lang.String;>, <java.nio.IntBuffer> null)
glCompileShader(<int> 0x2)
glCreateProgram() = 3
glAttachShader(<int> 0x3, <int> 0x1)
glAttachShader(<int> 0x3, <int> 0x2)
glLinkProgram(<int> 0x3)
glDeleteShader(<int> 0x1)
glDeleteShader(<int> 0x2)
glGenVertexArrays(<int> 0x1, <[I>, <int> 0x0)
glBindVertexArray(<int> 0x1)
glGetError() = 0
glViewport(<int> 0x0, <int> 0x0, <int> 0x180, <int> 0xA2)
glUseProgram(<int> 0x3)
glDrawArrays(<int> 0x0, <int> 0x0, <int> 0x1)
```

Although extremely useful during debugging, as with most debugging tools the composable pipeline incurs considerable overhead, and should not be enabled in production code.

There are other tricks for deducing the causes of runtime errors in shader code. A common result of shader runtime errors is for the output screen to be completely blank, essentially with no output at all. This can happen even if the error is a very small typo in a shader, yet it can be difficult to tell at which stage of the pipeline the error occurred. With no output at all, it's like looking for a needle in a haystack.

One useful trick in such cases is to temporarily replace the fragment shader with the one shown in Program 2.2. Recall that in that example, the fragment shader simply output a particular color—solid blue, for example. If the subsequent output is of the correct geometric form (but solid blue), the vertex shader is probably correct, and there is an error in the original fragment shader. If the output is still a blank screen, the error is more likely earlier in the pipeline, such as in the vertex shader.

In Appendix C we show how to use yet another useful debugging tool called *Nsight*, which is available for machines equipped with certain Nvidia graphics cards.

2.3 READING GLSL SOURCE CODE FROM FILES

So far, our GLSL shader code has been stored inline in strings. As our programs grow in complexity, this will become impractical. We should instead store our shader code in files and read them in.

Reading text files is a basic Java skill, and won't be covered here. However, for practicality, code to read shaders is provided in readShaderSource(), shown in Program 2.4. It reads the shader text file and returns an array of strings, where each string is one line of text from the file. It then determines the size of that array based on how many lines were read in. Note that here, createShaderProgram() replaces the version from Program 2.2.

In this example, the vertex and fragment shader code is now placed in the text files "vertShader.glsl" and "fragShader.glsl," respectively.

Program 2.4 Reading GLSL Source from Files

```
(....imports as before, plus the following...)
import java.io.File;
import java.io.IOException;
import java.util.Scanner;

public class Code extends JFrame implements GLEventListener
{  (..... declarations same as before, display() as before)

    private int createShaderProgram()
    {  (...... as before plus....)
        vshaderSource = readShaderSource("vertShader.glsl");
        fshaderSource = readShaderSource("fragShader.glsl");

        gl.glShaderSource(vertexShader, vshaderSource.length, vshaderSource, null, 0);
        gl.glShaderSource(fragmentShader, fshaderSource.length, fshaderSource, null, 0);
```

(....etc., building rendering program as before)
}

(..... main, constructor, reshape, init, dispose as before)

```
private String[ ] readShaderSource(String filename)
{   Vector<String> lines = new Vector<String>();
    Scanner sc;
    String[ ] program;
    try
    {   sc = new Scanner(new File(filename));
        while (sc.hasNext())
        {   lines.addElement(sc.nextLine());
        }
        program = new String[lines.size()];
        for (int i = 0; i < lines.size(); i++)
        {   program[i] = (String) lines.elementAt(i) + "\n";
        }
    }
    catch (IOException e)
    {   System.err.println("IOException reading file: " + e);
        return null;
    }
    return program;
} }
```

■2.4■ BUILDING OBJECTS FROM VERTICES

Ultimately we want to draw more than just a single point. We'd like to draw objects that are constructed of *many* vertices. Large sections of this book will be devoted to this topic. For now we just start with a simple example—we will define *three* vertices and use them to draw a *triangle*.

We can do this by making two small changes to Program 2.2 (actually, the version in Program 2.4 which reads the shaders from files): (a) modify the vertex shader so that *three different* vertices are output to the subsequent stages of the pipeline, and (b) modify the glDrawArrays() call to specify that we are using *three* vertices.

In the Java/JOGL application (specifically in the glDrawArrays() call) we specify GL_TRIANGLES (rather than GL_POINTS), and also specify that there are *three* vertices sent through the pipeline. This causes the vertex shader to run *three times*, and at each iteration, the built-in variable gl_VertexID is automatically incremented (it is initially set to 0). By testing the value of gl_VertexID, the shader is designed to output a different point each of the three times it is executed. Recall that the three points then pass through the *rasterization* stage, producing a filled-in triangle. The modifications are shown in Program 2.5 (the remainder of the code is the same as previously shown in Program 2.4).

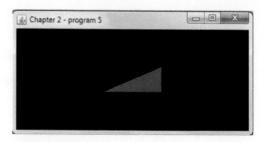

Figure 2.15
Drawing a simple triangle.

Program 2.5 Drawing a Triangle

Vertex Shader

```
#version 430
void main(void)
{   if (gl_VertexID == 0) gl_Position = vec4( 0.25, -0.25, 0.0, 1.0);
    else if (gl_VertexID == 1) gl_Position = vec4(-0.25, -0.25, 0.0, 1.0);
    else gl_Position = vec4( 0.25, 0.25, 0.0, 1.0);
}
```

Java/JOGL application – in display()

```
. . .
gl.glDrawArrays(GL_TRIANGLES, 0, 3);
```

2.5 ANIMATING A SCENE

Many of the techniques in this book can be *animated*. This is when things in the scene are moving or changing, and the scene is rendered repeatedly to reflect these changes in real time.

Recall from Section 2.1.1 that OpenGL makes a single call to init(), and then to display(), when it is initialized. After that, if there are changes to our scene, it becomes the programmer's responsibility to tell OpenGL to call display() again. This is done by invoking the display() function in the GLCanvas from the Java/JOGL application, as follows:

```
myCanvas.display();
```

That is, the GLCanvas has its own display() function. If we call it, the GLCanvas will then in turn call back the display() function in our Java/JOGL application. Technically, the two display()s are completely different functions, but they are intertwined.

One approach is to call display() whenever a change in the scene occurs. In a complex scene, this can become unwieldy. A better approach is to make this call repeatedly, without regard to whether or not anything in the scene has changed, and have our display() function alter what it draws over time. While this may at first seem inefficient, it actually leads to a more efficient and responsive program. Each rendering of our scene is then called a *frame*, and the frequency of calls to display() is the *frame rate*.

There are many ways to organize the code for animating a scene. One way is to create an "animator" class in Java, using either Timer, or Thread.sleep(), or better yet, a ScheduledThreadPoolExecutor.

An even simpler way to build the animator is to use one of the JOGL-specific animator classes:

- Animator
- FPSAnimator

These classes are designed specifically for animating 3D scenes. An FPSAnimator ("FPS" stands for "frames per second"), when instantiated, calls the display() function on a drawable object repeatedly, at a specified frame rate. An Animator (without the "FPS"), when instantiated, calls the display() function repeatedly, but not at any particular frame rate. The developers of JOGL recommend using Animator (instead of FPSAnimator), and handling the rate of movement within the application logic based on the elapsed time since the previous frame. Hence, that is how we will write our programs that are animated.

An example is shown in Program 2.6. We have taken the triangle from Program 2.5 and animated it so that it moves to the right, then moves to the left, back and forth. The Animator is instantiated by the Java/JOGL application in its constructor; the parameter on the Animator constructor call specifies the drawable object. After that, the application is free to make changes to the scene within the display() function. In this example, we don't consider the elapsed time, so the triangle may move more or less quickly depending on the speed of the computer (in future examples, we will use the elapsed time to ensure that they run at the same speed regardless of the computer).

In Program 2.6, the application's display() method maintains a variable "x" used to offset the triangle's X coordinate position. Its value changes each time display() is called (and thus is different for each frame), and it reverses direction each time it reaches 1.0 or -1.0. The value in x is copied to a corresponding variable called "offset" in the vertex shader. The mechanism that performs this copy uses something called a *uniform variable*, which we will study later in Chapter 4. It isn't necessary to understand the details of uniform variables yet. For now, just note that the Java/JOGL application first calls glGetUniformLocation() to get a pointer to the "offset" variable, and then calls glProgramUniform1f() to copy the value of x into offset. The vertex shader then adds the offset to the X coordinate of the triangle being drawn. Note also that the background is cleared at each call to display(), to avoid the triangle leaving a trail as it moves. Figure 2.16 illustrates the display at three time instances (of course, the movement can't be shown in a still figure).

Program 2.6 Simple Animation Example

Java/JOGL application:

```
//  same imports and declarations as before, plus the following:
import com.jogamp.opengl.util.*;
. . .
public class Code extends JFrame implements GLEventListener
{  // same declarations as before, plus:
    private float x = 0.0f;      // location of triangle
    private float inc = 0.01f;   // offset for moving the triangle

    public Code()
    {  //  same constructor as before, plus this at the end, after the call to setVisible(true).
        Animator animtr = new Animator(myCanvas);
        animtr.start();
    }

    public void display(GLAutoDrawable drawable)
    {  GL4 gl = (GL4) GLContext.getCurrentGL();
        gl.glClear(GL_DEPTH_BUFFER_BIT);
        gl.glClear(GL_COLOR_BUFFER_BIT);      // clear the background to black, each time
        gl.glUseProgram(renderingProgram);

        x += inc;                             // move the triangle along x axis
        if (x > 1.0f) inc = -0.01f;           // switch to moving the triangle to the left
        if (x < -1.0f) inc = 0.01f;           // switch to moving the triangle to the right
        int offsetLoc = gl.glGetUniformLocation(renderingProgram, "offset");  // retrieve pointer to "offset"
```

```
gl.glProgramUniform1f(renderingProgram, offsetLoc, x);    // send value in "x" to "offset"

gl.glDrawArrays(GL_TRIANGLES,0,3);
}
... // remaining functions, same as before
}
```

Vertex shader:

```
#version 430
uniform float offset;
void main(void)
{    if (gl_VertexID == 0) gl_Position = vec4( 0.25 + offset, -0.25, 0.0, 1.0);
     else if (gl_VertexID == 1) gl_Position = vec4(-0.25 + offset, -0.25, 0.0, 1.0);
     else gl_Position = vec4( 0.25 + offset, 0.25, 0.0, 1.0);
}
```

Note that in addition to adding code to animate the triangle, we have also added the following line at the beginning of the display() function:

```
gl.glClear(GL_DEPTH_BUFFER_BIT);
```

While not strictly necessary in this particular example, we have added it here and it will continue to appear in most of our applications. Recall from the discussion in Section 2.1.7 that *hidden surface removal* requires both a color buffer and a depth buffer. As we proceed to drawing progressively more complex 3D scenes, it will be necessary to initialize (clear) the depth buffer each frame, especially for scenes that are animated, to ensure that depth comparisons aren't affected by old depth data. It should be apparent from the example above that the command for clearing the depth buffer is essentially the same as for clearing the color buffer.

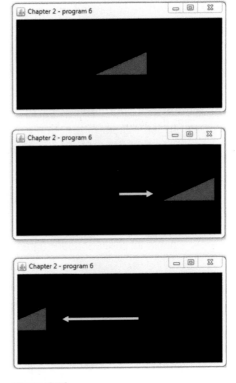

Figure 2.16
An animated, moving triangle.

2.6 ORGANIZING THE JAVA CODE FILES

So far, we have been placing all of the Java/JOGL application code in a single class file called "Code.java" and the GLSL shaders into files called "vertShader. glsl" and "fragShader.glsl." While we freely admit that naming any code module "Code" is almost laughably bad practice, we have adopted this naming convention in this book so that it is absolutely clear in every example which file contains the main block of Java/JOGL code relevant to the example being discussed. Throughout this textbook, it will always be called "Code.java." In practice, a name should of course be chosen that appropriately describes the task performed by the application.

However, as we proceed, there will be circumstances in which we create modules that will be useful in many different applications. Wherever appropriate, we will move those modules into separate files to facilitate reuse. For example, later we will define a Sphere class that will be useful in many different examples, and so it will be separated into its own file.

Similarly, as we encounter *functions* that we wish to reuse, we will place them in a class file called "Utils.java." We have already seen several functions that are appropriate to move into "Utils.java": the error-detecting modules described in Section 2.2 and the functions for reading in GLSL shader programs described in Section 2.3. The latter is particularly well suited to overloading, such that a "createShaderProgram()" function can be defined for each possible combination of pipeline shaders assembled in a given application:

- public int createShaderProgram(String vS, String fS)
- public int createShaderProgram(String vS, String gS, String fS)
- public int createShaderProgram(String vS, String tCS, String tES, String fS)
- public int createShaderProgram(String vS, String tCS, String tES, String gS, String fS)

The first case (above) supports shader programs which utilize only a vertex and fragment shader. The second supports those utilizing vertex, geometry, and fragment shaders. The third supports those using vertex, tessellation, and fragment shaders. And the fourth supports those using vertex, tessellation, geometry, and fragment shaders. The parameters accepted in each case are pathnames for the GLSL files containing the shader code. For example, the following call uses one of the overloaded functions to compile and link a shader pipeline program that includes a vertex and fragment shader. The completed program is placed in the variable "renderingProgram":

```
renderingProgram = Utils.createShaderProgram("vertShader.glsl", "fragShader.glsl");
```

These createShaderProgram() implementations can all be found on the accompanying CD (in the "Utils.java" file), and all of them incorporate the error-detecting modules from Section 2.2 as well. There is nothing new about them; they are simply organized in this way for convenience. As we move forward in the book, other similar functions will be added to Utils.java as we go along. The reader is strongly encouraged to examine the Utils.java file on the accompanying CD, and even add to it as desired. The programs found there are built from the methods as we learn them in the book, and studying their organization should serve to strengthen one's own understanding.

Regarding the functions in the "Utils.java" file, we have implemented them as static methods so that it isn't necessary to instantiate the Utils class. Readers may prefer to implement them as instance methods rather than static methods, depending on the architecture of the particular system being developed.

All of our shader files will be named with a ".glsl" extension.

SUPPLEMENTAL NOTES

There are many details of the OpenGL pipeline that we have not discussed in this introductory chapter. We have skipped a number of internal stages and have completely omitted how *textures* are processed. Our goal was to map out, as simply as possible, the framework in which we will be writing our code. As we proceed we will continue to learn additional details.

We have also deferred presenting code examples for tessellation and geometry. In later chapters we will build complete systems that show how to write practical shaders for each of the stages.

There are more sophisticated ways to organize the code for animating a scene, especially with respect to managing threads. Readers interested in designing a render loop (or "game loop") appropriate for a particular application are encouraged to consult some of the more specialized books on game engine design (e.g., [NY14]), and to peruse the related discussions on gamedev.net [GD17].

We ignored one detail on the glShaderSource() command. The fourth parameter is used to specify a "lengths array" that contains the integer string lengths of each line of code in the given shader program. If this parameter is set to null, as we have done, OpenGL will build this array automatically if the strings are null-terminated. JOGL ensures that strings sent to glShaderSource() are null-terminated. However, it is not uncommon to encounter applications that build these arrays manually rather than sending null.

The composable pipeline can also be configured within the Java/JOGL application code [JU16], rather than just enabling it on the command line (as was described in Section 2.2). This can be useful for utilizing the debugging and tracing tools based on interactive input (e.g., a user keystroke).

Throughout this book, the reader may at times wish to know one or more of OpenGL's upper limits. For example, the programmer might need to know the maximum number of outputs that can be produced by the geometry shader, or the maximum size that can be specified for rendering a point. Many such values are implementation-dependent, meaning that they can vary between different machines. OpenGL provides a mechanism for retrieving such limits using the glGet() command, which takes various forms depending on the type of the parameter being queried. For example, to find the maximum allowable point size, the following call will place the minimum and maximum values (for your machine's OpenGL implementation) into the first two elements of the float array named "size":

```
gl.glGetFloatv(GL_POINT_SIZE_RANGE, size, 0)
```

Many such queries are possible. Consult the OpenGL reference [OP16] documentation for examples.

In some cases, the reader may notice that an OpenGL call is defined as requiring a C pointer as one of its parameters. For example, this occurs in Program 2.2, in the following JOGL call:

```
gl.glGenVertexArrays(vao.length, vao, 0);
```

Looking up the corresponding OpenGL call to glGenVertexArrays() in the OpenGL documentation reveals the following definition:

```
glGenVertexArrays(GLsizei n, GLuint *arrays)
```

Here, notice that the second parameter (*arrays) is defined in OpenGL as a C pointer. While JOGL makes every effort to match the original OpenGL C calls, Java does not have pointers. Any parameter in OpenGL that is a pointer is changed in JOGL. In this case, the JOGL version utilizes an array instead, followed by an integer offset into the array. Whenever there is a discrepancy between a JOGL call and the original C call, consult the JOGL Javadoc for details on the revised parameter(s).

In this chapter, we have tried to describe each parameter on each OpenGL call. However, as the book proceeds, this will become unwieldy and we will sometimes not bother describing a parameter when we believe that doing so would complicate matters unnecessarily. This is because many OpenGL functions have a large number of parameters that are irrelevant to our examples. The reader should get used to using the JOGL/OpenGL documentation to fill in such details when necessary.

Exercises

2.1 Modify Program 2.2 to add animation that causes the drawn point to grow and shrink, in a cycle. Hint: use the glPointSize() function, with a variable as the parameter.

2.2 Modify Program 2.5 so that it draws an isosceles triangle (rather than the right triangle shown in Figure 2.15).

2.3 *(PROJECT)* Modify Program 2.5 to include the error-checking modules shown in Program 2.3. After you have that working, try inserting various errors into the shaders and observing both the resulting behavior and the error messages generated.

References

[GD17] Game Development Network, accessed December 2017, https://www .gamedev.net/

[GL16] GLUT and OpenGL Utility Libraries, accessed July 2016, https://www .opengl.org/resources/libraries/

[JU16] JOGL Users Guide, accessed July 2016, https://jogamp.org/jogl/doc/userguide/

[NY14] R. Nystrom, *Game Programming Patterns—Game Loop* (Genever Benning, 2014), accessed December 2017, http://gameprogrammingpatterns.com/game-loop.html

[OP16] OpenGL 4.5 Reference Pages, accessed July 2016, https://www.opengl.org/sdk/docs/man/

MATHEMATICAL FOUNDATIONS

Computer graphics makes heavy use of mathematics, particularly matrices and matrix algebra. Although we tend to consider 3D graphics programming to be among the most contemporary of technical fields (and in many respects it is), many of the techniques that are used actually date back hundreds of years. Some of them were first understood and codified by the great philosophers of the Renaissance era.

Virtually every facet of 3D graphics, every effect—movement, scale, perspective, texturing, lighting, shadows, and so on—will be accomplished largely mathematically. Therefore this chapter lays the groundwork upon which every subsequent chapter relies.

It is assumed the reader has a basic knowledge of matrix operations; a full coverage of basic matrix algebra is beyond the scope of this text. Therefore, if at any point a particular matrix operation is unfamiliar, it may be necessary to do some supplementary background reading to ensure full understanding before proceeding.

■3.1■ 3D COORDINATE SYSTEMS

3D space is generally represented with three axes: X, Y, and Z. The three axes can be arranged into two configurations, *right-handed* or *left-handed*. (The name derives from the orientation of the axes as if constructed by pointing the thumb and first two fingers of the right versus the left hand, at right angles.)

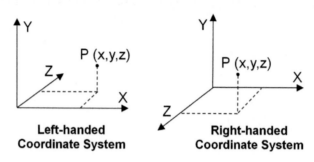

Figure 3.1
3D coordinate systems.

It is important to know which coordinate system your graphics programming environment uses. For example, the majority of coordinate systems in OpenGL are right-handed, whereas in Direct3D the majority are left-handed. Throughout this book, we will assume a right-handed configuration unless otherwise stated.

■3.2■ POINTS

Points in 3D space can be specified by listing the X, Y, Z values, using a notation such as (2, 8, -3). However, it turns out to be much more useful to specify points using *homogeneous* notation, a representation first described in the early 1800s. Points in homogeneous notation contain four values, the first three corresponding to X, Y, and Z, and the fourth, W, is always a fixed nonzero value, usually 1. Thus, we represent this point as (2, 8, -3, 1). As we will see shortly, homogeneous notation will make many of our graphics computations more efficient.

The appropriate GLSL data type for storing points in homogeneous 3D notation is vec4 ("vec" refers to *vector*, but it can also be used for a point). The JOML library includes classes appropriate for creating and storing three-element and four-element (homogeneous) points in the Java application, called Vector3f and

Vector4f, respectively. In some cases (as we will see), JOML adds the fourth element (set to 1.0) to a Vector3f when needed to carry out a homogeneous operation.

3.3 ■ MATRICES

A *matrix* is a rectangular array of values, and its elements are typically accessed by means of subscripts. The first subscript refers to the row number, and the second subscript refers to the column number, with the subscripts starting at 0. Most of the matrices that we will use for 3D graphics computations are of size 4x4, as shown in Figure 3.2.

$$\begin{bmatrix} A_{00} & A_{01} & A_{02} & A_{03} \\ A_{10} & A_{11} & A_{12} & A_{13} \\ A_{20} & A_{21} & A_{22} & A_{23} \\ A_{30} & A_{31} & A_{32} & A_{33} \end{bmatrix}$$

Figure 3.2
4x4 matrix.

The GLSL language includes a data type called mat4 that can be used for storing 4x4 matrices. Similarly, JOML includes a *class* called Matrix4f for instantiating and storing 4x4 matrices.

The *identity matrix* contains all zeros, with ones along the diagonal:

$$\begin{bmatrix} 1 & 0 & 0 & 0 \\ 0 & 1 & 0 & 0 \\ 0 & 0 & 1 & 0 \\ 0 & 0 & 0 & 1 \end{bmatrix}$$

Any item multiplied by the identity matrix is unchanged. In JOML, the identity matrix is available through the function Matrix4f.identity().

The *transpose* of a matrix is computed by interchanging its rows and columns. For example:

$$\begin{bmatrix} A_{00} & A_{01} & A_{02} & A_{03} \\ A_{10} & A_{11} & A_{12} & A_{13} \\ A_{20} & A_{21} & A_{22} & A_{23} \\ A_{30} & A_{31} & A_{32} & A_{33} \end{bmatrix} = \begin{bmatrix} A_{00} & A_{10} & A_{20} & A_{30} \\ A_{01} & A_{11} & A_{21} & A_{31} \\ A_{02} & A_{12} & A_{22} & A_{32} \\ A_{03} & A_{13} & A_{23} & A_{33} \end{bmatrix}^{T}$$

The JOML library and GLSL both have transpose functions: Matrix4f.transpose() and transpose(mat4), respectively.

Matrix addition is straightforward:

$$\begin{bmatrix} A+a & B+b & C+c & D+d \\ E+e & F+f & G+g & H+h \\ I+i & J+j & K+k & L+l \\ M+m & N+n & O+o & P+p \end{bmatrix} = \begin{bmatrix} A & B & C & D \\ E & F & G & H \\ I & J & K & L \\ M & N & O & P \end{bmatrix} + \begin{bmatrix} a & b & c & d \\ e & f & g & h \\ i & j & k & l \\ m & n & o & p \end{bmatrix}$$

In GLSL the **+** operator is overloaded on mat4 to support matrix addition.

There are various multiplication operations possible with matrices that are useful in 3D graphics. Matrix multiplication in general can be done either *left-to-right* or *right-to-left* (note that since these operations are different, it follows that matrix multiplication is not commutative). Most of the time we will use right-to-left multiplication.

In 3D graphics, multiplying a point by a matrix is in most cases done right-to-left, as follows:

$$\begin{pmatrix} AX+BY+CZ+D \\ EX+FY+GZ+H \\ IX+JY+KZ+L \\ MX+NY+OZ+P \end{pmatrix} = \begin{bmatrix} A & B & C & D \\ E & F & G & H \\ I & J & K & L \\ M & N & O & P \end{bmatrix} * \begin{pmatrix} X \\ Y \\ Z \\ 1 \end{pmatrix}$$

Note that we represent the point (X,Y,Z) in homogeneous notation as a one-column matrix.

GLSL and JOML support multiplying a point by a matrix. In JOML, when the point and the matrix are of compatible dimensions (such as a Vector4f and a Matrix4f) then Vector4f.mul(Matrix4f) is used. In cases where a point is stored in a Vector3f, the function Vector3f.mulPosition(Matrix4f) can be used, which will assume a fourth element (set to 1.0) in the vector before carrying out the multiplication. In GLSL vectors and matrices can be multiplied with the * operator.

Multiplying a 4x4 Matrix by another 4x4 matrix is done as follows:

$$\begin{bmatrix} A & B & C & D \\ E & F & G & H \\ I & J & K & L \\ M & N & O & P \end{bmatrix} * \begin{bmatrix} a & b & c & d \\ e & f & g & h \\ i & j & k & l \\ m & n & o & p \end{bmatrix} =$$

$$\begin{bmatrix} Aa+Be+Ci+Dm & Ab+Bf+Cj+Dn & Ac+Bg+Ck+Do & Ad+Bh+Cl+Dp \\ Ea+Fe+Gi+Hm & Eb+Ff+Gj+Hn & Ec+Fg+Gk+Ho & Ed+Fh+Gl+Hp \\ Ia+Je+Ki+Lm & Ib+Jf+Kj+Ln & Ic+Jg+Kk+Lo & Id+Jh+Kl+Lp \\ Ma+Ne+Oi+Pm & Mb+Nf+Oj+Pn & Mc+Ng+Ok+Po & Md+Nh+Ol+Pp \end{bmatrix}$$

Matrix multiplication is frequently referred to as **concatenation**, because as will be seen, it is used to combine a set of matrix transforms into a single matrix. This ability to combine matrix transforms is made possible because of the **associative** property of matrix multiplication. Consider the following sequence of operations:

New Point = Matrix$_1$ * (Matrix$_2$ * (Matrix$_3$ * Point))

Here, we multiply a point by Matrix$_3$, then multiply that result by Matrix$_2$, and that result finally by Matrix$_1$. The result is a new point. The associative property ensures that the above computation is equivalent to

New Point = (Matrix$_1$ * Matrix$_2$ * Matrix$_3$) * Point

Here we first multiply the three matrices together, forming the *concatenation* of Matrix$_1$, Matrix$_2$, and Matrix$_3$ (which itself is also a 4x4 matrix). If we refer to this concatenation as Matrix$_C$, we can rewrite the above operation as

New Point = Matrix$_C$ * Point

The advantage here, as we will see in Chapter 4, is that we will frequently need to apply the same sequence of matrix transformations to every point in our scene. By pre-computing the concatenation of all of those matrices once, we can reduce the total number of matrix operations needed manyfold.

GLSL and JOML both support matrix multiplication, in GLSL with the overloaded * operator, and in JOML with the function Matrix4f.mul(Matrix4f).

The **inverse** of a 4x4 matrix M is another 4x4 matrix, denoted M^{-1}, that has the following property under matrix multiplication:

M*(M^{-1}) = (M^{-1})*M = *identity matrix*

We won't present the details of computing the inverse here. However, it is worth knowing that determining the inverse of a matrix can be computationally expensive; fortunately, we will rarely need it. In the rare instances when we do, it is available in JOML through the function Matrix4f.invert() and in GLSL through the mat4.inverse() function.

◾3.4◾ TRANSFORMATION MATRICES

In graphics, matrices are typically used for performing *transformations* on objects. For example, a matrix can be used to move a point from one location to another. In this chapter we will learn several useful transformation matrices:

- *Translation*
- *Rotation*
- *Scale*
- *Projection*
- *Look-At*

An important property of our transformation matrices is that they are all of size 4x4. This is made possible by our decision to use the *homogeneous* notation. Otherwise, some of the transforms would be of diverse and incompatible dimensions. As we have seen, ensuring they are the same size is not just for convenience; it also makes it possible to combine them arbitrarily and pre-compute groups of transforms for improved performance.

◾3.4.1◾ Translation

A *translation* matrix is used to move items from one location to another. It consists of an identity matrix, with the X, Y, and Z movement(s) given in locations A_{03}, A_{13}, A_{23}. Figure 3.3 shows the form of a translation matrix, and its effect when multiplied by a homogeneous point; the result is a new point "moved" by the translate values.

$$\begin{pmatrix} X + T_X \\ Y + T_Y \\ Z + T_Z \\ 1 \end{pmatrix} = \begin{bmatrix} 1 & 0 & 0 & T_X \\ 0 & 1 & 0 & T_Y \\ 0 & 0 & 1 & T_Z \\ 0 & 0 & 0 & 1 \end{bmatrix} * \begin{pmatrix} X \\ Y \\ Z \\ 1 \end{pmatrix}$$

Figure 3.3
Translation matrix transform.

Note that point (X,Y,Z) is translated (or moved) to location ($X+T_x$, $Y+T_y$, $Z+T_z$) as a result of being multiplied by the translation matrix. Also note that multiplication is specified *right-to-left*.

For example, if we wish to move a group of points upward 5 units along the positive *Y* direction, we could build a translation matrix by taking an identity matrix and placing the value 5 in the T_Y position shown above. Then we simply multiply each of the points we wish to move by the matrix.

There are several functions in JOML for building translation matrices and for multiplying points by matrices, including the following relevant functions:

- *Matrix4f.settranslation(x,y,z)*
- *Vector4f.mul(Matrix4f)* or *Vector3f.mulPosition(Matrix4f)*

3.4.2 Scaling

A *scale* matrix is used to change the size of objects, or to move points toward or away from the origin. Although it may initially seem strange to scale a point, objects in OpenGL are defined by groups of points. So scaling an object involves expanding or contracting its set of points.

The scale matrix transform consists of an identity matrix, with the X, Y, and Z scale factors given in locations A_{00}, A_{11}, A_{22}. Figure 3.4 shows the form of a scale matrix, and its effect when multiplied by a homogeneous point; the result is a new point modified by the scale values.

$$\begin{pmatrix} X * S_X \\ Y * S_Y \\ Z * S_Z \\ 1 \end{pmatrix} = \begin{bmatrix} S_X & 0 & 0 & 0 \\ 0 & S_Y & 0 & 0 \\ 0 & 0 & S_Z & 0 \\ 0 & 0 & 0 & 1 \end{bmatrix} * \begin{pmatrix} X \\ Y \\ Z \\ 1 \end{pmatrix}$$

Figure 3.4
Scale matrix transform.

There are several functions in JOML for building scale matrices and multiplying points by scale matrix transforms, including the following relevant functions:

- *Matrix4f.scaling(x,y,z)*
- *Vector3f.mul(Matrix4f)*

Scaling can be used to switch coordinate systems. For example, we can use scale to determine what the left-hand coordinates would be, given a set of right-hand coordinates. From Figure 3.1 we see that negating the Z coordinate would toggle between right-hand and left-hand systems, so the scale matrix transform to accomplish this is

$$\begin{bmatrix} 1 & 0 & 0 & 0 \\ 0 & 1 & 0 & 0 \\ 0 & 0 & -1 & 0 \\ 0 & 0 & 0 & 1 \end{bmatrix}$$

3.4.3 Rotation

Rotation is a bit more complex, because rotating an item in 3D space requires specifying (a) an axis of rotation and (b) a rotation amount in degrees or radians.

In the mid-1700s, the mathematician Leonhard Euler showed that a rotation around any desired axis could be specified instead as a combination of rotations around the X, Y, and Z axes [EU76]. These three rotation angles, around the respective axes, have come to be known as *Euler angles*. The discovery, known as *Euler's Theorem*, is very useful to us, because rotations around each of the three axes can be specified using matrix transforms.

The three rotation transforms, around the X, Y, and Z axes, respectively, are shown in Figure 3.5. There are several functions in JOML for building and using rotation matrices as well:

- *Matrix4f.rotateX(radians)*
- *Matrix4f.rotateY(radians)*
- *Matrix4f.rotateZ(radians)*
- *Matrix4f.rotateXYZ(θx,θy,θz)*
- *Vector3f.mul(Matrix4f)*

In practice, using Euler angles to rotate an item around an arbitrary line in 3D space takes a couple of additional steps if the line doesn't pass through the origin. In general:

1. Translate the axis of rotation so that it goes through the origin.
2. Rotate by appropriate Euler angles around X, Y, and Z.
3. Undo the translation of Step 1.

Rotation around X by θ:

$$\begin{pmatrix} X' \\ Y' \\ Z' \\ 1 \end{pmatrix} = \begin{bmatrix} 1 & 0 & 0 & 0 \\ 0 & cos\theta & -sin\theta & 0 \\ 0 & sin\theta & cos\theta & 0 \\ 0 & 0 & 0 & 1 \end{bmatrix} * \begin{pmatrix} X \\ Y \\ Z \\ 1 \end{pmatrix}$$

Rotation around Y by θ:

$$\begin{pmatrix} X' \\ Y' \\ Z' \\ 1 \end{pmatrix} = \begin{bmatrix} cos\theta & 0 & sin\theta & 0 \\ 0 & 1 & 0 & 0 \\ -sin\theta & 0 & cos\theta & 0 \\ 0 & 0 & 0 & 1 \end{bmatrix} * \begin{pmatrix} X \\ Y \\ Z \\ 1 \end{pmatrix}$$

Rotation around Z by θ:

$$\begin{pmatrix} X' \\ Y' \\ Z' \\ 1 \end{pmatrix} = \begin{bmatrix} cos\theta & -sin\theta & 0 & 0 \\ sin\theta & cos\theta & 0 & 0 \\ 0 & 0 & 1 & 0 \\ 0 & 0 & 0 & 1 \end{bmatrix} * \begin{pmatrix} X \\ Y \\ Z \\ 1 \end{pmatrix}$$

Figure 3.5
Rotation transform matrices.

The three rotation transforms shown in Figure 3.5 each have the interesting property that the inverse rotation happens to equal the transpose of the matrix. This can be verified by examining the above matrices, recalling that $cos(-\theta) = cos(\theta)$ and $sin(-\theta) = -sin(\theta)$. This property will become useful later.

Euler angles can cause certain artifacts in some 3D graphic applications. For that reason it is often advisable to use *quaternions* for computing rotations. Many resources exist for those readers interested in exploring quaternions (e.g., [KU98]). Euler angles will suffice for most of our needs.

3.5 ▮ VECTORS

Vectors specify a *magnitude* and *direction*. They are not bound to a specific location; a vector can be "moved" without changing what it represents.

There are various ways to notate a vector, such as a line segment with an arrowhead at one end, or as a pair (magnitude, direction), or as the difference between two points. In 3D graphics, vectors are frequently represented as a single point in space, where the vector is the distance and direction from the origin to that point. In Figure 3.6, vector V (shown in red) can be specified either as the difference between points P1 and P2 or as an equivalent distance from the origin to P3. In all of our applications, we specify V as simply (x,y,z), the same notation used to specify the point P3.

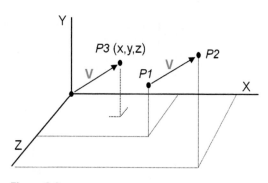

Figure 3.6
Two representations for a vector V.

It is convenient to represent a vector the same way as a point, because we can use our matrix transforms on points or vectors interchangeably. However, it also can be confusing. For this reason we sometimes will notate a vector with a small arrow above it (such as $\vec{V}$). Many graphics systems do not distinguish between a point and a vector at all, such as in GLSL and JOML, which provide data types vec3/vec4 and classes Vector3f/Vector4f (respectively) that can hold either points or vectors. Some systems (such as the graphicslib3D library used in a previous edition of this book) have separate point and vector classes, and enforce appropriate use of one or the other depending on the operation being done. It is an open debate as to whether it is clearer to use one data type for both or separate data types.

There are several vector operations that are used frequently in 3D graphics, for which there are functions available in JOML and GLSL. For example, assuming vectors A(u,v,w) and B(x,y,z):

Addition and Subtraction:

A ± B = (u ± x, v ± y, w ± z)
JOML: Vector3f.add(Vector3f)
GLSL: vec3 ± vec3

Normalize (change to length=1; *note the "^" notation above the "A"):*

$\hat{A}$ = A/|A| = A/sqrt(u^2+v^2+w^2), where |A| ≡ *length of vector A*
JOML: Vector3f.normalize()
GLSL: normalize(vec3) *or* normalize(vec4)

Dot Product:

A • B = ux + vy + wz
JOML: Vector3f.dot(Vector3f)
GLSL: dot(vec3,vec3) *or* dot(vec4,vec4)

Cross Product:

A x B = (vz-wy, wx-uz, uy-vx)
JOML: Vector3f.cross(Vector3f)
GLSL: cross(vec3,vec3)

Other useful vector functions are *magnitude* (which is available in both JOML and GLSL as length()) as well as *reflection* and *refraction* (both are available in GLSL; JOML includes reflection only).

We shall now take a closer look at the functions *dot product* and *cross product*.

3.5.1 Uses for *Dot Product*

Throughout this book, our programs make heavy use of the dot product. The most important and fundamental use is for finding the *angle between two vectors*. Consider two vectors $\vec{V}$ and $\vec{W}$, and say we wish to find the angle θ separating them.

$$\vec{V} \bullet \vec{W} = |\vec{V}| * |\vec{W}| * \cos(\theta)$$

$$\cos(\theta) = \frac{\vec{V} \bullet \vec{W}}{|\vec{V}| * |\vec{W}|}$$

Therefore, if $\vec{V}$ and $\vec{W}$ are normalized (i.e., of unit length—we use the "^" notation for normalization as shown earlier), then:

$$\cos(\theta) = \hat{V} \bullet \hat{W}$$

$$\theta = \arccos(\hat{V} \bullet \hat{W})$$

Interestingly, we will later see that often it is *cos(θ)* that we need, rather than θ itself. So both of the above derivations will be directly useful.

The dot product also has a variety of other uses:

- Finding a vector's magnitude: $\sqrt{\vec{V} \bullet \vec{V}}$
- Finding whether two vectors are perpendicular if $\vec{V} \bullet \vec{W} = 0$
- Finding whether two vectors are parallel if $\vec{V} \bullet \vec{W} = |\vec{V}| * |\vec{W}|$
- Finding whether two vectors are parallel but pointing in opposite directions: $\vec{V} \bullet \vec{W} = -|\vec{V}| * |\vec{W}|$
- Finding whether an angle between vectors lies in the range [-90°..+90°]: $\hat{V} \bullet \hat{W} > 0$
- Finding the minimum signed distance from point $P = (x,y,z)$ to plane $S = (a,b,c,d)$ (first, find unit vector normal to S, $\hat{n} = (\frac{a}{\sqrt{a^2+b^2+c^2}}, \frac{b}{\sqrt{a^2+b^2+c^2}}, \frac{c}{\sqrt{a^2+b^2+c^2}})$, and shortest distance $D = \frac{d}{\sqrt{a^2+b^2+c^2}}$ from the origin to the plane; then the minimum signed distance from P to S is $(\hat{n} \bullet P) + D$ and the sign of this distance determines on which side of the plane S point P lies)

3.5.2 Uses for *Cross Product*

An important property of the cross product of two vectors, which we will use extensively throughout this book, is that it produces a vector that is *normal* (perpendicular) to the plane defined by the original two vectors.

Any two non-collinear vectors define a plane. For example, consider two arbitrary vectors $\vec{V}$ and $\vec{W}$. Since vectors can be moved without changing their meaning, they can be moved so that their origins coincide. Figure 3.7 shows a plane defined by $\vec{V}$ and $\vec{W}$, and the normal vector resulting from their cross product. The direction of the resulting normal obeys the *right-hand rule,* wherein curling the fingers of one's right hand from $\vec{V}$ to $\vec{W}$ causes the thumb to point in the direction of the normal vector $\vec{R}$.

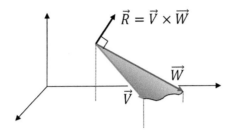

Figure 3.7
Cross product produces normal vector.

Note that the order is significant; $\vec{W} \times \vec{V}$ would produce a vector in the opposite direction from $\vec{R}$.

The ability to find normal vectors by using the cross product will become extremely useful later when we study *lighting*. In order to determine lighting effects, we will need to know *outward normals* associated with the model we are rendering. Figure 3.8 shows an example of a simple model made up of six points (vertices), and the computation employing cross product that determines the outward normal of one of its faces.

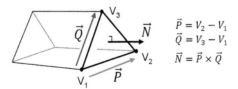

$$\vec{P} = V_2 - V_1$$
$$\vec{Q} = V_3 - V_1$$
$$\vec{N} = \vec{P} \times \vec{Q}$$

Figure 3.8
Computing outward normals.

■3.6■ LOCAL AND WORLD SPACE

The most common use for 3D graphics (with OpenGL or any other framework) is to simulate a three-dimensional world, place objects in it, and then view that simulated world on a monitor. The objects placed in the 3D world are usually modeled as collections of triangles. Later, in Chapter 6, we will dive into modeling. But we can start looking at the overall process now.

When building a 3D model of an object, we generally orient the model in the most convenient manner for describing it. For example, when modeling a sphere, we might orient the model with the sphere's center at the origin (0,0,0) and give it a convenient radius, such as 1. The space in which a model is defined is called its *local space*, or *model space*. OpenGL documentation uses the term *object space*.

The sphere might then be used as a piece of a larger model, such as becoming the head on a robot. The robot would, of course, be defined in its own local/model space. Positioning the sphere model into the robot model space can be done using the matrix transforms for scale, rotation, and translation, as illustrated in Figure 3.9. In this manner, complex models can be built hierarchically (this is developed further in Section 4.8 of Chapter 4, using a stack of matrices).

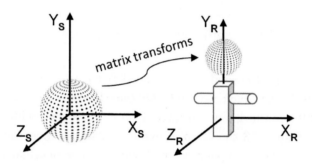

Figure 3.9
Model spaces for a sphere and a robot.

In the same manner, modeled objects are placed in a simulated world by deciding on the orientation and dimensions of that world, called *world space*. The matrix that positions and orients an object into world space is called a *model matrix*, or M.

3.7 ■ EYE SPACE AND THE SYNTHETIC CAMERA

So far, the transform matrices we have seen all operate in 3D space. Ultimately, however, we will want to display our 3D space—or a portion of it—on a 2D monitor. In order to do this, we need to decide on a vantage point. Just as we see our real world through our eyes from a particular point, in a particular direction, so too must we establish a position and orientation as the window into our virtual world. This vantage point is called "view" or "eye" space, or the "synthetic camera."

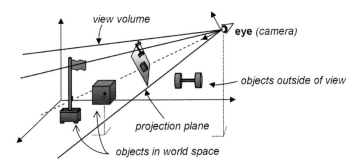

Figure 3.10
Positioning a camera in the 3D world.

As shown in Figures 3.10 and 3.12, viewing involves (a) placing the camera at some world location; (b) orienting the camera, which usually requires maintaining its own set of orthogonal axes $\vec{U}/\vec{V}/\vec{N}$; (c) defining a *view volume*; and (d) projecting objects within the volume onto a *projection plane*.

OpenGL includes a camera that is permanently fixed at the origin (0,0,0) and faces down the negative Z-axis, as shown in Figure 3.11.

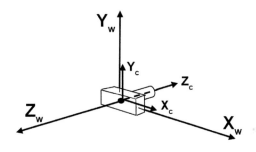

Figure 3.11
OpenGL fixed camera.

In order to use the OpenGL camera, one of the things we need to do is *simulate* moving it to some desired location and orientation. This is done by figuring out where our objects in the world are located relative to the desired camera position (i.e., where they are located in "camera space," as defined by the U, V, and N axes of the camera as illustrated in Figure 3.12). Given a point at world space location P_W, we need a transform to convert it to the equivalent point in camera space, making it *appear* as though we are viewing it from the desired camera location C_W. We do this by computing its camera space position P_C. Knowing that the OpenGL camera location is always at the fixed position (0,0,0), what transform would achieve this?

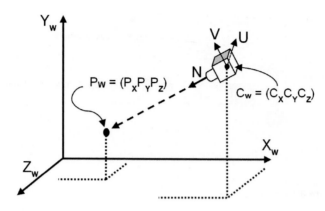

Figure 3.12
Camera orientation.

The necessary transforms are determined as follows:

1. Translate P_W by the negative of the desired camera location.
2. Rotate P_W by the negative of the desired camera orientation Euler angles.

We can build a single transform that does both the rotation and the translation in one matrix, called the *viewing transform* matrix, or V. The matrix V is produced by concatenating the two matrices T (a translation matrix containing the negative of the desired camera location) and R (a rotation matrix containing the negative of the desired camera orientation). In this case, working from right to left, we first translate world point P, then rotate it:

$$P_C = R * (T * P_W)$$

As we saw earlier, the associative rule allows us to group the operations instead thusly:

$$P_C = (R * T) * P_W$$

If we save the concatenation R*T in the matrix V, the operation now looks like

$$P_C = V * P_W$$

The complete computation and the exact contents of matrices T and R are shown in Figure 3.13 (we omit the derivation of matrix R—a derivation is available in [FV95]).

$$
\begin{pmatrix} X_C \\ Y_C \\ Z_C \\ 1 \end{pmatrix} = \overbrace{\begin{bmatrix} \hat{U}_X & \hat{U}_Y & \hat{U}_Z & 0 \\ \hat{V}_X & \hat{V}_Y & \hat{V}_Z & 0 \\ \hat{N}_X & \hat{N}_Y & \hat{N}_Z & 0 \\ 0 & 0 & 0 & 1 \end{bmatrix}}^{\substack{\text{negative of camera} \\ \text{rotation angles}}} * \overbrace{\begin{bmatrix} 1 & 0 & 0 & -C_X \\ 0 & 1 & 0 & -C_Y \\ 0 & 0 & 1 & -C_Z \\ 0 & 0 & 0 & 1 \end{bmatrix}}^{\substack{\text{negative of} \\ \text{camera location}}} * \begin{pmatrix} P_X \\ P_Y \\ P_Z \\ 1 \end{pmatrix}
$$

point P_C in eye space — R (rotation) — T (translation) — world point P_W

V (viewing transform)

Figure 3.13
Deriving a view matrix.

More commonly, the V matrix is concatenated with the model matrix M to form a single *model-view* (MV) matrix:

$$MV = V * M$$

Then, a point P_M in its own model space is transformed directly to camera space in one step as follows:

$$P_C = MV * P_M$$

The advantage of this approach becomes clear when one considers that, in a complex scene, we will need to perform this transformation not on just one point, but *on every vertex in the scene.* By pre-computing MV, transforming each point into view space will require us to do just *one* matrix multiplication per vertex, rather than two. Later, we will see that we can extend this process to pre-computing several matrix concatenations, reducing the per-vertex computations considerably.

3.8 ■ PROJECTION MATRICES

Now that we have established the camera, we can examine *projection matrices.* Two important projection matrices that we will now examine are (a) *perspective* and (b) *orthographic.*

3.8.1 The Perspective Projection Matrix

Perspective projection attempts to make a 2D picture appear 3D, by utilizing the concept of perspective to mimic what we see when we look at the real world. Objects that are close appear larger than objects that are far away, and in some cases, lines that are parallel in 3D space are no longer parallel when drawn with perspective.

Perspective was one of the great discoveries of the Renaissance era in the 1400–1500s, when artists started painting with more realism than did their predecessors.

An excellent example can be seen in Figure 3.14, the *Annunciation, with St. Emidius* by Carlo Crivelli, painted in 1486 (currently held at the National Gallery in London [CR86]). The intense use of perspective is clear—the receding lines of the left-facing wall of the building on the right are slanted toward each other dramatically. This creates the illusion of depth and 3D space, and in the process lines that are parallel in reality are not parallel in the picture. Also, the people in the foreground are larger than the people in the background. While today we take these devices for granted, finding a transformation matrix to accomplish this requires some mathematical analysis.

We achieve this effect by using a matrix transform that converts parallel lines into appropriate non-parallel lines. Such a matrix is called a *perspective matrix* or *perspective transform,* and is built by defining the four parameters of a *view volume.* Those parameters are (a) *aspect ratio,* (b) *field of view,* (c) *projection plane* or *near clipping plane,* and (d) *far clipping plane.*

Only objects between the *near* and *far* clipping planes are rendered. The near clipping plane also serves as the plane on which objects are *projected,* and is generally positioned close to the eye or camera (shown on the left in Figure 3.15). Selection of an appropriate value for the far clipping plane is discussed in Chapter 4. The *field of view* is the vertical angle of viewable space. The *aspect ratio* is the ratio width/height of the near and far clipping planes. The shape formed by these elements and shown in Figure 3.15 is called a *frustum.*

Figure 3.14
Crivelli's *Annunciation, with Saint Emidius* (1486).

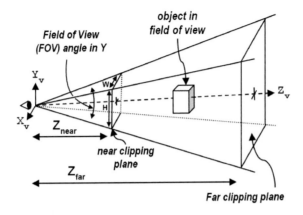

Figure 3.15
Perspective view volume or frustum.

The perspective matrix is used to transform points in 3D space to their appropriate position on the near clipping plane, and is built by first computing values q, A, B, and C, and then using those values to construct the matrix, as shown in Figure 3.16 (and derived in [FV95]).

$$q = \frac{1}{\tan(\frac{fieldOfView}{2})}$$

$$A = \frac{q}{aspectRatio}$$

$$B = \frac{Z_{near} + Z_{far}}{Z_{near} - Z_{far}}$$

$$C = \frac{2 * (Z_{near} * Z_{far})}{Z_{near} - Z_{far}}$$

$$\begin{bmatrix} A & 0 & 0 & 0 \\ 0 & q & 0 & 0 \\ 0 & 0 & B & C \\ 0 & 0 & -1 & 0 \end{bmatrix}$$

Figure 3.16
Building a perspective matrix.

Generating a perspective transform matrix is a simple matter, by simply inserting the described formulas into the cells of a 4x4 matrix. JOML also includes a function Matrix4f.setPerspective() for building a perspective matrix.

3.8.2 The Orthographic Projection Matrix

In *orthographic* projection, parallel lines remain parallel; that is, perspective isn't employed. Instead, objects that are within the view volume are projected directly, without any adjustment of their sizes due to their distances from the camera.

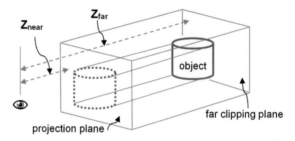

Figure 3.17
Orthographic projection.

An orthographic projection is a parallel projection in which all projections are at right angles with the projection plane. An orthographic matrix is built by defining the following parameters: (a) the distance Z_{near} from the camera to the projection plane, (b) the distance Z_{far} from the camera to the far clipping plane, and (c) values for L, R, T, and B, with L and R corresponding to the X coordinates of the left and right boundaries of the projection plane, respectively, and T and B corresponding to the Y coordinates of the top and bottom boundaries of the projection plane, respectively. The orthographic projection matrix, as derived in [FV95], is shown in Figure 3.18.

$$\begin{bmatrix} \dfrac{2}{R-L} & 0 & 0 & -\dfrac{R+L}{R-L} \\[2ex] 0 & \dfrac{2}{T-B} & 0 & -\dfrac{T+B}{T-B} \\[2ex] 0 & 0 & \dfrac{1}{Z_{far}-Z_{near}} & -\dfrac{Z_{near}}{Z_{far}-Z_{near}} \\[2ex] 0 & 0 & 0 & 1 \end{bmatrix}$$

Figure 3.18
Orthographic projection matrix.

Not all parallel projections are orthographic, but others are out of the scope of this textbook.

Parallel projections don't match what the eye sees when looking at the real world. But they are useful in a variety of situations, such as in casting shadows, performing 3D clipping, and in CAD (computer aided design)—the latter because they preserve measurement regardless of the placement of the objects. Regardless, the great majority of examples in this book use perspective projection.

3.9 ■ LOOK-AT MATRIX

The final transformation we will examine is the *look-at* matrix. This is handy when you wish to place the camera at one location and look toward a particular other location, as illustrated in Figure 3.19. Of course, it would be possible to achieve this using the methods we have already seen, but it is such a common operation that building one matrix transform to do it is often useful.

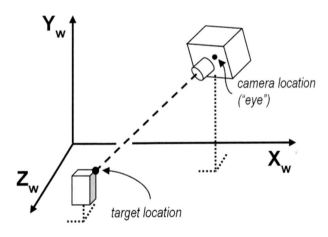

Figure 3.19
Elements of look-at.

A look-at transform still requires deciding on a camera orientation. We do this by specifying a vector approximating the general orientation desired (such as the world $\vec{Y}$ axis). Typically, a sequence of cross products can be used to then generate a suitable set of forward, side, and up vectors for the desired camera orientation. Figure 3.20 shows the computations, starting with the camera location (eye), target location, and initial up vector $\vec{Y}$, to build the look-at matrix, as derived in [FV95].

$$\overrightarrow{fwd} = normalize(eye - target)$$

$$\overrightarrow{side} = normalize(-\overrightarrow{fwd} \times \vec{Y})$$

$$\overrightarrow{up} = normalize(\overrightarrow{side} \times -\overrightarrow{fwd})$$

The look-at matrix then equals:

$$\begin{bmatrix} \overrightarrow{side}_X & \overrightarrow{side}_Y & \overrightarrow{side}_Z & -(\overrightarrow{side} \bullet \overrightarrow{eye}) \\ \overrightarrow{up}_X & \overrightarrow{up}_Y & \overrightarrow{up}_Z & -(\overrightarrow{up} \bullet \overrightarrow{eye}) \\ -\overrightarrow{fwd}_X & -\overrightarrow{fwd}_Y & -\overrightarrow{fwd}_Z & -(-\overrightarrow{fwd} \bullet \overrightarrow{eye}) \\ 0 & 0 & 0 & 1 \end{bmatrix}$$

Figure 3.20
Look-at matrix.

We could encode this as a simple Java/JOGL utility function that builds a look-at matrix, given specified values for camera location, target location, and the initial "up" vector $\vec{Y}$. Since JOML includes the function Matrix4f.setLookAt() for building a look-at matrix, we will simply use that. This function will be useful later in this textbook, particularly in Chapter 8 when we generate shadows.

3.10 GLSL FUNCTIONS FOR BUILDING MATRIX TRANSFORMS

Although JOML includes predefined functions for performing many of the 3D transformations covered in this chapter, such as translation, rotation, and scale, GLSL only includes basic matrix operations such as addition, concatenation, and so on. It is therefore sometimes necessary to write our own GLSL utility functions for building 3D transformation matrices when we need them to perform certain 3D computations in a shader. The appropriate datatype to hold such a matrix in GLSL is mat4.

The syntax for initializing mat4 matrices in GLSL loads values by columns. The first four values are put into the first column, the next four into the next column, and so forth, as illustrated in the following example:

```
mat4 translationMatrix =
    mat4(   1.0, 0.0, 0.0, 0.0,        // note this is the leftmost column, not the top row
            0.0, 1.0, 0.0, 0.0,
            0.0, 0.0, 1.0, 0.0,
            tx, ty, tz, 1.0 );
```

which builds the translation matrix described previously in Figure 3.3.

Program 3.1 includes five GLSL functions for building 4x4 translation, rotation, and scale matrices, each corresponding to formulas given earlier in this chapter. We will use some of these functions later in the book.

Program 3.1 Building Transformation Matrices in GLSL

```
// builds and returns a translation matrix
mat4 buildTranslate(float x, float y, float z)
{   mat4 trans = mat4(1.0, 0.0, 0.0, 0.0,
                      0.0, 1.0, 0.0, 0.0,
                      0.0, 0.0, 1.0, 0.0,
                      x, y, z, 1.0 );
    return trans;
}

// builds and returns a matrix that performs a rotation around the X axis
mat4 buildRotateX(float rad)
{   mat4 xrot = mat4(1.0, 0.0, 0.0, 0.0,
                     0.0, cos(rad), -sin(rad), 0.0,
                     0.0, sin(rad), cos(rad), 0.0,
                     0.0, 0.0, 0.0, 1.0 );
    return xrot;
}

// builds and returns a matrix that performs a rotation around the Y axis
mat4 buildRotateY(float rad)
{   mat4 yrot = mat4(cos(rad), 0.0, sin(rad), 0.0,
                     0.0, 1.0, 0.0, 0.0,
                     -sin(rad), 0.0, cos(rad), 0.0,
                     0.0, 0.0, 0.0, 1.0 );
    return yrot;
}

// builds and returns a matrix that performs a rotation around the Z axis
mat4 buildRotateZ(float rad)
{   mat4 zrot = mat4(cos(rad), -sin(rad), 0.0, 0.0,
                     sin(rad), cos(rad), 0.0, 0.0,
                     0.0, 0.0, 1.0, 0.0,
                     0.0, 0.0, 0.0, 1.0 );
    return zrot;
}
```

```
//  builds and returns a scale matrix
mat4 buildScale(float x, float y, float z)
{   mat4 scale = mat4(x, 0.0, 0.0, 0.0,
                      0.0, y, 0.0, 0.0,
                      0.0, 0.0, z, 0.0,
                      0.0, 0.0, 0.0, 1.0 );
    return scale;
}
```

SUPPLEMENTAL NOTES

In this chapter we have seen examples of applying matrix transformations to points. Later, we will also want to apply these same transforms to vectors. In order to accomplish a transform on a vector V equivalent to applying some matrix transform M to a point, it is necessary in the general case to compute the *inverse transpose* of M, denoted $(M^{-1})^T$, and multiply V by that matrix. In some cases, $M=(M^{-1})^T$, and in those cases it is possible to simply use M. For example, the basic rotation matrices we have seen in this chapter are equal to their own inverse transpose and can be applied directly to vectors (and therefore also to points). Thus, the examples in this book sometimes use $(M^{-1})^T$ when applying a transform to a vector, and sometimes simply use M.

Many of the JOML functions described in this section modify a specified matrix and (somewhat counterintuitively) return a reference to the same matrix, rather than building and returning a new matrix. This is for performance reasons, and will be discussed in greater detail in Chapter 4.

One of the things we haven't discussed in this chapter is techniques for moving the camera smoothly through space. This is very useful, especially for games and CGI movies, but also for visualization, virtual reality, and 3D modeling.

We didn't include complete derivations for all of the matrix transforms that were presented (they can be found in other sources, such as [FV95]). We strove instead for a concise summary of the point, vector, and matrix operations necessary for doing basic 3D graphics programming. As this book proceeds, we will encounter many practical uses for the methods presented.

Exercises

3.1 Modify Program 2.5 so that the vertex shader includes one of the buildRotate() functions from Program 3.1 and applies it to the points comprising the triangle. This should cause the triangle to be rotated from its original orientation. You don't need to animate the rotation.

3.2 *(RESEARCH)* At the end of Section 3.4 we indicated that Euler angles can in some cases lead to undesirable artifacts. The most common is called "gimbal lock." Describe gimbal lock, give an example, and explain why gimbal lock can cause problems.

3.3 *(RESEARCH)* One way of avoiding the artifacts that can manifest when using Euler angles is to use *quaternions*. We didn't study quaternions; however, JOML includes a Quaternionf class. Do some independent study on quaternions, and familiarize yourself with the related JOML Quaternionf class.

References

[**CR86**] C. Crivelli, *The Annunciation, with Saint Emidius* (1486), in the National Gallery, London, England, accessed July 2016, https://www.nationalgallery.org.uk/paintings/carlo-crivelli-the-annunciation-with-saint-emidius

[**EU76**] L. Euler, *Formulae generals pro translatione quacunque coporum rigidorum* (General formulas for the translation of arbitrary rigid bodies), Novi Commentarii academiae scientiarum Petropolitanae 20, 1776.

[**FV95**] J. Foley, A. van Dam, S. Feiner, and J. Hughes, *Computer Graphics—Principles and Practice*, 2nd ed. (Addison-Wesley, 1995).

[**KU98**] J. B. Kuipers, *Quaternions and Rotation Sequences* (Princeton University Press, 1998).

CHAPTER 4

MANAGING 3D GRAPHICS DATA

■ ■ ■ ■ ■

Using OpenGL to render 3D images generally involves sending several datasets through the OpenGL shader pipeline. For example, to draw a simple 3D object such as a *cube*, you will need to at least send the following items:

- the vertices for the cube model
- some transformation matrices to control the appearance of the cube's orientation in 3D space

To complicate matters a bit, there are *two* ways of sending data through the OpenGL pipeline:

- through a *buffer* to a *vertex attribute*, or
- directly to a *uniform variable*

It is important to understand exactly how these two mechanisms work, so as to use the appropriate method for each item we are sending through.

Let's start by rendering a simple cube.

◼ 4.1 ◼ BUFFERS AND VERTEX ATTRIBUTES

For an object to be drawn, its vertices must be sent to the vertex shader. Vertices are usually sent by putting them in a *buffer* on the Java side and associating that buffer with a *vertex attribute* declared in the shader. There are several steps to accomplish this, some of which only need to be done once, and some of which—if the scene is animated—must be done at every frame:

Done once—typically in init():

1. create a buffer
2. copy the vertices into the buffer

Done at each frame—typically in display():

1. enable the buffer containing the vertices
2. associate the buffer with a vertex attribute
3. enable the vertex attribute
4. use glDrawArrays(...) to draw the object

Buffers are typically created all at once at the start of the program, either in init() or in a function called by init(). In OpenGL, a buffer is contained in a *Vertex Buffer Object*, or *VBO*, which is declared and instantiated in the Java/JOGL application. A scene may require many VBOs, so it is customary to generate and then fill several of them in init(), so that they are available whenever your program needs to draw one or more of them.

A buffer interacts with a vertex attribute in a specific way. When glDrawArrays() is executed, the data in the buffer starts flowing, sequentially from the beginning of the buffer, through the vertex shader. As described in Chapter 2, the vertex shader executes *once per vertex*. A vertex in 3D space requires three values, so an appropriate vertex attribute in the shader to receive these three values would be of type vec3. Then, for each *three values* in the buffer, the shader is invoked, as illustrated in Figure 4.1.

A related structure in OpenGL is called a *Vertex Array Object*, or *VAO*. VAOs were introduced in version 3.0 of OpenGL and are provided as a way of organizing buffers and making them easier to manipulate in complex scenes. OpenGL requires at least one VAO to be created, and for our purposes one will be sufficient.

For example, suppose that we wish to display two objects. On the Java/JOGL side, we could do this by declaring a single VAO and an associated set of two VBOs (one per object), as follows:

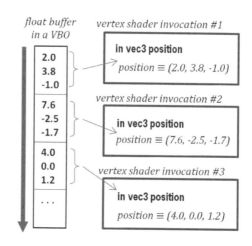

Figure 4.1
Data transmission between a VBO and a vertex attribute.

```
private int vao[ ] = new int[1];      // OpenGL requires these values be specified in arrays
private int vbo[ ] = new int[2];
...
gl.glGenVertexArrays(1, vao, 0);
gl.glBindVertexArray(vao[0]);
gl.glGenBuffers(2, vbo, 0);
```

The two OpenGL commands glGenVertexArrays() and glGenBuffers() create VAOs and VBOs, respectively, and return integer IDs for them. We store those IDs into the int arrays vao and vbo. The three parameters on each of them refer to how many are created, an array to hold the returned IDs, and an offset into that array (usually set to 0). The purpose of glBindVertexArrays() is to make the specified VAO "active" so that the generated buffers[1] will be associated with that VAO.

A buffer needs to have a corresponding *vertex attribute* variable declared in the vertex shader. Vertex attributes are generally the first variables declared in a

---

[1] Throughout this example, two buffers are declared, to emphasize that *usually* we will use several buffers. Later we will use the additional buffer(s) to store other information associated with the vertex, such as color. In the current case we are using only one of the declared buffers, so it would have been sufficient to declare just one VBO.

shader. In our cube example, a vertex attribute to receive the cube vertices could be declared in the vertex shader as follows:

```
layout (location = 0) in vec3 position;
```

The keyword in means "input" and indicates that this vertex attribute will be receiving values from a buffer (as we will see later, vertex attributes can also be used for "output"). As seen before, the "vec3" means that each invocation of the shader will grab *three* float values (presumably *x*, *y*, *z*, comprising a single vertex). The variable name is "position"; the "layout (location=0)" portion of the command is called a "layout qualifier" and is how we will associate the vertex attribute with a particular buffer. Thus this vertex attribute has an identifier 0 that we will use later for this purpose.

The manner in which we load the vertices of a model into a buffer (VBO) depends on where the model's vertex values are stored. In Chapter 6 we will see how models are commonly built in a modeling tool (such as *Blender* [BL16] or *Maya* [MA16]), exported to a standard file format (such as .obj—also described in Chapter 6), and imported into the Java/JOGL application. We will also see how a model's vertices can be calculated on the fly, or generated inside the pipeline, such as in the tessellation shader.

For now, let's say that we wish to draw a *cube*, and let's presume that the vertices of our cube are hardcoded in an array in the Java/JOGL application. In that case, we need to copy those values into one of our two buffers that we generated above. To do that, we need to (a) make that buffer (say, the 0th buffer) "active" with the OpenGL glBindBuffer() command, (b) copy the vertices into a Java FloatBuffer, and (c) use the glBufferData() command to copy the FloatBuffer into the active buffer (the 0th VBO in this case). Presuming that the vertices are stored in a float array named vPositions, the following JOGL code[2] would copy those values into the 0th VBO:

```
gl.glBindBuffer(GL_ARRAY_BUFFER, vbo[0]);
FloatBuffer vBuf = Buffers.newDirectFloatBuffer(vPositions);
gl.glBufferData(GL_ARRAY_BUFFER, vBuf.limit()*4, vBuf, GL_STATIC_DRAW);
```

---

[2] Note that here, for the first time, we are refraining from describing every parameter in one or more JOGL calls. As mentioned in Chapter 2, the reader is encouraged to utilize the OpenGL documentation for such details as needed.

Java has two types of buffers: *direct* and *non-direct*. For performance reasons, *direct* buffers should be used in JOGL applications. JOGL provides tools in the class com.jogamp.common.nio.Buffers that facilitate the use of direct buffers. In the example above, the JOGL function newDirectFloatBuffer() copies values from an array to a FloatBuffer, in this case the vertices of the cube to be drawn.

Next, we add code to display() that will cause the values in the buffer to be sent to the vertex attribute in the shader. We do this with the following three steps: (a) make that buffer "active" with the glBindBuffer() command as we did above, (b) associate the active buffer with a vertex attribute in the shader, and (c) enable the vertex attribute. The following three lines of code will accomplish these steps:

```
gl.glBindBuffer(GL_ARRAY_BUFFER, vbo[0]);          // make the 0ᵗʰ buffer "active"
gl.glVertexAttribPointer(0, 3, GL_FLOAT, false, 0, 0);   // associate 0ᵗʰ vertex attribute with active buffer
gl.glEnableVertexAttribArray(0);                   // enable the 0ᵗʰ vertex attribute
```

Now when we execute glDrawArrays(), data in the 0th VBO will be transmitted to the vertex attribute that has a layout qualifier with location 0. This sends the cube vertices to the shader.

4.2 ■ UNIFORM VARIABLES

Rendering a scene so that it appears 3D requires building appropriate transformation matrices, such as those described in Chapter 3, and applying them to each of the models' vertices. It is most efficient to apply the required matrix operations in the vertex shader, and it is customary to send these matrices from the Java/JOGL application to the shader in a *uniform variable*.

Uniform variables are declared in a shader by using the "uniform" keyword. The following example, declaring variables to hold model-view and projection matrices, will be suitable for our cube program:

```
uniform mat4 mv_matrix;
uniform mat4 proj_matrix;
```

The keyword "mat4" indicates that these are 4x4 matrices. Here we have named the variables mv_matrix to hold the model-view matrix and proj_matrix to hold the projection matrix. Since 3D transformations are 4x4, *mat4* is a commonly used datatype in GLSL shader uniforms.

Sending data from a Java/JOGL application to a uniform variable requires the following steps: (a) acquire a pointer to the uniform variable, and (b) associate a Java float buffer containing the desired values with the acquired uniform pointer. Assuming that the linked rendering program is saved in a variable called "renderingProgram" the following lines of code would specify that we will be sending model-view and projection matrices to the two uniforms mv_matrix and proj_matrix in our cube example:

```
mvLoc = gl.glGetUniformLocation(renderingProgram,"mv_matrix");   // get the locations of uniforms
pLoc = gl.glGetUniformLocation(renderingProgram,"proj_matrix");  //   in the shader program
gl.glUniformMatrix4fv(mLoc, 1, false, mvMat.get(vals));          // send matrix data to the
gl.glUniformMatrix4fv(pLoc, 1, false, pMat.get(vals));          //   uniform variables
```

The above example assumes that we have utilized the JOML utilities to build model-view and projection matrix transforms mvMat and pMat, as will be discussed in greater detail shortly. They are of type Matrix4f (a JOML class). The JOML function call get() copies those matrix values into the float buffer specified in the parameter (in this case, "vals"), and returns a reference to that float buffer, which is needed by glUniformMatrix4fv() to transfer those matrix values to the uniform variable.

▉4.3▉ INTERPOLATION OF VERTEX ATTRIBUTES

It is important to understand how *vertex attributes* are processed in the OpenGL pipeline versus how *uniform variables* are processed. Recall that immediately before the fragment shader is *rasterization*, where primitives (e.g., triangles) defined by vertices are converted to fragments. Rasterization *linearly interpolates vertex attribute* values so that the displayed pixels seamlessly connect the modeled surfaces.

By contrast, *uniform* variables behave like initialized constants and remain unchanged across each vertex shader invocation (i.e., for each vertex sent from the buffer). A uniform variable is not interpolated; it always contains the same value regardless of the number of vertices.

The interpolation done on vertex attributes by the rasterizer is useful in many ways. Later, we will use rasterization to interpolate colors, texture coordinates, and surface normals. It is important to understand that *all values sent through a buffer to a vertex attribute will be interpolated* further down the pipeline.

We have seen vertex attributes in a vertex shader declared as "in" to indicate that they receive values from a buffer. Vertex attributes may instead be declared as "out"; this means that they send their values forward toward the next stage in the pipeline. For example, the following declaration in a vertex shader specifies a vertex attribute named "color" that outputs a vec4:

```
out vec4 color;
```

It is not necessary to declare an "out" variable for the vertex positions, because OpenGL has a built-in out vec4 variable named gl_Position for that purpose. In the vertex shader, we apply the matrix transformations to the incoming vertex (declared earlier as position), assigning the result to gl_Position:

```
gl_Position = proj_matrix * mv_matrix * position;
```

The transformed vertices will then be automatically output to the rasterizer, with corresponding pixel locations ultimately sent to the fragment shader.

The rasterization process is illustrated in Figure 4.2. When specifying GL_TRIANGLES in the glDrawArrays() function, rasterization is done per triangle. Interpolation starts along the lines connecting the vertices, at a level of precision corresponding to the pixel display density. The pixels in the interior space of the triangle are then filled by interpolating along the horizontal lines connecting the edge pixels.

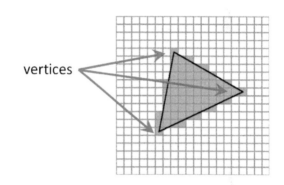

Figure 4.2
Rasterization of vertices.

4.4 ■ MODEL-VIEW AND PERSPECTIVE MATRICES

A fundamental step in rendering an object in 3D is to create appropriate transformation matrices and send them to uniform variables like we did in Section 4.2. We start by defining three matrices:

1. a *Model* matrix
2. a *View* matrix
3. a *Perspective* matrix

The *Model* matrix positions and orients the object in the world coordinate space. Each model has its own model matrix, and that matrix would need to be continuously rebuilt if the model moves.

The *View* matrix moves and rotates the models in the world to simulate the effect of a camera at a desired location. Recall from Chapter 2 that the OpenGL camera exists at location (0,0,0) and faces down the negative Z axis. To simulate the appearance of that camera being moved a certain way, we will need to move the objects themselves in the opposite way. For example, moving a camera to the right would cause the objects in the scene to appear to move to the left; although the OpenGL camera is fixed, we can make it appear as though we have moved it to the right by moving the objects to the left.

The *Perspective* matrix is a transform that provides the 3D effect according to the desired frustum, as described earlier in Chapter 3.

It is also important to understand when to compute each type of matrix. Matrices that never change can be built in init(), but those that change would need to be built in display() so that they are rebuilt for each frame. Let's assume that the models are animated and the camera is movable. Then:

- A model matrix needs to be created *for each model,* and *at each frame.*
- The view matrix needs to be created *once per frame* (because the camera can be moved), but is the same for all objects rendered during that frame.
- The perspective matrix is created once (in init()), using the screen window's width and height (and desired frustum parameters), and usually remains unchanged unless the window is resized.

Generating model and view transformation matrices then happens in the display() function, as follows:

1. Build the view matrix based on the desired camera location and orientation.
2. For each model, do the following:
    i. Build a model matrix based on the model's location and orientation.
    ii. Concatenate the model and view matrices into a single "MV" matrix.
    iii. Send the MV and projection matrices to the corresponding shader uniforms.

Technically, it isn't necessary to combine the model and view matrices into a single matrix. That is, they could be sent to the vertex shader in individual, separate matrices. However, there are certain advantages to combining them, while keeping the perspective matrix separate. For example, in the vertex shader, each vertex in the model is multiplied by the matrices. Since complex models may have hundreds or even thousands of vertices, performance can be improved by pre-multiplying the model and view matrices once before sending them to the vertex shader. Later, we will see the need to keep the perspective matrix separate for lighting purposes.

■4.5■ OUR FIRST 3D PROGRAM—A 3D CUBE

It's time to put all the pieces together! In order to build a complete Java/JOGL/ GLSL system to render our cube in a 3D "world," all of the mechanisms described so far will need to be put together and perfectly coordinated. We can reuse some of the code that we have seen previously in Chapter 2. Specifically, we won't repeat the following functions for reading in files containing shader code, compiling and linking them, and detecting GLSL errors; in fact, recall that we have moved them to a "Utils.java" file:

- createShaderProgram()
- readShaderSource()
- checkOpenGLError()
- printProgramLog()
- printShaderLog()

We will also need a utility function that builds a perspective matrix, given a specified field-of-view angle for the Y axis, the screen aspect ratio, and the desired near and far clipping planes (selecting appropriate values for near and far clipping planes is discussed in Section 4.9). While we could easily write such a function ourselves, JOML already includes one:

Matrix4f.setPerspective(*<field of view>*, *<aspect ratio>*, *<near plane>*, *<far plane>*);

We now build the complete 3D cube program, shown in Program 4.1.

Program 4.1 Plain Red Cube

Java/JOGL Application

```
import java.nio.*;
import javax.swing.*;
import java.lang.Math;
```

```java
import static com.jogamp.opengl.GL4.*;
import com.jogamp.opengl.*;
import com.jogamp.opengl.awt.GLCanvas;
import com.jogamp.common.nio.Buffers;
import com.jogamp.opengl.GLContext;
import org.joml.*;

public class Code extends JFrame implements GLEventListener
{   private GLCanvas myCanvas;

    private int renderingProgram;
    private int vao[ ] = new int[1];
    private int vbo[ ] = new int[2];
    private float cameraX, cameraY, cameraZ;
    private float cubeLocX, cubeLocY, cubeLocZ;

    // allocate variables used in display() function, so that they won't need to be allocated during rendering
    private FloatBuffer vals = Buffers.newDirectFloatBuffer(16);  // utility buffer for transferring matrices
    private Matrix4f pMat = new Matrix4f();         // perspective matrix
    private Matrix4f vMat = new Matrix4f();         // view matrix
    private Matrix4f mMat = new Matrix4f();         // model matrix
    private Matrix4f mvMat = new Matrix4f();        // model-view matrix
    private int mvLoc, projLoc;
    private float aspect;

    public Code()
    {   setTitle("Chapter4 - program1a");
        setSize(600, 600);
        myCanvas = new GLCanvas();
        myCanvas.addGLEventListener(this);
        this.add(myCanvas);
        this.setVisible(true);
    }

    public void init(GLAutoDrawable drawable)
    {   GL4 gl = (GL4) GLContext.getCurrentGL();
        renderingProgram = Utils.createShaderProgram("vertShader.glsl", "fragShader.glsl");
        setupVertices();
        cameraX = 0.0f; cameraY = 0.0f; cameraZ = 8.0f;
        cubeLocX = 0.0f; cubeLocY = -2.0f; cubeLocZ = 0.0f;   // shifted down the Y-axis to reveal perspective
    }

    // main(), reshape(), and dispose() are unchanged
    public static void main(String[ ] args) {  new Code();  }
    public void reshape(GLAutoDrawable drawable, int x, int y, int width, int height) { }
    public void dispose(GLAutoDrawable drawable) { }
```

```
public void display(GLAutoDrawable drawable)
{   GL4 gl = (GL4) GLContext.getCurrentGL();
    gl.glClear(GL_DEPTH_BUFFER_BIT);
    gl.glUseProgram(renderingProgram);

    // get references to the uniform variables for the MV and projection matrices
    mvLoc = gl.glGetUniformLocation(renderingProgram, "mv_matrix");
    projLoc = gl.glGetUniformLocation(renderingProgram, "proj_matrix");

    // build perspective matrix. This one has fovy=60, aspect ratio matches the screen window.
    // Values for near and far clipping planes can vary as discussed in Section 4.9
    aspect = (float) myCanvas.getWidth() / (float) myCanvas.getHeight();
    pMat.setPerspective((float) Math.toRadians(60.0f), aspect, 0.1f, 1000.0f);

    // build view matrix, model matrix, and model-view matrix
    vMat.translation(-cameraX, -cameraY, -cameraZ);

    mMat.translation(cubeLocX, cubeLocY, cubeLocZ);

    mvMat.identity();
    mvMat.mul(vMat);
    mvMat.mul(mMat);

    // copy perspective and MV matrices to corresponding uniform variables
    gl.glUniformMatrix4fv(mvLoc, 1, false, mvMat.get(vals));
    gl.glUniformMatrix4fv(projLoc, 1, false, pMat.get(vals));

    // associate VBO with the corresponding vertex attribute in the vertex shader
    gl.glBindBuffer(GL_ARRAY_BUFFER, vbo[0]);
    gl.glVertexAttribPointer(0, 3, GL_FLOAT, false, 0, 0);
    gl.glEnableVertexAttribArray(0);

    // adjust OpenGL settings and draw model
    gl.glEnable(GL_DEPTH_TEST);
    gl.glDepthFunc(GL_LEQUAL);
    gl.glDrawArrays(GL_TRIANGLES, 0, 36);
}

private void setupVertices()
{   GL4 gl = (GL4) GLContext.getCurrentGL();

    // 36 vertices of the 12 triangles making up a 2 x 2 x 2 cube centered at the origin
    float[ ] vertexPositions =
    {   -1.0f,  1.0f, -1.0f, -1.0f, -1.0f, -1.0f,  1.0f, -1.0f, -1.0f,
         1.0f, -1.0f, -1.0f,  1.0f,  1.0f, -1.0f, -1.0f,  1.0f, -1.0f,
         1.0f, -1.0f, -1.0f,  1.0f, -1.0f,  1.0f,  1.0f,  1.0f, -1.0f,
         1.0f, -1.0f,  1.0f,  1.0f,  1.0f,  1.0f,  1.0f,  1.0f, -1.0f,
         1.0f, -1.0f,  1.0f, -1.0f, -1.0f,  1.0f,  1.0f,  1.0f,  1.0f,
```

```
        -1.0f, -1.0f,  1.0f, -1.0f,  1.0f,  1.0f, 1.0f,  1.0f,  1.0f,
        -1.0f, -1.0f,  1.0f, -1.0f, -1.0f, -1.0f, -1.0f,  1.0f,  1.0f,
        -1.0f, -1.0f, -1.0f, -1.0f,  1.0f, -1.0f, -1.0f,  1.0f,  1.0f,
        -1.0f, -1.0f,  1.0f,  1.0f, -1.0f,  1.0f,  1.0f, -1.0f, -1.0f,
         1.0f, -1.0f, -1.0f, -1.0f, -1.0f, -1.0f, -1.0f, -1.0f,  1.0f,
        -1.0f,  1.0f, -1.0f,  1.0f,  1.0f, -1.0f,  1.0f,  1.0f,  1.0f,
         1.0f,  1.0f,  1.0f, -1.0f,  1.0f,  1.0f, -1.0f,  1.0f, -1.0f
    };

    gl.glGenVertexArrays(vao.length, vao, 0);
    gl.glBindVertexArray(vao[0]);
    gl.glGenBuffers(vbo.length, vbo, 0);

    gl.glBindBuffer(GL_ARRAY_BUFFER, vbo[0]);
    FloatBuffer vertBuf = Buffers.newDirectFloatBuffer(vertexPositions);
    gl.glBufferData(GL_ARRAY_BUFFER, vertBuf.limit()*4, vertBuf, GL_STATIC_DRAW);
  }
}
```

Vertex shader (file name: "vertShader.glsl")

```
#version 430

layout (location=0) in vec3 position;

uniform mat4 mv_matrix;
uniform mat4 proj_matrix;

void main(void)
{   gl_Position = proj_matrix * mv_matrix * vec4(position,1.0);
}
```

Fragment shader (file name: "fragShader.glsl")

```
#version 430

out vec4 color;

uniform mat4 mv_matrix;
uniform mat4 proj_matrix;

void main(void)
{   color = vec4(1.0, 0.0, 0.0, 1.0);
}
```

Figure 4.3
Output of Program 4.1: red cube positioned at (0,-2,0) viewed from (0,0,8).

Let's take a close look at the code in Program 4.1. It is important that we understand how *all* of the pieces work, *and how they work together*.

Start by examining the function near the end of the Java/JOGL listing, setupVertices(), called by init(). At the start of this function, an array is declared called vertexPositions that contains the 36 vertices comprising the cube. At first you might wonder why this cube has 36 vertices, when logically a cube should only require eight. The answer is that we need to build our cube out of triangles, and so each of the six cube faces needs to be built of two triangles, for a total of 6x2=12 triangles (see Figure 4.4). Since each triangle is specified by three vertices, this totals 36 vertices.

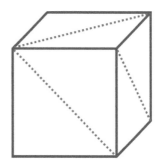

Figure 4.4
Cube made of triangles.

Since each vertex has three values (x,y,z), there are a total of 36x3=108 values in the array. It is true that each vertex participates in multiple triangles, but we still specify each vertex separately because for now we are sending each triangle's vertices down the pipeline separately.

The cube is defined in its own coordinate system, with (0,0,0) at its center, and with its corners ranging from -1.0 to +1.0 along the x, y, and z axes. The rest of the setupVertices() function sets up the VAO, two VBOs (although only one is used), and loads the cube vertices into the 0th VBO buffer.

Note that the init() function performs tasks that only need to be done once: reading in the shader code and building the rendering program, and loading the cube vertices into the buffer (by calling "setupVertices()"). Note that it also positions the cube and the camera in the world; later we will animate the cube and also see how to move the camera around, at which point we may need to remove this hardcoded positioning.

Now let's look at the display() function. Recall that display() may be called repeatedly and the rate at which it is called is referred to as the *frame rate*. That is, animation works by continually drawing and redrawing the scene, or frame, very quickly. It is usually necessary to clear the depth buffer before rendering a frame, so that hidden surface removal occurs properly (not clearing the depth buffer can sometimes result in every surface being removed, resulting in a completely black screen). By default, depth values in OpenGL range from 0.0 to 1.0. Clearing the depth buffer is done by calling glClear(GL_DEPTH_BUFFER_BIT), which fills the depth buffer with the default value (usually 1.0).

Next, display() enables the shaders by calling glUseProgram(), installing the GLSL code on the GPU. Recall this doesn't run the shader program, but it does enable subsequent OpenGL calls to determine the shader's *vertex attribute* and *uniform* locations. The display() function next gets the uniform variable locations; builds the perspective, view, and model matrices;[3] concatenates the view and model matrices into a single MV matrix; and assigns the perspective and MV matrices to their corresponding uniforms.

Next, display() enables the buffer containing the cube vertices and attaches it to 0th vertex attribute to prepare for sending the vertices to the shader.

The last thing display() does is draw the model by calling glDrawArrays(), specifying that the model is composed of triangles and has 36 total vertices. The call to glDrawArrays() is typically preceded by additional commands that adjust rendering settings for this model.[4] In this example, there are two such commands, both of which are related to depth testing. Recall from Chapter 2 that depth testing is used by OpenGL to perform hidden surface removal. Here we enable depth testing, and specify the particular depth test we wish OpenGL to use. The settings shown correspond to the description in Chapter 2; later in the book we will see other uses for these commands.

Finally, consider the shaders. First, note that they both include the same block of uniform variable declarations. Although this is not always required, it is often a good practice to include the same block of uniform variable declarations in all of the shaders within a particular rendering program.

Note also in the vertex shader the presence of the layout qualifier on the incoming vertex attribute position. Since the location is specified as "0" the display() function can reference this variable simply by using 0 in the first parameter of the glVertexAttribPointer() function call, and in the glEnableVertexAttribArray() function call. Note also that the position vertex attribute is declared as a vec3, and so it needs to be converted to a vec4 in order to be compatible with the 4x4 matrices with which it will be multiplied. This conversion is done with vec4(position,1.0), which builds a vec4 out of the variable named "position" and puts a value of 1.0 in the newly added fourth spot.

---

[3] An astute reader may notice that it shouldn't be necessary to build the perspective matrix every time display() is called, because its value doesn't change. This is partially true—the perspective matrix *would* need to be recomputed if the user were to *resize* the window while the program was running. In Section 4.11 we will handle this situation more efficiently, and in the process we will move the computation of the perspective matrix out of display() and into the init() function.

[4] Often, these calls may be placed in init() rather than in display(). However, it is necessary to place one or more of them in display() when drawing multiple objects with different properties. For simplicity, we always place them in display().

The multiplication in the vertex shader applies the matrix transforms to the vertex, converting it to camera space (note the right-to-left concatenation order). Those values are put in the built-in OpenGL output variable gl_Position and then proceed through the pipeline and are interpolated by the rasterizer.

The interpolated pixel locations (referred to as *fragments*) are then sent to the *fragment shader*. Recall that the primary purpose of the fragment shader is to set the color of an outputted pixel. In a manner similar to the vertex shader, the fragment shader processes the pixels one-by-one, with a separate invocation for each pixel. In this case, it outputs a hardcoded value corresponding to red. For reasons indicated earlier, the uniform variables have been included in the fragment shader even though they aren't being used there in this example.

An overview of the flow of data starting with the Java/JOGL application and passing through the pipeline is shown in Figure 4.5.

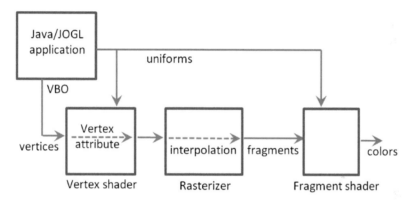

Figure 4.5
Data flow through Program 4.1.

Let's make a slight modification to the shaders. In particular, we will assign a color to each vertex according to its location and put that color in the outgoing vertex attribute varyingColor. The fragment shader is similarly revised to accept the incoming color (interpolated by the rasterizer) and use that to set the color of the output pixel. Note that the code also multiplies the location by one-half and then adds one-half to convert the range of values from [-1..+1] to [0..1]. Note also the use of the common convention of assigning variable names that include the word *varying* to programmer-defined interpolated vertex attributes. The changes in each shader are highlighted and the resulting output shown on the following page.

Revised vertex shader:

```
#version 430

layout (location=0) in vec3 position;
uniform mat4 mv_matrix;
uniform mat4 proj_matrix;

out vec4 varyingColor;

void main(void)
{   gl_Position = proj_matrix * mv_matrix * vec4(position,1.0);
    varyingColor = vec4(position,1.0) * 0.5 + vec4(0.5, 0.5, 0.5, 0.5);
}
```

Revised fragment shader:

```
#version 430

in vec4 varyingColor;

out vec4 color;
uniform mat4 mv_matrix;
uniform mat4 proj_matrix;

void main(void)
{   color = varyingColor;
}
```

Note that, because the colors are sent out from the vertex shader in a vertex attribute (varyingColor), *they too are interpolated* by the rasterizer! The effect of this can be seen in Figure 4.6, where the colors from corner to corner are clearly interpolated smoothly throughout the cube.

Note also that the "out" variable varyingColor in the vertex shader is also the "in" variable in the fragment shader. The two shaders know which variable from the vertex shader feeds which variable in the fragment shader because they have the same name—"varyingColor"—in both shaders.

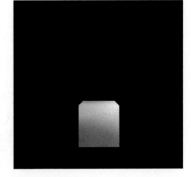

Figure 4.6
Cube with interpolated colors.

We can animate the cube using the Animator class as in Program 2.6, by building the model matrix using a varying translation and rotation based on the elapsed time. For example, the code in the display() function in Program 4.1 could be modified as follows (changes are highlighted):

```
gl.glClear(GL_DEPTH_BUFFER_BIT);
gl.glClear(GL_COLOR_BUFFER_BIT);

// use system time to generate slowly-increasing sequence of floating-point values
elapsedTime = System.currentTimeMills() – startTime;   // elapsedTime, startTime, and tf
tf = elapsedTime / 1000.0;                              // would all be declared of type double.
. . .
// use tf (time factor) to compute different translations in x, y, and z
mMat.identity();
mMat.translate((float)Math.sin(.35f*tf)*2.0f, (float)Math.sin(.52f*tf)*2.0f, (float)Math.sin(.7f*tf)*2.0f);
mMat.rotateXYZ(1.75f*(float)tf, 1.75f*(float)tf, 1.75f*(float)tf);   // the 1.75 adjusts the rotation speed
```

The use of elapsed time (and a variety of trigonometric functions) in the model matrix causes the cube to appear to tumble around in space. Note that adding this animation illustrates the importance of clearing the depth buffer each time through display() to ensure correct hidden surface removal. It also necessitates clearing the *color* buffer as shown; otherwise, the cube will leave a trail as it moves.

The translate() and rotateXYZ() functions are part of the JOML library. Note that in the code, translate() is called before rotate(). This results in a concatenation of the two transforms, with translation on the left and rotation on the right. When a vertex is subsequently multiplied by this matrix, the computation is right-to-left, meaning that the rotation is done first, followed by the translation. The order of application of transforms is significant and changing the order would result in different behavior. Figure 4.7 shows some of the frames that are displayed after animating the cube.

Figure 4.7
Animated ("tumbling") 3D cube.

4.6 ■ RENDERING MULTIPLE COPIES OF AN OBJECT

Before we tackle the general case of rendering a variety of models in a single scene, let's consider the simpler case of *multiple occurrences of the same model.* Suppose, for instance, that we wish to expand the previous example so that it renders a "swarm" of 24 tumbling cubes. We can do this by moving the portions of the code in display() that build the MV matrix and that draw the cube (shown below) into a loop that executes 24 times. We incorporate the loop variable into the cube's rotation and translation, so that each time the cube is drawn a different model matrix is built. (We also positioned the camera further down the positive Z axis so we can see all of the cubes and increased the multiplier from 2.0 to 8.0 to spread them out.) The resulting animated scene is shown in Figure 4.8.

```java
public void display(GLAutoDrawable drawable)
{   . . .
    timeFactor = elapsedTime/1000.0;

    for (i=0; i<24; i++)
    {   x = timeFactor + i;
        mMat.identity();
        mMat.translate((float)Math.sin(.35f*x)*8.0f, (float)Math.sin(.52f*x)*8.0f, (float)Math.
                                                                        sin((.70f*x)*8.0f));
        mMat.rotateXYZ(1.75f*(float)x, 1.75f*(float)x, 1.75f*(float)x);

        mvMat.identity();
        mvMat.mul(vMat);
        mvMat.mul(mMat);

        gl.glUniformMatrix4fv(mvLoc, 1, false, mvMat.get(vals));
        gl.glUniformMatrix4fv(projLoc, 1, false, pMat.get(vals));

        gl.glBindBuffer(GL_ARRAY_BUFFER, vbo[0]);
        gl.glVertexAttribPointer(0, 3, GL_FLOAT, false, 0, 0);
        gl.glEnableVertexAttribArray(0);

        gl.glEnable(GL_DEPTH_TEST);
        gl.glDepthFunc(GL_LEQUAL);
        gl.glDrawArrays(GL_TRIANGLES, 0, 36);
    }
}
```

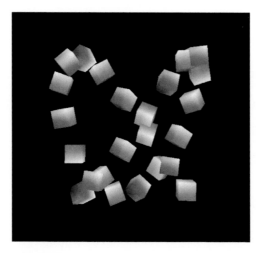

Figure 4.8
Multiple tumbling cubes.

4.6.1 Instancing

Instancing provides a mechanism for telling the graphics card to render multiple copies of an object using only a single Java call. This can result in a significant performance benefit, particularly when there are thousands or millions of copies of the object being drawn—such as when rendering many flowers in a field, or many zombies in an army.

We start by changing the glDrawArrays() call in our Java/JOGL application to glDrawArraysInstanced(). Now we can ask OpenGL to draw as many copies as we want. We can specify drawing 24 cubes as follows:

```
glDrawArraysInstanced(GL_TRIANGLES, 0, 36, 24);
```

When using instancing, the vertex shader has access to a built-in variable, gl_InstanceID, an integer that refers to which numeric instance of the object is currently being processed.

To replicate our previous tumbling cubes example using instancing, we will need to move the computations that build the different model matrices (previously inside a loop in display()) into the vertex shader. Since GLSL does not provide translate or rotate functions and we cannot make calls to JOML from inside a shader, we will need to use the utility functions from Program 3.1. We will also need to pass the "time factor" variable from the Java/JOGL application to the vertex shader in a uniform. We also need to pass the model and view matrices into separate uniforms because the rotation computations are applied to each cube's model matrix. The revisions, including those in the Java/JOGL application and those in the new vertex shader, are shown in Program 4.2.

Program 4.2 Instancing: 24 Animated Cubes

Vertex Shader:

```
#version 430
layout (location=0) in vec3 position;

uniform mat4 v_matrix;          // only the P and V matrices are sent from the appication
uniform mat4 proj_matrix;
uniform float tf;               // time factor for animation and placement of cubes

out vec4 varyingColor;

mat4 buildRotateX(float rad);   // declaration of matrix transformation utility functions
mat4 buildRotateY(float rad);   // (GLSL requires functions to be declared prior to invocation)
mat4 buildRotateZ(float rad);
mat4 buildTranslate(float x, float y, float z);

void main(void)
{   float x = gl_InstanceID + tf;   // value based on time factor, but different for each cube instance

    float a = sin(.35 * x) * 8.0;   // these are the x, y, and z components for the translation, below
    float b = sin(.52 * x) * 8.0;
    float c = sin(.70 * x) * 8.0;

    // build the rotation and translation matrices to be applied to this cube's model matrix
    mat4 localRotX = buildRotateX(1.75*x);
    mat4 localRotY = buildRotateY(1.75*x);
    mat4 localRotZ = buildRotateZ(1.75*x);
    mat4 localTrans = buildTranslate(a,b,c);

    // build the model matrix and then the model-view matrix
    mat4 newM_matrix = localTrans * localRotX * localRotY * localRotZ;
    mat4 mv_matrix = v_matrix * newM_matrix;

    gl_Position = proj_matrix * mv_matrix * vec4(position,1.0);
    varyingColor = vec4(position,1.0) * 0.5 + vec4(0.5, 0.5, 0.5, 0.5);
}

// utility function to build a translation matrix (from Chapter 3)
mat4 buildTranslate(float x, float y, float z)
{   mat4 trans = mat4( 1.0, 0.0, 0.0, 0.0,
```

```
                 0.0, 1.0, 0.0, 0.0,
                 0.0, 0.0, 1.0, 0.0,
                 x, y, z, 1.0 );
    return trans;
}
// similar functions included for rotation around the X, Y, and Z axes (also from Chapter 3)
 . . .
```

Java/JOGL Application (in display())

```
 . . .
// computations that build (and transform) mMat have been moved to the vertex shader.
// there is no longer any need to build an MV matrix in the Java/JOGL application.
gl.glUniformMatrix4fv(vLoc, 1, false, vMat.get(vals));          // the shader does need the V matrix.
int tfLoc = gl.glGetUniformLocation(renderingProgram, "tf");   // uniform for the time factor
gl.glUniform1f(tfLoc, (float)timeFactor);                      // (the shader needs that too)
 . . .
gl.glDrawArraysInstanced(GL_TRIANGLES, 0, 36, 24);
```

The resulting output of Program 4.2 is identical to that for the previous example and can be seen in Figure 4.8.

Instancing makes it possible to greatly expand the number of copies of an object; in this example animating *100,000* cubes is still feasible even for a modest GPU. The changes to the code—mainly just a few modified constants to spread the large number of cubes further apart—are as follows:

Vertex Shader:

```
 . . .
float a = sin(203.0 * i/8000.0) * 403.0;
float b = cos(301.0 * i/4001.0) * 401.0;
float c = sin(400.0 * i/6003.0) * 405.0;
 . . .
```

Java/JOGL Application

```
 . . .
cameraZ = 420.0f;  // move camera further down the Z axis to view the increased number of cubes
 . . .
gl.glDrawArraysInstanced(GL_TRIANGLES, 0, 36, 100000);
```

The resulting output is shown in Figure 4.9.

Figure 4.9
Instancing: 100,000 animated cubes.

4.7 RENDERING MULTIPLE DIFFERENT MODELS IN A SCENE

To render more than one model in a single scene, a simple approach is to use a separate buffer for each model. Each model will need its own model matrix, and thus a new model-view matrix will be generated for each model that we render. There will also need to be separate calls to glDrawArrays() for each model. There are changes both in init() and in display().

Another consideration is whether or not we will need different shaders—or a different rendering program—for each of the objects we wish to draw. As it turns out, *in many cases we can use the same shaders* (and thus the same rendering program) for the various objects we are drawing. We usually only need to employ different rendering programs for the various objects if they are built of different primitives (such as lines instead of triangles), or if there are complex lighting or other effects involved. For now, that isn't the case, so we can reuse the same vertex and fragment shaders, and just modify our Java/JOGL application to send each model down the pipeline when display() is called.

Let's proceed by adding a simple pyramid, so our scene includes both a single cube and a pyramid. The code is shown in Program 4.3. A few of the key details are highlighted, such as where we specify one or the other buffer and where we specify the number of vertices contained in the model. Note that the pyramid is composed of six triangles—four on the sides and two on the bottom, totaling 6×3=18 vertices.

The resulting scene, containing both the cube and the pyramid, is shown in Figure 4.10.

Program 4.3 Cube and Pyramid

```
private void setupVertices()
{   GL4 gl = (GL4) GLContext.getCurrentGL();

    float[ ] cubePositions =
    { -1.0f,  1.0f, -1.0f, -1.0f, -1.0f, -1.0f, 1.0f, -1.0f, -1.0f,
       1.0f, -1.0f, -1.0f, 1.0f,  1.0f, -1.0f, -1.0f,  1.0f, -1.0f,
              ... same as before, for the rest of the cube vertices
    };

    // pyramid with 18 vertices, comprising 6 triangles (four sides, and two on the bottom)

    float[ ] pyramidPositions =
    {   -1.0f, -1.0f, 1.0f, 1.0f, -1.0f, 1.0f, 0.0f, 1.0f, 0.0f,     // front face
         1.0f, -1.0f, 1.0f, 1.0f, -1.0f, -1.0f, 0.0f, 1.0f, 0.0f,     // right face
         1.0f, -1.0f, -1.0f, -1.0f, -1.0f, -1.0f, 0.0f, 1.0f, 0.0f,    // back face
        -1.0f, -1.0f, -1.0f, -1.0f, -1.0f, 1.0f, 0.0f, 1.0f, 0.0f,     // left face
        -1.0f, -1.0f, -1.0f, 1.0f, -1.0f, 1.0f, -1.0f, -1.0f, 1.0f,    // base – left front
         1.0f, -1.0f, 1.0f, -1.0f, -1.0f, -1.0f, 1.0f, -1.0f, -1.0f    // base – right back
    };
    gl.glGenVertexArrays(vao.length, vao, 0);
    gl.glBindVertexArray(vao[0]);
    gl.glGenBuffers(vbo.length, vbo, 0);

    gl.glBindBuffer(GL_ARRAY_BUFFER, vbo[0]);
    FloatBuffer cubeBuf = Buffers.newDirectFloatBuffer(cubePositions);
    gl.glBufferData(GL_ARRAY_BUFFER, cubeBuf.limit()*4, cubeBuf, GL_STATIC_DRAW);

    gl.glBindBuffer(GL_ARRAY_BUFFER, vbo[1]);
    FloatBuffer pyrBuf = Buffers.newDirectFloatBuffer(pyramidPositions);
    gl.glBufferData(GL_ARRAY_BUFFER, pyrBuf.limit()*4, pyrBuf, GL_STATIC_DRAW);
}

public void display(GLAutoDrawable drawable)
{   ... clear the color and depth buffers as before (not shown here)
```

. . . use rendering program and obtain uniform locations as before (not shown here)

```
//  set up the projection and view matrices
aspect = (float) myCanvas.getWidth() / (float) myCanvas.getHeight();
pMat.setPerspective((float) Math.toRadians(60.0f), aspect, 0.1f, 1000.0f);

vMat.translation(-cameraX,-cameraY,-cameraZ);

//  draw the cube (use buffer #0)
mMat.translation(cubeLocX, cubeLocY, cubeLocZ);

mvMat.identity();
mvMat.mul(vMat);
mvMat.mul(mMat);

gl.glUniformMatrix4fv(mvLoc, 1, false, mvMat.get(vals));
gl.glUniformMatrix4fv(projLoc, 1, false, pMat.get(vals));

gl.glBindBuffer(GL_ARRAY_BUFFER, vbo[0]);
gl.glVertexAttribPointer(0, 3, GL_FLOAT, false, 0, 0);
gl.glEnableVertexAttribArray(0);

gl.glEnable(GL_DEPTH_TEST);
gl.glDepthFunc(GL_LEQUAL);

gl.glDrawArrays(GL_TRIANGLES, 0, 36);

//  draw the pyramid (use buffer #1)
mMat.translation(pyrLocX, pyrLocY, pyrLocZ);

mvMat.identity();
mvMat.mul(vMat);
mvMat.mul(mMat);

gl.glUniformMatrix4fv(mvLoc, 1, false, mvMat.get(vals));
gl.glUniformMatrix4fv(projLoc, 1, false, pMat.get(vals));
                                            // (repeated for clarity)

gl.glBindBuffer(GL_ARRAY_BUFFER, vbo[1]);
gl.glVertexAttribPointer(0, 3, GL_FLOAT, false, 0, 0);
gl.glEnableVertexAttribArray(0);

gl.glEnable(GL_DEPTH_TEST);
gl.glDepthFunc(GL_LEQUAL);

gl.glDrawArrays(GL_TRIANGLES, 0, 18);
}
```

Figure 4.10
3D cube and pyramid.

A few other minor details to note regarding Program 4.3:

- The variables pyrLocX, pyrLocY, and pyrLocZ need to be declared in the class and initialized in init() to the desired pyramid location, as was done for the cube location.

- The view matrix vMat is built at the top of display() and then used in both the cube's and the pyramid's model-view matrices.

- The vertex and fragment shaders are not shown—they are unchanged from Section 4.5.

4.8 ■ MATRIX STACKS

So far, the models we have rendered have each been constructed of a single set of vertices. It is often desired, however, to build complex models by assembling smaller simple models. For example, a model of a "robot" could be created by separately drawing the head, body, legs, and arms, where each is a separate model. An object built in this manner is often called a *hierarchical model*. The tricky part of building hierarchical models is keeping track of all the model-view matrices, and making sure they stay perfectly coordinated—otherwise the robot might fly apart into pieces!

Hierarchical models are useful not only for building complex objects—they can also be used to generate complex scenes. For example, consider how our planet earth revolves around the sun, and in turn how the moon revolves around the earth. Such a scene is shown in Figure 4.11.[5] Computing the moon's actual path through space could be complex. However, if we can *combine* the transforms representing the two simple circular paths—the moon's path around the earth and the earth's path around the sun—we avoid having to explicitly compute the moon trajectory.

---

[5] Yes, we know that the moon doesn't revolve in this "vertical" trajectory around the earth, but rather in one that is more coplanar with the earth's revolution around the sun. We chose this orbit to make our program's execution clearer.

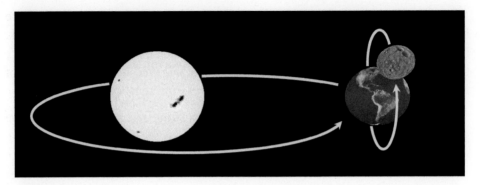

Figure 4.11
Animated planetary system.
Source: Sun and earth textures are from [HT16]; the moon texture is from [NA16].

It turns out that we can do this fairly easily with a *matrix stack*. A matrix stack is, as its name implies, a stack of transformation matrices. As we will see, matrix stacks make it easy to create and manage complex hierarchical objects and scenes, where transforms can be built upon (and removed from) other transforms.

OpenGL has a built-in matrix stack, but as part of the older fixed-function (nonprogrammable) pipeline it has long been deprecated. It was nicely devised and convenient to use, and happily a similar Java class is available in JOML, called Matrix4fStack, patterned after the one that became popular in older versions of OpenGL [OL16]. As we will see, many of the model, view, and model-view matrices that would normally be needed in a complex scene can be replaced by a single instance of Matrix4fStack.

We will first examine the basic commands for instantiating and utilizing a matrix stack, then use Matrix4fStack to build a complex animated scene. Some important Matrix4fStack functions include the following:

- pushMatrix()—makes a copy of the top matrix and pushes the copy onto the stack
- popMatrix()—removes and returns the top matrix
- get(v)—copies values in the topmost matrix to buffer v and returns a reference to the buffer (the topmost matrix is not removed from the stack)
- rotate(d,x,y,z) ⎫
- scale(x,y,z) ⎬ apply directly to the top matrix in the stack
- translate(x,y,z) ⎭

Matrix4fStack is designed as a subclass of Matrix4f, and thus inherits all of the functions defined in Matrix4f. If one of those functions is called on a Matrix4fStack, it is applied to the matrix at the top of the stack (in fact, the functions get(), rotate(), scale(), and translate() listed above are examples of this mechanism, as are many of the other JOML matrix functions, such as matrix concatenation).

Now, rather than building transforms by creating instances of Matrix4f, we instead use the pushMatrix() command to create new matrices at the top of the stack. Desired transforms are then applied as needed to the newly created matrix on the top of the stack.

The first matrix pushed on the stack is frequently the VIEW matrix. The matrices above it are model-view matrices of increasing complexity; that is, they have an increasing number of model transforms applied to them. These transforms can either be applied directly or by first concatenating other matrices.

In our planetary system example, the matrix positioned immediately above the VIEW matrix would be the sun's MV matrix. The matrix on top of that matrix would be the earth's MV matrix, *which consists of a copy of the sun's MV matrix with the earth's model matrix transforms applied to it*. That is, the earth's MV matrix is built by incorporating the planet's transforms into the sun's transforms. Similarly, the moon's MV matrix sits on top of the planet's MV matrix and is constructed by applying the moon's model matrix transforms to the planet's MV matrix immediately below it.

After rendering the moon, a second "moon" could be rendered by "popping" the first moon's matrix off of the stack (restoring the top of the stack to the planet's model-view matrix) and then repeating the process for the second moon.

The basic approach is as follows:

1. When a new object is introduced relative to a parent object, do a "pushMatrix()" call.
2. Apply the new object's transforms; i.e., multiply a transform to the matrix at the top of the stack.
3. When an object or subobject has finished being drawn, call "popMatrix()" to remove its model-view matrix from atop the matrix stack.

In later chapters we will learn how to create spheres and make them look like planets and moons. For now, to keep things simple, we will build a "planetary system" using our pyramid and a couple of cubes.

Here is an overview of how a display() function using a matrix stack is typically organized:

Setup	• Instantiate the matrix stack.
Camera	• Push a new matrix onto the stack. (this will instantiate an empty VIEW matrix).
	• Apply transform(s) to the view matrix on the top of the stack.
Parent	• Push a new matrix onto the stack (this will be the parent MV matrix—for the first parent, it duplicates the view matrix).
	• Apply transforms to incorporate the parent's M matrix into the duplicated view matrix.
	• Send the topmost matrix ("get") to the MV uniform variable in the vertex shader.
	• Draw the parent object.
Child	• Push a new matrix onto the stack. This will be the child's MV matrix, duplicating the parent MV matrix.
	• Apply transforms to incorporate the child's M matrix into the duplicated parent MV matrix.
	• Send the topmost matrix ("get") to the MV uniform variable in the vertex shader.
	• Draw the child object.
Cleanup	• Pop the child's MV matrix off the stack.
	• Pop the parent's MV matrix off the stack.
	• Pop the VIEW matrix off the stack.

Note that the pyramid ("sun") rotation on its axis is in its own local coordinate space, and should not be allowed to affect the "children" (the planet and moon, in this case). Therefore, the sun's rotation (shown in the image below) is pushed onto the stack, but then after drawing the sun, it must be removed (popped) from the stack.

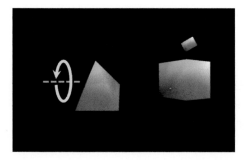

The big cube's (planet) revolution around the sun (left image, below) will affect the moon's movement, and so it is pushed on the stack and remains there when drawing the moon as well. By contrast, the planet's rotation on its axis (right image, below) is local and does not affect the moon, so it is popped off the stack before drawing the moon.

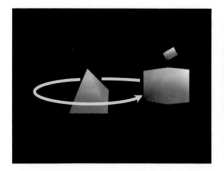
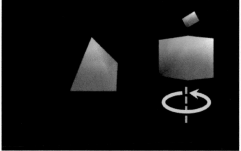

Similarly, we would push transforms onto the stack for the moon's rotations (around the planet and on its axis), indicated in the following images.

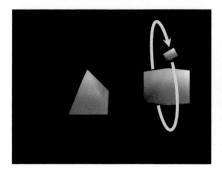
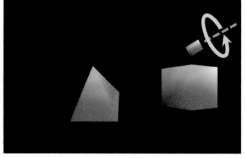

Here is the sequence of steps for the "planet":

- **pushMatrix()**—This will be the portion of the planet's MV matrix that will also affect children.

- **translate(...)**—This will incorporate the planet movement around the sun into the planet's MV matrix. In this example we use trigonometry to calculate the planet movement as a translation.

- **pushMatrix()**—This will be the planet's complete MV matrix, also including its axis rotation.

- **rotate(...)**—This will incorporate the planet's axis rotation (this will later be popped and not affect children).

- **get()**—This will obtain the MV matrix and then send it to the MV uniform.

- Draw the planet.

- **popMatrix()**—This removes the planet MV matrix off the stack, exposing underneath it an earlier copy of the planet MV matrix that doesn't include the planet's axis rotation (so that only the planet's translation will affect the moon).

We now can write the complete display() routine, shown in Program 4.4.

Program 4.4 Simple Solar System Using Matrix Stack

```
private Matrix4fStack mvStack = new Matrix4fStack(5);
public void display(GLAutoDrawable drawable)
{   // setup of background, depth buffer, rendering program, and proj matrices unchanged

    tf = elapsedTime/1000.0;  // time factor, as before
    . . .
    // push view matrix onto the stack
    mvStack.pushMatrix();
    mvStack.translate(-cameraX, -cameraY, -cameraZ);

    // -------------------- pyramid == sun -------------------------------------
    mvStack.pushMatrix();
    mvStack.translate(0.0f, 0.0f, 0.0f);              // sun's position
    mvStack.pushMatrix();
    mvStack.rotate((float)tf, 1.0f, 0.0f, 0.0f);      // sun's rotation on its axis
    gl.glUniformMatrix4fv(mvLoc, 1, false, mvStack.get(vals));
    gl.glBindBuffer(GL_ARRAY_BUFFER, vbo[1]);
    gl.glVertexAttribPointer(0, 3, GL_FLOAT, false, 0, 0);
    gl.glEnableVertexAttribArray(0);
    gl.glEnable(GL_DEPTH_TEST);
```

```
gl.glDrawArrays(GL_TRIANGLES, 0, 18);        // draw the sun
mvStack.popMatrix();                         // remove the sun's axial rotation from the stack

//---------------------- cube == planet -------------------------------------
mvStack.pushMatrix();
mvStack.translate((float)Math.sin(tf)*4.0f, 0.0f, (float)Math.cos(tf)*4.0f); // planet moves around sun
mvStack.pushMatrix();
mvStack.rotate((float)tf, 0.0f, 1.0f, 0.0f);                   // planet axis rotation
gl.glUniformMatrix4fv(mvLoc, 1, false, mvStack.get(vals));
gl.glBindBuffer(GL_ARRAY_BUFFER, vbo[0]);
gl.glVertexAttribPointer(0, 3, GL_FLOAT, false, 0, 0);
gl.glEnableVertexAttribArray(0);
gl.glDrawArrays(GL_TRIANGLES, 0, 36);        // draw the planet
mvStack.popMatrix();                         // remove the planet's axial rotation from the stack

//---------------------- smaller cube == moon -------------------------------
mvStack.pushMatrix();
mvStack.translate(0.0f, (float)Math.sin(tf)*2.0f, (float)Math.cos(tf)*2.0f);  // moon moves around planet
mvStack.rotate((float)tf, 0.0f, 0.0f, 1.0f);                   // moon's rotation on its axis
mvStack.scale(0.25f, 0.25f, 0.25f);                           // make the moon smaller
gl.glUniformMatrix4fv(mvLoc, 1, false, mvStack.get(vals));
gl.glBindBuffer(GL_ARRAY_BUFFER, vbo[0]);
gl.glVertexAttribPointer(0, 3, GL_FLOAT, false, 0, 0);
gl.glEnableVertexAttribArray(0);
gl.glDrawArrays(GL_TRIANGLES, 0, 36);        // draw the moon

// remove moon scale/rotation/position, planet position, sun position, and view matrices from stack
mvStack.popMatrix();  mvStack.popMatrix();  mvStack.popMatrix();  mvStack.popMatrix();
}
```

The matrix stack operations have been highlighted. There are several details worth noting:

- We have introduced a *scale* operation in a model matrix. We want the moon to be a smaller cube than the planet, so we use a call to scale() when building the MV matrix for the moon.

- In this example, we are using the trigonometric operations sin() and cos() to compute the revolution of the planet around the sun (as a translation), and also for the moon around the planet.

- The two buffers #0 and #1 contain cube and pyramid vertices, respectively.

- Note the use of the get() function call within the glUniformMatrix() command. The get() call retrieves the values in the matrix on top of the stack, and those values are then sent to the uniform variable (in this case, the sun, planet, and then moon's MV matrices).

The vertex and fragment shaders are not shown—they are unchanged from the previous example. We also moved the initial position of the pyramid (sun) and the camera to center the scene on the screen.

■4.9■ COMBATING "Z-FIGHTING" ARTIFACTS

Recall that when rendering multiple objects, OpenGL uses the *Z-buffer algorithm* (shown earlier in Figure 2.14) for performing hidden surface removal. Ordinarily, this resolves which object surfaces are visible and rendered to the screen versus which surfaces lie behind other objects and thus should not be rendered, by choosing a pixel's color to be that of the corresponding fragment closest to the camera.

However, there can be occasions when two object surfaces in a scene overlap and lie in coincident planes, making it problematic for the Z-buffer algorithm to determine which of the two surfaces should be rendered (since neither is "closest" to the camera). When this happens, floating point rounding errors can lead to some portions of the rendered surface using the color of one of the objects and other portions using the color of the other object. This artifact is known as *Z-fighting* or *depth-fighting*, because the effect is the result of rendered fragments "fighting" over mutually corresponding pixel entries in the Z-buffer. Figure 4.12 shows an example of Z-fighting between two boxes with overlapping coincident (top) faces.

Situations like this often occur when creating terrain or shadows. It is often possible to predict Z-fighting in such instances, and a common way of correcting it in these cases is to move one object slightly, so that the surfaces are no longer coplanar. We will see an example of this in Chapter 8.

Z-fighting can also occur due to limited precision of the values in the depth buffer. For each pixel processed by the Z-buffer algorithm, the accuracy of its depth information is limited by the number of bits available for storing

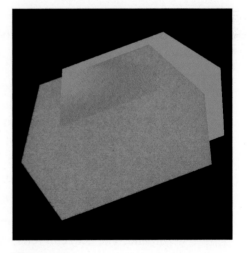

Figure 4.12
Z-fighting example.

it in the depth buffer. The greater the range between near and far clipping planes used to build the perspective matrix, the more likely two objects' points with similar (but not equal) actual depths will be represented by the same numeric value in the depth buffer. Therefore, it is up to the programmer to select near and far clipping plane values to minimize the distance between the two planes, while still ensuring that all objects essential to the scene lie within the viewing frustum.

It is also important to understand that, due to the effect of the perspective transform, changing the near clipping plane value can have a greater impact on the likelihood of Z-fighting artifacts than making an equivalent change in the far clipping plane. Therefore, it is advisable to avoid selecting a near clipping plane that is too close to the eye.

Previous examples in this book have simply used values of 0.1 and 1000 (in our calls to perspective()) for the near and far clipping planes. These may need to be adjusted for your scene.

4.10 ■ OTHER OPTIONS FOR PRIMITIVES

OpenGL supports a number of primitive types—so far we have seen two: GL_TRIANGLES and GL_POINTS. In fact, there are several others. All of the available primitive types supported in OpenGL fall into the categories of *triangles*, *lines*, *points*, and *patches*. Here is a complete list:

Triangle primitives:

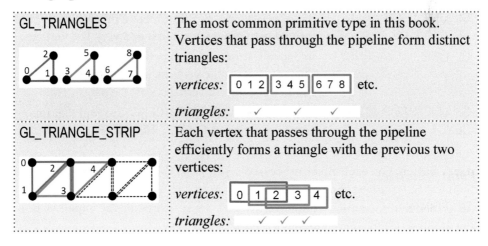

GL_TRIANGLE_FAN 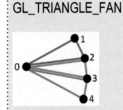	Each pair of vertices that passes through the pipe-line forms a triangle with the very first vertex: *vertices:* 0 1 2 3 4 etc. *triangles:* 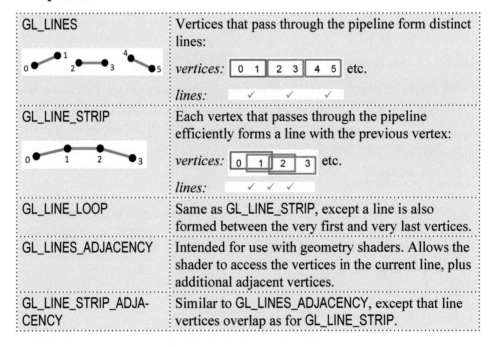
GL_TRIANGLES_ ADJACENCY	Intended only for use with geometry shaders. Allows the shader to access the vertices in the current triangle, plus additional adjacent vertices.
GL_TRIANGLE_STRIP_ ADJACENCY	Intended only for use with geometry shaders. Similar to GL_TRIANGLES_ADJACENCY, except that tri-angle vertices overlap as for GL_TRIANGLE_STRIP.

Line primitives:

GL_LINES	Vertices that pass through the pipeline form distinct lines: *vertices:* 0 1 2 3 4 5 etc. *lines:* ✓ ✓ ✓
GL_LINE_STRIP	Each vertex that passes through the pipeline efficiently forms a line with the previous vertex: *vertices:* 0 1 2 3 etc. *lines:* ✓ ✓ ✓
GL_LINE_LOOP	Same as GL_LINE_STRIP, except a line is also formed between the very first and very last vertices.
GL_LINES_ADJACENCY	Intended for use with geometry shaders. Allows the shader to access the vertices in the current line, plus additional adjacent vertices.
GL_LINE_STRIP_ADJA-CENCY	Similar to GL_LINES_ADJACENCY, except that line vertices overlap as for GL_LINE_STRIP.

Point primitives:

GL_POINTS	Each vertex that passes through the pipeline is a point.

Patch primitives:

GL_PATCH	Intended for use only with tessellation shaders. Indicates that a set of vertices passes from the vertex shader to the tessellation control shader, where they are typically used to shape a tessellated grid into a curved surface.

4.11 ■ CODING FOR PERFORMANCE

As the complexity of our 3D scenes grows, we will become increasingly concerned with performance. We have already seen a few instances where coding decisions were made in the interest of speed, such as when we used instancing and when we moved expensive computations into the shaders.

Actually, the code we have presented has already also included some additional optimizations that we haven't yet discussed, some of which are facilitated by the JOML math library. We now explore these and other important techniques.

4.11.1 Minimizing Dynamic Memory Allocation

The critical module in our Java/JOGL applications, with respect to performance, is clearly the display() function. This is the function that is called repeatedly during any animation or real-time rendering, and it is thus in this function (or in any function that it calls) where we must strive for maximum efficiency.

One important way of keeping overhead in the display() function to a minimum is by avoiding any steps that require memory allocation. Obvious examples of things to avoid thus would include the following:

- instantiating objects
- declaring variables
- allocating buffers

The reader is encouraged to review each of the programs that we have developed so far and note that every variable used in the display() function was declared, and its space allocated, *before* the display() function was ever actually called. Another example is Matrix4fStack, in which JOML requires allocation of the maximum stack size up front, so that the entire stack is allocated ahead of time, so the "push" operations done in display() don't allocate space dynamically. In fact, we now minimize the number of declarations or instantiations of any kind that appear in display(). For example, Program 4.1 included the following block of code early in its listing:

```
// allocate variables used in display(), so they aren't allocated during rendering
private FloatBuffer vals = Buffers.newDirectFloatBuffer(16);   // for transfering matrices
private Matrix4f pMat = new Matrix4f();          // perspective matrix
private Matrix4f vMat = new Matrix4f();          // view matrix
private Matrix4f mMat = new Matrix4f();          // model matrix
private Matrix4f mvMat = new Matrix4f();         // model-view matrix
private int mvLoc, projLoc;
private float aspect;
```

Note that we purposely placed a comment at the top of the block indicating that these variables are pre-allocated for later use in the display() function (although we are only explicitly pointing that out now).

There are other, more subtle examples. For example, function calls that convert data from one type to another may in some cases instantiate and return the newly converted data. It is thus important to understand the behaviors of any library functions called from display().

Fortunately, the math library we are using, JOML, has been carefully designed to eliminate (or at least minimize) memory allocation as a result of calling its functions, while still providing needed capabilities for OpenGL. Most of its functions operate directly on the object from which the function is invoked, or on one of its parameters (rather than building an answer and returning it), and thus in either case allowing for the space holding the result to be pre-allocated.

An example of how cleverly JOML was designed to maximize performance in this way is seen in the calls to glUniformMatrix4fv(). Let's take a closer look at one such call, that transfers the model-view matrix to a uniform variable:

```
gl.glUniformMatrix4fv(mvLoc, 1, false, mvMat.get(vals));
```

Recall that the variable mvMat is of type Matrix4f, and that we wish to send the values in that matrix to the shader uniform pointed to by mvLoc. As expected, the JOML library has provided a get() function for retrieving the matrix values. We might ordinarily expect such a "get" function to return those values in an object such as an array (as is done in other math libraries such as glm or graphicslib3D). However, JOML instead requires that a *parameter* be included on the call to get(), and then uses this parameter as the destination where it will place the retrieved matrix values. What makes this so clever is that the JOML get() function *also returns a reference to the user-supplied destination object*, so that the call to get() can be placed directly into the glUniformMatrix4fv() call (which is expecting such a reference). Note also that we have declared and allocated this destination variable "vals" in the declaration block outside of display() (along with all of the other variables used in display()). In a sense, the get() is actually doing a sort of "put," but when implemented in this manner clearly fulfils the needs of a "get" function in this OpenGL setting, albeit much more efficiently.

In keeping with the recommendations of JOML developers, we have used the form of get() that expects a FloatBuffer as the destination parameter. JOGL allows for transferring either a buffer or an array to a structured uniform variable (such as mat4 or vec4). But performance is slightly better when using buffers, particularly here because JOML forces the use of only direct NIO buffers, as opposed to buffers that are wrappers for Java primitive types.

4.11.2 Pre-Computing the Perspective Matrix

Another optimization that can be done to reduce overhead in the display() function is to move the computation of the perspective matrix into the init() function. We mentioned this possibility earlier in Section 4.5 (well, in a footnote). While this is certainly easy to do, there is one slight complication. Although it is not normally necessary to recompute the perspective matrix, it *would* be necessary if the user running the application *resizes* the window (such as by dragging the window corner resize handle).

Fortunately, JOGL automatically makes a call to reshape() whenever the window is resized. So far, we have left the reshape() function empty—now we have a use for it. We simply move the code that computes the perspective matrix into init(), and also copy it into reshape().

Consider, for example, Program 4.1. If we reorganize the code so as to remove the computation of the perspective matrix from display(), then the revised versions of the init(), display(), and reshape() functions would be as follows:

```
public void init(GLAutoDrawable drawable)
{   // same as earlier, plus the following two lines:
    aspect = (float) myCanvas.getWidth() / (float) myCanvas.getHeight();
    pMat.setPerspective((float) Math.toRadians(60.0f), aspect, 0.1f, 1000.0f);
}

public void display(GLAutoDrawable drawable)
{   // same as earlier, except with the following lines removed:
    // build perspective matrix
    aspect = (float) myCanvas.getWidth() / (float) myCanvas.getHeight();
    pMat.setPerspective((float) Math.toRadians(60.0f), aspect, 0.1f, 1000.0f);
    // the rest of the function is unchanged
}

public void reshape(GLAutoDrawable drawable, int x, int y, int width, int height)
{   GL4 gl = (GL4) GLContext.getCurrentGL();
    aspect = (float) width / (float) height;     // new window width & height are provided by the callback
    gl.glViewport(0, 0, width, height);          // sets region of screen associated with the frame buffer
    pMat.setPerspective((float) Math.toRadians(60.0f), aspect, 0.1f, 1000.0f);
}
```

4.11.3 Back-Face Culling

Another way of improving rendering efficiency is to take advantage of OpenGL's ability to do *back-face culling*. When a 3D model is entirely "closed," meaning the interior is never visible (such as for the cube and for the pyramid), then it turns out that those portions of the outer surface that are angled away from the viewer will always be obscured by some other portion of the same model. That is, those triangles that face away from the viewer cannot possibly be seen (they would be overwritten by hidden surface removal anyway), and thus there is no reason to rasterize or render them.

We can ask OpenGL to identify and "cull" (not render) back-facing triangles with the command glEnable(GL_CULL_FACE). We can also disable face culling with glDisable(GL_CULL_FACE). By default, face culling is disabled, so if you want OpenGL to cull back-facing triangles, you must enable it.

When face culling is enabled, by default triangles are rendered only if they are *front-facing*. Also by default a triangle is considered front-facing if its three vertices progress in a *counterclockwise* direction (based on the order that they were defined in the buffer) as viewed from the OpenGL camera. Triangles whose vertices progress in a clockwise direction (as viewed from the OpenGL camera) are *back-facing*, and are not rendered. This counterclockwise definition of "front-facing" is sometimes called the *winding order*, and can be set explicitly using the function call glFrontFace(GL_CCW) for counterclockwise (the default) or glFrontFace(GL_CW) for clockwise. Similarly, whether it is the front-facing or the back-facing triangles that are rendered can also be set explicitly. Actually, for this purpose we specify which ones are *not* to be rendered—that is, which ones are "culled." We can specify that the back-facing triangles be culled (although this would be unnecessary because it is the default) by calling glCullFace(GL_BACK). Alternatively, we can specify instead that the front-facing triangles be culled, or even that all of the triangles be culled, by replacing the parameter GL_BACK with either GL_FRONT or GL_FRONT_AND_BACK, respectively.

As we will see in Chapter 6, 3D models are typically designed so that the outer surface is constructed of triangles with the same winding order—most commonly counterclockwise—so that if culling is enabled, then by default the portion of the model's outer surface that faces the camera is rendered. Since by default OpenGL assumes the winding order is counterclockwise, if a model is designed to be displayed with a *clockwise* winding order, it is up to the programmer to call gl_FrontFace(GL_CW) to account for this if back-face culling is enabled.

Note that in the case of GL_TRIANGLE_STRIP, the winding order of each triangle alternates. OpenGL compensates for this by "flipping" the vertex sequence when building each successive triangle, as follows: 0-1-2, then 2-1-3, 2-3-4, 4-3-5, 4-5-6, and so on.

Back-face culling improves performance by ensuring that OpenGL doesn't spend time rasterizing and rendering surfaces that are never intended to be seen. Most of the examples we have seen in this chapter are so small that there is little motivation to enable face culling (an exception is the example shown in Figure 4.9, with the 100,000 instanced animated cubes, which may pose a performance challenge on some systems). In practice, it is common for most 3D models to be "closed," and so it is customary to routinely enable back-face culling. For example, we can add back-face culling to Program 4.3 by modifying the display() function as follows:

```
public void display(GLAutoDrawable drawable)
{   ...
    gl.glEnable(GL_CULL_FACE);

    // draw the cube
    ...
    gl.glEnable(GL_DEPTH_TEST);
    gl.glDepthFunc(GL_LEQUAL);
    gl.glFrontFace(GL_CW);              // the cube vertices have clockwise winding order
    gl.glDrawArrays(GL_TRIANGLES, 0, 36);

    // draw the pyramid
    ...
    gl.glEnable(GL_DEPTH_TEST);
    gl.glDepthFunc(GL_LEQUAL);
    gl.glFrontFace(GL_CCW);            // the pyramid vertices have counter-clockwise winding order
    gl.glDrawArrays(GL_TRIANGLES, 0, 18);
}
```

Properly setting the winding order is important when using back-face culling. An incorrect setting, such as GL_CW when it should be GL_CCW, can lead to the interior of an object being rendered rather than its exterior, which in turn can produce distortion similar to that of an incorrect perspective matrix.

Efficiency isn't the only reason for doing face culling. In later chapters we will see other uses, such as for those circumstances when we want to see the *inside* of a 3D model or when using transparency.

SUPPLEMENTAL NOTES

JOML has a huge variety of functions for performing translation, rotation, and scaling. For example, JOML's functions "translate()" and "translation()" are slightly different. The first concatenates a translation onto an existing matrix, whereas the second builds a translation matrix. We have used both of these functions in our examples, and there are many others to choose from. The reader should be careful to double-check that the JOML function being used does exactly what is desired.

As mentioned in this chapter, when using Java buffers it is advisable to ensure that only direct buffers are used. For example, it is tempting to use the Java FloatBuffer.wrap() function to put vertex data stored in an array into a buffer. However, wrap() produces a *non-direct* buffer, in which the resulting buffer is a wrapper for data that is still stored in an array.[6] One approach for copying the data into a *direct* buffer is to allocate a direct ByteBuffer, use ByteBuffer.asFloatBuffer() to view it as a FloatBuffer, and then use a loop with the put() command to copy the data one at a time. As described earlier, the JOGL com.jogamp.common.nio.Buffers class makes it easier to populate direct buffers by providing convenience methods for loading array data into a variety of buffer types:

```
newDirectByteBuffer(byte[ ])
newDirectCharBuffer(char[ ])
newDirectDoubleBuffer(double[ ])
newDirectFloatBuffer(float[ ])
newDirectIntBuffer(int[ ])
newDirectLongBuffer(long[ ])
newDirectShortBuffer(short[ ])
```

Using the above JOGL methods for populating buffers with vertex data (that is, data intended to be used by JOGL applications) also insures correct native byte ordering. It also ensures correct size allocation and makes an explicit allocation unnecessary.

There is a myriad of other capabilities and structures available for managing and utilizing data in OpenGL/JOGL/GLSL, and we have only scratched the surface in this chapter. We haven't, for example, described a *uniform block*, which is a mechanism for organizing uniform variables similar to a *struct* in C. Uniform blocks can even be set up to receive data from buffers. Another powerful mechanism is a *shader storage block*, which is essentially a buffer into which a shader can write.

An excellent reference on the many options for managing data (albeit in C++) is the *OpenGL SuperBible* [SW15], particularly the chapter entitled "Data" (Chapter 5 in the seventh edition). It also describes many of the details and options

---

[6] Using non-direct buffers is actually allowable in JOGL. However, when a non-direct buffer is passed to a JOGL method, JOGL will convert it to a direct buffer, and this conversion incurs a performance penalty.

for the various commands that we have covered. The first two example programs in this chapter, Program 4.1 and Program 4.2, were inspired by similar examples in the *SuperBible*.

There are other types of data that we will need to learn how to manage and how to send down the OpenGL pipeline. One of these is a *texture*, which contains color image data (such as in a photograph) that can be used to "paint" the objects in our scene. We will study texture images in Chapter 5. Another important buffer that we will study further is the *depth buffer* (or Z-buffer). This will become important when we study shadows in Chapter 8. We still have much to learn about managing graphics data in OpenGL!

Exercises

4.1 *(PROJECT)* Modify Program 4.1 to replace the cube with some other simple 3D shape of your own design. Be sure to properly specify the number of vertices in the glDrawArrays() command.

4.2 *(PROJECT)* In Program 4.1, the "view" matrix is defined in the display() function simply as the negative of the camera location:

vMat.identity().translate(-cameraX, -cameraY, -cameraZ);

Replace this code with an implementation of the computation shown in Figure 3.13. This will allow you to position the camera by specifying a camera position and three orientation axes. You will find it necessary to store the vectors U,V,N described in Section 3.7. Then, experiment with different camera viewpoints, and observe the resulting appearance of the rendered cube.

4.3 *(PROJECT)* Modify Program 4.4 to include a second "planet," which is your custom 3D shape from Exercise 4.1. Make sure that your new "planet" is in a different orbit than the existing planet, so that they don't collide.

4.4 *(PROJECT)* Modify Program 4.4 so that the "view" matrix is constructed using the "look-at" function (as described in Section 3.9). Then experiment with setting the "look-at" parameters to various locations, such as looking at the sun (in which case the scene should appear normal), looking at the planet, or looking at the moon.

4.5 *(RESEARCH)* Propose a practical use for glCullFace(GL_FRONT_AND_BACK).

References

[BL16] Blender, The Blender Foundation, accessed July 2016, https://www
.blender.org/

[HT16] J. Hastings-Trew, *JHT's Planetary Pixel Emporium*, accessed July 2016,
http://planetpixelemporium.com/

[MA16] Maya, AutoDesk, Inc., accessed July 2016, http://www.autodesk.com/
products/maya/overview

[NA16] NASA 3D Resources, accessed July 2016, http://nasa3d.arc.nasa.gov/

[OL16] Legacy OpenGL, accessed July 2016, https://www.opengl.org/wiki/
Legacy_OpenGL

[SW15] G. Sellers, R. Wright Jr., and N. Haemel, *OpenGL SuperBible:
Comprehensive Tutorial and Reference*, 7th ed. (Addison-Wesley, 2015).

TEXTURE MAPPING

Texture mapping is the technique of overlaying an image across a rasterized model surface. It is one of the most fundamental and important ways of adding realism to a rendered scene.

Texture mapping is so important that there is hardware support for it, allowing for very high performance resulting in real-time photorealism. *Texture Units* are hardware components designed specifically for texturing, and modern graphics cards typically come with several texture units included.

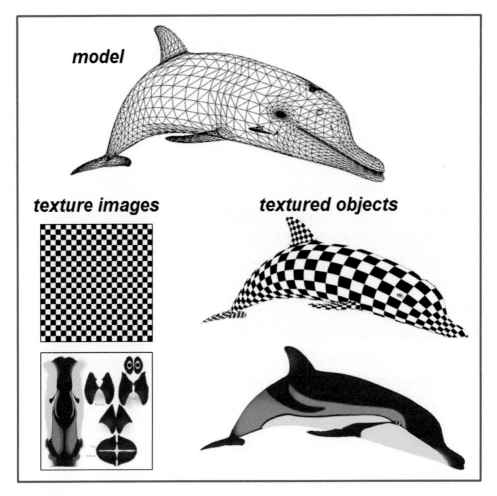

Figure 5.1
Texturing a dolphin model with two different images [TU16].

5.1 LOADING TEXTURE IMAGE FILES

There are a number of datasets and mechanisms that need to be coordinated to accomplish texture mapping efficiently in JOGL/GLSL:

- a *texture object* to hold the texture image (in this chapter we consider only 2D images)
- a special uniform *sampler* variable so that the vertex shader can access the texture
- a buffer to hold the *texture coordinates*

- a vertex attribute for passing the texture coordinates down the pipeline
- a *texture unit* on the graphics card

A texture image can be a picture of anything. It can be a picture of something man-made or occurring in nature, such as cloth, grass, or a planetary surface, or it could be a geometric pattern, such as the checkerboard in Figure 5.1. In video-games and animated movies, texture images are commonly used to paint faces and clothing on characters or skin on creatures such as on the dolphin in Figure 5.1.

Images are typically stored in image files, such as .jpg, .png, .gif, or .tiff. In order to make a texture image available to shaders in the OpenGL pipeline, we need to extract the colors from the image and put them into an OpenGL *texture object* (a built-in OpenGL structure for holding a texture image).

Java has some useful image file tools in its imageio and awt packages that can be used to read texture images. The steps are as follows: (a) read the image data into a ByteBuffer, using the JOGL buffer tools we saw in Chapter 4, (b) use glGenTextures() to instantiate a texture object and assign it an integer ID, (c) call glBindTexture() to make the newly created texture object active, (d) load the previously read-in image data into the texture object with the glTexImage2D() command, and (e) adjust the texture settings using the glTexParameter() function. The result is an integer ID referencing the now available OpenGL texture object. We will walk through these steps at the end of this chapter.

However, JOGL includes its own tools for working with textures that make it considerably simpler to load a texture image file into an OpenGL texture object. Those tools are found in the JOGL classes Texture, TextureIO, and TextureData.

Texturing an object starts by declaring a variable of type Texture. This is a JOGL class; a JOGL Texture object serves as a wrapper for an OpenGL texture object. Next, we call newTexture()—a static method in the TextureIO class—to actually generate the texture object. The newTexture() function accepts an image file name as one of its parameters (several standard image file types are supported, including the four mentioned above). These steps are implemented in the following function:

```
public static int loadTexture(String textureFileName)
{   Texture tex = null;
    try { tex = TextureIO.newTexture(new File(textureFileName), false); }
    catch (Exception e) { e.printStackTrace(); }
    int textureID = tex.getTextureObject();
    return textureID;
}
```

We will use this function often, so we add it our Utils.java utility class. The Java/JOGL application then simply calls the above loadTexture() function to create the OpenGL texture object as follows:

int myTexture = Utils.loadTexture("image.jpg");

where image.jpg is a texture image file and myTexture is an integer ID for the resulting OpenGL texture object.

5.2 TEXTURE COORDINATES

Now that we have a means for loading a texture image into OpenGL, we need to specify how we want the texture to be applied to the rendered surface of an object. We do this by specifying *texture coordinates* for each vertex in our model.

Texture coordinates are references to the pixels in a (usually 2D) texture image. Pixels in a texture image are referred to as *texels*, in order to differentiate them from the pixels being rendered on the screen. Texture coordinates are used to map points on a 3D model to locations in a texture. Each point on the surface of the model has, in addition to (x,y,z) coordinates that place it in 3D space, texture coordinates (s,t) that specify which texel in the texture image provides its color. Thus, the surface of the object is "painted" by the texture image. The orientation of a texture across the surface of an object is determined by the assignment of texture coordinates to object vertices.

In order to use texture mapping, *it is necessary to provide texture coordinates for every vertex* in the object to be textured. OpenGL will use these texture coordinates to determine the color of each rasterized pixel in the model, by looking up the color stored at the referenced texel in the image. In order to ensure that every pixel in your rendered model is painted with an appropriate texel from the texture image, *the texture coordinates are put into a vertex attribute so that they are also interpolated by the rasterizer.* In that way the texture image is interpolated, or filled in, along with the model vertices.

For each set of vertex coordinates (x,y,z) passing through the vertex shader, there will be an accompanying set of texture coordinates (s,t). We will thus set up two buffers, one for the vertices (with three components x, y, and z in each entry) and one for the corresponding texture coordinates (with two components s and t in each entry). Each vertex shader invocation thus receives one vertex, now comprising both its spatial coordinates and its corresponding texture coordinates.

Texture coordinates are most often 2D (OpenGL does support some other dimensionalities but we won't cover them in this chapter). It is assumed that the image is rectangular, with location (0,0) at the lower left and (1,1) at the upper right.[1] Texture coordinates, then, should ideally have values in the range (0,1).

Consider the example shown in Figure 5.2. The cube model, recall, is constructed of triangles. The four corners of one side of the cube are highlighted, but remember that it takes two triangles to specify each square side. The texture coordinates for each of the *six* vertices that specify this one cube side are listed alongside the four corners, with the corners at the upper left and lower right each comprising a pair of vertices. A texture image is also shown. The texture coordinates (indexed by s and t) have mapped portions of the image (the texels) onto the rasterized pixels of the front face of the model. Note that all of the intervening pixels in between the vertices have been painted with the intervening texels in the image. This is achieved because the texture coordinates are sent to the fragment shader in a *vertex attribute*, and thus are *also interpolated* just like the vertices themselves.

In this example, we purposely specified texture coordinates that result in an oddly painted surface, for purposes of illustration. If you look closely, you can also see that the image appears slightly stretched—that is because the aspect ratio of the texture image doesn't match the aspect ratio of the cube face relative to the given texture coordinates.

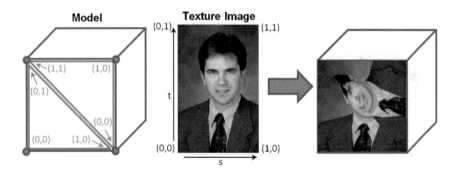

Figure 5.2
Texture coordinates.

---

[1] This is the orientation that OpenGL texture objects assume. However, this is different from the orientation of an image stored in many standard image file formats, in which the origin is at the upper left. Reorienting the image by flipping it vertically so that it corresponds to OpenGL's expected format is one of the operations performed by the JOGL newTexture() call that we made from the loadTexture() function.

For simple models like cubes or pyramids, selecting texture coordinates is relatively easy. But for more complex curved models with lots of triangles, it isn't practical to determine them by hand. In the case of curved geometric shapes, such as a sphere or torus, texture coordinates can be computed algorithmically or mathematically. In the case of a model built with a modeling tool such as Maya [MA16] or Blender [BL16], such tools offer "UV-mapping" (which is outside the scope of this book) to make this task easier.

Let us return to rendering our pyramid, only this time texturing it with an image of bricks. We will need to specify (a) an OpenGL texture object to hold the texture image, (b) texture coordinates for the model vertices, (c) a buffer for holding the texture coordinates, (d) vertex attributes so that the vertex shader can receive and forward the texture coordinates through the pipeline, (e) a texture unit on the graphics card for holding the texture object, and (f) a *uniform sampler* variable for accessing the texture unit in GLSL, which we will see shortly. These are each described in the next sections.

5.3 CREATING A TEXTURE OBJECT

Suppose the image shown here is stored in a file named "brick1.jpg" [LU16].

As shown previously, we can load this image by calling our loadTexture() function, as follows:

```
int brickTexture = Utils.loadTexture("brick1.jpg");
```

Recall that texture objects are identified by integer IDs, so brickTexture is of type int.

5.4 CONSTRUCTING TEXTURE COORDINATES

Our pyramid has four triangular sides and a square on the bottom. Although geometrically this only requires five (5) points, we have been rendering it with triangles. This requires four triangles for the sides and two triangles for the square bottom, for a total of six triangles. Each triangle has three vertices, for a total of 6*3=18 vertices that must be specified in the model.

We have already listed the pyramid's geometric vertices in Program 4.3 in the float array pyramid_positions[ ]. There are many ways that we could orient our texture coordinates so as to draw our bricks onto the pyramid. One simple (albeit imperfect) way would be to make the top center of the image correspond to the peak of the pyramid, as follows:

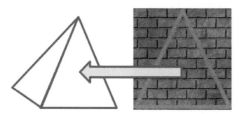

We can do this for all four of the triangle sides. We also need to paint the bottom square of the pyramid, which comprises two triangles. A simple and reasonable approach would be to texture it with the entire area from the picture (the pyramid has been tipped back and is sitting on its side):

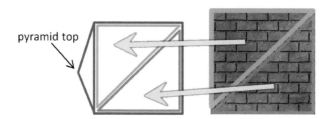

The corresponding set of vertex and texture coordinates using this very simple strategy, for the first eight of the pyramid vertices from Program 4.3, is shown in Figure 5.3.

```
        vertices              texture coordinates
    (-1.0,-1.0, 1.0)         (0,   0)    // front face
    ( 1.0,-1.0, 1.0)         (1,   0)
    (   0, 1.0,   0)         (.5,  1)
    ( 1.0,-1.0, 1.0)         (0,   0)    // right face
    ( 1.0,-1.0,-1.0)         (1,   0)
    (   0, 1.0,   0)         (.5,  1)
    ( 1.0,-1.0,-1.0)         (0,   0)    // back face
    (-1.0,-1.0,-1.0)         (1,   0)
    (   0, 1.0,   0)         (.5,  1)
    etc.
```

Figure 5.3
Texture coordinates for the pyramid (partial list).

■ 5.5 ■ LOADING TEXTURE COORDINATES INTO BUFFERS

We can load the texture coordinates into a VBO in a similar manner as seen previously for loading the vertices. In setupVertices(), we add the following declaration of the texture coordinate values:

```
float[ ] pyrTextureCoordinates =
{   0.0f, 0.0f, 1.0f, 0.0f, 0.5f, 1.0f,   0.0f, 0.0f, 1.0f, 0.0f, 0.5f, 1.0f,   // top and right faces
    0.0f, 0.0f, 1.0f, 0.0f, 0.5f, 1.0f,   0.0f, 0.0f, 1.0f, 0.0f, 0.5f, 1.0f,   // back and left faces
    0.0f, 0.0f, 1.0f, 1.0f, 0.0f, 1.0f,   1.0f, 1.0f, 0.0f, 0.0f, 1.0f, 0.0f };  // base triangles
```

Then, after the creation of at least two VBOs (one for the vertices and one for the texture coordinates), we add the following lines of code to load the texture coordinates into VBO #1:

```
gl.glBindBuffer(GL_ARRAY_BUFFER, vbo[1]);
FloatBuffer pTexBuf = Buffers.newDirectFloatBuffer(pyrTextureCoordinates);
gl.glBufferData(GL_ARRAY_BUFFER, pTexBuf.limit()*4, pTexBuf, GL_STATIC_DRAW);
```

■ 5.6 ■ USING THE TEXTURE IN A SHADER: SAMPLER VARIABLES AND TEXTURE UNITS

To maximize performance, we will want to perform the texturing in hardware. This means that our fragment shader will need a way of accessing the texture object that we created in the Java/JOGL application. The mechanism for doing this is via a special GLSL tool called a *uniform sampler variable*. This is a variable designed for instructing a texture unit on the graphics card as to which texel to extract or "sample" from a loaded texture object.

Declaring a sampler variable in the shader is easy—just add it to your set of uniforms:

```
layout (binding=0) uniform sampler2D samp;
```

Ours is named "samp"; the "layout (binding=0)" portion of the declaration specifies that this sampler is to be associated with texture unit 0.

A texture unit (and associated sampler) can be used to sample whichever texture object you wish, and that can change at runtime. Your display() function will need to specify which texture object you want the texture unit to sample for the current frame. So each time you draw an object, you will need to activate a texture unit and bind it to a particular texture object, as follows:

```
gl.glActiveTexture(GL_TEXTURE0);
gl.glBindTexture(GL_TEXTURE_2D, brickTexture);
```

The number of available texture units depends on how many are provided on the graphics card. According to the OpenGL API documentation, OpenGL version 4.5 requires that this be at least 16 per shader stage and at least 80 total units across all stages [OP16]. In this example, we have made the 0th texture unit active by specifying GL_TEXTURE0 in the glActiveTexture() call.

To actually perform the texturing, we will need to modify how our fragment shader outputs colors. Previously, our fragment shader either output a constant color, or it obtained colors from a vertex attribute. This time instead, we need to use the interpolated texture coordinates received from the vertex shader (through the rasterizer) to sample the texture object, by calling the texture() function as follows:

```
in vec2 tc;          // texture coordinates
. . .
color = texture(samp, tc);
```

▪5.7▪ TEXTURE MAPPING: EXAMPLE PROGRAM

Program 5.1 combines the previous steps into a single program. The result, showing the pyramid textured with the brick image, appears in Figure 5.4. Two rotations (not shown in the code listing) were added to the pyramid's model matrix to expose the underside of the pyramid.

It is now a simple matter to replace the brick texture image with other texture images, as desired, simply by changing the filename in the load-Texture() call. For example, if we replace "brick1.jpg" with the image file "ice.jpg" [LU16], we get the result shown in Figure 5.5.

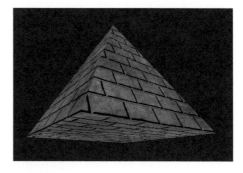

Figure 5.4
Pyramid texture mapped with brick image.

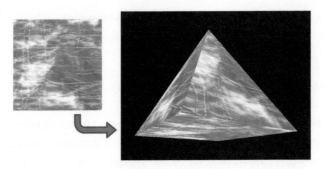

Figure 5.5
Pyramid texture mapped with "ice" image.

Program 5.1 Pyramid with Brick Texture

JAVA/JOGL Application

```
//  the following additional imports will be necessary for the texture functions:
import java.io.*;
import java.nio.*;
import com.jogamp.opengl.util.texture.*;

public class Code extends JFrame implements GLEventListener
{   // previous declarations and constructor code applies. We just need to add declarations for the texture:
    . . .
    private int brickTexture;
    . . .
    public Code()
    {   // unchanged . . .
    }
    public void display(GLAutoDrawable drawable)
    {   GL4 gl = (GL4) GLContext.getCurrentGL();
        . . .
        // setup of background color, depth buffer.
        // PROJ matrix moved to init() and reshape() as described in Chapter 2
        . . .
        // this time we are drawing only the pyramid.
        // setup of M and MV matrices is unchanged.
        . . .
        // activate buffer #0, which contains the vertices
        gl.glBindBuffer(GL_ARRAY_BUFFER, vbo[0]);
        gl.glVertexAttribPointer(0, 3, GL_FLOAT, false, 0, 0);
        gl.glEnableVertexAttribArray(0);
```

```
// activate buffer #1, which contains the texture coordinates
gl.glBindBuffer(GL_ARRAY_BUFFER, vbo[1]);
gl.glVertexAttribPointer(1, 2, GL_FLOAT, false, 0, 0);
gl.glEnableVertexAttribArray(1);

// activate texture unit #0 and bind it to the brick texture object
gl.glActiveTexture(GL_TEXTURE0);
gl.glBindTexture(GL_TEXTURE_2D, brickTexture);

gl.glEnable(GL_DEPTH_TEST);
gl.glDepthFunc(GL_LEQUAL);

gl.glDrawArrays(GL_TRIANGLES, 0, 18);
}


public void init(GLAutoDrawable drawable)
{   // setup of rendering program, camera and object location unchanged
    . . .
    brickTexture = Utils.loadTexture("brick1.jpg");
}

private void setupVertices()
{   GL4 gl = (GL4) GLContext.getCurrentGL();
    float[ ] pyramidPositions = {  /* data as listed previously in Program 4.2 */ };
    float[ ] pyrTextureCoordinates =
    {   0.0f, 0.0f, 1.0f, 0.0f, 0.5f, 1.0f,     0.0f, 0.0f, 1.0f, 0.0f, 0.5f, 1.0f,
        0.0f, 0.0f, 1.0f, 0.0f, 0.5f, 1.0f,     0.0f, 0.0f, 1.0f, 0.0f, 0.5f, 1.0f,
        0.0f, 0.0f, 1.0f, 1.0f, 0.0f, 1.0f,     1.0f, 1.0f, 0.0f, 0.0f, 1.0f, 0.0f };

    // . . . generate the VAO as before, and at least two VBOs, then load the two buffers as follows:
    gl.glBindBuffer(GL_ARRAY_BUFFER, vbo[0]);
    FloatBuffer pyrBuf = Buffers.newDirectFloatBuffer(pyramidPositions);
    gl.glBufferData(GL_ARRAY_BUFFER, pyrBuf.limit()*4, pyrBuf, GL_STATIC_DRAW);

    gl.glBindBuffer(GL_ARRAY_BUFFER, vbo[1]);
    FloatBuffer pTexBuf = Buffers.newDirectFloatBuffer(pyrTextureCoordinates);
    gl.glBufferData(GL_ARRAY_BUFFER, pTexBuf.limit()*4, pTexBuf, GL_STATIC_DRAW);
}
    . . .   // remainder of the class definition and utility functions here
}
```

Vertex shader

```
#version 430
layout (location=0) in vec3 pos;
layout (location=1) in vec2 texCoord;
out vec2 tc;         // texture coordinate output to rasterizer for interpolation
```

```
uniform mat4 mv_matrix;
uniform mat4 proj_matrix;
layout (binding=0) uniform sampler2D samp;      // not used in vertex shader

void main(void)
{   gl_Position = proj_matrix * mv_matrix * vec4(pos,1.0);
    tc = texCoord;
}
```

Fragment shader

```
#version 430
in vec2 tc;            // interpolated incoming texture coordinate
out vec4 color;
uniform mat4 mv_matrix;
uniform mat4 proj_matrix;
layout (binding=0) uniform sampler2D samp;

void main(void)
{   color = texture(samp, tc);
}
```

▄▄5.8▄▄ MIPMAPPING

Texture mapping commonly produces a variety of undesirable artifacts in the rendered image. This is because the resolution or aspect ratio of the texture image rarely matches that of the region in the scene being textured.

A very common artifact occurs when the image resolution is *less than* that of the region being drawn. In this case, the image would need to be stretched to cover the region, becoming blurry (and possibly distorted). This can sometimes be combated, depending on the nature of the texture, by assigning the texture coordinates differently so that applying the texture requires less stretching. Another solution is to use a higher resolution texture image.

The reverse situation is when the resolution of the image texture is *greater than* that of the region being drawn. It is probably not at all obvious why this would pose a problem, but it does! In this case, noticeable *aliasing* artifacts can occur, giving rise to strange-looking false patterns, or "shimmering" effects in moving objects.

Aliasing is caused by *sampling errors*. It is most often associated with signal processing, where an inadequately sampled signal appears to have different properties (such as wavelength) than it actually does when it is reconstructed. An example is shown in Figure 5.6. The original waveform is shown in red. The yellow dots along the waveform represent the samples. If they are used to reconstruct the wave, and if there aren't enough of them, they can define a different wave (shown in blue).

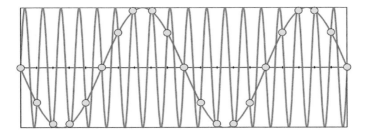

Figure 5.6
Aliasing due to inadequate sampling.

Similarly, in texture-mapping, when a high-resolution (and highly detailed) image is sparsely sampled (such as when using a uniform sampler variable), the colors retrieved will be inadequate to reflect the actual detail in the image, and may instead seem random. If the texture image has a repeated pattern, aliasing can result in a *different* pattern being produced than the one in the original image. If the object being textured is moving, rounding errors in texel lookup can result in constant changes in the sampled pixel at a given texture coordinate, producing an unwanted sparkling effect across the surface of the object being drawn.

Figure 5.7 shows a tilted close-up rendering of the top of a cube which has been textured by a large, high-resolution image of a checkerboard.

Aliasing is evident near the top of the image, where the undersampling of the checkerboard has produced a "striped" effect. Although we can't show it here in a still image, if this

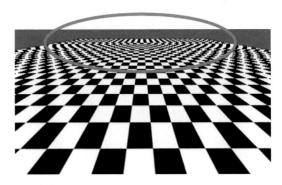

Figure 5.7
Aliasing in a texture map.

Figure 5.8
"Sparkling" in a texture map.

were an animated scene, the patterns would likely undulate between various incorrect patterns such as this one.

Another example appears in Figure 5.8, in which the cube has been textured with an image of the surface of the moon [HT16]. At first glance, this image appears sharp and full of detail. However, some of the detail at the upper right of the image is false and causes "sparkling" as the cube object (or the camera) moves. (Unfortunately, we can't show the sparkling effect clearly in a still image.)

These and similar sampling error artifacts can be largely corrected by a technique called *mipmapping*, in which different versions of the texture image are created at various resolutions. OpenGL then uses the texture image that most closely matches the resolution at the point being textured. Even better, colors can be averaged between the images closest in resolution to that of the region being textured. Results of applying mipmapping to the images in Figure 5.7 and Figure 5.8 are shown in Figure 5.9.

 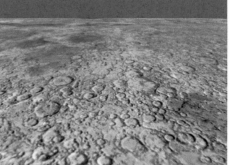

Figure 5.9
Mipmapped results.

Mipmapping works by a clever mechanism for storing a series of successively lower-resolution copies of the same image, in a texture image one-third larger than the original image. This is achieved by storing the R, G, and B components of the image separately in three-fourths of the texture image space, then repeating the process in the remaining one-fourth-sized image space for the same image at one-fourth the original resolution. This subdividing repeats until the remaining quadrant is too small to contain any useful image data. An example image and a visualization of the resulting mipmap is shown in Figure 5.10.

Figure 5.10
Mipmapping an image.

This method of stuffing several images into a small space (well, just a bit bigger than the space needed to store the original image) is how mipmapping got its name. MIP stands for *multum in parvo* [WI83], which is Latin for "much in a small space."

When actually texturing an object, the mipmap can be sampled in several ways. In OpenGL, the manner in which the mipmap is sampled can be chosen by setting the GL_TEXTURE_MIN_FILTER parameter to the desired *minification* technique, which is one of the following:

- **GL_NEAREST_MIPMAP_NEAREST**
  chooses the mipmap with the resolution most similar to that of the region of pixels being textured. It then obtains the nearest texel to the desired texture coordinates.

- **GL_LINEAR_MIPMAP_NEAREST**
  chooses the mipmap with the resolution most similar to that of the region of pixels being textured. It then interpolates the four texels nearest to the texture coordinates. This is called "linear filtering."

- **GL_NEAREST_MIPMAP_LINEAR**
  chooses the two mipmaps with resolutions nearest to that of the region of pixels being textured. It then obtains the nearest texel to the texture coordinates from each mipmap and interpolates them. This is called "bilinear filtering."

- **GL_LINEAR_MIPMAP_LINEAR**
  chooses the two mipmaps with resolutions nearest to that of the region of pixels being textured. It then interpolates the four nearest texels in each mipmap and interpolates those two results. This is called "trilinear filtering" and is illustrated in Figure 5.11.

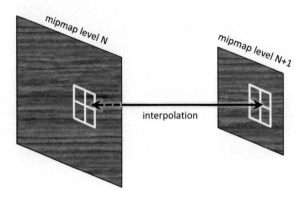

Figure 5.11
Trilinear filtering.

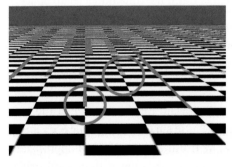

Figure 5.12
Linear filtering artifacts.

Trilinear filtering is usually preferable, as lower levels of blending often produce artifacts, such as visible separations between mipmap levels. Figure 5.12 shows a close-up of the checkerboard using mipmapping with only linear filtering enabled. Note the circled artifacts, where the vertical lines suddenly change from thick to thin at a mipmap boundary. By contrast, the example in Figure 5.9 used trilinear filtering.

Mipmapping is richly supported in OpenGL. There are mechanisms provided for building your own mipmap levels or having OpenGL build them for you. In most cases, the mipmaps built automatically by OpenGL are sufficient. This is done by adding the following lines of code to the Utils.loadTexture() function (described earlier in Section 5.1), immediately after the getTextureObject() function call:

```
gl.glBindTexture(GL_TEXTURE_2D, textureID);
gl.glTexParameteri(GL_TEXTURE_2D, GL_TEXTURE_MIN_FILTER, GL_LINEAR_MIPMAP_LINEAR);
gl.glGenerateMipmap(GL_TEXTURE_2D);
```

This tells OpenGL to generate the mipmaps. The brick texture is made active with the glBindTexture() call, and then the glTexParameteri() function call enables one of the minification factors listed above, such as GL_LINEAR_MIPMAP_LINEAR shown in the above call, which enables trilinear filtering.

Once the mipmap is built, the filtering option can be changed (although this is rarely necessary) by calling glTexParameteri() again, such as in the display function. Mipmapping can even be disabled by selecting GL_NEAREST or GL_LINEAR.

For critical applications, it is possible to build the mipmaps yourself, using whatever is your preferred image editing software. They can then be added as mipmap levels when creating the texture object by repeatedly calling OpenGL's glTexImage2D() function, or JOGL's updateSubImage() function, for each mipmap level. Further discussion of this approach is outside the scope of this book.

5.9 ANISOTROPIC FILTERING

Mipmapped textures can sometimes appear more blurry than non-mipmapped textures, especially when the textured object is rendered at a heavily tilted viewing angle. We saw an example of this back in Figure 5.9, where reducing artifacts with mipmapping led to reduced detail (compared with Figure 5.8).

This loss of detail occurs because when an object is tilted, its primitives appear smaller along one axis (i.e., width vs. height) than along the other. When OpenGL textures a primitive, it selects the mipmap appropriate for the *smaller* of the two axes (to avoid "sparkling" artifacts). In Figure 5.9 the surface is tilted heavily away from the viewer, so each rendered primitive will utilize the mipmap appropriate for its reduced *height*, which is likely to have a resolution lower than appropriate for its *width*.

One way of restoring some of this lost detail is to use *anisotropic filtering* (AF). Whereas standard mipmapping samples a texture image at a variety of square resolutions (e.g., 256x256, 128x128, etc.), AF samples the textures at a number of rectangular resolutions as well, such as 256x128, 64x128, and so on. This enables viewing at various angles while retaining as much detail in the texture as possible.

Anisotropic filtering is more computationally expensive than standard mipmapping, and is not a required part of OpenGL. However, most graphics cards support AF (this is referred to as an *OpenGL extension*), and OpenGL does provide both a way of querying the card to see if it supports AF and a way of accessing AF if it does. The code is added immediately after generating the mipmap:

```
. . .
// if mipmapping
gl.glBindTexture(GL_TEXTURE_2D, textureID);
gl.glTexParameteri(GL_TEXTURE_2D, GL_TEXTURE_MIN_FILTER, GL_LINEAR_MIPMAP_LINEAR);
gl.glGenerateMipmap(GL_TEXTURE_2D);

// if also anisotropic filtering
if (gl.isExtensionAvailable("GL_EXT_texture_filter_anisotropic"))
{   float anisoSetting[ ] = new float[1];
    gl.glGetFloatv(GL_MAX_TEXTURE_MAX_ANISOTROPY_EXT, anisoSetting, 0);
    gl.glTexParameterf(GL_TEXTURE_2D, GL_TEXTURE_MAX_ANISOTROPY_EXT, anisoSetting[0]);
}
```

Figure 5.13
Anisotropic filtering.

The call to gl.isExtensionAvailable() tests whether the graphics card supports AF. If it does, we set it to the maximum degree of sampling supported, a value retrieved using glGetFloatv() as shown. It is then applied to the active texture object using glTexParameterf(). The result is shown in Figure 5.13. Note that much of the lost detail from Figure 5.8 has been restored, while still removing the sparkling artifacts.

5.10 WRAPPING AND TILING

So far we have assumed that texture coordinates all fall in the range (0,1). However, OpenGL actually supports texture coordinates of any value. There are several options for specifying what happens when texture coordinates fall outside the range (0,1). The desired behavior is set using glTexParameteri(), and the options are as follows:

- **GL_REPEAT**: The integer portion of the texture coordinates are ignored, generating a repeating or "tiling" pattern. This is the default behavior.
- **GL_MIRRORED_REPEAT**: The integer portion is ignored, except that the coordinates are reversed when the integer portion is odd, so the repeating pattern alternates between normal and mirrored.
- **GL_CLAMP_TO_EDGE**: Coordinates less than 0 and greater than 1 are set to 0 and 1, respectively.
- **GL_CLAMP_TO_BORDER**: Texels outside of (0,1) will be assigned some specified border color.

For example, consider a pyramid in which the texture coordinates have been defined in the range (0,5) rather than the range (0,1). The default behavior (GL_REPEAT), using the texture image shown previously in Figure 5.2, would result in the texture repeating five times across the surface (sometimes called "tiling"), as shown in Figure 5.14.

Figure 5.14
Texture coordinate wrapping with GL_REPEAT.

To make the tiles' appearance alternate between normal and mirrored, we can specify the following:

```
gl.glTexParameteri(GL_TEXTURE_2D, GL_TEXTURE_WRAP_S, GL_MIRRORED_REPEAT);
gl.glTexParameteri(GL_TEXTURE_2D, GL_TEXTURE_WRAP_T, GL_MIRRORED_REPEAT);
```

Specifying that values less than 0 and greater than 1 be set to 0 and 1, respectively, can be done by replacing **GL_MIRRORED_REPEAT** with **GL_CLAMP_TO_EDGE**.

Specifying that values less than 0 and greater than 1 result in a "border" color can be done as follows:

```
gl.glTexParameteri(GL_TEXTURE_2D, GL_TEXTURE_WRAP_S, GL_CLAMP_TO_BORDER);
gl.glTexParameteri(GL_TEXTURE_2D, GL_TEXTURE_WRAP_T, GL_CLAMP_TO_BORDER);
float[ ] redColor = new float[ ] { 1.0f, 0.0f, 0.0f, 1.0f };
gl.glTexParameterfv(GL_TEXTURE_2D, GL_TEXTURE_BORDER_COLOR, redColor, 0);
```

The effect of each of these options (mirrored repeat, clamp to edge, and clamp to border), with texture coordinates ranging from −2 to +3, are shown, respectively (left to right), in Figure 5.15.

Figure 5.15
Textured pyramid with various wrapping options.

In the center example (clamp to edge), the pixels along the edges of the texture image are replicated outward. Note that as a side effect, the lower-left and lower-right regions of the pyramid faces obtain their color from the lower-left and lower-right pixels of the texture image, respectively.

5.11 PERSPECTIVE DISTORTION

We have seen that as texture coordinates are passed from the vertex shader to the fragment shader, they are interpolated as they pass through the rasterizer. We have also seen that this is the result of the automatic linear interpolation that is always performed on vertex attributes.

However, in the case of texture coordinates, linear interpolation can lead to noticeable distortion in a 3D scene with perspective projection.

Consider a rectangle made of two triangles and textured with a checkerboard image, facing the camera. As the rectangle is rotated around the X axis, the top part of the rectangle tilts away from the camera, while the lower part of the rectangle swings closer to the camera. Thus, we would expect the squares at the top to become smaller and the squares at the bottom to become larger. However, linear interpolation of the texture coordinates will instead cause the height of *all* squares to be equal. The distortion is exacerbated along the diagonal defining the two triangles that make up the rectangle. The resulting distortion is shown in Figure 5.16.

Fortunately, there are algorithms for correcting perspective distortion, and by default, OpenGL applies a *perspective correction* algorithm [OP14] during rasterization. Figure 5.17 shows the same rotating checkerboard, properly rendered by OpenGL.

Figure 5.16
Texture perspective distortion.

Figure 5.17
OpenGL perspective correction.

Although not common, it is possible to disable OpenGL's perspective correction by adding the keyword "noperspective" in the declaration of the vertex attribute containing the texture coordinates. This has to be done in both the vertex and fragment shaders. For example, the vertex attribute in the vertex shader would be declared as follows:

```
noperspective out vec2 texCoord;
```

The corresponding attribute in the fragment shader would be declared

```
noperspective in vec2 texCoord;
```

This second syntax was in fact used to produce the distorted checkerboard in Figure 5.16.

5.12 LOADING TEXTURE IMAGE FILES USING JAVA AWT CLASSES

Throughout the rest of this textbook we use the JOGL Texture, TextureIO, and TextureData classes as described earlier in this chapter to load texture image data into OpenGL texture objects. However, it is possible to load texture image file data into OpenGL textures *directly*, using Java AWT classes and some additional OpenGL commands. The process is quite a bit more complicated, so for simplicity and clarity we will use the JOGL classes in this book whenever possible. However, it is useful to understand the process (and the particular commands) one could use in lieu of the JOGL texture classes. For example, the JOGL texture classes don't support 3D textures, so as we will see later, building an OpenGL 3D texture object will require doing many of the steps ourselves in Java. We will also use some of these steps when building skyboxes, as described in Chapter 9.

Building a texture-loading function analogous to the one in Program 5.1 without using JOGL texture classes is shown in Program 5.2. To avoid confusion, we will call it loadTextureAWT().[2] It starts by calling two utility functions (also shown). The first one is getBufferedImage(), which reads the specified image file, assumed to be in a recognized format such as .jpg or .png, and returns a Java BufferedImage containing the image file data. The second utility function, getRGBAPixelData(), extracts the RGBA pixel colors from the specified BufferedImage and returns them in a byte array organized in the form expected by OpenGL. It is in this function that we may or may not flip the image vertically (specified by a boolean parameter) as described earlier, depending on the application.

The loadTextureAWT() function then continues by copying the byte array returned from getRGBAPixelData() into a Java ByteBuffer, using the JOGL Buffers. newDirectByteBuffer() method described in Chapter 4. It then creates the texture object, in a manner similar to the steps we used for creating VBOs. Textures, like buffers, are given integer IDs by calling glGenTextures(). Here, the variable textureID is used to hold the ID of a generated texture object. Next, the texture object is made active by calling glBindTexture(), and then we load the previously read-in image data into the active texture object by using the glTexImage2D() command. Note the first parameter on this call specifies the type of texture object—in this case GL_TEXTURE_2D (later we will use this command to create other types of

---

[2] We chose the name "loadTextureAWT()" for this function because it uses several classes from the Java AWT package.

OpenGL textures, such as texture cube maps in Chapter 9 and 3D textures in Chapter 14). The next command, glTexParameteri(), can be used to adjust some of the texture settings, such as building mipmaps. When loadTextureAWT() finishes, it returns the integer ID for the now available OpenGL texture object, as we did in Program 5.1.

Assuming that we have placed all of the relevant code in the Utils.java utilities class, the following single call to loadTextureAWT() then creates the integer ID for the OpenGL texture object:

int brickTexture = Utils.loadTextureAWT("brick1.jpg");

Program 5.2 Java AWT Routines for Loading Texture Images

```java
public static int loadTextureAWT(String textureFileName)
{   GL4 gl = (GL4) GLContext.getCurrentGL();
    BufferedImage textureImage = getBufferedImage(textureFileName);
    byte[ ] imgRGBA = getRGBAPixelData(textureImage, true);
    ByteBuffer rgbaBuffer = Buffers.newDirectByteBuffer(imgRGBA);

    int[ ] textureIDs = new int[1];                         // array to hold generated texture IDs
    gl.glGenTextures(1, textureIDs, 0);
    int textureID = textureIDs[0];                          // ID for the 0th texture object
    gl.glBindTexture(GL_TEXTURE_2D, textureID);             // specifies the active 2D texture
    gl.glTexImage2D(GL_TEXTURE_2D, 0, GL_RGBA,              // MIPMAP level, color space
        textureImage.getWidth(), textureImage.getHeight(), 0 // image size, border (ignored)
        GL_RGBA, GL_UNSIGNED_BYTE,                          // pixel format and data type
        rgbaBuffer);                                        // buffer holding texture data
    gl.glTexParameteri(GL_TEXTURE_2D, GL_TEXTURE_MIN_FILTER, GL_LINEAR);
    return textureID;
}

private static BufferedImage getBufferedImage(String fileName)
{   BufferedImage img;
    try { img = ImageIO.read(new File(fileName)); }
    catch (IOException e)
    {   System.err.println("Error reading '" + fileName + "'"); throw new RuntimeException(e); }
    return img;
}

private static byte[ ] getRGBAPixelData(BufferedImage img, boolean flip)
{   byte[ ] imgRGBA;
    int height = img.getHeight(null);
    int width = img.getWidth(null);
```

```
WritableRaster raster =
    Raster.createInterleavedRaster(DataBuffer.TYPE_BYTE, width, height, 4, null);
ComponentColorModel colorModel = new ComponentColorModel(
    ColorSpace.getInstance(ColorSpace.CS_sRGB),
    new int[ ] { 8, 8, 8, 8 }, true, false,          // bits, has Alpha, isAlphaPreMultiplied
    ComponentColorModel.TRANSLUCENT,                 // transparency
    DataBuffer.TYPE_BYTE);                           // data transfer type

BufferedImage newImage = new BufferedImage(colorModel, raster, false, null);
Graphics2D g = newImage.createGraphics();

//   use an affine transform to "flip" the image to conform to OpenGL orientation.
//   In Java the origin is at the upper left. In OpenGL the origin is at the lower left.
if (flip)
{   AffineTransform gt = new AffineTransform();
    gt.translate(0, height);
    gt.scale(1, -1d);
    g.transform(gt);
}
g.drawImage(img, null, null);
g.dispose();

DataBufferByte dataBuf = (DataBufferByte) raster.getDataBuffer();
imgRGBA = dataBuf.getData();
return imgRGBA;
}
```

SUPPLEMENTAL NOTES

Researchers have developed a number of uses for texture units beyond just texturing models in a scene. In later chapters, we will see how texture units can be used for altering the way light reflects off an object, making it appear bumpy. We can also use a texture unit to store "height maps" for generating terrain and for storing "shadow maps" to efficiently add shadows to our scenes. These uses will be described in subsequent chapters.

Shaders can also *write to textures*, allowing shaders to modify texture images, or even copy part of one texture into some portion of another texture.

Mipmaps and anisotropic filtering are not the only tools for reducing aliasing artifacts in textures. *Full-scene anti-aliasing* (FSAA) and other supersampling methods, for example, can also improve the appearance of textures in a 3D scene.

Although not part of the OpenGL core, they are supported on many graphics cards through OpenGL's extension mechanism [OE16].

There is an alternative mechanism for configuring and managing textures and samplers. Version 3.3 of OpenGL introduced *sampler objects* (sometimes called *"sampler states"*—not to be confused with sampler variables) that can be used to hold a set of texture settings independent of the actual texture object. Sampler objects are attached to texture units and allow for conveniently and efficiently changing texture settings. The examples shown in this textbook are sufficiently simple that we decided to omit coverage of sampler objects. For interested readers, usage of sampler objects is easy to learn, and there are many excellent online tutorials (such as [GE11]).

The JOGL Texture class makes a number of OpenGL texture-related functions available directly, without extracting the actual OpenGL texture object as we did in this chapter. For example, there are bind() and setTexParameter() functions that invoke the OpenGL functions glBindTexture() and glSetTexParameter(). We will explore more of the functionality in the JOGL texture classes later in the book when we study cube maps and 3D textures. An excellent source of information on the JOGL Texture, TextureIO, and TextureData classes is their extensive Javadoc pages.

Exercises

5.1 Modify Program 5.1 by adding the "noperspective" declaration to the texture coordinate vertex attributes, as described in Section 5.11. Then rerun the program and compare the output with the original. Is any perspective distortion evident?

5.2 Using a simple "paint" program (such as Windows "Paint" or GIMP [GI16]), draw a freehand picture of your own design. Then use your image to texture the pyramid in Program 5.1.

5.3 *(PROJECT)* Modify Program 4.4 so that the "sun," "planet," and "moon" are textured. You may continue to use the shapes already present, and you may use any texture you like. Texture coordinates for the cube are available by searching through some of the posted code examples, or you can build them yourself by hand (although that is a bit tedious).

References

[BL16] Blender, The Blender Foundation, accessed July 2016, https://www
.blender.org/

[GE11] Geeks3D, "OpenGL Sampler Objects: Control Your Texture Units,"
September 8, 2011, accessed July 2016, http://www.geeks3d.com/20110908/

[GI16] GNU Image Manipulation Program, accessed July 2016, http://www
.gimp.org

[HT16] J. Hastings-Trew, *JHT's Planetary Pixel Emporium*, accessed July 2016,
http://planetpixelemporium.com/

[LU16] F. Luna, *Introduction to 3D Game Programming with DirectX 12*, 2nd ed.
(Mercury Learning, 2016).

[MA16] Maya, AutoDesk, Inc., accessed July 2016, http://www.autodesk.com/
products/maya/overview

[OE16] OpenGL Registry, The Khronos Group, accessed July 2016, https://www
.opengl.org/registry/

[OP14] OpenGL Graphics System: A Specification (version 4.4), M. Segal and
K. Akeley, March 19, 2014, accessed July 2016, https://www.opengl.org/
registry/doc/glspec44.core.pdf

[OP16] OpenGL 4.5 Reference Pages, accessed July 2016, https://www.opengl
.org/sdk/docs/man/

[TU16] J. Turberville, Studio 522 Productions, Scottsdale, AZ, www.studio522
.com (dolphin model developed 2016).

[WI83] L. Williams, "Pyramidal Parametrics," *Computer Graphics* 17, no. 3
(July 1983).

3D MODELS

So far we have dealt only with very simple 3D objects, such as cubes and pyramids. These objects are so simple that we have been able to explicitly list all of the vertex information in our source code and place it directly into buffers.

However, most interesting 3D scenes include objects that are too complex to continue building them as we have, by hand. In this chapter, we will explore more complex object models, how to build them, and how to load them into our scenes.

3D modeling is itself an extensive field, and our coverage here will necessarily be very limited. We will focus on the following two topics:

- *building models procedurally*
- *loading models produced externally*

While this only scratches the surface of the rich field of 3D modeling, it will give us the capability to include a wide variety of complex and realistically detailed objects in our scenes.

6.1 PROCEDURAL MODELS—BUILDING A SPHERE

Some types of objects, such as spheres, cones, and so forth, have mathematical definitions that lend themselves to algorithmic generation. Consider for example a circle of radius R; coordinates of points around its perimeter are well-defined (Figure 6.1).

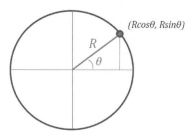

Figure 6.1
Points on a circle.

We can systematically use our knowledge of the geometry of a circle to algorithmically build a sphere model. Our strategy is as follows:

1. Select a *precision* representing a number of circular "horizontal slices" through the sphere. See the left side of Figure 6.2.
2. Subdivide the circumference of each circular slice into some number of points. See the right side of Figure 6.2. More points and horizontal slices produces a more accurate and smoother model of the sphere. In our model, *each slice will have the same number of points.*

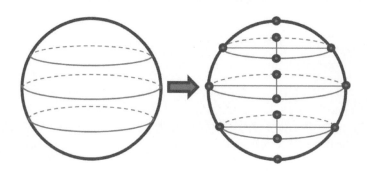

Figure 6.2
Building circle vertices.

3. Group the vertices into triangles. One approach is to step through the vertices, building two triangles at each step. For example, as we move along the row of the five colored vertices on the sphere in Figure 6.3, for each of those five vertices we build the two triangles shown in the corresponding color (the steps are described in greater detail below).

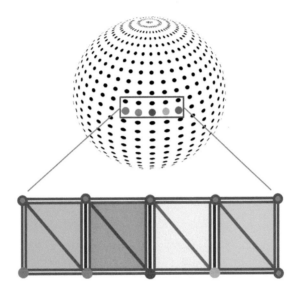

Figure 6.3
Grouping vertices into triangles.

4. Select texture coordinates depending on the nature of our texture images. In the case of a sphere, there exist many topographical texture images, such as the one shown in Figure 6.4 [VE16] for planet earth. If we assume this sort of texture image, then by imagining the image "wrapped" around the sphere as shown in Figure 6.5, we can assign texture coordinates to each vertex according to the resulting corresponding positions of the texels in the image.

Figure 6.4
Topographical texture image [VE16].

Figure 6.5
Sphere texture coordinates.

5. It is also often desirable to generate *normal vectors*—vectors that are *perpendicular to the model's surface*—for each vertex. We will use them soon, in Chapter 7, for *lighting*.

Determining normal vectors can be tricky, but in the case of a sphere, the vector pointing from the center of the sphere to a vertex happens to conveniently equal the normal vector for that vertex! Figure 6.6 illustrates this property (the center of the sphere is indicated with a "star").

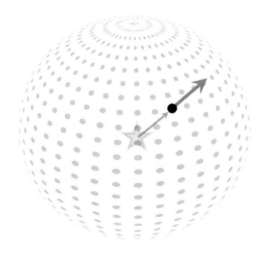

Figure 6.6
Sphere vertex normal vectors.

Some models define triangles using *indices*. Note in Figure 6.3 that each vertex appears in multiple triangles, which would lead to each vertex being specified multiple times. Rather than doing this, we instead store each vertex once, and then specify indices for each corner of a triangle, referencing the desired vertices. Since we will store a vertex's location, texture coordinates, and normal vector, this can facilitate memory savings for large models.

The vertices are stored in a one-dimensional array, starting with the vertices in the bottommost horizontal slice. When using indexing, the associated array of indices includes an entry for each triangle corner. The contents are integer references (specifically, subscripts) into the vertex array. Assuming that each slice contains n vertices, the vertex array would look as shown in Figure 6.7, along with an example portion of the corresponding index array.

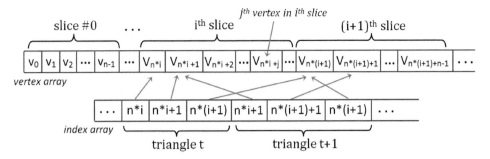

Figure 6.7
Vertex array and corresponding index array.

We can then traverse the vertices in a circular fashion around each horizontal slice, starting at the bottom of the sphere. As we visit each vertex, we build two triangles forming a square region above and to its right, as shown earlier in Figure 6.3. The processing is thus organized into nested loops, as follows:

> for each horizontal slice i in the sphere (i ranges from 0 through all the slices in the sphere)
> { for each vertex j in slice i (j ranges from 0 through all the vertices in the slice)
> { calculate indices for two triangles which point to neighboring vertices to the right,
> above, and to the above-right of vertex j
> } }

For example, consider the "red" vertex from Figure 6.3 (repeated in Figure 6.8). The vertex in question is at the lower left of the yellow triangles shown in Figure 6.8 and, given the loops just described, would be indexed by $i*n+j$, where i is the slice currently being processed (the outer loop), j is the vertex currently being processed within that slice (the inner loop), and n is the number of vertices per slice. Figure 6.8 shows this vertex (in red) along with its three relevant neighboring vertices, each with formulas showing how they would be indexed.

These four vertices are then used to build the two triangles (shown in yellow) generated for this (red) vertex. The six entries in the index table for these two triangles are indicated in the figure in the order shown by the numbers 1 through 6. Note that entries

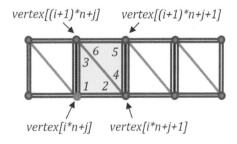

Figure 6.8
Indices generated for the jth vertex in the ith slice (*n = number of vertices per slice*).

3 and 6 both refer to the same vertex, which is also the case for entries 2 and 4. The two triangles thus defined when we reach the vertex highlighted in red (i.e., vertex[i*n+j]) are built out of these six vertices—one with entries marked 1, 2, 3, referencing vertices vertex[i*n+j], vertex[i*n+j+1], and vertex[(i+1)*n+j], and one with entries marked 4, 5, 6, referencing the three vertices vertex[i*n+j+1], vertex[(i+1)*n+j+1], and vertex[(i+1)*n+j].

Program 6.1 shows the implementation of our sphere model as a class named Sphere. The center of the resulting sphere is at the origin. Code for using Sphere is also shown. Note that each vertex is stored as a set of instances of the JOML classes Vector2f and Vector3f (this is different from previous examples, where vertices were stored in float arrays). Vector2f and Vector3f include methods for obtaining the x, y, and z vertex components as float values, which are then put into float buffers as before.

Note the calculation of triangle indices in the Sphere class, as described earlier in Figure 6.8. The variable "prec" refers to the "precision," which in this case is used both for the number of sphere slices and the number of vertices per slice. Because the texture map wraps completely around the sphere, we will need an extra coincident vertex at each of the points where the left and right edges of the texture map meet. Thus, the total number of vertices is (prec+1)*(prec+1). Since six triangle indices are generated per vertex, the total number of indices is prec*prec*6.

Program 6.1 Procedurally Generated Sphere

Sphere class

```
import org.joml.*;
import static java.lang.Math.*;

public class Sphere
{   private int numVertices, numIndices, prec;   // prec = precision
    private int[ ] indices;
    private Vector3f[ ] vertices;
    private Vector2f[ ] texCoords;
    private Vector3f[ ] normals;

    public Sphere(int p)
    {   prec = p;
        initSphere();
    }
```

```
private void initSphere()
{   numVertices = (prec+1) * (prec+1);
    numIndices = prec * prec * 6;
    indices = new int[numIndices];
    vertices = new Vector3f[numVertices];
    texCoords = new Vector2f[numVertices];
    normals = new Vector3f[numVertices];
    for (int i=0; i<numVertices; i++)
    {   vertices[i] = new Vector3f();
        texCoords[i] = new Vector2f();
        normals[i] = new Vector3f();
    }

    // calculate triangle vertices
    for (int i=0; i<=prec; i++)
    {   for (int j=0; j<=prec; j++)
        {   float y = (float) cos(toRadians(180-i*180/prec));
            float x = -(float) cos(toRadians(j*360/(float)prec)) * (float)abs(cos(asin(y)));
            float z = (float) sin(toRadians(j*360/(float)prec)) * (float)abs(cos(asin(y)));
            vertices[i*(prec+1)+j].set(x,y,z);
            texCoords[i*(prec+1)+j].set((float)j/prec, (float)i/prec);
            normals[i*(prec+1)+j].set(x,y,z);
        }   }

    // calculate triangle indices
    for(int i=0; i<prec; i++)
    {   for(int j=0; j<prec; j++)
        {   indices[6*(i*prec+j)+0] = i*(prec+1)+j;
            indices[6*(i*prec+j)+1] = i*(prec+1)+j+1;
            indices[6*(i*prec+j)+2] = (i+1)*(prec+1)+j;
            indices[6*(i*prec+j)+3] = i*(prec+1)+j+1;
            indices[6*(i*prec+j)+4] = (i+1)*(prec+1)+j+1;
            indices[6*(i*prec+j)+5] = (i+1)*(prec+1)+j;
}   }   }
    public int getNumIndices() { return numIndices; }
    public int getNumVertices() { return numIndices; }
    public int[ ] getIndices() { return indices; }
    public Vector3f[ ] getVertices() { return vertices; }
    public Vector2f[ ] getTexCoords() { return texCoords; }
    public Vector3f[ ] getNormals() { return normals; }
}
```

Using the Sphere class

```
private void setupVertices()
{   GL4 gl = (GL4) GLContext.getCurrentGL();

    mySphere = new Sphere(24);
    numSphereVerts = mySphere.getIndices().length;

    int[ ] indices = mySphere.getIndices();
    Vector3f[ ] vert = mySphere.getVertices();
    Vector2f[ ] tex  = mySphere.getTexCoords();
    Vector3f[ ] norm = mySphere.getNormals();

    float[ ] pvalues = new float[indices.length*3];   // vertex positions
    float[ ] tvalues = new float[indices.length*2];    // texture coordinates
    float[ ] nvalues = new float[indices.length*3];   // normal vectors

    for (int i=0; i<indices.length; i++)
    {   pvalues[i*3] = (float) (vert[indices[i]]).x;
        pvalues[i*3+1] = (float) (vert[indices[i]]).y;
        pvalues[i*3+2] = (float) (vert[indices[i]]).z;

        tvalues[i*2] = (float) (tex[indices[i]]).x;
        tvalues[i*2+1] = (float) (tex[indices[i]]).y;

        nvalues[i*3] = (float) (norm[indices[i]]).x;
        nvalues[i*3+1]= (float)(norm[indices[i]]).y;
        nvalues[i*3+2]=(float) (norm[indices[i]]).z;
    }

    gl.glGenVertexArrays(vao.length, vao, 0);
    gl.glBindVertexArray(vao[0]);
    gl.glGenBuffers(3, vbo, 0);

    // put the vertices into buffer #0
    gl.glBindBuffer(GL_ARRAY_BUFFER, vbo[0]);
    FloatBuffer vertBuf = Buffers.newDirectFloatBuffer(pvalues);
    gl.glBufferData(GL_ARRAY_BUFFER, vertBuf.limit()*4, vertBuf, GL_STATIC_DRAW);

    // put the texture coordinates into buffer #1
    gl.glBindBuffer(GL_ARRAY_BUFFER, vbo[1]);
    FloatBuffer texBuf = Buffers.newDirectFloatBuffer(tvalues);
    gl.glBufferData(GL_ARRAY_BUFFER, texBuf.limit()*4, texBuf, GL_STATIC_DRAW);

    // put the normals into buffer #2
    gl.glBindBuffer(GL_ARRAY_BUFFER, vbo[2]);
    FloatBuffer norBuf = Buffers.newDirectFloatBuffer(nvalues);
    gl.glBufferData(GL_ARRAY_BUFFER, norBuf.limit()*4, norBuf, GL_STATIC_DRAW);
}
```

in display()

```
. . .
gl.glDrawArrays(GL_TRIANGLES, 0, numSphereVerts);
. . .
```

When using the Sphere class, we will need three values for each vertex position and normal vector, but only two values for each texture coordinate. This is reflected in the declarations for the arrays (pvalues, tvalues, and nvalues) that are later populated with values obtained by calls to Sphere functions and loaded into the buffers.

It is important to note that although indexing is used in the process of building the sphere, the ultimate sphere vertex data stored in the VBOs doesn't utilize indexing. Rather, as setupVertices() loops through the sphere indices, it generates separate (often redundant) vertex entries in the VBO for each of the index entries. OpenGL does have a mechanism for indexing vertex data; for simplicity we didn't use it in this example, but we will use OpenGL's indexing in the next example.

Figure 6.9 shows the output of Program 6.1, with a precision of 48. The texture from Figure 6.5 has been loaded as described in Chapter 5.

Figure 6.9
Textured sphere model.

Many other models can be created procedurally, from geometric shapes to real-world objects. One of the most well-known is the *"Utah teapot"* [CH16], which was developed in 1975 by Martin Newell, using a variety of Bézier curves and surfaces. The *OpenGL Utility Toolkit* (or *"GLUT"*) [GL16] even includes procedures for drawing teapots(!) (see Figure 6.10). We don't cover GLUT in this book, but Bézier surfaces are covered in Chapter 11.

Figure 6.10
OpenGL GLUT teapot.

6.2 ■ OPENGL INDEXING—BUILDING A TORUS

6.2.1 ■ The Torus

Algorithms for producing a *torus* can be found on various websites. Paul Baker gives a step-by-step description for defining a circular slice, and then rotating the slice around a circle to form a donut [PP07]. Figure 6.11 shows two views—from the side and from above.

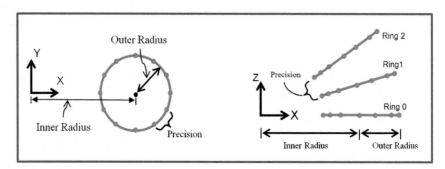

Figure 6.11
Building a torus.

The way that the torus vertex positions are generated is rather different from what was done to build the sphere. For the torus, the algorithm positions a vertex to the right of the origin, and then rotates that vertex in a circle on the XY plane using a rotation around the Z axis to form a "ring." The ring is then moved outward by the "inner radius" distance. Texture coordinates and normal vectors are computed for each of these vertices as they are built. An additional vector tangent to the surface of the torus (called the *tangent vector*) is also generated for each vertex.

Vertices for additional torus rings are formed by rotating the original ring around the Y axis. Tangent and normal vectors for each resulting vertex are computed by also rotating the tangent and normal vectors of the original ring around the Y axis. After the vertices are created, they are traversed from ring to ring, and for each vertex two triangles are generated. The generation of six index table entries comprising the two triangles is done in a similar manner as we did for the sphere.

Our strategy for choosing texture coordinates for the remaining rings will be to arrange them so that the S axis of the texture image wraps halfway around the horizontal perimeter of the torus, and then repeats for the other half. As we rotate around the Y axis generating the rings, we specify a variable ring that starts at 1 and increases up to the specified precision (again dubbed "prec"). We then set the S texture coordinate value to ring*2.0/prec, causing S to range between 0.0 and 2.0, then subtract 1.0 whenever the texture coordinate is greater than 1.0. The motivation for this approach is to avoid having the texture image appear overly "stretched" horizontally. If instead we did want the texture to stretch completely around the torus, we would simply remove the "*2.0" multiplier from the texture coordinate computation.

Building a torus class in Java/JOGL could be done in a virtually identical manner as for the Sphere class. However, we have the opportunity to take advantage of the indices that we created while building the torus by using OpenGL's support for vertex indexing (we could have also done this for the sphere, but we didn't). For very large models with thousands of vertices, using OpenGL indexing can result in improved performance, and so we will describe how to do that next.

6.2.2 Indexing in OpenGL

In both our sphere and torus models, we generate an array of integer indexes referencing into the vertex array. In the case of the sphere, we used the list of indices to build a complete set of individual vertices and loaded them into a VBO just as we did for examples in earlier chapters. Instantiating the torus and loading its vertices, normals, etc. into buffers could be done in a similar manner as was done in Program 6.1, but instead we will use OpenGL's indexing.

When using OpenGL indexing, we also load the indices themselves into a VBO. We generate one additional VBO for holding the indices. Since each index value is simply an integer reference, we first copy the index array into a Java IntBuffer, and then use glBufferData() to load the IntBuffer into the added VBO, specifying that the VBO is of type GL_ELEMENT_ARRAY_BUFFER (this tells OpenGL that the VBO contains indices). The code that does this can be added to setupVertices():

```
int[ ] indices = myTorus.getIndices();    // the torus index accessor returns the indices as an int array
. . .
gl.glBindBuffer(GL_ELEMENT_ARRAY_BUFFER, vbo[3]);    // vbo #3 is the additional added vbo
IntBuffer idxBuf = Buffers.newDirectIntBuffer(indices);
gl.glBufferData(GL_ELEMENT_ARRAY_BUFFER, idxBuf.limit()*4, idxBuf, GL_STATIC_DRAW);
```

In the display() method, we replace the glDrawArrays() call with a call to glDrawElements(), which tells OpenGL to utilize the index VBO for looking up the vertices to be drawn. We also enable the VBO that contains the indices by using glBindBuffer(), specifying which VBO contains the indices and that it is a GL_ELEMENT_ARRAY_BUFFER. The code is as follows:

```
int numIndices = myTorus.getNumIndices();
gl.glBindBuffer(GL_ELEMENT_ARRAY_BUFFER, vbo[3]);
gl.glDrawElements(GL_TRIANGLES, numTorusIndices, GL_UNSIGNED_INT, 0);
```

Interestingly, the shaders used for drawing the sphere continue to work, unchanged, for the torus, even with the changes that we made in the Java/JOGL application to implement indexing. OpenGL is able to recognize the presence of a GL_ELEMENT_ARRAY_BUFFER and utilize it to access the vertex attributes.

Program 6.2 shows a class named Torus based on Baker's implementation. The "inner" and "outer" variables refer to the corresponding inner and outer radius in Figure 6.11. The prec ("precision") variable has a similar role as in the sphere, with analogous computations for number of vertices and indices. By contrast, determining normal vectors is much more complex than it was for the sphere. We have used the strategy given in Baker's description, wherein two tangent vectors are computed (dubbed *sTangent* and *tTangent* by Baker, although more commonly referred to as "tangent" and "bitangent"); their cross product forms the normal.

We will use this torus class (and the sphere class described earlier) in many examples throughout the remainder of the textbook.

Program 6.2 Procedurally Generated Torus

Torus class

```
public class Torus
{
    private int numVertices, numIndices, prec;
    private int[ ] indices;
    private Vector3f[ ] vertices;
    private Vector2f[ ] texCoords;
    private Vector3f[ ] normals;
    private float inner, outer;
    private Vector3f[ ] sTangents, tTangents;

    public Torus()
    {   prec = 48;
        inner = 0.5f;
```

```java
        outer = 0.2f;
        initTorus();
}

public Torus(float innerRadius, float outerRadius, int precision)
{   inner = innerRadius; outer=outerRadius; prec=precision;
    initTorus();
}

private void initTorus()
{   numVertices = (prec+1) * (prec+1);
    numIndices = prec * prec * 6;
    indices = new int[numIndices];
    vertices = new Vector3f[numVertices];
    texCoords = new Vector2f[numVertices];
    normals = new Vector3f[numVertices];
    sTangents = new Vector3f[numVertices];
    tTangents = new Vector3f[numVertices];

    for (int i=0; i<numVertices; i++)
    {   vertices[i] = new Vector3f();
        texCoords[i] = new Vector2f();
        normals[i] = new Vector3f();
        sTangents[i] = new Vector3f();
        tTangents[i] = new Vector3f();
    }

    // calculate first ring.
    for (int i=0; i<prec+1; i++)
    {   float amt = (float) toRadians(i*360.0f/prec);

        // build the ring by rotating points around the origin, then moving them outward
        Vector3f ringPos = new Vector3f(outer, 0.0f, 0.0f);
        ringPos.rotateAxis(amt, 0.0f, 0.0f, 1.0f);
        ringPos.add(new Vector3f(inner, 0.0f, 0.0f));
        vertices[i].set(ringPos);

        // compute texture coordinates for each vertex in the ring
        texCoords[i].set(0.0f, ((float)i)/((float)prec));

        // compute tangents and normal vectors for each vertex in the ring
        tTangents[i] = new Vector3f(0.0f, -1.0f, 0.0f);        // The first tangent vector starts as the -Y axis,
        tTangents[i].rotateAxis(amt, 0.0f, 0.0f, 1.0f);        //   and is then rotated around the Z axis.
        sTangents[i].set(0.0f, 0.0f, -1.0f);                   // The second tangent is -Z in each case.
        normals[i] = tTangents[i].cross(sTangents[i]);         // The cross product produces the normal
    }
```

```java
// rotate the first ring about the Y axis to get the other rings
for (int ring=1; ring<prec+1; ring++)
{   for (int vert=0; vert<prec+1; vert++)
    {   // rotate the vertex positions of the original ring around the Y axis
        float amt = (float) toRadians((float)ring*360.0f/prec);
        Vector3f vp = new Vector3f(vertices[vert]);
        vp.rotateAxis(amt, 0.0f, 1.0f, 0.0f);
        vertices[ring*(prec+1)+vert].set(vp);

        // compute the texture coordinates for the vertices in the new rings
        texCoords[ring*(prec+1)+vert].set((float)ring*2.0f/(float)prec, texCoords[vert].y());
        if (texCoords[ring*(prec+1)+i].x > 1.0f) texCoords[ring*(prec+1)+i].x -= 1.0f;

        // rotate the tangent and bitangent vectors around the Y axis
        sTangents[ring*(prec+1)+vert].set(sTangents[vert]);
        sTangents[ring*(prec+1)+vert].rotateAxis(amt, 0.0f, 1.0f, 0.0f);
        tTangents[ring*(prec+1)+vert].set(tTangents[vert]);
        tTangents[ring*(prec+1)+vert].rotateAxis(amt, 0.0f, 1.0f, 0.0f);

        // rotate the normal vector around the Y axis
        normals[ring*(prec+1)+vert].set(normals[vert]);
        normals[ring*(prec+1)+vert].rotateAxis(amt, 0.0f, 1.0f, 0.0f);
    }   }

// calculate triangle indices corresponding to the two triangles built per vertex
for(int ring=0; ring<prec; ring++)
{   for(int vert=0; vert<prec; vert++)
    {   indices[((ring*prec+vert)*2)  *3+0]= ring*(prec+1)+vert;
        indices[((ring*prec+vert)*2)  *3+1]=(ring+1)*(prec+1)+vert;
        indices[((ring*prec+vert)*2)  *3+2]= ring*(prec+1)+vert+1;
        indices[((ring*prec+vert)*2+1)*3+0]= ring*(prec+1)+vert+1;
        indices[((ring*prec+vert)*2+1)*3+1]=(ring+1)*(prec+1)+vert;
        indices[((ring*prec+vert)*2+1)*3+2]=(ring+1)*(prec+1)+vert+1;
    }   }

// accessors for the torus indices and vertices
int getNumIndices() { return numIndices; }
public int[ ] getIndices() { return indices; }
public int getNumVertices() { return numVertices; }
public Vector3f[ ] getVertices() { return vertices; }
public Vector2f[ ] getTexCoords() { return texCoords; }
public Vector3f[ ] getNormals() { return normals; }
public Vector3f[ ] getStangents() { return sTangents; }
public Vector3f[ ] getTtangents() { return tTangents; }
}
```

Using the Torus class (with OpenGL indexing)

```
myTorus = new Torus(0.5f, 0.2f, 48);     // in init(), or in setupVertices(), or in the top level declarations
...
private void setupVertices()
{   GL4 gl = (GL4) GLContext.getCurrentGL();

    numTorusVertices = myTorus.getNumVertices();
    numTorusIndices = myTorus.getNumIndices();

    Vector3f[ ] vertices = myTorus.getVertices();
    Vector2f[ ] texCoords = myTorus.getTexCoords();
    Vector3f[ ] normals = myTorus.getNormals();
    int[ ] indices = myTorus.getIndices();

    float[ ] pvalues = new float[vertices.length*3];
    float[ ] tvalues = new float[texCoords.length*2];
    float[ ] nvalues = new float[normals.length*3];

    for (int i=0; i<numTorusVertices; i++)
    {   pvalues[i*3]   = (float) vertices[i].x;          // vertex position
        pvalues[i*3+1] = (float) vertices[i].y;
        pvalues[i*3+2] = (float) vertices[i].z;
        tvalues[i*2]   = (float) texCoords[i].x;         // texture coordinates
        tvalues[i*2+1] = (float) texCoords[i].y;
        nvalues[i*3]   = (float) normals[i].x;           // normal vector
        nvalues[i*3+1] = (float) normals[i].y;
        nvalues[i*3+2] = (float) normals[i].z;
    }
    gl.glGenVertexArrays(vao.length, vao, 0);
    gl.glBindVertexArray(vao[0]);
    gl.glGenBuffers(4, vbo, 0);                          // generate VBOs as before, plus one for indices

    gl.glBindBuffer(GL_ARRAY_BUFFER, vbo[0]);            // vertex positions
    FloatBuffer vertBuf = Buffers.newDirectFloatBuffer(pvalues);
    gl.glBufferData(GL_ARRAY_BUFFER, vertBuf.limit()*4, vertBuf, GL_STATIC_DRAW);

    gl.glBindBuffer(GL_ARRAY_BUFFER, vbo[1]);            // texture coordinates
    FloatBuffer texBuf = Buffers.newDirectFloatBuffer(tvalues);
    gl.glBufferData(GL_ARRAY_BUFFER, texBuf.limit()*4, texBuf, GL_STATIC_DRAW);

    gl.glBindBuffer(GL_ARRAY_BUFFER, vbo[2]);            // normal vectors
    FloatBuffer norBuf = Buffers.newDirectFloatBuffer(nvalues);
    gl.glBufferData(GL_ARRAY_BUFFER, norBuf.limit()*4, norBuf, GL_STATIC_DRAW);

    gl.glBindBuffer(GL_ELEMENT_ARRAY_BUFFER, vbo[3]);              // indices
```

```
IntBuffer idxBuf = Buffers.newDirectIntBuffer(indices);
gl.glBufferData(GL_ELEMENT_ARRAY_BUFFER, idxBuf.limit()*4, idxBuf, GL_STATIC_DRAW);
}
```

in display()

```
. . .
gl.glBindBuffer(GL_ELEMENT_ARRAY_BUFFER, vbo[3]);
gl.glDrawElements(GL_TRIANGLES, numTorusIndices, GL_UNSIGNED_INT, 0);
```

Note in the code that uses the Torus class that the loop in setupVertices() now stores the data associated with each vertex once, rather than once for each index entry (as was the case in the sphere example). This difference is also reflected in the declared array sizes for the data being entered into the VBOs. Also note that in the torus example, rather than using the index values when retrieving vertex data, they are simply loaded into VBO #3. Since that VBO is designated as a GL_ELEMENT_ARRAY_BUFFER, OpenGL knows that that VBO contains vertex indices.

Figure 6.12 shows the result of instantiating a torus and texturing it with the brick texture.

Figure 6.12
Procedurally generated torus.

▋6.3▋ LOADING EXTERNALLY PRODUCED MODELS

Complex 3D models, such as characters found in videogames or computer-generated movies, are typically produced using modeling tools. Such "DCC" (digital content creation) tools make it possible for people (such as artists) to build arbitrary shapes in 3D space and automatically produce the vertices, texture coordinates, vertex normals, and so on. There are too many such tools to list, but some examples are Maya, Blender, Lightwave, and Cinema4D, among many others. Blender is free and open source. Figure 6.13 shows an example Blender screen during the editing of a 3D model.

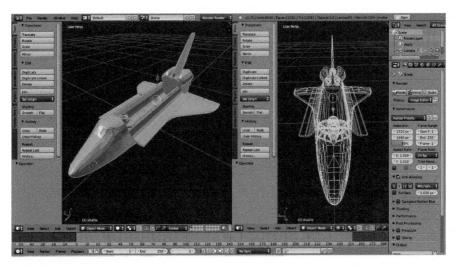

Figure 6.13
Example Blender model creation [BL16].

In order for us to use a DCC-created model in our OpenGL scenes, that model needs to be saved (exported) in a format that we can read (import) into our program. There are several standard 3D model file formats; again, there are too many to list, but some examples are Wavefront (.obj), 3D Studio Max (.3ds), Stanford Scanning Repository (.ply), and Ogre3D (.mesh), to name a few. Arguably the simplest is Wavefront (usually dubbed OBJ), so we will examine that one.

OBJ files are simple enough that we can develop a basic importer relatively easily. In an OBJ file, lines of text specify vertex geometric data, texture coordinates, normals, and other information. It has some limitations—for example, OBJ files have no way of specifying model animation.

Lines in an OBJ file start with a character tag indicating what kind of data is on that line. Some common tags include

- v – geometric (vertex location) data
- vt – texture coordinates

- vn – vertex normal
- f – face (typically vertices in a triangle)

Other tags make it possible to store the object name, materials it uses, curves, shadows, and many other details. We will limit our discussion to the four tags listed above, which are sufficient for importing a wide variety of complex models.

Suppose we use Blender to build a simple pyramid such as the one we developed for Program 4.3. Figure 6.14 is a screenshot of a similar pyramid being created in Blender.

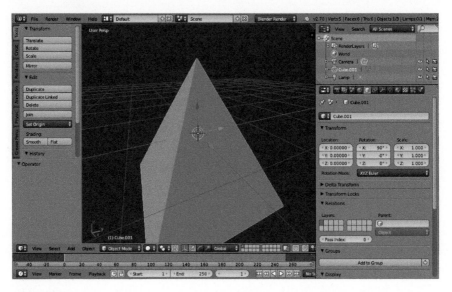

Figure 6.14
Pyramid built in Blender.

In Blender, if we now *export* our pyramid model, specify .obj format, and also set Blender to output texture coordinates and vertex normals, an OBJ file is created that includes all of this information. The resulting OBJ file is shown in Figure 6.15. (The actual values of the texture coordinates can vary depending on how the model is built.)

We have color-coded the important sections of the OBJ file for reference. The lines at the top beginning with "#" are comments placed there by Blender, which our importer ignores. This is followed by a line beginning with "o" giving the name of the object. Our importer can ignore this line as well. Later, there is a line

```
# Blender v2.70 (sub 0) OBJ File: ''
# www.blender.org
o Pyramid
v 1.000000 -1.000000 -1.000000
v 1.000000 -1.000000 1.000000
v -1.000000 -1.000000 1.000000
v -1.000000 -1.000000 -1.000000
v 0.000000 1.000000 0.000000
vt 0.515829 0.258220
vt 0.515829 0.750612
vt 0.023438 0.750612
vt 0.370823 0.790246
vt 0.820312 0.388210
vt 0.820312 0.991264
vt 0.566135 0.988689
vt 0.015625 0.742493
vt 0.566135 0.496298
vt 0.015625 0.250102
vt 0.566135 0.003906
vt 1.000000 0.000000
vt 1.000000 0.603054
vt 0.550510 0.402036
vt 0.023438 0.258220
vn 0.000000 -1.000000 0.000000
vn 0.894427 0.447214 0.000000
vn -0.000000 0.447214 0.894427
vn -0.894427 0.447214 -0.000000
vn 0.000000 0.447214 -0.894427
s off
f 2/1/1 3/2/1 4/3/1
f 1/4/2 5/5/2 2/6/2
f 2/7/3 5/8/3 3/9/3
f 3/9/4 5/10/4 4/11/4
f 5/12/5 1/13/5 4/14/5
f 1/15/1 2/1/1 4/3/1
```

Figure 6.15
Exported OBJ file for the pyramid.

beginning with "s" that specifies that the faces shouldn't be smoothed (our code will also ignore lines starting with "s").

The first substantive set of lines in the OBJ file are those starting with "v" (colored blue). They specify the X, Y, and Z local spatial coordinates of the five vertices of our pyramid model relative to the origin, which in this case is at the center of the pyramid.

The values colored red (starting with "vt") are the various texture coordinates. The reason that the list of texture coordinates is longer than the list of vertices is that some of the vertices participate in more than one triangle, and in those cases different texture coordinates might be used.

The values colored green (starting with "vn") are the various normal vectors. This list too is often longer than the list of vertices (although not in this example), again because some of the vertices participate in more than one triangle, and in those cases different normal vectors might be used.

The values colored purple (starting with "f"), near the bottom of the file, specify the triangles (i.e., "faces"). In this example, each face (triangle) has three elements, each with three values separated by "/" (OBJ allows other formats as well). The values for each element are indices into the lists of vertices, texture coordinates, and normal vectors, respectively. For example, the third face is

f 2/7/3 5/8/3 3/9/3

This indicates that the second, fifth, and third vertices from the list of vertices (in blue) comprise a triangle (note that OBJ indices start at 1). The corresponding texture coordinates are the seventh, eighth, and ninth from the list of texture coordinates in the section colored red. All three vertices have the same normal vector, the third in the list of normals in the section colored green.

Models in OBJ format are not required to have normal vectors, or even texture coordinates. If a model does not have texture coordinates or normals, the face values would specify only the vertex indices:

f 2 5 3

If a model has texture coordinates, but not normal vectors, the format would be as follows:

f 2/7 5/8 3/9

And, if the model has normals but not texture coordinates, the format would be

f 2//3 5//3 3//3

It is not unusual for a model to have tens of thousands of vertices. There are hundreds of such models available for download on the Internet for nearly every conceivable application, including models of animals, buildings, cars, planes, mythical creatures, people, and so on.

Programs of varying sophistication that can import an OBJ model are available on the Internet. Alternatively, it is relatively easy to write a very simple OBJ loader function that can handle the basic tags we have seen (v, vt, vn, and f). Program 6.3 shows one such loader, albeit a *very* limited one. It incorporates a class to hold an arbitrary imported model, which in turn calls the importer.

Before we describe the code in our simple OBJ importer, we must warn the reader of its limitations:

- It only supports models that include *all three* face attribute fields. That is, vertex positions, texture coordinates, and normals *must all* be present and in the form f #/#/# #/#/# #/#/#.

- The material tag is ignored—texturing must be done using the methods described in Chapter 5.

- Only OBJ models comprising a single triangle mesh are supported (the OBJ format supports composite models, but our simple importer does not).

- It assumes that elements on each line are separated by exactly one space.

If you have an OBJ model that doesn't satisfy all of the above criteria and you wish to import it using the simple loader in Program 6.3, it *may* still be feasible to do so. It is often possible to load such a model into Blender, and then export it to another OBJ file that accommodates the loader's limitations. For instance, if the model doesn't include normal vectors, it is possible to have Blender produce normal vectors while it exports the revised OBJ file.

Another limitation of our OBJ loader has to do with indexing. Observe in the previous descriptions that the "face" tag allows for the possibility of mix-and-matching vertex positions, texture coordinates, and normal vectors. For example, two different "face" rows may include indices which point to the same v entry, but different vt entries. Unfortunately, OpenGL's indexing mechanism does not support this level of flexibility—index entries in OpenGL can only point to a particular vertex *along with its attributes*. This complicates writing an OBJ model loader somewhat, as we cannot simply copy the references in the triangle face entries into an index array. Rather, using OpenGL indexing would require ensuring that entire *combinations* of v, vt, and vn values for a face entry each have their own references in the index array. A simpler, albeit less efficient, alternative is to create a new vertex for every triangle face entry. We opt for this simpler approach here in the interest of clarity, despite the space-saving advantage of using OpenGL indexing (especially when loading larger models).

The ModelImporter class includes a parseOBJ() function that reads in each line of an OBJ file one-by-one, handling separately the four cases v, vt, vn, and f. In each case, the subsequent numbers on the line are extracted, first by using substring() to skip the initial v, vt, vn, or f character(s) and then using the iterator returned by the split() function to extract each subsequent parameter value, storing them in an ArrayList. As the face (f) entries are processed, the vertices are built, with corresponding entries in parallel arrays for vertex positions, texture coordinates, and normal vectors.

The ModelImporter class is embedded in the ImportedModel class, which simplifies loading and accessing the vertices of an OBJ file by putting the imported vertices into arrays of Vector3f and Vector2f objects. Recall these are JOML classes; we use them here to store vertex positions, texture coordinates, and normal vectors. The accessors in the ImportedModel class then make them available to the Java/JOGL application in much the same manner as was done in the Sphere and Torus classes.

Following the ModelImporter and ImportedModel classes is an example sequence of calls for loading an OBJ file and then transferring the vertex information into a set of VBOs for subsequent rendering.

Figure 6.16 shows a rendered model of the space shuttle, downloaded as an OBJ file from the NASA website [NA16], imported using the code from Program 6.3 and textured using the code from Program 5.1 with the associated NASA texture image file, with anisotropic filtering. This texture image is an example of the use of *UV-mapping*, where texture coordinates in the model are carefully mapped to particular regions of the texture image. (As mentioned in Chapter 5, the details of UV-mapping are outside the scope of this book.)

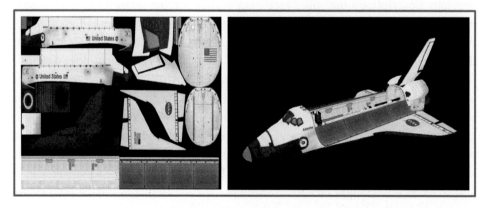

Figure 6.16
NASA space shuttle model with texture.

Program 6.3 Simple (Limited) OBJ Loader

ImportedModel class

```
public class ImportedModel
{   private Vector3f[ ] vertices;
    private Vector2f[ ] texCoords;
    private Vector3f[ ] normals;
    private int numVertices;

    public ImportedModel(String filename)
    {   ModelImporter modelImporter = new ModelImporter();
        try
        {   modelImporter.parseOBJ(filename);      // uses modelImporter to get vertex information
            numVertices  = modelImporter.getNumVertices();
            float[ ] verts  = modelImporter.getVertices();
            float[ ] tcs  = modelImporter.getTextureCoordinates();
            float[ ] normals  = modelImporter.getNormals();

            vertices = new Vector3f[numVertices];
            texCoords = new Vector2f[numVertices];
            normals = new Vector3f[numVertices];

            for(int i=0; i<vertices.length; i++)
            {   vertices[i] = new Vector3f();
                vertices[i].set(verts[i*3], verts[i*3+1], verts[i*3+2]);
                texCoords[i] = new Vector2f();
                texCoords[i].set(tcs[i*2], tcs[i*2+1]);
                normals[i] = new Vector3f();
                normals[i].set(norm[i*3], norm[i*3+1], norm[i*3+2]);
            }
        } catch (IOException e)
        { e.printStackTrace();
    }  }
    public int getNumVertices() { return numVertices; }      // accessors
    public Vector3f[ ] getVertices() { return vertices; }
    public Vector2f[ ] getTexCoords() { return texCoords; }
    public Vector3f[ ] getNormals() { return normals; }
```

ModelImporter nested class

```
    private class ModelImporter
    {   // values as read in from OBJ file
        private ArrayList<Float> vertVals = new ArrayList<Float>();
        private ArrayList<Float> stVals = new ArrayList<Float>();
        private ArrayList<Float> normVals = new ArrayList<Float>();
```

```java
// values stored for later use as vertex attributes
private ArrayList<Float> triangleVerts = new ArrayList<Float>();
private ArrayList<Float> textureCoords = new ArrayList<Float>();
private ArrayList<Float> normals = new ArrayList<Float>();

public void parseOBJ(String filename) throws IOException
{   InputStream input = ModelImporter.class.getResourceAsStream(filename);
    BufferedReader br = new BufferedReader(new InputStreamReader(input));
    String line;
    while ((line = br.readLine()) != null)
    {   if(line.startsWith("v"))                          // vertex position ("v" case)
        {   for(String s : (line.substring(2)).split(" "))
            {   vertVals.add(Float.valueOf(s));           // extract the vertex position values
        }   }
        else if(line.startsWith("vt"))                    // texture coordinates ("vt" case)
        {   for(String s : (line.substring(3)).split(" "))
            {   stVals.add(Float.valueOf(s));             // extract the texture coordinate values
        }   }
        else if(line.startsWith("vn"))                    // vertex normals ("vn" case)
        {   for(String s : (line.substring(3)).split(" "))
            {   normVals.add(Float.valueOf(s));           // extract the normal vector values
        }   }
        else if(line.startsWith("f"))                     // triangle faces ("f" case)
        {   for(String s : (line.substring(2)).split(" "))
            {   String v = s.split("/")[0];               // extract triangle face references
                String vt = s.split("/")[1];
                String vn = s.split("/")[2];

                int vertRef = (Integer.valueOf(v)-1)*3;
                int tcRef = (Integer.valueOf(vt)-1)*2;
                int normRef = (Integer.valueOf(vn)-1)*3;

                triangleVerts.add(vertVals.get(vertRef));   // build array of vertices
                triangleVerts.add(vertVals.get(vertRef+1));
                triangleVerts.add(vertVals.get(vertRef+2));

                textureCoords.add(stVals.get(tcRef));       // build array of
                textureCoords.add(stVals.get(tcRef+1));     // texture coordinates.

                normals.add(normVals.get(normRef));         //... and normals
                normals.add(normVals.get(normRef+1));
                normals.add(normVals.get(normRef+2));
    }   }   }
    input.close();
}
```

```
    //  accessors for retrieving the number of vertices, the vertices themselves,
    //  and the corresponding texture coordinates and normals (only called once per model)

    public int getNumVertices() { return (triangleVerts.size()/3); }

    public float[ ] getVertices()
    {    float[ ] p = new float[triangleVerts.size()];
         for(int i = 0; i < triangleVerts.size(); i++)
         {  p[i] = triangleVerts.get(i);
         }
         return p;
    }
    // similar accessors for texture coordinates and normal vectors go here
}  }
```

Using the Model Importer

```
. . .
myModel = new ImportedModel("shuttle.obj");              // in init()

. . .
private void setupVertices()
{   GL4 gl = (GL4) GLContext.getCurrentGL();

    numObjVertices = myModel.getNumVertices();
    Vector3f[ ] vertices = myModel.getVertices();
    Vector2f[ ] texCoords = myModel.getTexCoords();
    Vector3f[ ] normals = myModel.getNormals();

    float[ ] pvalues = new float[numObjVertices*3];      // vertex positions
    float[ ] tvalues = new float[numObjVertices*2];      // texture coordinates
    float[ ] nvalues = new float[numObjVertices*3];      // normal vectors

    for (int i=0; i<numObjVertices; i++)
    {   pvalues[i*3]     = (float) (vertices[i]).x();
        pvalues[i*3+1]  = (float) (vertices[i]).y();
        pvalues[i*3+2]  = (float) (vertices[i]).z();
        tvalues[i*2]     = (float) (texCoords[i]).x();
        tvalues[i*2+1]  = (float) (texCoords[i]).y();
        nvalues[i*3]     = (float) (normals[i]).x();
        nvalues[i*3+1]  = (float) (normals[i]).y();
        nvalues[i*3+2]  = (float) (normals[i]).z();
    }
    gl.glGenVertexArrays(vao.length, vao, 0);
    gl.glBindVertexArray(vao[0]);
    gl.glGenBuffers(vbo.length, vbo, 0);
```

```
// VBO for vertex locations
gl.glBindBuffer(GL_ARRAY_BUFFER, vbo[0]);
FloatBuffer vertBuf = Buffers.newDirectFloatBuffer(pvalues);
gl.glBufferData(GL_ARRAY_BUFFER, vertBuf.limit()*4, vertBuf, GL_STATIC_DRAW);

// VBO for texture coordinates
gl.glBindBuffer(GL_ARRAY_BUFFER, vbo[1]);
FloatBuffer texBuf = Buffers.newDirectFloatBuffer(tvalues);
gl.glBufferData(GL_ARRAY_BUFFER, texBuf.limit()*4, texBuf, GL_STATIC_DRAW);

// VBO for normal vectors
gl.glBindBuffer(GL_ARRAY_BUFFER, vbo[2]);
FloatBuffer norBuf = Buffers.newDirectFloatBuffer(nvalues);
gl.glBufferData(GL_ARRAY_BUFFER, norBuf.limit()*4,norBuf, GL_STATIC_DRAW);
}
```

in display():

```
. . .
gl.glDrawArrays(GL_TRIANGLES, 0, myModel.getNumVertices());
```

SUPPLEMENTAL NOTES

Although we discussed the use of DCC tools for creating 3D models, we didn't discuss how to use such tools. While such instruction is outside the scope of this text, there is a wealth of tutorial video material and documentation for all of the popular tools such as Blender and Maya.

The topic of 3D modeling is itself a rich field of study. Our coverage in this chapter has been just a rudimentary introduction, with emphasis on its relationship to OpenGL. Many universities offer entire courses in 3D modeling, and readers interested in learning more are encouraged to consult some of the popular resources that offer greater detail (e.g., [BL16], [CH11], [VA12]).

We reiterate that the OBJ importer we presented in this chapter is limited and can only handle a subset of the features supported by the OBJ format. Although sufficient for our needs, it will fail on some OBJ files. In those cases it would be necessary to first load the model into Blender (or Maya, etc.) and re-export it as an OBJ file that complies with the importer's limitations as described earlier in this chapter.

Exercises

6.1 Modify Program 4.4 so that the "sun," "planet," and "moon" are textured *spheres*, such as the ones shown in Figure 4.11.

6.2 *(PROJECT)* Modify your program from Exercise 6.1 so that the imported NASA shuttle object from Figure 6.16 also orbits the "sun." You'll want to experiment with the scale and rotation applied to the shuttle to make it look realistic.

6.3 *(RESEARCH & PROJECT)* Learn the basics of how to use Blender to create a 3D object of your own. To make full use of Blender with your OpenGL applications, you'll want to learn how to use Blender's UV-unwrapping tools to generate texture coordinates and an associated texture image. You can then export your object as an OBJ file and load it using the code from Program 6.3.

References

[BL16] Blender, The Blender Foundation, accessed July 2016, https://www .blender.org/

[CH11] A. Chopine, *3D Art Essentials: The Fundamentals of 3D Modeling, Texturing, and Animation* (Focal Press, 2011).

[CH16] Computer History Museum, accessed July 2016, http://www .computerhistory.org/revolution/computer-graphics-music-and-art/15/206

[GL16] GLUT and OpenGL Utility Libraries, accessed July 2016, https://www .opengl.org/resources/libraries/

[NA16] NASA 3D Resources, accessed July 2016, http://nasa3d.arc.nasa.gov/

[PP07] P. Baker, *Paul's Projects*, 2007, accessed July 2016, www.paulsprojects.net

[VA12] V. Vaughan, *Digital Modeling* (New Riders, 2012).

[VE16] Visible Earth, NASA Goddard Space Flight Center Image, accessed July 2016, http://visibleearth.nasa.gov

LIGHTING

■ ■ ■ ■ ■ ■

Light affects the appearance of our world in varied and sometimes dramatic ways. When a flashlight shines on an object, we expect it to appear brighter on the side facing the light. The earth on which we live is itself brightly lit where it faces the sun at noon, but as it turns, that daytime brightness gradually fades into evening, until becoming completely dark at midnight.

Objects also respond differently to light. Besides having different colors, objects can have different reflective characteristics. Consider two objects, both green, but one is made of cloth versus the other made of polished steel—the latter will appear more "shiny."

7.1 LIGHTING MODELS

Light is the product of photons being emitted by high energy sources and subsequently bouncing around until some of the photons reach our eyes. Unfortunately, it is computationally infeasible to emulate this natural process, as it would require simulating and then tracking the movement of a huge number of photons, adding many objects (and matrices) to our scene. What we need is a *lighting model*.

Lighting models are sometimes called *shading models*, although in the presence of shader programming, that can be a bit confusing. Sometimes the term *reflection model* is used, complicating the terminology further. We will try to stick to whichever terminology is simplest and most practical.

The most common lighting models today are called "ADS" models, because they are based on three types of reflection labeled A, D, and S:

- **A**mbient reflection simulates a low-level illumination that equally affects everything in the scene.
- **D**iffuse reflection brightens objects to various degrees depending on the light's angle of incidence.
- **S**pecular reflection conveys the shininess of an object by strategically placing a highlight of appropriate size on the object's surface where light is reflected most directly toward our eyes.

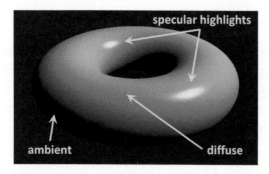

Figure 7.1
ADS Lighting contributions.

ADS models can be used to simulate different lighting effects and a variety of materials.

Figure 7.1 illustrates the ambient, diffuse, and specular contributions of a positional light on a shiny gold torus.

Recall that a scene is ultimately drawn by having the fragment shader output a color for each pixel on the screen. Using an ADS lighting model requires specifying contributions due to lighting on a pixel's RGBA output value. Factors include the following:

- the type of light source and its ambient, diffuse, and specular characteristics
- the object material's ambient, diffuse, and specular characteristics
- the object material's specified "shininess"
- the angle at which the light hits the object
- the angle from which the scene is being viewed

7.2 ■ LIGHTS

There are many types of lights, each with different characteristics and requiring different steps to simulate their effects. Some types include:

- Global (usually called "global ambient" because it includes only an ambient component)
- Directional (or "distant")
- Positional (or "point source")
- Spotlight

Global ambient light is the simplest type of light to model. Global ambient light has no source position—the light is equal everywhere, at each pixel on every object in the scene, regardless of where the objects are. Global ambient lighting simulates the real-world phenomenon of light that has bounced around so many times that its source and direction are undeterminable. Global ambient light has only an ambient component, specified as an RGBA value; it has no diffuse or specular components. For example, global ambient light can be defined as follows:

```
float[ ] globalAmbient = new float[ ] { 0.6f, 0.6f, 0.6f, 1.0f };
```

RGBA values range from 0 to 1, so global ambient light is usually modeled as dim white light, where each of the RGB values are set to the same fractional value between 0 and 1, with the alpha set to 1.

Directional, or *distant* light also doesn't have a source location, but it does have a *direction*. It is useful for situations where the source of the light is so far away that the light rays are effectively parallel, such as light coming from the sun. In many such situations we may only be interested in modeling the light, and not the object that produces the light. The effect of directional light on an object depends on the light's angle of impact; objects are brighter on the side facing a directional light than on a tangential or opposite side. Modeling directional light requires specifying its direction (as a vector) and its ambient, diffuse, and specular characteristics (as RGBA values). A red directional light pointing down the negative Z axis might be specified as follows:

```
float[ ] dirLightAmbient = new float[ ] { 0.1f, 0.0f, 0.0f, 1.0f };
float[ ] dirLightDiffuse = new float[ ] { 1.0f, 0.0f, 0.0f, 1.0f };
float[ ] dirLightSpecular = new float[ ] { 1.0f, 0.0f, 0.0f, 1.0f };
float[ ] dirLightDirection = new float[ ] { 0.0f, 0.0f, -1.0f };
```

It might seem redundant to include an ambient contribution for a light when we already have global ambient light. The separation of the two, however, is intentional and noticeable when the light is "on" or "off." When "on," the total ambient contribution would be increased, as expected. In the above example, we have included only a small ambient contribution for the light. It is important to balance the two contributions, depending on the needs of your scene.

A *positional* light has a specific location in the 3D scene. Light sources that are near the scene, such as lamps, candles, and so forth, are examples. Like directional lights, the effect of a positional light depends on angle of impact; however, its direction is not specified, as it is different for each vertex in our scene. Positional lights may also incorporate *attenuation factors,* in order to model how their intensity diminishes with distance. As with the other types of lights we have seen, positional lights have ambient, diffuse, and specular properties specified as RGB values. A red positional light at location (5,2,-3) could for example be specified as follows:

```
float[ ] posLightAmbient = new float[ ] { 0.1f, 0.0f, 0.0f, 1.0f };
float[ ] posLightDiffuse = new float[ ] { 1.0f, 0.0f, 0.0f, 1.0f };
float[ ] posLightSpecular = new float[ ] { 1.0f,0.0f, 0.0f, 1.0f };
float[ ] posLightLocation = new float[ ] { 5.0f, 2.0f, -3.0f };
```

Attenuation factors can be modeled in a variety of ways. One way is to include tunable non-negative parameters for *constant, linear,* and *quadratic* attenuation (k_c, k_l, and k_q, respectively). These parameters are then combined, taking into account the distance (d) from the light source:

$$attenuationFactor = \frac{1}{k_c + k_l d + k_q d^2}$$

Multiplying this factor by the light intensity causes the intensity to be decreased the greater the distance is to the light source. Note that k_c should always be set greater than or equal to 1, so that the attenuation factor will always be in the range [0..1] and approach 0 as the distance d increases.

Spotlights have both a position and a direction. The effect of the spotlight's "cone" can be simulated using a *cutoff angle* θ between 0° and 90°, specifying the half-width of the light beam, and a *falloff exponent* to model the variation of intensity across the angle of the beam. As shown in Figure 7.2, we determine the angle

ϕ between the spotlight's direction and a vector from the spotlight to the pixel. We then compute an *intensity factor* by raising the cosine of ϕ to the falloff exponent when ϕ is less than θ (when ϕ is greater than θ the intensity factor is set to 0). The result is an intensity factor that ranges from 0 to 1. The falloff exponent adjusts the rate at which the intensity factor tends to 0 as the angle ϕ increases. The intensity factor is then multiplied by the light's intensity to simulate the cone effect.

A red spotlight at location (5,2,-3) pointing down the negative Z axis could be specified as follows:

```
float[ ] spotLightAmbient = new float[ ] { 0.1f, 0.0f, 0.0f, 1.0f };
float[ ] spotLightDiffuse = new float[ ] { 1.0f, 0.0f, 0.0f, 1.0f };
float[ ] spotLightSpecular = new float[ ] { 1.0f, 0.0f, 0.0f, 1.0f };
float[ ] spotLightLocation = new float[ ] { 5.0f, 2.0f, -3.0f };
float[ ] spotLightDirection = new float[ ] { 0.0f, 0.0f, -1.0f };
float[ ] spotLightCutoff = 20.0f;
float[ ] spotLightExponent = 10.0f;
```

Spotlights also can include attenuation factors. We haven't shown them in the above settings, but defining them can be done in the same manner as described earlier for positional lights.

Historically, spotlights have been iconic in computer graphics since Pixar's popular animated short *Luxo Jr.* appeared in 1986 [DI16].

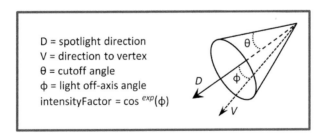

Figure 7.2
Spotlight components.

When designing a system containing many types of lights, a programmer should consider creating a class hierarchy, such as defining a "Light" class and subclasses for "Global Ambient," "Directional," "Positional," and "Spotlight." Because spotlights share characteristics of both directional and positional lights, it can be a bit tricky settling on a class hierarchy given Java's absence of multiple inheritance. In a previous edition of this book, we used a library called graphicslib3D which included container classes for each of these types of lights, in which SpotLight was a subclass of PositionalLight. Our examples are sufficiently simple that we omit building such a class hierarchy for lighting in this edition.

7.3 ■ MATERIALS

The "look" of the objects in our scene has so far been handled exclusively by color and texture. The addition of lighting allows us to also consider the *reflectance* characteristics of the surfaces. By that, we mean how the object interacts with our ADS lighting model. This can be modeled by considering each object to be "made of" a certain *material*.

Materials can be simulated in an ADS lighting model by specifying four values, three of which we are already familiar with—*ambient*, *diffuse*, and *specular* RGB colors. The fourth is called *shininess*, which, as we will see, is used to build an appropriate specular highlight for the intended material. ADS and shininess values have been developed for many different types of common materials. For example, "pewter" can be specified as follows:

```
float[ ] pewterMatAmbient = new float[ ] { .11f, .06f, .11f, 1.0f };
float[ ] pewterMatDiffuse = new float[ ] { .43f, .47f, .54f, 1.0f };
float[ ] pewterMatSpecular = new float[ ] { .33f, .33f, .52f, 1.0f };
float pewterMatShininess = 9.85f;
```

ADS RGBA values for a few other materials are given in Figure 7.3 (from [BA16]).

Sometimes other properties are included in the material properties. *Transparency* is handled in the RGBA specifications in the fourth (or "alpha") channel, which specifies an opacity; a value of 1.0 represents completely opaque and 0.0 represents completely transparent. For most materials it is simply set to 1.0, although for certain materials a slight transparency plays a role. For example, in Figure 7.3, note that the materials "jade" and "pearl" include a small amount of transparency (values slightly less than 1.0) to add realism.

Emissiveness is also sometimes included in an ADS material specification. This is useful when simulating a material that emits its own light, such as phosphorescent materials.

material	ambient RGBA diffuse RGBA specular RGBA	shininess
Gold	0.24725, 0.1995, 0.0745, 1.0 0.75164, 0.60648, 0.22648, 1.0 0.62828, 0.5558, 0.36607, 1.0	51.2
Jade	0.135, 0.2225, 0.1575, 0.95 0.54, 0.89, 0.63, 0.95 0.3162, 0.3162, 0.3162, 0.95	12.8
Pearl	0.25, 0.20725, 0.20725, 0.922 1.00, 0.829, 0.829, 0.922 0.2966, 0.2966, 0.2966, 0.922	11.264
Silver	0.19225, 0.19225, 0.19225, 1.0 0.50754, 0.50754, 0.50754, 1.0 0.50827, 0.50827, 0.50827, 1.0	51.2

Figure 7.3
Material ADS coefficients.

When an object is rendered that doesn't have a texture, it is often desirable to specify material characteristics. For that reason, it will be very convenient to have a few predefined materials available to us. We thus add the following lines of code to our "Utils.java" utility program:

```
// GOLD material - ambient, diffuse, specular, and shininess
public static float[ ] goldAmbient()  { return (new float [ ] {0.2473f,  0.1995f, 0.0745f, 1} ); }
public static float[ ] goldDiffuse()  { return (new float [ ] {0.7516f,  0.6065f, 0.2265f, 1} ); }
public static float[ ] goldSpecular() { return (new float [ ] {0.6283f,  0.5559f, 0.3661f, 1} ); }
public static float goldShininess()  { return 51.2f; }

// SILVER material - ambient, diffuse, specular, and shininess
public static float[ ] silverAmbient()  { return (new float [ ] {0.1923f,  0.1923f,  0.1923f, 1} ); }
public static float[ ] silverDiffuse()  { return (new float [ ] {0.5075f,  0.5075f,  0.5075f, 1} ); }
public static float[ ] silverSpecular() { return (new float [ ] {0.5083f,  0.5083f,  0.5083f, 1} ); }
public static float silverShininess()  { return 51.2f; }

// BRONZE material - ambient, diffuse, specular, and shininess
public static float[ ] bronzeAmbient()  { return (new float [ ] {0.2125f, 0.1275f, 0.0540f, 1} ); }
public static float[ ] bronzeDiffuse()  { return (new float [ ] {0.7140f,  0.4284f, 0.1814f, 1} ); }
public static float[ ] bronzeSpecular() { return (new float [ ] {0.3936f,  0.2719f, 0.1667f, 1} ); }
public static float bronzeShininess()  { return 25.6f; }
```

This makes it very easy to specify that an object has, say, a "gold" material, in either the init() function or in the top-level declarations, as follows:

```
float[ ] matAmbient = Utils.goldAmbient();
float[ ] matDiffuse = Utils.goldDiffuse();
float[ ] matSpecular = Utils.goldSpecular();
float matShininess = Utils.goldShininess();
```

Note that our code for light and material properties described so far in these sections does not actually perform lighting. It merely provides a way to specify and store desired light and material properties for elements in a scene. We still need to actually compute the lighting ourselves. This is going to require some serious mathematical processing in our shader code. So let's now dive into the nuts-and-bolts of implementing ADS lighting in our Java/JOGL and GLSL graphics programs.

7.4 ADS LIGHTING COMPUTATIONS

As we draw our scene, recall that each vertex is transformed so as to simulate a 3D world on a 2D screen. Pixel colors are the result of rasterization, as well as texturing and interpolation. We must now incorporate the additional step of adjusting those rasterized pixel colors to effect the lighting and materials in our scene. The basic ADS computation that we need to perform is to determine the reflection intensity *(I)* for each pixel in our scene. This computation takes the following form:

$$I_{observed} = I_{ambient} + I_{diffuse} + I_{specular}$$

That is, we need to compute and sum the ambient, diffuse, and specular reflection contributions for each pixel, for each light source. This will of course depend on the type of light(s) in our scene and the type of material associated with the rendered model.

Ambient contribution is the simplest. It is the product of the specified ambient light and the specified ambient coefficient of the material:

$$I_{ambient} = Light_{ambient} * Material_{ambient}$$

Keeping in mind that light and material intensities are specified via RGB values, the computation is more precisely

$$I_{ambient}^{red} = Light_{ambient}^{red} * Material_{ambient}^{red}$$

$$I_{ambient}^{green} = Light_{ambient}^{green} * Material_{ambient}^{green}$$

$$I_{ambient}^{blue} = Light_{ambient}^{blue} * Material_{ambient}^{blue}$$

Diffuse contribution is more complex because it depends on the angle of incidence between the light and the surface. Lambert's Cosine Law (published in 1760) specifies that the amount of light that reflects from a surface is proportional to the cosine of the light's angle of incidence. This can be modeled as follows:

$$I_{diffuse} = Light_{diffuse} * Material_{diffuse} * cos(\theta)$$

As before, the actual computations involve red, green, and blue components.

Determining the angle of incidence θ requires us to (a) find a vector from the pixel being drawn to the light source (or, similarly, a vector opposite the light direction) and (b) find a vector that is normal (perpendicular) to the surface of the object being rendered. Let's denote these vectors $\vec{L}$ and $\vec{N}$, respectively, as shown in Figure 7.4.

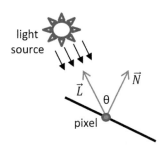

Figure 7.4
Angle of light incidence.

Depending on the nature of the lights in the scene, $\vec{L}$ could be computed by negating the light direction vector or by computing a vector from the location of the pixel to the location of the light source. Determining vector $\vec{N}$ may be trickier—normal vectors may be available for the vertices in the model being rendered, but if the model doesn't include normals, $\vec{N}$ would need to be estimated geometrically based on the locations of neighboring vertices. For the rest of the chapter, we will assume that the model being rendered includes normal vectors for each vertex (this is common in models constructed with modeling tools such as Maya or Blender).

It turns out that, in this case, it isn't necessary to compute θ itself. What we really desire is cos(θ), and recall from Chapter 3 that this can be found using the *dot product*. Thus, the diffuse contribution can be computed as follows:

$$I_{diffuse} = Light_{diffuse} * Material_{diffuse} * (\widehat{N} \bullet \widehat{L})$$

The diffuse contribution is only relevant when the surface is exposed to the light, which occurs when -90 < θ < 90—that is, when cos(θ) > 0. Thus we must replace the rightmost term above with

$$max\ ((\widehat{N} \bullet \widehat{L}),\, 0)$$

Specular contribution determines whether the pixel being rendered should be brightened because it is part of a "specular highlight." It involves not only the angle of incidence of the light source but also the angle between the reflection of the light on the surface and the viewing angle of the "eye" relative to the object's surface.

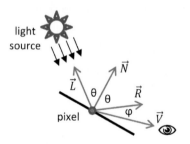

Figure 7.5
View angle incidence.

In Figure 7.5, $\vec{R}$ represents the direction of reflection of the light, and $\vec{V}$ (called the *view vector*) is a vector from the pixel to the eye. Note that $\vec{V}$ is the negative of the vector from the eye to the pixel (in camera space, the eye is at the origin). The smaller the angle φ between $\vec{R}$ and $\vec{V}$, the more the eye is on-axis, or "looking into" the reflection, and the more this pixel contributes to the specular highlight (and thus the brighter it should appear).

The manner in which φ is used to compute the specular contribution depends on the desired "shininess" of the object being rendered. Objects that are extremely shiny, such as a mirror, have very small specular highlights—that is, they reflect the incoming light to the eye exactly. Materials that are less shiny have specular highlights that are more "spread out," and thus more pixels are a part of the highlight.

Shininess is generally modeled with a *falloff* function that expresses how quickly the specular contribution reduces to zero as the angle φ grows. We can use *cos(φ)* to model falloff, and increase or decrease the shininess by using powers of the cosine function, such as $\cos(φ)$, $\cos^2(φ)$, $\cos^3(φ)$, $\cos^{10}(φ)$, $\cos^{50}(φ)$, and so on, as illustrated in Figure 7.6.

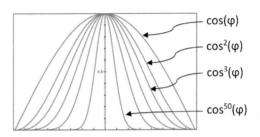

Figure 7.6
Shininess modeled as cosine exponent.

Note that the higher the value of the exponent, the faster the falloff, and thus the smaller the specular contribution of pixels with light reflections that are off-axis from the viewing angle.

We call the exponent *n*, as used in the *cos^n(φ)* falloff function, the *shininess factor* for a specified material. Note back in Figure 7.3 that shininess factors for each of the materials listed are specified in the rightmost column.

We now can specify the full specular calculation:

$$I_{spec} = Light_{spec} * Material_{spec} * \max(0, (\hat{R} \bullet \hat{V})^n)$$

Note that we use the max() function in a similar manner as we did for the diffuse computation. In this case, we need to ensure that the specular contribution does not ever utilize negative values for cos(φ), which could produce strange artifacts such as "darkened" specular highlights.

And of course as before, the actual computations involve red, green, and blue components.

7.5 IMPLEMENTING ADS LIGHTING

The computations described in Section 7.4 have so far been mostly theoretical, as they have assumed that we can perform them for every pixel. This is complicated by the fact that normal ($\vec{N}$) vectors are typically available to us only for the vertices that define the models, not for each pixel. Thus we need to either compute normals for each pixel, which could be time-consuming, or find some way of estimating the values that we need to achieve a sufficient effect.

One approach is called "faceted shading" or "flat shading." Here we assume that every pixel in each rendered primitive (i.e., polygon or triangle) has the same lighting value. Thus we need only do the lighting computations for one vertex in each polygon in the model, and then copy those lighting values across the nearby rendered pixels on a per-polygon or per-triangle basis.

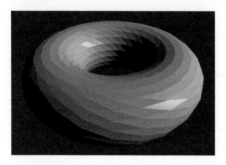

Faceted shading is rarely used today, because the resulting images tend to not look very realistic and because modern hardware makes more accurate computations feasible. An example of a faceted-shaded torus, in which each triangle behaves as a flat reflective surface, is shown in Figure 7.7.

Figure 7.7
Torus with faceted shading.

Although faceted shading can be adequate in some circumstances (or used as a deliberate effect), usually a better approach is "smooth shading," in which the lighting intensity is computed for each pixel. Smooth shading is feasible because of the parallel processing done on modern graphics cards and because of the interpolated rendering that takes place in the OpenGL graphics pipeline.

We will examine two popular methods for smooth shading: *Gouraud shading* and *Phong shading*.

7.5.1 Gouraud Shading

The French computer scientist Henri Gouraud published a smooth shading algorithm in 1971 that has come to be known as *Gouraud shading* [GO71]. It is particularly well suited to modern graphics cards, because it takes advantage of the automatic interpolated rendering that is available in 3D graphics pipelines such as in OpenGL. The process for Gouraud shading is as follows:

1. Determine the color of each *vertex*, incorporating the lighting computations.

2. Allow those colors to be interpolated across intervening pixels through the normal rasterization process (which will also in effect interpolate the lighting contributions).

In OpenGL, this means that most of the lighting computations will be done in the vertex shader. The fragment shader will simply be a pass-through, so as to reveal the automatically interpolated lighted colors.

Figure 7.8 outlines the strategy we will use to implement our Gouraud shader in OpenGL, for a scene with a torus and one positional light. The strategy is then implemented in Program 7.1.

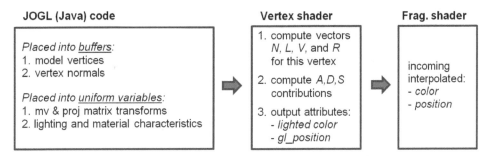

Figure 7.8
Implementing Gouraud shading.

Program 7.1 Torus with Positional Light and Gouraud Shading

```
public class Code extends JFrame implements GLEventListener
{   private GLCanvas myCanvas;
    // declarations for building shaders and rendering program, as before.
    // declaration of one VAO, two VBOs, Torus object, and Torus and camera location as before.
    // Utils.java class now has gold, silver, and bronze material accessors added.

    . . .
    // allocate variables for display() function
    private FloatBuffer vals = Buffers.newDirectFloatBuffer(16);
    private Matrix4f pMat = new Matrix4f();         // perspective matrix
    private Matrix4f vMat = new Matrix4f();         // view matrix
    private Matrix4f mMat = new Matrix4f();         // model matrix
    private Matrix4f mvMat = new Matrix4f();        // model-view matrix
    private Matrix4f invTrMat = new Matrix4f();     // inverse-transpose matrix for converting normals

    private int mvLoc, projLoc, nLoc;
    private int globalAmbLoc, ambLoc, diffLoc, specLoc, posLoc,
        mAmbLoc, mDiffLoc, mSpecLoc, mShiLoc;  // locations of shader uniform variables
```

```
private Vector3f currentLightPos = new Vector3f();     // current light position as Vector3f
private float[ ] lightPos = new float[3];              // current light position as float array

//  initial light location
private Vector3f initialLightLoc = new Vector3f(5.0f, 2.0f, 2.0f);

// properties of white light (global and positional) used in this scene
float[ ] globalAmbient = new float[ ] { 0.6f, 0.6f, 0.6f, 1.0f };
float[ ] lightAmbient = new float[ ] { 0.1f, 0.1f, 0.1f, 1.0f };
float[ ] lightDiffuse = new float[ ] { 1.0f, 1.0f, 1.0f, 1.0f };
float[ ] lightSpecular = new float[ ] { 1.0f, 1.0f, 1.0f, 1.0f };

// gold material properties
float[ ] matAmb = Utils.goldAmbient();
float[ ] matDif = Utils.goldDiffuse();
float[ ] matSpe = Utils.goldSpecular();
float matShi = Utils.goldShininess();

private void setupVertices()
{   . . .
    // This function is unchanged from the previous chapter.
    // The following portion is repeated for clarity, because we now will actually use the normals vectors:
    gl.glBindBuffer(GL_ARRAY_BUFFER, vbo[2]);
    FloatBuffer norBuf = Buffers.newDirectFloatBuffer(nvalues);
    gl.glBufferData(GL_ARRAY_BUFFER, norBuf.limit()*4, norBuf, GL_STATIC_DRAW);
}

public void display(GLAutoDrawable drawable)
{   // setup of GL4 object, clearing of depth buffer, and load rendering program as in earlier examples.
    . . .
    mvLoc = gl.glGetUniformLocation(renderingProgram, "mv_matrix");
    projLoc = gl.glGetUniformLocation(renderingProgram, "proj_matrix");
    nLoc = gl.glGetUniformLocation(renderingProgram, "norm_matrix");

    //  setup of projection and view matrices as in earlier examples.
    . . .
    // build the MODEL matrix based on the torus location
    mMat.translation(torusLoc.x(), torusLoc.y(), torusLoc.z());
    mMat.rotateX((float)Math.toRadians(35.0f));          // rotate the torus to make it easier to see

    // set up lights
    currentLightPos.set(initialLightLoc);
    installLights(vMat);

    // build the MODEL-VIEW (MV) matrix by concatenating matrices v and m, as before
    . . .
```

```
// build the inverse-transpose of the MV matrix, for transforming normal vectors
mvMat.invert(invTrMat);
invTrMat.transpose(invTrMat);

// put the MV, PROJ, and Inverse-transpose(normal) matrices into the corresponding uniforms
gl.glUniformMatrix4fv(mvLoc, 1, false, mvMat.get(vals));
gl.glUniformMatrix4fv(projLoc, 1, false, pMat.get(vals));
gl.glUniformMatrix4fv(nLoc, 1, false, invTrMat.get(vals));

// bind the vertices buffer (VBO #0) to vertex attribute #0 in the vertex shader
gl.glBindBuffer(GL_ARRAY_BUFFER, vbo[0]);
gl.glVertexAttribPointer(0, 3, GL_FLOAT, false, 0, 0);
gl.glEnableVertexAttribArray(0);

// bind the normals buffer (in VBO #2) to vertex attribute #1 in the vertex shader
gl.glBindBuffer(GL_ARRAY_BUFFER, vbo[2]);
gl.glVertexAttribPointer(1, 3, GL_FLOAT, false, 0, 0);
gl.glEnableVertexAttribArray(1);

gl.glEnable(GL_CULL_FACE);
gl.glFrontFace(GL_CCW);
gl.glEnable(GL_DEPTH_TEST);
gl.glDepthFunc(GL_LEQUAL);
gl.glBindBuffer(GL_ELEMENT_ARRAY_BUFFER, vbo[3]);
gl.glDrawElements(GL_TRIANGLES, numTorusIndices, GL_UNSIGNED_INT, 0);
}

private void installLights(Matrix4f vMatrix)
{   GL4 gl = (GL4) GLContext.getCurrentGL();

// convert light's position to view space, and save it in a float array
currentLightPos.mulPosition(vMatrix);
lightPos[0]=currentLightPos.x();
lightPos[1]=currentLightPos.y();
lightPos[2]=currentLightPos.z();

// get the locations of the light and material fields in the shader
globalAmbLoc = gl.glGetUniformLocation(renderingProgram, "globalAmbient");
ambLoc = gl.glGetUniformLocation(renderingProgram, "light.ambient");
diffLoc = gl.glGetUniformLocation(renderingProgram, "light.diffuse");
specLoc = gl.glGetUniformLocation(renderingProgram, "light.specular");
posLoc = gl.glGetUniformLocation(renderingProgram, "light.position");
mAmbLoc = gl.glGetUniformLocation(renderingProgram, "material.ambient");
mDiffLoc = gl.glGetUniformLocation(renderingProgram, "material.diffuse");
mSpecLoc = gl.glGetUniformLocation(renderingProgram, "material.specular");
mShiLoc = gl.glGetUniformLocation(renderingProgram, "material.shininess");
```

```
    // set the uniform light and material values in the shader
    gl.glProgramUniform4fv(renderingProgram, globalAmbLoc, 1, globalAmbient, 0);
    gl.glProgramUniform4fv(renderingProgram, ambLoc, 1, lightAmbient, 0);
    gl.glProgramUniform4fv(renderingProgram, diffLoc, 1, lightDiffuse, 0);
    gl.glProgramUniform4fv(renderingProgram, specLoc, 1, lightSpecular, 0);
    gl.glProgramUniform3fv(renderingProgram, posLoc, 1, lightPos, 0);
    gl.glProgramUniform4fv(renderingProgram, mAmbLoc, 1, matAmb, 0);
    gl.glProgramUniform4fv(renderingProgram, mDiffLoc, 1, matDif, 0);
    gl.glProgramUniform4fv(renderingProgram, mSpecLoc, 1, matSpe, 0);
    gl.glProgramUniform1f(renderingProgram, mShiLoc, matShi);
  }
  // init(), constructor, main(), dispose() and reshape() are all the same as before.
}
```

Most of the elements of Program 7.1 should be familiar. The torus, light, and materials properties are defined. Torus vertices and associated normals are loaded into buffers. The display() function is similar to that in previous programs, except that it also sends the light and material information to the vertex shader. To do this, it calls installLights(), which loads the light viewspace location and light and material ADS characteristics into corresponding uniform variables to make them available to the shaders. Note that we declared these uniform location variables ahead of time, for performance reasons.

An important detail is that the transformation matrix MV, used to move vertex positions into view space, doesn't always properly adjust *normal vectors* into view space. Simply applying the MV matrix to the normals doesn't guarantee that they will remain perpendicular to the object surface. The correct transformation is the *inverse transpose* of MV, as described earlier in the supplemental notes to Chapter 3. In Program 7.1, this additional matrix, named "invTrMat," is sent to the shaders in a uniform variable.

The variable lightPos contains the light's position in camera space. We only need to compute this once per frame, so we do it in installLights() (called from display()) rather than in the shader.

The shaders are shown in the following continuation of program 7.1. The vertex shader utilizes some notations that we haven't yet seen. Note for example the vector addition done at the end of the vertex shader—vector addition (and subtraction) was shown in Chapter 3 and is available as shown here in GLSL. We will discuss some of the other notations after presenting the shaders.

Program 7.1 (continued)

Vertex Shader

```
#version 430
layout (location=0) in vec3 vertPos;
layout (location=1) in vec3 vertNormal;
out vec4 varyingColor;

struct PositionalLight
{   vec4 ambient;
    vec4 diffuse;
    vec4 specular;
    vec3 position;
};
struct Material
{   vec4 ambient;
    vec4 diffuse;
    vec4 specular;
    float shininess;
};
uniform vec4 globalAmbient;
uniform PositionalLight light;
uniform Material material;
uniform mat4 mv_matrix;
uniform mat4 proj_matrix;
uniform mat4 norm_matrix;   // for transforming normals

void main(void)
{   vec4 color;

    // convert vertex position to view space,
    // convert normal to view space, and
    // calculate view space light vector (from vertex to light)
    vec4 P = mv_matrix * vec4(vertPos,1.0);
    vec3 N = normalize((norm_matrix * vec4(vertNormal,1.0)).xyz);
    vec3 L = normalize(light.position - P.xyz);

    // view vector is equivalent to the negative of view space vertex position
    vec3 V = normalize(-P.xyz);

    //  R is reflection of -L with respect to surface normal N
    vec3 R = reflect(-L,N);

    // ambient, diffuse, and specular contributions
    vec3 ambient = ((globalAmbient * material.ambient) + (light.ambient * material.ambient)).xyz;
```

```
    vec3 diffuse = light.diffuse.xyz * material.diffuse.xyz * max(dot(N,L), 0.0);
    vec3 specular =
        material.specular.xyz * light.specular.xyz * pow(max(dot(R,V), 0.0f), material.shininess);

    // send the color output to the fragment shader
    varyingColor = vec4((ambient + diffuse + specular), 1.0);

    // send the position to the fragment shader, as before
    gl_Position = proj_matrix * mv_matrix * vec4(vertPos,1.0);
}
```

Fragment Shader

```
#version 430
in vec4 varyingColor;
out vec4 fragColor;

//  uniforms match those in the vertex shader,
//  but aren't used directly in this fragment shader

struct PositionalLight
{   vec4 ambient;
    vec4 diffuse;
    vec4 specular;
    vec3 position;
};
struct Material
{   vec4 ambient;
    vec4 diffuse;
    vec4 specular;
    float shininess;
};
uniform vec4 globalAmbient;
uniform PositionalLight light;
uniform Material material;
uniform mat4 mv_matrix;
uniform mat4 proj_matrix;
uniform mat4 norm_matrix;

void main(void)
{   fragColor = varyingColor;
}
```

The output of Program 7.1 is shown in Figure 7.9.

The vertex shader contains our first example of using the struct notation. A GLSL "struct" is like a datatype; it has a name and a set of fields. When a variable is declared using the name of a struct, it then contains those fields, which are accessed using the "." notation. For example, variable "light" is declared of type

Figure 7.9
Torus with Gouraud shading.

"PositionalLight" so we can thereafter refer to its fields light.ambient, light.diffuse, and so forth.

Also note the field selector notation ".xyz" that is used in several places in the vertex shader. This is a shortcut for converting a vec4 to an equivalent vec3 containing only its first three elements.

The vertex shader is where most of the lighting computations are performed. For each vertex, the appropriate matrix transforms are applied to the vertex position and associated normal vector, and vectors for light direction ($\vec{L}$) and reflection ($\vec{R}$) are computed. The ADS computations described in Section 7.4 are then performed, resulting in a color for each vertex (called varyingColor in the code). The colors are interpolated as part of the normal rasterization process. The fragment shader is then a simple pass-through. The lengthy list of uniform variable declarations is also present in the fragment shader (for reasons described earlier in Chapter 4), but none of them are actually used there.

Note the use of the GLSL functions normalize(), which converts a vector to unit length and is necessary for proper application of the dot product, and reflect(), which computes the reflection of one vector about another.

Artifacts are evident in the output torus shown in Figure 7.9. Specular highlights have a blocky, faceted appearance. This artifact is more pronounced if the object is in motion (we can't illustrate that here).

Gouraud shading is susceptible to other artifacts. If the specular highlight is entirely contained within one of the model's triangles—that is, if it doesn't contain at least one of the model vertices—then it may disappear entirely. The specular component is calculated per-vertex, so if a model vertex with a specular contribution does not exist, none of the rasterized pixels will include specular light either.

7.5.2 Phong Shading

Bui Tuong Phong developed a smooth shading algorithm while a graduate student at the University of Utah and described it in his 1973 dissertation [PH73] and published it in [PH75]. The structure of the algorithm is similar to the algorithm for Gouraud shading, except that the lighting computations are done *per-pixel* rather than per-vertex. Since the lighting computations require a normal vector $\vec{N}$ and a light vector $\vec{L}$, which are only available in the model on a per-vertex basis, Phong shading is often implemented using a clever "trick," whereby $\vec{N}$ and $\vec{L}$ are computed in the vertex shader and *interpolated* during rasterization. Figure 7.10 outlines the strategy.

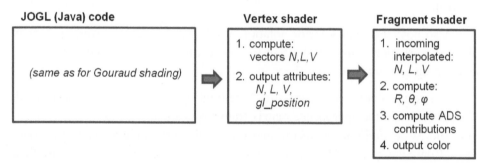

Figure 7.10
Implementing Phong shading.

The Java/JOGL code is completely unchanged. Some of the computations previously done in the vertex shader are now moved into the fragment shader. The effect of interpolating normal vectors is illustrated in Figure 7.11.

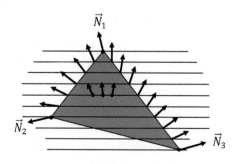

Figure 7.11
Interpolation of normal vectors.

We now are ready to implement our torus with positional lighting, using Phong shading. Most of the code is identical to that used for Gouraud shading. Since the Java/JOGL code is unchanged, we present only the revised vertex and fragment shaders, shown in Program 7.2. Examining the output of Program 7.2, as shown in Figure 7.12, Phong shading corrects the artifacts present in Gouraud shading.

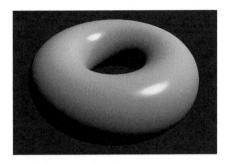

Figure 7.12
Torus with Phong shading.

Program 7.2 Torus with Phong Shading

Vertex Shader

```
#version 430
layout (location=0) in vec3 vertPos;
layout (location=1) in vec3 vertNormal;
out vec3 varyingNormal;        // eye-space vertex normal
out vec3 varyingLightDir;      // vector pointing to the light
out vec3 varyingVertPos;       // vertex position in eye space

// structs and uniforms same as for Gouraud shading
. . .
void main(void)
{   // output vertex position, light direction, and normal to the rasterizer for interpolation
    varyingVertPos=(mv_matrix * vec4(vertPos,1.0)).xyz;
    varyingLightDir = light.position - varyingVertPos;
    varyingNormal=(norm_matrix * vec4(vertNormal,1.0)).xyz;

    gl_Position=proj_matrix * mv_matrix * vec4(vertPos,1.0);
}
```

Fragment Shader

```
#version 430
in vec3 varyingNormal;
in vec3 varyingLightDir;
in vec3 varyingVertPos;
out vec4 fragColor;

// structs and uniforms same as for Gouraud shading
. . .
```

```
void main(void)
{   // normalize the light, normal, and view vectors:
    vec3 L = normalize(varyingLightDir);
    vec3 N = normalize(varyingNormal);
    vec3 V = normalize(-varyingVertPos);

    // compute light reflection vector with respect to N:
    vec3 R = normalize(reflect(-L, N));
    // get the angle between the light and surface normal:
    float cosTheta = dot(L,N);
    // angle between the view vector and reflected light:
    float cosPhi = dot(V,R);

    // compute ADS contributions (per pixel), and combine to build output color:
    vec3 ambient = ((globalAmbient * material.ambient) + (light.ambient * material.ambient)).xyz;
    vec3 diffuse = light.diffuse.xyz * material.diffuse.xyz * max(cosTheta,0.0);
    vec3 specular =
        light.specular.xyz * material.specular.xyz * pow(max(cosPhi,0.0), material.shininess);

    fragColor = vec4((ambient + diffuse + specular), 1.0);
}
```

Although Phong shading offers better realism than Gouraud shading, it does so while incurring a performance cost. One optimization to Phong shading was proposed by James Blinn in 1977 [BL77] and is referred to as the *Blinn-Phong* reflection model. It is based on the observation that one of the most expensive computations in Phong shading is determining the reflection vector $\vec{R}$.

Blinn observed that the vector $\vec{R}$ itself actually is not needed—$\vec{R}$ is only produced as a means of determining the angle φ. It turns out that φ can be found without computing $\vec{R}$, by instead computing a vector $\vec{H}$ that is halfway between $\vec{L}$ and $\vec{V}$. As shown in Figure 7.13, the angle α between $\vec{H}$ and $\vec{N}$ is conveniently equal to ½(φ). Although α isn't identical to φ, Blinn showed that reasonable results can be obtained by using α instead of φ.

The "halfway" vector $\vec{H}$ is most easily determined by finding $\vec{L} + \vec{V}$ (see Figure 7.14), after which cos(α) can be found using the dot product $\widehat{H} \bullet \widehat{N}$.

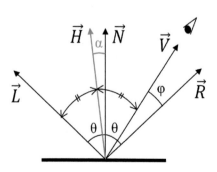

Figure 7.13
Blinn-Phong reflection.

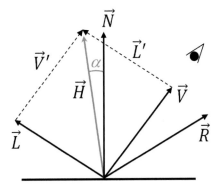

Figure 7.14
Blinn-Phong computation.

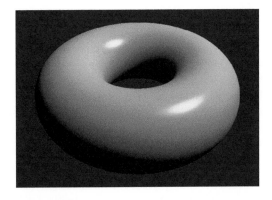

Figure 7.15
Torus with Blinn-Phong shading.

The computations can be done in the fragment shader, or even in the vertex shader (with some tweaks) if necessary for performance. Figure 7.15 shows the torus rendered using Blinn-Phong shading; the quality is largely indistinguishable from Phong shading, with substantial performance cost savings.

Program 7.3 shows the revised vertex and fragment shaders for converting the Phong shading example shown in Program 7.2 to Blinn-Phong shading. As before, there is no change to the Java/JOGL code.

Program 7.3 Torus with Blinn-Phong Shading

Vertex Shader

```
. . .
// half-vector "H" is an additional output varying
out vec3 varyingHalfVector;
. . .
void main(void)
{  // computations same as before, plus the following that computes L+V
    varyingHalfVector = normalize(normalize(varyingLightDir) + normalize(-varyingVertPos)).xyz;

    // (the rest of the vertex shader is unchanged)
}
```

Fragment Shader

```
. . .
in vec3 varyingHalfVector;
. . .
```

```
void main(void)
{   // note that it is no longer necessary to compute R in the fragment shader
    vec3 L = normalize(varyingLightDir);
    vec3 N = normalize(varyingNormal);
    vec3 V = normalize(-varyingVertPos);
    vec3 H = normalize(varyingHalfVector);
    . . .
    // get angle between the normal and the halfway vector
    float cosPhi = dot(H,N);

    // halfway vector H was computed in the vertex shader, and then interpolated by the rasterizer
    vec3 ambient = ((globalAmbient * material.ambient) + (light.ambient * material.ambient)).xyz;
    vec3 diffuse = light.diffuse.xyz * material.diffuse.xyz * max(cosTheta,0.0);
    vec3 specular =
        light.specular.xyz * material.specular.xyz * pow(max(cosPhi,0.0), material.shininess*3.0);
        // the multiplication by 3.0 at the end is a "tweak" to improve the specular highlight.
    fragColor = vec4((ambient + diffuse + specular), 1.0);
}
```

Figure 7.16
External models with Phong shading.

Figure 7.16 shows two examples of the effect of Phong shading on more complex externally generated models. The top image shows a rendering of an OBJ model of a dolphin created by Jay Turberville at Studio 522 Productions [TU16]. The bottom image is a rendering of the well-known "Stanford Dragon," the result of a 3D scan done in 1996 of an actual figurine [ST96]. Both models were rendered using the "gold" material we placed in our "Utils.java" class. The Stanford dragon is widely used for testing graphics algorithms and hardware because of its size—it contains over 800,000 triangles.

7.6 ■ COMBINING LIGHTING AND TEXTURES

So far, our lighting model has assumed that we are using lights with specified ADS values to illuminate objects made of material that has also been defined with ADS values. However, as we saw in Chapter 5, some objects may instead have surfaces defined by texture images. Therefore, we need a way of combining colors retrieved by sampling a texture and colors produced from a lighting model.

The manner in which we combine lighting and textures depends on the nature of the object and the purpose of its texture. There are several scenarios, including the following:

- The texture image very closely reflects the actual appearance of the object's surface.
- The object has both a material and a texture.
- The texture contains shadow or reflection information (covered in Chapters 8 and 9).
- There are multiple lights and/or multiple textures involved.

Let's consider the first case, where we have a simple textured object and we wish to add lighting to it. One simple way of accomplishing this in the fragment shader is to remove the material specification entirely and to use the texel color returned from the texture sampler in place of the material ADS values. The following is one such strategy (expressed in pseudocode):

```
fragColor = textureColor * ( ambientLight + diffuseLight ) + specularLight
```

Here the texture color contributes to the ambient and diffuse computation, while the specular color is defined entirely by the light. It is common to set the specular contribution solely based on the light color, especially for metallic or "shiny" surfaces. However, some less shiny surfaces, such as cloth or unvarnished wood (and even a few metals, such as gold) have specular highlights that include the color of the object surface. In those cases, a suitable slightly modified strategy would be

```
fragColor = textureColor * ( ambientLight + diffuseLight + specularLight )
```

There are also cases in which an object has an ADS material that is supplemented by a texture image, such as an object made of silver that has a texture that adds some tarnish to the surface. In those situations, the standard ADS model with both light and material, as described in previous sections, can be combined with the texture color using a weighted sum. For example:

```
textureColor = texture(sampler, texCoord)
lightColor = (ambLight * ambMaterial) + (diffLight * diffMaterial) + specLight
fragColor  = 0.5 * textureColor + 0.5 * lightColor
```

This strategy for combining lighting, materials, and textures can be extended to scenes involving multiple lights and/or multiple textures. For example:

```
texture1Color = texture(sampler1, texCoord)
texture2Color = texture(sampler2, texCoord)
light1Color = (ambLight1 * ambMaterial) + (diffLight1 * diffMaterial) + specLight1
light2Color = (ambLight2 * ambMaterial) + (diffLight2 * diffMaterial) + specLight2
fragColor  =  0.25 * texture1Color
           +  0.25 * texture2Color
           +  0.25 * light1Color
           +  0.25 * light2Color
```

Figure 7.17 shows the Studio 522 dolphin with a UV-mapped texture image (produced by Jay Turberville [TU16]) and the NASA shuttle model we saw earlier in Chapter 6. Both textured models are enhanced with Blinn-Phong lighting, without the inclusion of materials, and with specular highlights that utilize light only. In both cases, the relevant output color computation in the fragment shader is

```
vec4 texColor = texture(sampler, texCoord);
fragColor = texColor * (globalAmbient + lightAmb + lightDiff * max(dot(L,N),0.0))
          + lightSpec * pow(max(dot(H,N),0.0), matShininess*3.0);
```

Note that it is possible for the computation that determines fragColor to produce values greater than 1.0. When that happens, OpenGL clamps the computed value to 1.0.

SUPPLEMENTAL NOTES

The faceted-shaded torus shown in Figure 7.7 was created by adding the "flat" interpolation qualifier to the corresponding normal vector vertex attribute declarations in the vertex and fragment shaders. This instructs the rasterizer to *not* perform interpolation on the specified variable, and instead assign the same value

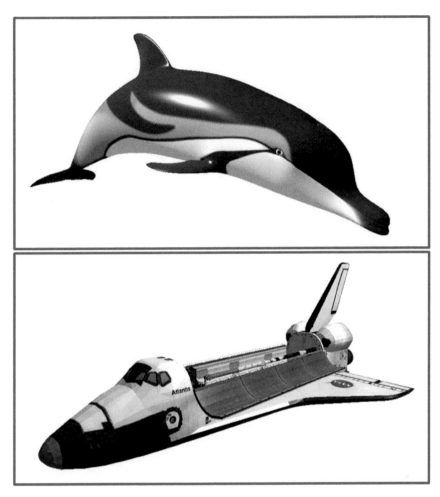

Figure 7.17
Combining lighting and textures.

for each fragment (by default it chooses the value associated with the first vertex in the triangle). In the Phong shading example, this could be done as follows:

```
flat out vec3 varyingNormal;        in the vertex shader, and
flat in vec3 varyingNormal;         in the fragment shader.
```

An important kind of light source that we haven't discussed is a *distributed light* or *area light*, which is a light that is characterized by having a source that occupies an area rather than being a single point location. A real-world example would be a fluorescent tube-style light commonly found in an office or classroom. Interested readers can find more details about area lights in [MH02].

HISTORICAL NOTE

We took the liberty of oversimplifying some of the terminology in this chapter, with respect to the contributions of Gouraud and Phong. Gouraud is credited with *Gouraud shading*—the notion of generating a smoothly curved surface appearance by computing light intensities at vertices and allowing the rasterizer to interpolate these values (sometimes called "smooth shading"). Phong is credited with *Phong shading*, another form of smooth shading that instead interpolates normals and computes lighting per-pixel. Phong is also credited with pioneering the successful incorporation of specular highlights into smooth shading. For this reason, the ADS lighting model, when applied to computer graphics, is often referred to as the *Phong Reflection Model*. So our example of Gouraud shading is, more accurately, Gouraud shading with a Phong reflection model. Since Phong's reflection model has become so ubiquitous in 3D graphics programming, it is common to demonstrate Gouraud shading in the presence of Phong reflection, although it is a bit misleading because Gouraud's original 1971 work did not, for example, include any specular component.

Exercises

7.1 *(PROJECT)* Modify Program 7.1 so that the light can be positioned by moving the mouse. After doing this, move the mouse around and note the movement of the specular highlight and the appearance of the Gouraud shading artifacts. You may find it convenient to render a point (or small object) at the location of the light source.

7.2 Repeat Exercise 7.1, but applied to Program 7.2. This should only require substituting the shaders for Phong shading into your solution to Exercise 7.1. The improvement from Gouraud to Phong shading should be even more apparent here, when the light is being moved around.

7.3 *(PROJECT)* Modify Program 7.2 so that it incorporates TWO positional lights, placed in different locations. The fragment shader will need to blend the diffuse and specular contributions of each of the lights. Try using a weighted sum, similar to the one shown in Section 7.6. You can also try simply adding them and clamping the result so it doesn't exceed the maximum light value.

7.4 *(RESEARCH AND PROJECT)* Replace the positional light in Program 7.2 with a "spot" light, as described in Section 7.2. Experiment with the settings for *cutoff angle* and *falloff exponent*, and observe the effects.

References

[BA16] N. Barradeu, accessed July 2016, http://www.barradeau.com/nicoptere/dump/materials.html

[BL77] J. Blinn, "Models of Light Reflection for Computer Synthesized Pictures," *Proceedings of the 4th Annual Conference on Computer Graphics and Interactive Techniques*, 1977.

[DI16] *Luxo Jr.* (Pixar, © Disney), accessed July 2016, http://www.pixar.com/short_films/Theatrical-Shorts/Luxo-Jr.#

[GO71] H. Gouraud, "Continuous Shading of Curved Surfaces," *IEEE Transactions on Computers* C-20, no. 6 (June 1971).

[MH02] T. Akenine-Möller and E. Haines, *Real-Time Rendering*, 2nd ed. (A. K. Peters, 2002).

[PH73] B. Phong, "Illumination of Computer-Generated Images" (PhD thesis, University of Utah, 1973).

[PH75] B. Phong, "Illumination for Computer Generated Pictures," *Communications of the ACM* 18, no. 6 (June 1975): 311–317.

[ST96] Stanford Computer Graphics Laboratory, 1996, accessed July 2016, http://graphics.stanford.edu/data/3Dscanrep/

[TU16] J. Turberville, Studio 522 Productions, Scottsdale, AZ, www.studio522.com (dolphin model developed 2016).

SHADOWS

8.1 THE IMPORTANCE OF SHADOWS

In Chapter 7, we learned how to add lighting to our 3D scenes. However, we didn't actually add light—instead, we simulated the effects of light on objects—using the ADS model—and modified how we drew those objects accordingly.

The limitations of this approach become apparent when we use it to light more than one object in the same scene. Consider the scene in Figure 8.1, which includes both our brick-textured torus and a ground plane (the ground plane is the top of a giant cube with a grass texture from [LU16]).

At first glance our scene may appear reasonable. However, closer examination reveals that there is something very important missing. In particular, it is impossible to discern the distance between the torus and the large textured cube below it. Is the torus floating above the cube, or is it resting on top of the cube?

Figure 8.1
Scene without shadows.

The reason we cannot answer this question is due to the lack of *shadows* in the scene. We expect to see shadows, and our brain uses shadows to help build a more complete mental model of the objects we see and where they are located.

Consider the same scene, shown in Figure 8.2, with shadows incorporated. It is now obvious that the torus is resting on the ground plane in the left example and floating above it in the right example.

Figure 8.2
Lighting with shadows.

8.2 PROJECTIVE SHADOWS

A variety of interesting methods have been devised for adding shadows to 3D scenes. One method that is well suited to drawing shadows on a ground plane (such as our image in Figure 8.1) and relatively computationally inexpensive is called *projective shadows*. Given a point light source position (X_L, Y_L, Z_L), an object to render, and a plane on which the object's shadow is to be cast, it is possible to derive a transformation matrix that will convert points (X_W, Y_W, Z_W) on the object to corresponding shadow points $(X_S, 0, Z_S)$ on the plane. The resulting "shadow polygon" is then drawn, typically as a dark object blended with the texture on the ground plane, as illustrated in Figure 8.3.

The advantages of projective shadow casting are its efficiency and simplicity of implementation. However, it only works on a flat plane—the method can't be used to cast shadows on a curved surface or on other objects. It is still useful for performance-intensive applications involving outdoor scenes, such as in many video games.

Development of projective shadow transformation matrices is discussed in [AS14], [BL88], and [KS16].

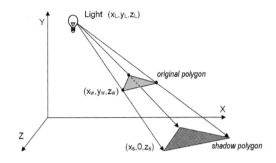

Figure 8.3
Projective shadow.

▮8.3▮ SHADOW VOLUMES

Another important method, proposed by Crow in 1977, is to identify the spatial volume shadowed by an object, and reduce the color intensity of polygons inside the intersection of the shadow volume with the view volume [CR77]. Figure 8.4 shows a cube in a shadow volume, so the cube would be drawn darker.

Shadow volumes have the advantage of being highly accurate, with fewer artifacts than other methods. However, finding the shadow volume, and then computing whether each polygon is inside of it, is computationally expensive even on modern GPU hardware. Geometry shaders can be used to generate shadow volumes, and the *stencil buffer*[1] can be used to determine whether a pixel is within the volume. Some graphics cards include hardware support for optimizing certain shadow volume operations.

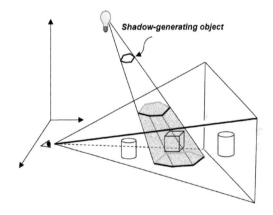

Figure 8.4
Shadow volume.

----

[1] The *stencil buffer* is a third buffer—along with the color buffer and the z-buffer—accessible through OpenGL. The stencil buffer is not described in this textbook.

8.4 SHADOW MAPPING

One the most practical and popular methods for casting shadows is called *shadow mapping*. Although it is not always as accurate as shadow volumes (and is often accompanied by pesky artifacts), shadow mapping is easier to implement, can be used in a wide variety of situations, and enjoys powerful hardware support.

We would be remiss if we failed to clarify our use of the word *easier* in the previous paragraph. Although shadow mapping is simpler than shadow volumes (both conceptually and in practice), it is by no means "easy"! Students often find shadow mapping among the most difficult techniques to implement in a 3D graphics course. Shader programs are by nature difficult to debug, and shadow mapping requires the perfect coordination of several components and shader modules. *Be advised that successful implementation of shadow mapping will be greatly facilitated by liberal use of the debugging tools described earlier in Section 2.2.*

Shadow mapping is based on a very simple and clever idea—namely, anything that cannot be seen by the *light* is in shadow. That is, if object #1 blocks the light from reaching object #2, it is the same as the light not being able to "see" object #2.

The reason this idea is so powerful is that we already have a method for determining if something can be "seen"—the hidden surface removal algorithm (HSR) using the Z-buffer, as described in Section 2.1.7. So a strategy for finding shadows is to temporarily move the camera to the location of the light, apply the Z-buffer HSR algorithm, and then use the resulting depth information to find shadows.

Rendering our scene will require two passes: one to render the scene from the point of view of the light (but not actually drawing it to the screen) and a second pass to render it from the point of view of the camera. The purpose of pass one is to generate a Z-buffer from the light's point of view. After completing pass one, we need to retain the Z-buffer and use it to help us generate shadows in pass two. Pass two actually draws the scene.

Our strategy is now becoming more refined:

- *(Pass 1) Render the scene from the light's position. The depth buffer then contains, for each pixel, the distance between the light and the nearest object to it.*
- *Copy the depth buffer to a separate "shadow buffer."*

- *(Pass 2) Render the scene normally. For each pixel, look up the corresponding position in the shadow buffer. If the distance to the point being rendered is greater than the value retrieved from the shadow buffer, then the object being drawn at this pixel is further from the light than the object nearest the light, and therefore this pixel is in shadow.*

When a pixel is found to be in shadow, we need to make it darker. One simple and effective way of doing this is to render only its ambient lighting, ignoring its diffuse and specular components.

The method described above is often called "shadow buffering." The term "shadow mapping" arises when, in the second step, we instead copy the depth buffer into a *texture*. When a texture object is used in this way, we will refer to it as a *shadow texture*, and OpenGL has support for shadow textures in the form of a sampler2DShadow type (discussed below). This allows us to leverage the power of hardware support for texture units and sampler variables (i.e., "texture mapping") in the fragment shader to quickly perform the depth lookup in pass 2. Our strategy now is revised:

- *(Pass 1) as before.*
- *Copy the depth buffer into a <u>texture</u>.*
- *(Pass 2) as before, except that the shadow buffer is now a <u>shadow</u> <u>texture</u>.*

Let's now implement these steps.

8.4.1 Shadow Mapping (Pass One)—"Draw" Objects from Light Position

In step one, we first move our camera to the light's position, and then render the scene. Our goal here is *not* to actually draw the scene on the display, but to complete just enough of the rendering process that the depth buffer is properly filled. Thus it will not be necessary to generate colors for the pixels, and so our first pass will utilize a vertex shader, but the fragment shader does nothing.

Of course, moving the camera involves constructing an appropriate *view* matrix. Depending on the contents of the scene, we will need to decide on an appropriate *direction* to view the scene from the light. Typically, we would want this direction to be toward the region that would ultimately be rendered in step 3. This is often application specific—in our scenes, we will generally be pointing the camera from the light to the origin.

Several important details need to be handled in pass one:

- Configure the buffer and shadow texture.
- Disable color output.
- Build a look-at matrix from the light toward the objects in view.
- Enable the GLSL pass one shader program, containing only the simple vertex shader shown in Figure 8.5 that expects to receive an MVP matrix. In this case, the MVP matrix will include the object's model matrix M, the look-at matrix computed in the previous step (serving as the view matrix V), and the perspective matrix P. We call this MVP matrix "shadowMVP" because it is based on the point of view of the light rather than the camera. Since the view from the light isn't actually being displayed, the pass one shader program's fragment shader doesn't do anything.
- For each object, create the shadowMVP matrix, and call glDrawArrays(). It is not necessary to include textures or lighting in pass one, because objects are not rendered to the screen.

```
#version 430          // vertex shader
layout (location=0) in vec3 vertPos;
uniform mat4 shadowMVP;


void main(void)
{    gl_Position = shadowMVP * vec4(vertPos,1.0);
}
```

```
#version 430          // fragment shader
void main(void) { }
```

Figure 8.5
Shadow mapping pass 1 vertex and fragment shaders.

8.4.2 Shadow Mapping (Intermediate Step)—Copying the Z-Buffer to a Texture

OpenGL offers two methods for putting Z-buffer depth data into a texture unit. The first method is to generate an empty shadow texture, and then use the command glCopyTexImage2D() to copy the active depth buffer into the shadow texture.

The second method is to build a "custom framebuffer" back in pass one (rather than use the default Z-buffer) and attach the shadow texture to it using the command glFrameBufferTexture(). This command was introduced into OpenGL, in version 3.0, to further support shadow mapping. When using this approach, it isn't necessary to "copy" the Z-buffer into a texture, because the buffer already has a texture attached to it, and so the depth information is put into the texture by OpenGL automatically. This is the method we will use in our implementation.

8.4.3 Shadow Mapping (Pass Two)—Rendering the Scene with Shadows

Much of pass two will resemble what we saw in Chapter 7. Namely, it is here that we render our complete scene and all of the items in it, along with the lighting, materials, and any textures adorning the objects in the scene. We also need to add the necessary code to determine, for each pixel, whether or not it is in shadow.

An important feature of pass two is that it utilizes two MVP matrices. One is the standard MVP matrix that tranforms object coordinates into screen coordinates (as seen in most of our previous examples). The other is the shadowMVP matrix that was generated in pass one for use in rendering from the light's point of view—this will now be used in pass two for looking up depth information from the shadow texture.

A complication arises in pass two when we try to look up pixels in a texture map. The OpenGL camera utilizes a [-1..+1] coordinate space, whereas texture maps utilize a [0..1] space. A common solution is to build an additional matrix transform, typically called B, that converts (or "biases," hence the name) from camera space to texture space. Deriving B is fairly simple—a scale by one-half followed by a translate by one-half.

The B matrix is as follows:

$$B = \begin{bmatrix} 0.5 & 0 & 0 & 0.5 \\ 0 & 0.5 & 0 & 0.5 \\ 0 & 0 & 0.5 & 0.5 \\ 0 & 0 & 0 & 1 \end{bmatrix}$$

B is then concatenated onto the shadowMVP matrix for use in pass two, as follows:

shadowMVP2 = [B] [shadowMVP$_{(pass1)}$]

Assuming that we use the method whereby a shadow texture has been attached to our custom framebuffer, OpenGL provides some relatively simple tools for determining whether each pixel is in shadow as we draw the objects. The following is a summary of the details handled in pass two:

- Build the "B" transform matrix for converting from light to texture space (actually this is more appropriately done in init()).
- Enable the shadow texture for look-up.
- Enable color output.
- Enable the GLSL pass two rendering program, containing both vertex and fragment shaders.
- Build MVP matrix for the object being drawn based on the camera position (as normal).
- Build the shadowMVP2 matrix (incorporating the B matrix, as described earlier)—the shaders will need it to look up pixel coordinates in the shadow texture.
- Send the matrix transforms to shader uniform variables.
- Enable buffers containing vertices, normal vectors, and texture coordinates (if used), as usual.
- Call glDrawArrays().

In addition to their rendering duties, the vertex and fragment shaders have additional tasks:

- The vertex shader converts vertex positions from camera space to light space and sends the resulting coordinates to the fragment shader in a vertex attribute so that they will be interpolated. This makes it possible to retrieve the correct values from the shadow texture.

- The fragment shader calls the textureProj() function, which returns a 0 or 1 indicating whether or not the pixel is in shadow (this mechanism is explained later). If it is in shadow, the shader outputs a darker pixel by not including its diffuse and specular contributions.

Shadow mapping is such a common task that GLSL provides a special type of sampler variable called a sampler2DShadow (as previously mentioned) that can be attached to a shadow texture in the Java/JOGL application. The textureProj() function is used to look up values from a shadow texture and is similar to texture() which we saw previously in Chapter 5, except that it uses a vec3 to index the texture rather than the usual vec2. Since a pixel coordinate is a vec4, it is necessary to project that onto 2D texture space in order to look up the depth value in the shadow texture map. As we will see below, textureProj() does all of this for us.

The remainder of the vertex and fragment shader code implements Blinn-Phong shading. These shaders are shown in Figures 8.6 and 8.7, with the added code for shadow mapping highlighted.

Let's examine more closely how we use OpenGL to perform the depth comparison between the pixel being rendered and the value in the shadow texture. We start in the vertex shader with vertex coordinates in model space, which we multiply by shadowMVP2 to produce shadow texture coordinates that correspond to vertex coordinates projected into light space, previously generated from the light's point of view. The interpolated (3D) light space coordinates (x,y,z) are used in the

```
#version 430
layout (location=0) in vec3 vertPos;
layout (location=1) in vec3 vertNormal;

out vec3 varyingNormal, varyingLightDir, varyingVertPos, varyingHalfVec;
out vec4 shadow_coord;

struct PositionalLight { vec4 ambient, diffuse, specular; vec3 position; };
struct Material { vec4 ambient, diffuse, specular; float shininess; };
uniform vec4 globalAmbient;
uniform PositionalLight light;        // light's position is assumed to be in eye space
uniform Material material;
uniform mat4 mv_matrix;
uniform mat4 proj_matrix;
uniform mat4 norm_matrix;
uniform mat4 shadowMVP2;
layout (binding=0) uniform sampler2DShadow shTex;

void main(void)
{    varyingVertPos = (mv_matrix * vec4(vertPos,1.0)).xyz;
     varyingLightDir = light.position - varyingVertPos;
     varyingNormal = (norm_matrix * vec4(vertNormal,1.0)).xyz;
     varyingHalfVec = (varyingLightDir - varyingVertPos).xyz;
     shadow_coord = shadowMVP2 * vec4(vertPos,1.0);
     gl_Position = proj_matrix * mv_matrix * vec4(vertPos,1.0);
}
```

Figure 8.6
Shadow mapping pass 2 vertex shader.

```
#version 430
in vec3 varyingNormal, varyingLightDir, varyingVertPos, varyingHalfVec;
in vec4 shadow_coord;
out vec4 fragColor;

// same structs and uniforms as in the vertex shader
. . .
void main(void)
{    vec3 L = normalize(varyingLightDir);
     vec3 N = normalize(varyingNormal);
     vec3 V = normalize(-varyingVertPos);
     vec3 H = normalize(varyingHalfVec);

     float notInShadow = textureProj(shTex, shadow_coord);

     fragColor = globalAmbient * material.ambient + light.ambient * material.ambient;
     If (notInShadow == 1.0)
     {    fragColor += light.diffuse * material.diffuse * max(dot(L,N),0.0)
          + light.specular * material.specular
          * pow(max(dot(H,N),0.0),material.shininess*3.0);
     }
}
```

Figure 8.7
Shadow mapping pass 2 fragment shader.

fragment shader as follows. The z component represents the distance from the light to the pixel. The (x,y) components are used to retrieve the depth information stored in the (2D) shadow texture. This retrieved value (the distance to the object nearest the light) is compared with z. This comparison produces a "binary" result that tells us whether the pixel we are rendering is further from the light than the object nearest the light (i.e., whether the pixel is in shadow).

If in OpenGL we use glFrameBufferTexture() as described earlier and we enable *depth testing*, then using a sampler2DShadow and textureProj() as shown in the fragment shader (Figure 8.7) will exactly what we need. That is, textureProj() will output either 0.0 or 1.0 depending on the depth comparison. Based on this value, we can then in the fragment shader omit the diffuse and specular contributions when the pixel is further from the light than the object nearest the light, effectively creating the shadow when appropriate. An overview is shown in Figure 8.8.

We are now ready to build our JOGL application to work with the previously described shaders.

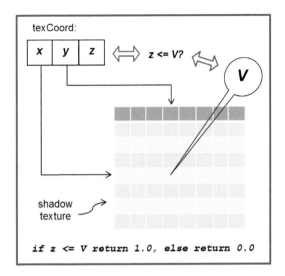

Figure 8.8
Automatic depth comparison.

8.5 A SHADOW MAPPING EXAMPLE

Consider the scene in Figure 8.9 that includes a torus and a pyramid. A positional light has been placed on the left (note the specular highlights—the pyramid *should* cast a shadow on the torus).

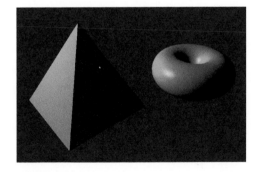

Figure 8.9
Lighted scene without shadows.

To clarify the development of the example, our first step will be to *render pass one to the screen* to make sure it is working properly. To do this, we will temporarily add a simple fragment shader (it will not be included in the final version) to pass one that just outputs a constant color (e.g., red); for example:

```
#version 430
out vec4 fragColor;
void main(void)
{   fragColor = vec4(1.0, 0.0, 0.0, 0.0);
}
```

Let's assume that the origin of the scene above is situated at the center of the figure, in between the pyramid and the torus. In pass one we place the camera at the light's position (at the left in Figure 8.10) and point it toward (0,0,0). If we then draw the objects in red, it produces the output shown at the right in Figure 8.10. Note the torus near the top—from this vantage point it is partially behind the pyramid.

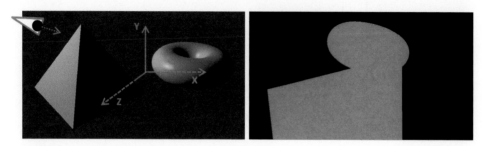

Figure 8.10
Pass one: Scene (left) from light's point of view (right).

The complete two-pass JOGL code with lighting and shadow mapping is shown in Program 8.1.

Program 8.1 Shadow Mapping

```
//  Much is the same as we have seen before. New sections to support shadows are highlighted.
//  The imports necessary for lighting, etc., would be included at the start, are the same as before,
//  and are not shown here.

public class Code extends JFrame implements GLEventListener
{  // variable declarations for rendering programs, buffers, shader sources, etc., would go here.
    . . .
    private ImportedModel pyramid = new ImportedModel("pyr.obj");   // define the pyramid
    private Torus myTorus = new Torus(0.6f, 0.4f, 48);              // define the torus
    private int numPyramidVertices, numTorusVertices, numTorusIndices;

    . . .
    // locations of torus, pyramid, camera, and light
    private Vector3f torusLoc = new Vector3f(1.6, 0.0, -0.3);
    private Vector3f pyrLoc = new Vector3f(-1.0, 0.1, 0.3);
    private Vector3f cameraLoc = new Vector3f(0.0, 0.2, 6.0);
    private Vector3f lightLoc = new Vector3f(-3.8f, 2.2f, 1.1f);

    // properties of white light (global and positional) used in this scene
    private float[ ] globalAmbient = new float[ ] { 0.7f, 0.7f, 0.7f, 1.0f };
```

```
private float[ ] lightAmbient = new float[ ] { 0.0f, 0.0f, 0.0f, 1.0f };
private float[ ] lightDiffuse = new float[ ] { 1.0f, 1.0f, 1.0f, 1.0f };
private float[ ] lightSpecular = new float[ ] { 1.0f, 1.0f, 1.0f, 1.0f };

// gold material for the pyramid
private float[ ] goldMatAmb = Utils.goldAmbient();
private float[ ] goldMatDif = Utils.goldDiffuse();
private float[ ] goldMatSpe = Utils.goldSpecular();
private float goldMatShi = Utils.goldShininess();

// bronze material for the torus
private float[ ] bronzeMatAmb = Utils.bronzeAmbient();
private float[ ] bronzeMatDif = Utils.bronzeDiffuse();
private float[ ] bronzeMatSpe = Utils.bronzeSpecular();
private float bronzeMatShi = Utils.bronzeShininess();

// variables used in display() for transfering light to shaders
private float[ ] curAmb, curDif, curSpe, matAmb, matDif, matSpe;
private float curShi, matShi;

// shadow-related variables
private int screenSizeX, screenSizeY;
private int [ ] shadowTex = new int [1];
private int [ ] shadowBuffer = new int [1];
private Matrix4f lightVmat = new Matrix4f();
private Matrix4f lightPmat = new Matrix4f();
private Matrix4f shadowMVP1 = new Matrix4f();
private Matrix4f shadowMVP2 = new Matrix4f();
private Matrix4f b = new Matrix4f();

// light and camera view matrix transforms are all declared here (mMat, vMat, etc.) of type Matrix4f.
// Other variables used in display() are also declared here.
. . .
public Code()
{   // The constructor is unchanged from Program 7-3, and so it is not shown here.
    // This example assumes that Animator() is being used.
}

// The init() routine performs the usual calls to compile shaders and initialize objects.
// It also calls setupShadowBuffers() to instantiate the buffers related to shadow-mapping.
// Lastly, it builds the B matrix for converting from light space to texture space.

public void init(GLAutoDrawable drawable)
{   GL4 gl = (GL4) GLContext.getCurrentGL();

    renderingProgram1 = Utils.createShaderProgram("code/vert1shader.glsl", "code/frag1shader.glsl");
    renderingProgram2 = Utils.createShaderProgram("code/vert2shader.glsl", "code/frag2shader.glsl");
```

```java
    setupVertices();
    setupShadowBuffers();

    b.set (
        0.5f, 0.0f, 0.0f, 0.0f,
        0.0f, 0.5f, 0.0f, 0.0f,
        0.0f, 0.0f, 0.5f, 0.0f,
        0.5f, 0.5f, 0.5f, 1.0f);
}

private void setupShadowBuffers()
{   GL4 gl = (GL4) GLContext.getCurrentGL();
    screenSizeX = myCanvas.getWidth();
    screenSizeY = myCanvas.getHeight();

    // create the custom frame buffer
    gl.glGenFramebuffers(1, shadowBuffer, 0);

    // create the shadow texture and configure it to hold depth information.
    // these steps are similar to those in Program 5.2
    gl.glGenTextures(1, shadowTex, 0);
    gl.glBindTexture(GL_TEXTURE_2D, shadowTex[0]);
    gl.glTexImage2D(GL_TEXTURE_2D, 0, GL_DEPTH_COMPONENT32,
        screenSizeX, screenSizeY, 0, GL_DEPTH_COMPONENT, GL_FLOAT, null);
    gl.glTexParameteri(GL_TEXTURE_2D, GL_TEXTURE_MIN_FILTER, GL_LINEAR);
    gl.glTexParameteri(GL_TEXTURE_2D, GL_TEXTURE_MAG_FILTER, GL_LINEAR);
    gl.glTexParameteri(GL_TEXTURE_2D, GL_TEXTURE_COMPARE_MODE,
                                      GL_COMPARE_REF_TO_TEXTURE);
    gl.glTexParameteri(GL_TEXTURE_2D, GL_TEXTURE_COMPARE_FUNC, GL_LEQUAL);
}

private void setupVertices()
{   // same as in earlier examples. This function creates the VAO, the VBOs, and then
    // loads vertices and normal vectors for the torus and pyramid into the buffers.
}

// The display() function manages the setup of the custom frame buffer and the shadow texture
// in preparation for pass 1 and pass 2 respectively. New shadow-related features are highlighted.

public void display(GLAutoDrawable drawable)
{   GL4 gl = (GL4) GLContext.getCurrentGL();
    gl.glClear(GL_COLOR_BUFFER_BIT);
    gl.glClear(GL_DEPTH_BUFFER_BIT);

    // set up perspective matrix for the camera, either here or in init()

    // set up view and perspective matrix from the light point of view, for pass 1
    lightVmat.identity().setLookAt(lightloc, origin, up);                // vector from light to origin
    lightPmat.identity().setPerspective((float) Math.toRadians(60.0f), aspect, 0.1f, 1000.0f);
```

```
// make the custom frame buffer current, and associate it with the shadow texture
gl.glBindFramebuffer(GL_FRAMEBUFFER, shadowBuffer[0]);
gl.glFramebufferTexture(GL_FRAMEBUFFER, GL_DEPTH_ATTACHMENT, shadowTex[0], 0);

// disable drawing colors, but enable the depth computation
gl.glDrawBuffer(GL_NONE);
gl.glEnable(GL_DEPTH_TEST);

passOne();

// restore the default display buffer, and re-enable drawing
gl.glBindFramebuffer(GL_FRAMEBUFFER, 0);
gl.glActiveTexture(GL_TEXTURE0);
gl.glBindTexture(GL_TEXTURE_2D, shadowTex[0]);
gl.glDrawBuffer(GL_FRONT);                  // re-enables drawing colors

passTwo();
}

// What follows now are the methods for the first and second passes.
// They are largely identical to things we have seen before.
// Shadow-related additions are highlighted.

public void passOne()
{   GL4 gl = (GL4) GLContext.getCurrentGL();

// renderingProgram1 includes the pass one vertex and fragment shaders
gl.glUseProgram(renderingProgram1);

// the following blocks of code render the torus to establish the depth buffer from the light
// point of view

mMat.identity();
mMat.translate(torusLoc.x(), torusLoc.y(), torusLoc.z());
mMat.rotateX((float)Math.toRadians(25.0f));          // slight rotation for viewability

// we are drawing from the light's point of view, so we use the light's P and V matrices
shadowMVP1.identity();
shadowMVP1.mul(lightPmat);
shadowMVP1.mul(lightVmat);
shadowMVP1.mul(mMat);
sLoc = gl.glGetUniformLocation(renderingProgram1, "shadowMVP");
gl.glUniformMatrix4fv(sLoc, 1, false, shadowMVP1.get(vals));

// we only need to set up torus vertices buffer – we don't need its textures or normals for
// pass one.
gl.glBindBuffer(GL_ARRAY_BUFFER, vbo[0]);
gl.glVertexAttribPointer(0, 3, GL_FLOAT, false, 0, 0);
gl.glEnableVertexAttribArray(0);
```

```
gl.glClear(GL_DEPTH_BUFFER_BIT);
gl.glEnable(GL_CULL_FACE);
gl.glFrontFace(GL_CCW);
gl.glEnable(GL_DEPTH_TEST);
gl.glDepthFunc(GL_LEQUAL);

gl.glBindBuffer(GL_ELEMENT_ARRAY_BUFFER, vbo[4]);     // vbo[4] contains torus indices
gl.glDrawElements(GL_TRIANGLES, numTorusIndices, GL_UNSIGNED_INT, 0);

// repeat for the pyramid (but don't clear the GL_DEPTH_BUFFER_BIT).
//  The pyramid is not indexed, so we use glDrawArrays() rather than glDrawElements()
 . . .
gl.glDrawArrays(GL_TRIANGLES, 0, numPyramidVertices);
}

public void passTwo()
{   GL4 gl = (GL4) GLContext.getCurrentGL();

// renderingProgram2 includes the pass two vertex and fragment shaders
gl.glUseProgram(renderingProgram2);

// draw the torus – this time we need to include lighting, materials, normals, etc.
// We also need to provide MVP tranforms for BOTH camera space and light space.
mvLoc = gl.glGetUniformLocation(renderingProgram2, "mv_matrix");
projLoc = gl.glGetUniformLocation(renderingProgram2, "proj_matrix");
nLoc = gl.glGetUniformLocation(renderingProgram2, "norm_matrix");
sLoc = gl.glGetUniformLocation(renderingProgram2, "shadowMVP");
curAmb = bronzeMatAmb;        // the torus is bronze
curDif = bronzeMatDif;
curSpe = bronzeMatSpe;
curShi = bronzeMatShi;

vMat.identity().setTranslation(-cameraLoc.x(), -cameraLoc.y(), -cameraLoc.z());
currentLightPos.set(lightLoc);
installLights(renderingProgram2, vMat);

mMat.identity();
mMat.translate(torusLoc.x(), torusLoc.y(), torusLoc.z());
mMat.rotateX((float)Math.toRadians(25.0f));         // slight rotation for viewability

// build the MV matrix for the torus from the camera's point of view
mvMat.identity();
mvMat.mul(vMat);
mvMat.mul(mMat);
mvMat.invert(invTrMat);
invTrMat.transpose(invTrMat);
```

```
// build the MVP matrix for the torus from the light's point of view
shadowMVP2.identity();
shadowMVP2.mul(b);
shadowMVP2.mul(lightPmat);
shadowMVP2.mul(lightVmat);
shadowMVP2.mul(mMat);

// put the MV and PROJ matrices into the corresponding uniforms
gl.glUniformMatrix4fv(mvLoc, 1, false, mvMat.get(vals));
gl.glUniformMatrix4fv(projLoc, 1, false, pMat.get(vals));
gl.glUniformMatrix4fv(nLoc, 1, false, invTrMat.get(vals));
gl.glUniformMatrix4fv(sLoc, 1, false, shadowMVP2.get(vals));

// set up torus vertices and normals buffers (and texture coordinates buffer if used)
gl.glBindBuffer(GL_ARRAY_BUFFER, vbo[0]);          // torus vertices
gl.glVertexAttribPointer(0, 3, GL_FLOAT, false, 0, 0);
gl.glEnableVertexAttribArray(0);

gl.glBindBuffer(GL_ARRAY_BUFFER, vbo[2]);          // torus normals
gl.glVertexAttribPointer(1, 3, GL_FLOAT, false, 0, 0);
gl.glEnableVertexAttribArray(1);

gl.glClear(GL_DEPTH_BUFFER_BIT);
gl.glEnable(GL_CULL_FACE);
gl.glFrontFace(GL_CCW);
gl.glEnable(GL_DEPTH_TEST);
gl.glDepthFunc(GL_LEQUAL);

gl.glBindBuffer(GL_ELEMENT_ARRAY_BUFFER, vbo[4]);   // vbo[4] contains torus indices
gl.glDrawElements(GL_TRIANGLES, numTorusIndices, GL_UNSIGNED_INT, 0);

// repeat for the pyramid (but don't clear the GL_DEPTH_BUFFER_BIT)
. . .
// The pyramid is not indexed, so we use glDrawArrays() rather than glDrawElements()
gl.glDrawArrays(GL_TRIANGLES, 0, numPyramidVertices);
}
```

Program 8.1 shows the relevant portions of the Java/JOGL application that interact with the pass one and pass two shaders previously detailed. Not shown are the usual modules for reading in and compiling the shaders, building the models and their related buffers, installing the positional light's ADS characteristics in the shaders, and performing the perspective and look-at matrix computations. Those are unchanged from previous examples.

8.6 SHADOW MAPPING ARTIFACTS

Although we have implemented all of the basic requirements for adding shadows to our scene, running Program 8.1 produces mixed results, as shown in Figure 8.11.

Figure 8.11
Shadow "acne."

The good news is that our pyramid is now casting a shadow on the torus! Unfortunately, this success is accompanied by a severe artifact. There are wavy lines covering many of the surfaces in the scene. This is a common byproduct of shadow mapping and is called *shadow acne*, or *erroneous self-shadowing*.

Shadow acne is caused by rounding errors during depth testing. The texture coordinates computed when looking up the depth information in a shadow texture often don't exactly match the actual coordinates. Thus, the lookup may return the depth for a neighboring pixel, rather than the one being rendered. If the distance to the neighboring pixel is further, then our pixel will appear to be in shadow even if it isn't.

Shadow acne can also be caused by differences in precision between the texture map and the depth computation. This too can lead to rounding errors and subsequent incorrect assessment of whether or not a pixel is in shadow.

Fortunately, fixing shadow acne is fairly easy. Since shadow acne typically occurs on surfaces that are *not* in shadow, a simple trick is to move every pixel slightly closer to the light during pass one, and then move them back to their normal positions for pass two. This is usually sufficient to compensate for either type of rounding error. An easy way is to call glPolygonOffset() in the display() function, as shown in Figure 8.12 (highlighted).

Adding these few lines of code to our display() function improves the output of our program considerably, as shown in Figure 8.13. Note also that with the artifacts gone, we can now see that the inner circle of the torus displays a small correctly cast shadow on itself.

Although fixing shadow acne is easy, sometimes the repair causes new artifacts. The "trick" of moving the object before pass one can sometimes cause a gap to appear inside an object's shadow. An example of this is shown in Figure 8.14. This

```
public void display(GLAutoDrawable drawable)
{ GL4 gl = (GL4) GLContext.getCurrentGL();

   // clearing the depth and color buffers as before goes here
   . . .
   // setting up matrices for camera and light points of view as before goes here
   . . .
   gl.glBindFramebuffer(GL_FRAMEBUFFER, shadowBuffer[0]);
   gl.glFramebufferTexture(GL_FRAMEBUFFER, GL_DEPTH_ATTACHMENT,shadowTex[0], 0);

   gl.glDrawBuffer(GL_NONE);
   gl.glEnable(GL_DEPTH_TEST);

   // for reducing shadow artifacts
   gl.glEnable(GL_POLYGON_OFFSET_FILL);
   gl.glPolygonOffset(2.0f, 4.0f);

   passOne();

   gl.glDisable(GL_POLYGON_OFFSET_FILL);

   gl.glBindFramebuffer(GL_FRAMEBUFFER, 0);
   gl.glActiveTexture(GL_TEXTURE0);
   gl.glBindTexture(GL_TEXTURE_2D, shadowTex[0]);
   gl.glDrawBuffer(GL_FRONT);

   passTwo();
}
```

Figure 8.12
Combating shadow acne.

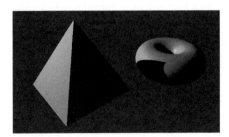

Figure 8.13
Rendered scene with shadows.

Figure 8.14
"Peter Panning."

artifact is often called "Peter Panning," because sometimes it causes the shadow of a resting object to inappropriately separate from the object's base (thus making portions of the object's shadow detach from the rest of the shadow, reminiscent of J. M. Barrie's character Peter Pan [PP16]). Fixing this artifact requires adjusting the glPolygonOffset() parameters. If they are too small, shadow acne can appear; if too large, Peter Panning happens.

There are many other artifacts that can happen during shadow mapping. For example, shadows can *repeat* as a result of the region of the scene being rendered in pass one (into the shadow buffer) being different from the region of the scene rendered in pass two (they are from different vantage points). Because of this difference, those portions of the scene rendered in pass two that fall outside the region rendered in pass one will attempt to access the shadow texture using texture coordinates outside of the range [0..1]. Recall that the default behavior in this case is GL_REPEAT, which can result in incorrectly duplicated shadows.

One possible solution is to add the following lines of code to setupShadowBuffers(), to set the texture wrap mode to "clamp to edge":

```
gl.glTexParameteri(GL_TEXTURE_2D, GL_TEXTURE_WRAP_S, GL_CLAMP_TO_EDGE);
gl.glTexParameteri(GL_TEXTURE_2D, GL_TEXTURE_WRAP_T, GL_CLAMP_TO_EDGE);
```

This causes values outside of a texture edge to be clamped to the value at edge (instead of repeating). Note that this approach can introduce its own artifacts; namely, when a shadow exists at the edge of the shadow texture, clamping to the edge can produce a "shadow bar" extending to the edge of the scene.

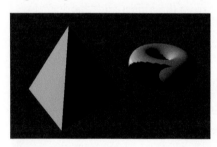

Figure 8.15
Jagged shadow edges.

Another common error is *jagged shadow edges*. This can happen when the shadow being cast is significantly larger than the shadow buffer can accurately represent. This usually depends on the location of the objects and light(s) in the scene. In particular, it commonly occurs when the light source is relatively distant from the objects involved. An example is shown in Figure 8.15.

Eliminating jagged shadow edges is not as simple as for the previous artifacts. One technique is to move the light position closer to the scene during pass one, and then return it to the correct position in pass two. Another approach that is often effective is to employ one of the "soft shadow" methods that we will discuss next.

8.7 SOFT SHADOWS

The methods presented thus far are limited to producing *hard shadows*. These are shadows with sharp edges. However, most shadows that occur in the real world are *soft shadows*. That is, their edges are blurred to various degrees. In this section, we will explore the appearance of soft shadows as they occur in the real world, and then describe a commonly used algorithm for simulating them in OpenGL.

8.7.1 Soft Shadows in the Real World

There are many causes of soft shadows, and there are many types of soft shadows. One thing that commonly causes soft shadows in nature is that real-world light sources are rarely points—more often they occupy some area. Another cause is the accumulation of imperfections in materials and surfaces, and the role that the objects themselves play in generating ambient light through their own reflective properties.

Figure 8.16 shows a photograph of an object casting a soft shadow on a table top. Note that this is *not* a 3D computer rendering, but an actual photograph of an object, taken in the home of one of the authors.

There are two aspects to note about the shadow in Figure 8.16:

- The shadow is "softer" the further it is from the object and "harder" the closer it is to the object. This is apparent when comparing the shadow near the legs of the object versus the wider portion of the shadow at the right region of the image.
- The shadow appears slightly darker the closer it is to the object.

The dimensionality of the light source itself can lead to soft shadows. As shown in Figure 8.17, the various regions across the light source cast slightly different shadows. Those areas where the various shadows differ are called the *penumbra* and comprise the soft regions at the edges of the shadow.

Figure 8.16
Soft shadow real-world example.

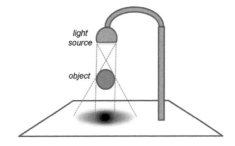

Figure 8.17
Soft shadow penumbra effect.

8.7.2 Generating Soft Shadows—Percentage Closer Filtering (PCF)

There are various ways of simulating the penumbra effect to generate soft shadows in software. One of the simplest and most common is called *percentage closer filtering* (PCF). In PCF, we sample the shadow texture at several surrounding locations to estimate what percentage of nearby locations are in shadow. Depending on how many of the nearby locations are in shadow, we increase or decrease the degree of lighting contribution for the pixel being rendered. The entire computation can be done in the fragment shader, and that is the only place where we have to change any of the code. PCF also can be used to reduce jagged line artifacts.

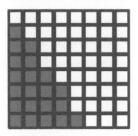

Figure 8.18
Hard shadow rendering.

Before we study the actual PCF algorithm, let's first look at a simple similar motivating example to illustrate the goal of PCF. Consider the set of output fragments (pixels) shown in Figure 8.18, whose colors are being computed by the fragment shader.

Suppose that the darkened pixels are in shadow, as computed using shadow mapping. Instead of simply rendering the pixels as shown (i.e., with or without the diffuse and specular components included), suppose that we had access to neighboring pixel information, so that we could see how many of the neighboring pixels are in shadow. For example, consider the particular pixel highlighted in yellow in Figure 8.19, which according to Figure 8.18 is not in shadow.

In the nine-pixel neighborhood of the highlighted pixel, three of the pixels are in shadow and six are not. Thus, the color of the rendered pixel could be

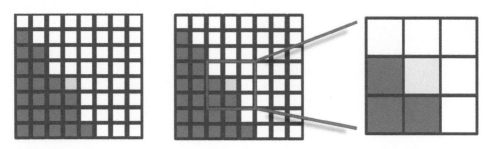

Figure 8.19
PCF sampling for a particular pixel.

computed as the sum of the ambient contribution at that pixel, plus six-ninths of the diffuse and specular contributions, resulting in a fairly (but not completely) brightened pixel. Repeating this process throughout the grid would produce pixel colors approximately as shown in Figure 8.20. Note that for those pixels whose neighborhoods are entirely in (or out of) shadow, the resulting color is the same as for standard shadow mapping.

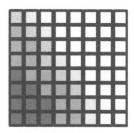

Figure 8.20
Soft shadow rendering.

Unlike the example just shown, implementations of PCF do not sample every pixel within a certain vicinity of the pixel being rendered. There are two reasons for this: (a) we'd like to perform this computation in the fragment shader, but the fragment shader does not have access to other pixels, and (b) obtaining a sufficiently broad penumbra effect (say, 10 to 20 pixels wide) would require sampling hundreds of nearby pixels for each pixel being rendered.

PCF addresses these two issues as follows. First, rather than attempting to access nearby pixels, we instead sample nearby *texels* in the shadow map. The fragment shader can do this because even though it doesn't have access to nearby pixel values, it does have access to the entire shadow map. Second, to achieve a sufficiently broad penumbra effect, a moderate number of nearby shadow map texels are sampled, each at some modest distance from the texel corresponding to the pixel being rendered.

The width of the penumbra and the number of points sampled can be tuned depending on the scene and performance requirements. For example, the image shown in Figure 8.21 was generated using PCF, with each pixel's brightness determined by sampling 64 nearby shadow map texels at various distances from the pixel's texel.

The accuracy or smoothness of our soft shadows depends on the number of nearby texels sampled. Thus, there is a tradeoff between performance and quality—the more points sampled, the better the results, but the more computational overhead is incurred. Depending on the complexity of the scene and the frame rate required for a given application, there is often a corresponding practical limit to the quality that

Figure 8.21
Soft shadow rendering—64 samples per pixel.

can be achieved. Samping 64 points per pixel, such as in Figure 8.21, is usually impractical.

A commonly used algorithm for implementing PCF is to sample four nearby texels per pixel, with the samples selected at specified offset distances from the texel which corresponds to the pixel. As we process each pixel, we alter the offsets used to determine which four texels are sampled. Altering the offsets in a staggered manner is sometimes called *dithering*, and aims to make the soft shadow boundary appear less "blocky" than it ordinarily would given the small number of sample points.

A common approach is to assume one of four different offset patterns—we can choose which pattern to use for a given pixel by computing the pixel's glFragCoord mod 2. Recall that glFragCoord is of type vec2, containing the x and y coordinates of the pixel location; the result of the mod computation is then one of four values: (0,0), (0,1), (1,0), or (1,1). We use this result to select one of our four different offset patterns in texel space (i.e., in the shadow map).

The offset patterns are typically specified in the x and y directions with different combinations of -1.5, -0.5, $+0.5$, and $+1.5$ (these can also be scaled as desired). More specifically, the four usual offset patterns for each of the cases resulting from the glFragCoord mod 2 computation are

case (0,0) sample points:	case (0,1) sample points:	case (1,0) sample points:	case (1,1) sample points:
$(s_x-1.5, s_y+1.5)$	$(s_x-1.5, s_y+0.5)$	$(s_x-0.5, s_y+1.5)$	$(s_x-0.5, s_y+0.5)$
$(s_x-1.5, s_y-0.5)$	$(s_x-1.5, s_y-1.5)$	$(s_x-0.5, s_y-0.5)$	$(s_x-0.5, s_y-1.5)$
$(s_x+0.5, s_y+1.5)$	$(s_x+0.5, s_y+0.5)$	$(s_x+1.5, s_y+1.5)$	$(s_x+1.5, s_y+0.5)$
$(s_x+0.5, s_y-0.5)$	$(s_x+0.5, s_y-1.5)$	$(s_x+1.5, s_y-0.5)$	$(s_x+1.5, s_y-1.5)$

S_x and S_y refer to the location (S_x, S_y) in the shadow map corresponding to the pixel being rendered, identified as shadow_coord in the code examples throughout this chapter. These four offset patterns are illustrated in Figure 8.22, with each case shown in a different color. In each case, the texel corresponding to the pixel being rendered is at the origin of the graph for that case. Note that when shown together in Figure 8.23, the staggering/dithering of the offsets is apparent.

Let's walk through the entire computation for a particular pixel. Assume the pixel being rendered is located at glFragCoord = (48,13). We start by determining the four shadow map sample points for the pixel. To do that, we would compute vec2(48,13) mod 2, which equals (0,1). From that we would choose the offsets shown

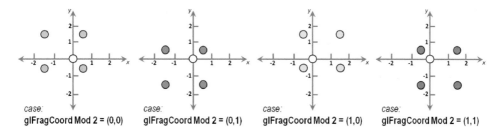

Figure 8.22
Dithered four-pixel PCF sampling cases.

for case (0,1), shown in green in Figure 8.22, and the specific points to be sampled in the shadow map (assuming that no scaling of the offsets has been specified) would be

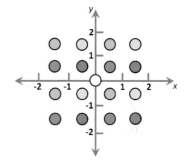

- (shadow_coord.x–1.5, shadow_coord.y+0.5)
- (shadow_coord.x–1.5, shadow_coord.y–1.5)
- (shadow_coord.x+0.5, shadow_coord.y+0.5)
- (shadow_coord.x+0.5, shadow_coord.y–1.5)

(Recall that shadow_coord is the location of the texel in the shadow map corresponding to the pixel being rendered—shown as a white circle in Figures 8.22 and 8.23.)

Figure 8.23
Dithered four-pixel PCF sampling (four cases shown together).

We next call textureProj() on each of these four points, which in each case returns either 0.0 or 1.0 depending on whether or not that sampled point is in shadow. We sum the four results and divide by 4.0 to determine the percentage of sampled points which are in shadow. This percentage is then used as a multiplier to determine the amount of diffuse and specular lighting to be applied when rendering the current pixel.

Despite the small sampling size—only 4 samples per pixel—this dithered approach can often produce surprisingly good soft shadows. Figure 8.24 was generated using 4-point dithered PCF. While not

Figure 8.24
Soft shadow rendering—four samples per pixel, dithered.

quite as good as the 64-point sampled version shown previously in Figure 8.21, it renders considerably faster.

In the next section, we develop the GLSL fragment shader that produced both this 4-sample dithered PCF soft shadow and the previously shown 64-sample PCF soft shadow.

8.7.3 A Soft Shadow/PCF Program

As mentioned earlier, the soft shadow computation can be done entirely in the fragment shader. Program 8.2 shows the fragment shader that replaces the one in Figure 8.7. The PCF additions are highlighted.

Program 8.2 Percentage Closer Filtering (PCF)

Fragment Shader

```
#version 430
// all variable declarations are unchanged
. . .

// Returns the shadow depth value for a texel at distance (x,y) from shadow_coord. Recall that
// shadow_coord is the location in the shadow map corresponding to the current pixel being rendered.

float lookup(float ox, float oy)
{   float t = textureProj(shadowTex,
        shadow_coord + vec4(ox * 0.001 * shadow_coord.w, oy * 0.001 * shadow_coord.w,
        -0.01, 0.0));   // the third parameter (-0.01) is an offset to counteract shadow acne
    return t;
}

void main(void)
{   float shadowFactor = 0.0;
    vec3 L = normalize(vLightDir);
    vec3 N = normalize(vNormal);
    vec3 V = normalize(-vVertPos);
    vec3 H = normalize(vHalfVec);

    // ----- this section produces a 4-sample dithered soft shadow
    float swidth = 2.5;          // tunable amount of shadow spread
    // produces one of 4 sample patterns depending on glFragCoord mod 2
    vec2 offset = mod(floor(gl_FragCoord.xy), 2.0) * swidth;
    shadowFactor += lookup(-1.5*swidth + offset.x,  1.5*swidth - offset.y);
```

```
shadowFactor += lookup(-1.5*swidth + offset.x, -0.5*swidth - offset.y);
shadowFactor += lookup( 0.5*swidth + offset.x,  1.5*swidth - offset.y);
shadowFactor += lookup( 0.5*swidth + offset.x, -0.5*swidth - offset.y);
shadowFactor = shadowFactor / 4.0;     // shadowFactor is an average of the four sampled points

// ----- this section, if un-commented, produces a 64-sample hi resolution soft shadow
//   float swidth = 2.5;        // tunable amount of shadow spread
//   float endp = swidth*3.0 +swidth/2.0;
//   for (float m=-endp ; m<=endp ; m=m+swidth)
//   {   for (float n=-endp ; n<=endp ; n=n+swidth)
//       {       shadowFactor += lookup(m,n);
//   }   }
//   shadowFactor = shadowFactor / 64.0;

vec4 shadowColor = globalAmbient * material.ambient + light.ambient * material.ambient;

vec4 lightedColor = light.diffuse * material.diffuse * max(dot(L,N),0.0)
                  + light.specular * material.specular
                  * pow(max(dot(H,N),0.0),material.shininess*3.0);

fragColor = vec4((shadowColor.xyz + shadowFactor*(lightedColor.xyz)),1.0);
}
```

The fragment shader shown in Program 8.2 contains code for both the 4-sample and 64-sample PCF soft shadows. First, a function lookup() is defined to make the sampling process more convenient. It makes a call to the GLSL function textureProj() that does a lookup in the shadow texture, but offset by a specified amount (ox,oy). The offset is multiplied by 1/windowsize, which here we have simply hardcoded to .001 assuming a window size of 1000×1000 pixels.[2]

The 4-sample dithered computation appears highlighted in main() and follows the algorithm described in the previous section. A scale factor swidth has been added that can be used to adjust the size of the "soft" region at the edge of the shadows.

The 64-sample code follows, and is commented out. It can be used instead of the 4-sample computation, by uncommenting it and instead commenting out the 4-sample code. The swidth scale factor in the 64-sample code is used as a step size in the nested loop that samples points at various distances from the

---

[2] We have also multiplied the offset by the w component of the shadow coordinate, because OpenGL automatically divides the input coordinate by w during texture lookup. This operation, called *perspective divide*, is one which we have ignored up to this point. It must be accounted for here. For more information on *perspective divide*, see [LO12].

pixel being rendered. For example, using the value of swidth shown (2.5), points would be sampled along each axis at distances of 1.25, 3.75, 6.25, and 8.25 in both directions—then scaled based on the window size (as described earlier) and used as texture coordinates into the shadow texture. With this many samples, dithering is generally not necessary to obtain good results.

Figure 8.25 shows our running torus/pyramid shadow mapping example, incorporating PCF soft shadowing with the fragment shader from Program 8.2, for both 4-sample and 64-sample approaches. The value chosen for swidth is scene dependent; for the torus/pyramid example it was set to 2.5, whereas for the dolphin example shown previously in Figure 8.21, swidth was set to 8.0.

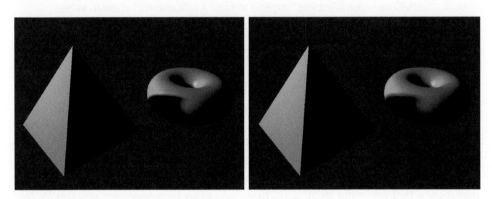

Figure 8.25
PCF Soft shadow rendering—4 samples per pixel, dithered (left), and 64 samples per pixel, not dithered (right).

SUPPLEMENTAL NOTES

In this chapter we have only given the most basic of introductions to the world of shadows in 3D graphics. Even using the basic shadow mapping methods presented here will likely require further study if used in more complex scenes.

For example, when adding shadows to a scene in which some of the objects are textured, it is necessary to ensure that the fragment shader properly distinguishes between the shadow texture and other textures. A simple way of doing this is to bind them to different texture units, such as

```
layout (binding = 0) uniform sampler2DShadow shTex;
layout (binding = 1) uniform sampler2D otherTexture;
```

Then the JOGL application can refer to the two samplers by their binding values.

When a scene utilizes multiple lights, multiple shadow textures are necessary—one for each light source. And a *pass one* will need to be performed for each one, with the results blended in pass two.

Although we have used perspective projection at each phase of shadow mapping, it is worth noting that *orthographic* projection is often preferred when the light source is distant and directional, rather than the positional light we utilized.

Generating realistic shadows is a rich and complex area of computer graphics, and many of the available techniques are outside the scope of this text. Readers interested in more detail are encouraged to investigate more specialized resources such as [ES12], [GP10], and [MI16].

Section 8.7.3 contains an example of a GLSL *function* (aside from the "main"). As in the C language, functions must be defined before (or "above") where they are called, or else a forward declaration must be provided. In the example, a forward declaration isn't required because the function has been defined above the call to it.

Exercises

8.1 In Program 8.1, experiment with different settings for glPolygonOffset(), and observe the effects on shadow artifacts such as Peter Panning.

8.2 *(PROJECT)* Modify Program 8.1 so that the *light* can be positioned by moving the mouse, similar to Exercise 7.1. You will probably notice that some lighting positions exhibit shadow artifacts, while others look fine.

8.3 *(PROJECT)* Add animation to Program 8.1, such that either the objects or the light (or both) move around on their own—such as one revolving around the other. The shadow effects will be more pronounced if you add a ground plane to the scene, such as the one illustrated in Figure 8.14.

8.4 *(PROJECT)* Modify Program 8.2 to replace the hardcoded values 0.001 in the lookup() function, with the more accurate values of 1.0/shadowbufferwidth and 1.0/shadowbufferheight. Observe to what degree this change makes a difference (or not) for various window sizes.

8.5 *(RESEARCH)* More sophisticated implementations of percentage closer filtering (PCF) take into account the relative distance between the light and the shadow versus the light and the occluder. Doing this can make soft shadows more realistic, by allowing their penumbra to change in size as the light moves closer or further from the occluder (or as the occluder moves closer or further from the shadow). Study existing methods for incorporating this capability, and add it to Program 8.2.

References

[AS14] E. Angel and D. Shreiner, *Interactive Computer Graphics: A Top-Down Approach with WebGL*, 7th ed. (Pearson, 2014).

[BL88] J. Blinn, "Me and My (Fake) Shadow," *IEEE Computer Graphics and Applications* 8, no. 2 (1988).

[CR77] F. Crow, "Shadow Algorithms for Computer Graphics," *Proceedings of SIGGRAPH '77* 11, no. 2 (1977).

[ES12] E. Eisemann, M. Schwarz, U. Assarsson, and M. Wimmer, *Real-Time Shadows* (CRC Press, 2012).

[GP10] *GPU Pro* (series), ed. Wolfgang Engel (A. K. Peters, 2010–2016).

[KS16] J. Kessenich, G. Sellers, and D. Shreiner, *OpenGL Programming Guide: The Official Guide to Learning OpenGL, Version 4.5 with SPIR-V*, 9th ed. (Addison-Wesley, 2016).

[LO12] *Understanding OpenGL's Matrices*, Learn OpenGL ES (2012), accessed May 2018, http://www.learnopengles.com/tag/perspective-divide/

[LU16] F. Luna, *Introduction to 3D Game Programming with DirectX 12*, 2nd ed. (Mercury Learning, 2016).

[MI16] *Common Techniques to Improve Shadow Depth Maps* (Microsoft Corp., 2016), accessed July 2016, https://msdn.microsoft.com/en-us/library/windows/desktop/ee416324(v=vs.85).aspx

[PP16] Peter Pan, Wikipedia, accessed July 2016, https://en.wikipedia.org/wiki/Peter_Pan

SKY AND BACKGROUNDS

■ ■ ■ ■ ■

The realism in an outdoor 3D scene can often be improved by generating a realistic effect at the horizon. As we look beyond our nearby buildings and trees, we are accustomed to seeing large distant objects such as clouds, mountains, or the sun (or at night, the moon and stars). However, adding such objects to our scene as individual models may come at an unacceptable performance cost. A *skybox* or *skydome* provides a relatively simple way of efficiently generating a convincing horizon.

9.1 SKYBOXES

The concept of a *skybox* is a remarkably clever and simple one:

1. Instantiate a cube object.
2. Texture the cube with the desired environment.
3. Position the cube so it surrounds the camera.

We already know how to do all of these steps. There are a few additional details, however.

• *How do we make the texture for our horizon?*

A cube has six faces, and we will need to texture all of them. One way is to use six image files and six texture units. Another common (and efficient) way is to use a single image that contains textures for all six faces, such as shown in Figure 9.1.

Figure 9.1
Six-faced skybox texture cube map.

An image that can texture all six faces of a cube with a single texture unit is an example of a *texture cube map*. The six portions of the cube map correspond to the top, bottom, front, back, and two sides of the cube. When "wrapped" around the cube, it acts as a horizon for a camera placed inside the cube, as shown in Figure 9.2.

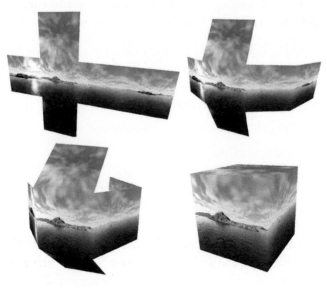

Figure 9.2
Cube map wrapping around the camera.

Texturing the cube with a texture cube map requires specifying appropriate texture coordinates. Figure 9.3 shows the distribution of texture coordinates that are in turn assigned to each of the cube vertices.

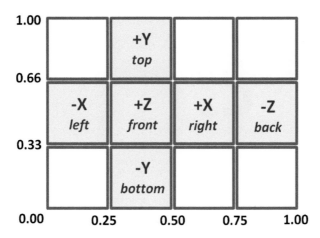

Figure 9.3
Cube map texture coordinates.

- *How do we make the skybox appear "distant"?*

Another important factor in building a skybox is ensuring that the texture appears as a distant horizon. At first, one might assume this would require making the skybox very large. However, it turns out that this isn't desirable because it would stretch and distort the texture. Instead, it is possible to make the skybox *appear* very large (and thus distant) by using the following two-part trick:

- ○ Disable depth testing, and render the skybox first (re-enabling depth testing when rendering the other objects in the scene).
- ○ Move the skybox with the camera (if the camera moves).

By drawing the skybox first with depth testing disabled, the depth buffer will still be filled completely with 1.0's (i.e., maximally far away). Thus all other objects in the scene will be fully rendered; that is, none of the other objects will be blocked by the skybox. This causes the walls of the skybox to appear farther away than every other object, *regardless of the actual size of the skybox*. The actual skybox cube itself can be quite small, as long as it is moved along with the camera whenever the camera moves. Figure 9.4 shows viewing a simple scene (actually just a brick-textured torus) from inside a skybox.

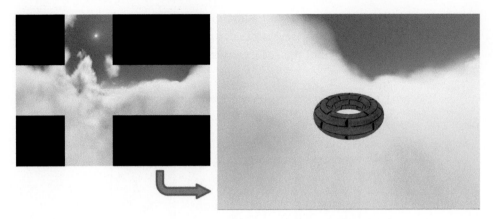

Figure 9.4
Viewing a scene from inside a skybox.

It is instructive to carefully examine Figure 9.4 in relation to the previous Figures 9.2 and 9.3. Note that the portion of the skybox that is visible in the scene is the rightmost section of the cube map. This is because the camera has been placed in the default orientation, facing in the negative Z direction, and is therefore looking at the *back* of the skybox cube (and so labeled in Figure 9.3). Also note that this back portion of the cube map appears horizontally reversed when rendered in the scene; this is because the "back" portion of the cube map has been folded around the camera and thus appears flipped sideways, as shown in Figure 9.2.

- *How do we construct the texture cube map?*

Building a texture cube map image, from artwork or photos, requires care to avoid "seams" at the cube face junctions and to create proper perspective so that the skybox will appear realistic and undistorted. Many tools exist for assisting in this regard: Terragen, Autodesk 3ds Max, Blender, and Adobe Photoshop have tools for building or working with cube maps. There are also many websites offering a variety of off-the-shelf cube maps—some for a price, some for free.

9.2 SKYDOMES

Another way of building a horizon effect is to use a *skydome*. The basic idea is the same as for a skybox, except that instead of using a textured cube, we use a textured *sphere* (or half a sphere). As was done for the skybox, we render the skydome first (with depth testing disabled) and keep the camera positioned at

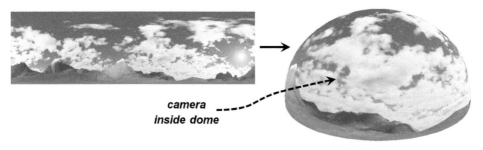

Figure 9.5
Skydome with camera placed inside.

the center of the skydome. (The skydome texture in Figure 9.5 was made using Terragen [TE16].)

Skydomes have some advantages over skyboxes. For example, they are less susceptible to distortion and seams (although spherical distortion at the poles must be accounted for in the texture image). One disadvantage of a skydome is that a sphere or dome is a more complex model than a cube, with many more vertices and a potentially varying number of vertices depending on the desired precision.

When using a skydome to represent an outdoor scene, it is usually combined with a ground plane or some sort of terrain. When using a skydome to represent a scene in space, such as a starfield, it is often more practical to use a sphere, such as shown in Figure 9.6 (a dashed line has been added for clarity in visualizing the sphere).

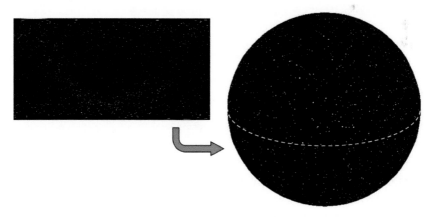

Figure 9.6
Skydome of stars using a sphere (starfield from [BO01]).

9.3 ■ IMPLEMENTING A SKYBOX

Despite the advantages of a skydome, skyboxes are still more common. They also are better supported in OpenGL, which is advantageous when doing *environment mapping* (covered later in this chapter). For these reasons, we will focus on skybox implementation.

There are two methods for implementing a skybox: building a simple one from scratch or using the cube map facilities in OpenGL. Each has its advantages, so we will cover both.

9.3.1 ■ Building a Skybox from Scratch

We have already covered almost everything needed to build a simple skybox. A cube model was presented in Chapter 4; we can assign the texture coordinates as shown earlier in this chapter in Figure 9.3. We saw how to read in textures and how to position objects in 3D space. We will see how to easily enable and disable depth testing (it's a single line of code).

Program 9.1 shows the code organization for our simple skybox, with a scene consisting of just a single textured torus. Texture coordinate assignments and calls to enable/disable depth testing are highlighted.

Program 9.1 Simple Skybox

```
public class Code extends JFrame implements GLEventListener,
{
    //  all variable declarations, constructor, and init() same as before
    . . .
    public void display(GLAutoDrawable drawable)
    {   // clear color and depth buffers, and create projection and camera view matrix as before
        . . .
        gl.glUseProgram(renderingProgram);
        // Prepare to draw the skybox first.  The M matrix places the skybox at the camera location
        mMat.identity().setTranslation(cameraLoc.x(), cameraLoc.y(), cameraLoc.z());

        // build the MODEL-VIEW matrix
        mvMat.identity();
        mvMat.mul(vMat);
        mvMat.mul(mMat);

        // put MV and PROJ matrices into uniforms, as before
        . . .
```

```
// set up buffer containing vertices
gl.glBindBuffer(GL_ARRAY_BUFFER, vbo[0]);
gl.glVertexAttribPointer(0,3, GL_FLOAT, false, 0, 0);
gl.glEnableVertexAttribArray(0);

// set up buffer containing texture coordinates
gl.glBindBuffer(GL_ARRAY_BUFFER, vbo[1]);
gl.glVertexAttribPointer(1,2, GL_FLOAT, false, 0, 0);
gl.glEnableVertexAttribArray(1);

// activate the skybox texture
gl.glActiveTexture(GL_TEXTURE0);
gl.glBindTexture(GL_TEXTURE_2D, skyboxTexture);
gl.glEnable(GL_CULL_FACE);
gl.glFrontFace(GL_CCW);          // cube has CW winding order, but we are viewing its interior

gl.glDisable(GL_DEPTH_TEST);
gl.glDrawArrays(GL_TRIANGLES, 0, 36);  // draw the skybox without depth testing
gl.glEnable(GL_DEPTH_TEST);

// now draw desired scene objects as before
. . .
gl.glDrawElements( . . . );          // as before for scene objects
}

private void setupVertices()
{   // cube_vertices defined same as before
    // cube texture coordinates for the skybox as they appear in Figure 9.3
    float[ ] cubeTextureCoord =
    {   1.00f, 0.66f, 1.00f, 0.33f, 0.75f, 0.33f,   // back face lower right
        0.75f, 0.33f, 0.75f, 0.66f, 1.00f, 0.66f,   // back face upper left
        0.75f, 0.33f, 0.50f, 0.33f, 0.75f, 0.66f,   // right face lower right
        0.50f, 0.33f, 0.50f, 0.66f, 0.75f, 0.66f,   // right face upper left
        0.50f, 0.33f, 0.25f, 0.33f, 0.50f, 0.66f,   // front face lower right
        0.25f, 0.33f, 0.25f, 0.66f, 0.50f, 0.66f,   // front face upper left
        0.25f, 0.33f, 0.00f, 0.33f, 0.25f, 0.66f,   // left face lower right
        0.00f, 0.33f, 0.00f, 0.66f, 0.25f, 0.66f,   // left face upper left
        0.25f, 0.33f, 0.50f, 0.33f, 0.50f, 0.00f,   // bottom face upper right
        0.50f, 0.00f, 0.25f, 0.00f, 0.25f, 0.33f,   // bottom face lower left
        0.25f, 1.00f, 0.50f, 1.00f, 0.50f, 0.66f,   // top face upper right
        0.50f, 0.66f, 0.25f, 0.66f, 0.25f, 1.00f    // top face lower left
    };
    // set up buffers for cube and scene objects as usual
}
// modules for loading shaders, textures, etc. as before
}
```

Standard texturing shaders are now used for all objects in the scene, including the cube map:

Vertex Shader

```
#version 430
layout (location = 0) in vec3 position;
layout (location = 1) in vec2 tex_coord;
out vec2 tc;
uniform mat4 mv_matrix;
uniform mat4 proj_matrix;
layout (binding = 0) uniform sampler2D s;

void main(void)
{   tc = tex_coord;
    gl_Position = proj_matrix * mv_matrix * vec4(position,1.0);
}
```

Fragment Shader

```
#version 430
in vec2 tc;
out vec4 fragColor;
uniform mat4 mv_matrix;
uniform mat4 proj_matrix;
layout (binding = 0) uniform sampler2D s;

void main(void)
{   fragColor = texture(s,tc);
}
```

The output of Program 9.1 is shown in Figure 9.7, for each of two different cube map textures.

As mentioned earlier, skyboxes are susceptible to image distortion and *seams*. Seams are lines that are sometimes visible where two texture images meet, such as along the edges of the cube. Figure 9.8 shows an example of a seam in the upper part of the image that is an artifact of running Program 9.1. Avoiding seams requires careful construction of the cube map image and assignment of precise texture coordinates. There exist tools for reducing seams along image edges (such as [Gl16]); however, this topic is outside the scope of this book.

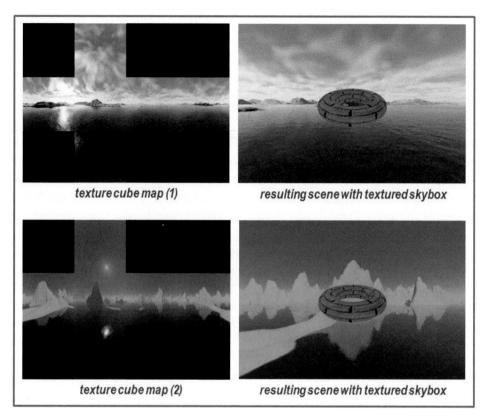

texture cube map (1)　　　resulting scene with textured skybox

texture cube map (2)　　　resulting scene with textured skybox

Figure 9.7
Simple skybox results.

Figure 9.8
Skybox "seam" artifact.

9.3.2 Using OpenGL Cube Maps

Another way to build a skybox is to use an OpenGL *texture cube map*. OpenGL cube maps are a bit more complex than the simple approach we saw in the previous section. There are advantages, however, to using OpenGL cube maps, such as seam reduction and support for environment mapping.

OpenGL texture cube maps are similar to *3D textures* that we will study later, in that they are accessed using three texture coordinates—often labeled (*s,t,r*)—rather than two as we have been doing thus far. Another unique characteristic of OpenGL texture cube maps is that the images in them are oriented with texture coordinate (0,0,0) at the upper left (rather than the usual lower left) of the texture image; this is often a source of confusion.

Whereas the method shown in Program 9.1 reads in a single image for texturing the cube map, the loadCubeMap() function shown in Program 9.2 reads in six separate cube face image files. There are two approaches we could use to read in the six image files and then build the cube map. We could use the JOGL TextureIO and TextureData classes as we did throughout Chapter 5 or we could use the AWT tools described at the end of Chapter 5. In this chapter, we choose the latter approach as it affords more flexibility with respect to whether or not we vertically flip the textures to accomodate the aforementioned difference in texture coordinate orientation.

In the loadCubeMap() function, the six texture image files are read in using the getRGBAPixelData() function described back in Section 5.12. We set its second parameter to false, so that it doesn't flip the textures vertically—this is because OpenGL automatically does a vertical flip for texture cube maps.

After reading in the textures and converting them to ByteBuffers, we then generate a single texture of type GL_TEXTURE_CUBE_MAP. OpenGL requires that we specify the size of the texture images using the glTexStorage2D() function—in this case they are 1024×1024 (they must be square). Finally, the loadCubeMap() function uses glTexSubImage2D() to assign each texture to a cube face.

The init() function now includes a call to enable GL_TEXTURE_CUBE_MAP_SEAMLESS, which tells OpenGL to attempt to blend adjoining edges of the cube to reduce or eliminate seams. In display(), the cube's vertices are sent down the pipeline as before, but this time it is unnecessary to send the cube's texture coordinates. As we will see, this is because an OpenGL texture cube map usually uses the cube's vertex positions as its texture coordinates. After disabling depth testing, the cube is drawn. Depth testing is then re-enabled for the rest of the scene.

The completed OpenGL texture cube map is referenced by an int identifier. As was the case for shadow mapping, artifacts along a border can be reduced by setting the texture wrap mode to "clamp to edge." In this case it can help further reduce seams. Note that this is set for all three texture coordinates (s, t, and r).

The texture is accessed in the fragment shader with a special type of sampler called a samplerCube. In a texture cube map, the value returned from the sampler is the texel "seen" from the origin as viewed along the direction vector (s,t,r). As a result, we can usually simply use the incoming interpolated vertex positions as the texture coordinates. In the vertex shader, we assign the cube vertex positions into the outgoing texture coordinate attribute so that they will be interpolated when they reach the fragment shader. Note also in the vertex shader that we convert the incoming view matrix to 3×3, and then back to 4×4. This "trick" effectively removes the translation component, while retaining the rotation (recall that translation values are found in the fourth column of a transformation matrix). This fixes the cube map at the camera location, while still allowing the synthetic camera to "look around."

Program 9.2 OpenGL Cube Map Skybox

Java/JOGL application

```
. . .
public void init(GLAutoDrawable drawable)
{   GL4 gl = (GL4) GLContext.getCurrentGL();

    // rendering programs and shaders for the torus, and for the cubemap
    renderingProgram = Utils.createShaderProgram("vertShader.glsl", "fragShader.glsl");
    renderingProgramCubeMap = Utils.createShaderProgram("vertCShader.glsl", "fragCShader.glsl");

    setupVertices();

    brickTexture = Utils.loadTexture("brick1.jpg");  // texture for the torus in the scene
    gl.glBindTexture(GL_TEXTURE_2D, brickTexture);
    gl.glTexParameteri(GL_TEXTURE_2D, GL_TEXTURE_WRAP_S, GL_REPEAT);
    gl.glTexParameteri(GL_TEXTURE_2D, GL_TEXTURE_WRAP_T, GL_REPEAT);

    skyboxTexture = Utils.loadCubeMap("cubeMap");        // folder containing the skybox textures
    gl.glEnable(GL_TEXTURE_CUBE_MAP_SEAMLESS);
}
public void display(GLAutoDrawable drawable)
{   //  clear color and depth buffers, projection and camera view matrix as before.
    . . .
    // draw cube map first – note that it now requires a different rendering program
    gl.glUseProgram(renderingProgramCubeMap);

    // put the P and V matrices into their corresponding uniforms.
    . . .
```

```
    // set up vertices buffer for cube (buffer for texture coordinates not necessary)
    gl.glBindBuffer(GL_ARRAY_BUFFER, vbo[0]);
    gl.glVertexAttribPointer(0, 3, GL_FLOAT, false, 0, 0);
    gl.glEnableVertexAttribArray(0);

    // make the cube map the active texture
    gl.glActiveTexture(GL_TEXTURE0);
    gl.glBindTexture(GL_TEXTURE_CUBE_MAP, skyboxTexture);

    // disable depth testing, and then draw the cube map
    gl.glEnable(GL_CULL_FACE);
    gl.glFrontFace(GL_CCW);
    gl.glDisable(GL_DEPTH_TEST);
    gl.glDrawArrays(GL_TRIANGLES, 0, 36);
    gl.glEnable(GL_DEPTH_TEST);

    // draw remainder of the scene
    . . .
}


public int loadCubeMap(String dirName)
{   GL4 gl = (GL4) GLContext.getCurrentGL();

    // assumes that the six file names are xp, xn, yp, yn, zp, and zn and are JPG format
    String topFile = dirName + File.separator + "yp.jpg";
    String leftFile = dirName + File.separator + "xn.jpg";
    String backFile = dirName + File.separator + "zn.jpg";
    String rightFile = dirName + File.separator + "xp.jpg";
    String frontFile = dirName + File.separator + "zp.jpg";
    String bottomFile = dirName + File.separator + "yn.jpg";

    BufferedImage topImage = getBufferedImage(topFile);
    BufferedImage leftImage = getBufferedImage(leftFile);
    BufferedImage frontImage = getBufferedImage(frontFile);
    BufferedImage rightImage = getBufferedImage(rightFile);
    BufferedImage backImage = getBufferedImage(backFile);
    BufferedImage bottomImage = getBufferedImage(bottomFile);

    // getRGBAPixel is from Chapter 5. This time image NOT flipped because OpenGL does it for us
    byte[ ] topRGBA = getRGBAPixelData(topImage, false);
    byte[ ] leftRGBA = getRGBAPixelData(leftImage, false);
    byte[ ] frontRGBA = getRGBAPixelData(frontImage, false);
    byte[ ] rightRGBA = getRGBAPixelData(rightImage, false);
    byte[ ] backRGBA = getRGBAPixelData(backImage, false);
    byte[ ] bottomRGBA = getRGBAPixelData(bottomImage, false);
```

```
ByteBuffer topWrappedRGBA = ByteBuffer.wrap(topRGBA);
ByteBuffer leftWrappedRGBA = ByteBuffer.wrap(leftRGBA);
ByteBuffer frontWrappedRGBA = ByteBuffer.wrap(frontRGBA);
ByteBuffer rightWrappedRGBA = ByteBuffer.wrap(rightRGBA);
ByteBuffer backWrappedRGBA = ByteBuffer.wrap(backRGBA);
ByteBuffer bottomWrappedRGBA = ByteBuffer.wrap(bottomRGBA);

int[ ] textureIDs = new int[1];
gl.glGenTextures(1, textureIDs, 0);
int textureID = textureIDs[0];

gl.glBindTexture(GL_TEXTURE_CUBE_MAP, textureID);
gl.glTexStorage2D(GL_TEXTURE_CUBE_MAP, 1, GL_RGBA8, 1024, 1024);

// attach the image texture to each face of the currently active OpenGL texture ID
gl.glTexSubImage2D(GL_TEXTURE_CUBE_MAP_POSITIVE_X, 0, 0, 0, 1024, 1024,
        GL_RGBA, GL.GL_UNSIGNED_BYTE, rightWrappedRGBA);
gl.glTexSubImage2D(GL_TEXTURE_CUBE_MAP_NEGATIVE_X, 0, 0, 0, 1024, 1024,
        GL_RGBA, GL.GL_UNSIGNED_BYTE, leftWrappedRGBA);
gl.glTexSubImage2D(GL_TEXTURE_CUBE_MAP_NEGATIVE_Y, 0, 0, 0, 1024, 1024,
        GL_RGBA, GL.GL_UNSIGNED_BYTE, bottomWrappedRGBA);
gl.glTexSubImage2D(GL_TEXTURE_CUBE_MAP_POSITIVE_Y, 0, 0, 0, 1024, 1024,
        GL_RGBA, GL.GL_UNSIGNED_BYTE, topWrappedRGBA);
gl.glTexSubImage2D(GL_TEXTURE_CUBE_MAP_POSITIVE_Z, 0, 0, 0, 1024, 1024,
        GL_RGBA, GL.GL_UNSIGNED_BYTE, frontWrappedRGBA);
gl.glTexSubImage2D(GL_TEXTURE_CUBE_MAP_NEGATIVE_Z, 0, 0, 0, 1024, 1024,
        GL_RGBA, GL.GL_UNSIGNED_BYTE, backWrappedRGBA);

// to help reduce seams
gl.glTexParameteri(GL_TEXTURE_CUBE_MAP, GL_TEXTURE_WRAP_S, GL_CLAMP_TO_EDGE);
gl.glTexParameteri(GL_TEXTURE_CUBE_MAP, GL_TEXTURE_WRAP_T, GL_CLAMP_TO_EDGE);
gl.glTexParameteri(GL_TEXTURE_CUBE_MAP, GL_TEXTURE_WRAP_R, GL_CLAMP_TO_EDGE);

return textureID;
}
```

Vertex shader

```
#version 430
layout (location = 0) in vec3 position;
out vec3 tc;

uniform mat4 v_matrix;
uniform mat4 proj_matrix;
layout (binding = 0) uniform samplerCube samp;
```

```
void main(void)
{
    tc = position;                              // texture coordinates are simply the vertex coordinates
    mat4 vrot_matrix = mat4(mat3(v_matrix));   // removes translation from view matrix
    gl_Position = proj_matrix * vrot_matrix * vec4(position, 1.0);
}
```

Fragment shader

```
#version 430
in vec3 tc;
out vec4 fragColor;

uniform mat4 v_matrix;
uniform mat4 proj_matrix;
layout (binding = 0) uniform samplerCube samp;

void main(void)
{   fragColor = texture(samp,tc);
}
```

9.4 ENVIRONMENT MAPPING

When we looked at lighting and materials, we considered the "shininess" of objects. However, we never modeled *very* shiny objects, such as a mirror or something made out of chrome. Such objects don't just have small specular highlights; they actually reflect their surroundings. When we look at them, we see things in the room, or sometimes even our own reflection. The ADS lighting model doesn't provide a way of simulating this effect.

Texture cube maps, however, offer a relatively simple way to simulate reflective surfaces—at least partially. The trick is to *use the cube map to texture the reflective object itself.*[1] Doing this so that it appears realistic requires finding texture coordinates that correspond to the part of the surrounding environment we should see reflected in the object from our vantage point.

Figure 9.9 illustrates the strategy of using a combination of the view vector and the normal vector to calculate a *reflection vector* which is then used to look up a texel from the cube map. The reflection vector can thus be used to access the texture cube map directly. When the cube map performs this function, it is referred to as an *environment map.*

[1] This same trick is also possible in those cases where a skydome is being used instead of a skybox, by texturing the reflective object with the skydome texture image.

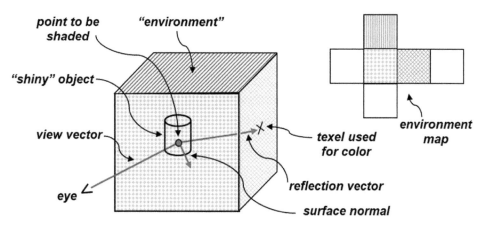

Figure 9.9
Environment mapping overview.

We computed reflection vectors earlier when we studied Blinn-Phong lighting. The concept here is similar, except that now we are using the reflection vector to look up a value from a texture map. This technique is called *environment mapping*, or *reflection mapping*. If the cube map is implemented using the second method we described (in Section 9.3.2—that is, as an OpenGL GL_TEXTURE_CUBE_MAP), then OpenGL can perform the environment mapping lookup in the same manner as was done for texturing the cube map itself. We use the view vector and the surface normal to compute a reflection of the view vector off the object's surface. The reflection vector can then be used to sample the texture cube map image directly. The lookup is facilitated by the OpenGL samplerCube; recall from the previous section that the samplerCube is indexed by a view direction vector. The reflection vector is thus well suited for looking up the desired texel.

The implementation requires a relatively small amount of additional code. Program 9.3 shows the changes that would be made to the display() and init() functions and the relevant shaders for rendering a "reflective" torus using environment mapping. The changes are highlighted. It is worth noting that if Blinn-Phong lighting is present, many of these additions would likely already be present. The only truly new section of code is in the fragment shader (in the main() method).

In fact, it might at first appear as if the highlighted code in Program 9.3 (i.e., the yellow sections) aren't really new at all. Indeed, we have seen nearly identical code before, when we studied lighting. However, in this case, the normal and reflection vectors are used for an entirely different purpose. Previously they were used to implement the ADS lighting model. Here they are instead used to compute texture coordinates for environment mapping. We highlighted these lines of code so that the reader can more easily track the use of normals and reflection computations for this new purpose.

The result, showing an environment-mapped "chrome" torus, is shown in Figure 9.10.

Figure 9.10
Example of environment mapping to create a reflective torus.

Program 9.3 Environment Mapping

```
public void display(GLAutoDrawable drawable)
{   //   the code for drawing the cube map is unchanged.
    . . .
    //   the changes are all in drawing the torus:

    gl.glUseProgram(renderingProgram);

    //   uniform locations for matrix transforms, including the transform for normals
    mvLoc = gl.glGetUniformLocation(renderingProgram, "mv_matrix");
    projLoc = gl.glGetUniformLocation(renderingProgram, "proj_matrix");
    nLoc = gl.glGetUniformLocation(renderingProgram, "norm_matrix");

    //   build the MODEL matrix, as before
    mMat.identity();
    mMat.translate(torusLoc.x(), torusLoc.y(), torusLoc.z());
```

```
// build the MODEL-VIEW matrix, as before
mvMat.identity();
mvMat.mul(vMat);
mvMat.mul(mMat);
mvMat.invert(invTrMat);
invTrMat.transpose(invTrMat);

// the normals transform is now included in the uniforms:
gl.glUniformMatrix4fv(mvLoc, 1, false, mvMat.get(vals));
gl.glUniformMatrix4fv(pLoc, 1, false, pMat.get(vals));
gl.glUniformMatrix4fv(nLoc, 1, false, invTrMat.get(vals));

// activate the torus vertices buffer, as before
gl.glBindBuffer(GL_ARRAY_BUFFER, vbo[1]);
gl.glVertexAttribPointer(0, 3, GL_FLOAT, false, 0, 0);
gl.glEnableVertexAttribArray(0);

// we need to activate the torus normals buffer:
gl.glBindBuffer(GL_ARRAY_BUFFER, vbo[2]);
gl.glVertexAttribPointer(1, 3, GL_FLOAT, false, 0, 0);
gl.glEnableVertexAttribArray(1);

// the torus texture is now the cube map
gl.glActiveTexture(GL_TEXTURE0);
gl.glBindTexture(GL_TEXTURE_CUBE_MAP, skyboxTexture);

// drawing the torus is otherwise unchanged
gl.glClear(GL_DEPTH_BUFFER_BIT);
gl.glEnable(GL_CULL_FACE);
gl.glFrontFace(GL_CCW);
gl.glDepthFunc(GL_LEQUAL);

gl.glBindBuffer(GL_ELEMENT_ARRAY_BUFFER, vbo[3]);
gl.glDrawElements(GL_TRIANGLES, numTorusIndices, GL_UNSIGNED_INT, 0);
}
```

Vertex shader

```
#version 430
layout (location = 0) in vec3 position;
layout (location = 1) in vec3 normal;
out vec3 varyingNormal;
out vec3 varyingVertPos;
uniform mat4 mv_matrix;
uniform mat4 proj_matrix;
uniform mat4 norm_matrix;
layout (binding = 0) uniform samplerCube tex_map;
```

```
void main(void)
{   varyingVertPos = (mv_matrix * vec4(position,1.0)).xyz;
    varyingNormal = (norm_matrix * vec4(normal,1.0)).xyz;
    gl_Position = proj_matrix * mv_matrix * vec4(position,1.0);
}
```

Fragment shader

```
#version 430
in vec3 varyingNormal;
in vec3 varyingVertPos;
out vec4 fragColor;
uniform mat4 mv_matrix;
uniform mat4 proj_matrix;
uniform mat4 norm_matrix;
layout (binding = 0) uniform samplerCube tex_map;

void main(void)
{   vec3 r = -reflect(normalize(-varyingVertPos), normalize(varyingNormal));
    fragColor = texture(tex_map, r);
}
```

Although two sets of shaders are required for this scene—one set for the cube map and another set for the torus—only the shaders used to draw the torus are shown in Program 9.3. This is because the shaders used for rendering the cube map are unchanged from Program 9.2. The changes made to Program 9.2, resulting in Program 9.3, are summarized as follows:

*in **init()**:*

- A buffer of normals for the torus is created (actually done in setupVertices(), called by init()).
- The buffer of texture coordinates for the torus is no longer needed.

*in **display()**:*

- The matrix for transforming normals (dubbed "norm_matrix" in Chapter 7) is created and linked to the associated uniform variable.
- The torus normal buffer is activated.
- The texture cube map is activated as the texture for the torus (rather than the "brick" texture).

*in the **vertex shader**:*

- The normal vectors and norm_matrix are added.
- The transformed vertex and normal vector are output in preparation for computing the reflection vector, similar to what was done for lighting and shadows.

*in the **fragment shader**:*

- The reflection vector is computed in a similar way to what was done for lighting.
- The output color is retrieved from the texture (now the cube map), with the lookup texture coordinate now being the reflection vector.

The resulting rendering shown in Figure 9.10 is an excellent example of how a simple trick can achieve a powerful illusion. By simply painting the background on an object, we have made the object look "metallic," when no such ADS material modeling has been done at all. It has also given the appearance that light is reflecting off of the object, even though no ADS lighting whatsoever has been incorporated into the scene. In this example, there even seems to be a specular highlight on the lower left of the torus, because the cube map includes the sun's reflection off of the water.

SUPPLEMENTAL NOTES

Throughout this chapter, we avoided JOGL's texturing tools when building our cube map. However, using JOGL's TextureIO and TextureData classes for this purpose can dramatically shorten the code in the loadCubeMap() function. This is done by first creating the texture cube map:

```
Texture tex = new Texture(GL_TEXTURE_CUBE_MAP);
```

Each of the six texture image files are loaded, for example as follows:

```
TextureData leftFile = TextureIO.newTextureData(glProfile, new File("code/left.jpg"), false, "jpg");
```

Then, each texure is assigned to a cube face:

```
tex.updateImage(gl, leftFile, GL_TEXTURE_CUBE_MAP_NEGATIVE_X);
```

The drawback of this approach is that it isn't as easy to control whether or not a texture image is being flipped vertically, because nowhere do we have direct access to the individual texture objects comprising the cube map. In some cases, it is necessary to provide vertically flipped versions of the original six texture images.

A major limitation of environment mapping, as presented in this chapter, is that it only generates a reflection of the cube map. Other objects rendered in the scene are not reflected in the reflection-mapped object. Depending on the nature of the scene, this might or might not be acceptable. If other objects are present that must be reflected in a mirror or chrome object, other methods must be used. A common approach utilizes the stencil buffer (mentioned earlier in Chapter 8) and is described in various web tutorials ([GR16], [NE14], and [OV12], for example), but is outside the scope of this text.

We didn't include an implementation of skydomes, although they are in some ways arguably simpler than skyboxes and can be less susceptible to distortion. Even environment mapping is simpler—at least the math—but the OpenGL support for cube maps often makes skyboxes more practical. We will generate a skydome later in Chapter 14 when we simulate clouds.

Of the topics covered in the later sections of this textbook, skyboxes and skydomes are arguably among the simplest conceptually. However, getting them to look convincing can consume a lot of time. We have dealt only briefly with some of the issues that can arise (such as seams), but depending on the texture image files used, other issues can occur, requiring additional repair. This is especially true when the scene is animated or when the camera can be moved interactively.

We also glossed over the generation of usable and convincing texture cube map images. There are excellent tools for doing this, one of the most popular being Terragen [TE16]. All of the cube maps in this chapter were made by the authors (except for the starfield in Figure 9.6), using Terragen [TE16].

Exercises

9.1 *(PROJECT)* In Program 9.2, add the ability to move the camera around with the mouse or keyboard. To do this, you will need to utilize the code you developed earlier in Exercise 4.2 for constructing a view matrix. You'll also need to assign mouse or keyboard actions to functions that move the camera forward and backward, and functions that rotate the camera on one or more of its axes (you'll need to write these functions too). After doing this, you should be able to "fly around" in your scene, noting that the skybox always appears to remain at the distant horizon.

9.2 Draw labels on the six cube map image files to confirm that the correct orientation is being achieved. For example, you could draw axis labels on the images, such as the following:

Also use your "labeled" cube map to verify that the reflections in the environment-mapped torus are being rendered correctly.

9.3 *(PROJECT)* Add animation to Program 9.3 so that one (or more) environment-mapped object(s) in the scene rotate or tumble. The simulated reflectivity of the object should be apparent as the skybox texture moves on the object's surface.

9.4 *(PROJECT)* Modify Program 9.3 so that the object in the scene blends environment mapping with a texture. Use a weighted sum in the fragment shader, as described in Chapter 7.

9.5 *(RESEARCH & PROJECT)* Learn the basics of how to use Terragen [TE16] to create a simple cube map. This generally entails making a "world" with the desired terrain and atmospheric patterns (in Terragen), and then positioning Terragen's synthetic camera to save six images representing the front, back, right, left, top, and bottom views. Use your images in Programs 9.2 and 9.3 to see how they appear as cube maps and with environment mapping. The free version of Terragen is quite sufficient for this exercise.

References

[BO01] P. Bourke, "Representing Star Fields," June 2001, accessed July 2016, http://paulbourke.net/miscellaneous/starfield/

[GI16] GNU Image Manipulation Program, accessed July 2016, http://www.gimp.org

[GR16] OpenGL Resources, "Planar Reflections and Refractions Using the Stencil Buffer," accessed July 2016, https://www.opengl.org/archives/resources/code/samples/advanced/advanced97/notes/node90.html

[NE14] NeHeProductions, "Clipping and Reflections Using the Stencil Buffer," 2014, accessed July 2016, http://nehe.gamedev.net/tutorial/clipping__reflections_using_the_stencil_buffer/17004/

[OV12] A. Overvoorde, "Depth and Stencils," 2012, accessed July 2016, https://open.gl/depthstencils

[TE16] Terragen, Planetside Software, LLC, accessed July 2016, http://planetside.co.uk/

ENHANCING SURFACE DETAIL

Suppose we want to model an object with an irregular surface—like the bumpy surface of an orange, the wrinkled surface of a raisin, or the cratered surface of the moon. How would we do it? So far, we have learned two potential methods: (a) we could model the entire irregular surface, which would often be impractical (a highly cratered surface would require a huge number of vertices), or (b) we could apply a texture map image of the irregular surface to a smooth version of the object. The second option is often effective. However, if the scene includes lights and the lights (or camera angle) move, it becomes quickly obvious that the object is statically textured (and smooth) because the light and dark areas on the texture wouldn't change, as they would if the object was actually bumpy.

In this chapter we are going to explore several related methods for using lighting effects to make objects *appear* to have realistic surface texture, even if the underlying object model is smooth. We will start by examining *bump mapping* and *normal mapping*, which can add considerable realism to the objects in our scenes when it would be too computationally expensive to include tiny surface details in the object models. We will also look at ways of actually perturbing the vertices in a smooth surface through *height mapping*, which is useful for generating *terrain* (and other uses).

10.1 BUMP MAPPING

In Chapter 7, we saw how surface normals are critical to creating convincing lighting effects. Light intensity at a pixel is determined largely by the reflection angle, taking into account the light source location, camera location, and the normal vector at the pixel. Thus, we can avoid generating detailed vertices corresponding to a bumpy or

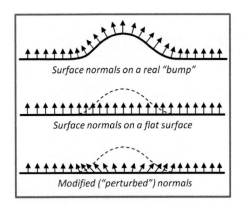

Figure 10.1
Perturbed normal vectors for bump mapping.

Figure 10.2
Procedural bump mapping example.

wrinkled surface if we can find a way of generating the corresponding normals.

Figure 10.1 illustrates the concept of modified normals corresponding to a single "bump."

Thus, if we want to make an object look as though it has bumps (or wrinkles, craters, etc.), one way is to compute the *normals* that would exist on such a surface. Then when the scene is lit, the lighting would produce the desired illusion. This was first proposed by Blinn in 1978 [BL78], and became practical with the advent of the capability of performing per-pixel lighting computations in a fragment shader.

An example is illustrated in the vertex and fragment shaders shown in Program 10.1, which produces a torus with a "golf-ball" surface as shown in Figure 10.2. The code is almost identical to what we saw previously in Program 7.2. The only significant change is in the fragment shader—the incoming interpolated normal vectors (named "varyingNormal" in the original program) are altered with bumps calculated using a sine wave function in the X, Y, and Z axes applied to the original (untransformed) vertices of the torus model. Note that the vertex shader therefore now needs to pass these untransformed vertices down the pipeline.

Altering the normals in this manner, with a mathematical function computed at runtime, is called *procedural bump mapping*.

Program 10.1 Procedural Bump Mapping

Vertex Shader

```
#version 430
//  same as Phong shading, but add this output vertex attribute:
out vec3 originalVertex;
. . .
```

```
void main(void)
{   //   include this pass-through of original vertex for interpolation:
    originalVertex = vertPos;
    . . .
}
```

Fragment Shader

```
#version 430
//  same as Phong shading, but add this input vertex attribute:
in vec3 originalVertex;
. . .
void main(void)
{   . . .
    // add the following to perturb the incoming normal vector:
    float a = 0.25;                    // a controls height of bumps
    float b = 100.0;                   // b controls width of bumps
    float x = originalVertex.x;
    float y = originalVertex.y;
    float z = originalVertex.z;
    N.x = varyingNormal.x + a*sin(b*x);  // perturb incoming normal using sine function
    N.y = varyingNormal.y + a*sin(b*y);
    N.z = varyingNormal.z + a*sin(b*z);
    N = normalize(N);
    // lighting computations and output fragColor (unchanged) now utilize the perturbed normal N
    . . .
}
```

▄10.2▄ NORMAL MAPPING

An alternative to bump mapping is to replace the normals using a lookup table. This allows us to construct bumps for which there is no mathematical function, such as the bumps corresponding to the craters on the moon. A common way of doing this is called *normal mapping*.

To understand how this works, we start by noting that a vector can be stored to reasonable precision in three bytes, one for each of the X, Y, and Z components. This makes it possible to store normals in a color image file, with the R, G, and B components corresponding to X, Y, and Z. RGB values in an image are stored in bytes and are usually interpreted as values in the range [0..1], whereas vectors can have positive or negative component values. If we restrict normal vector components to the range [-1..+1], a simple conversion to enable storing a normal vector N as a pixel in an image file is

$$R = (N_X + 1)/2$$
$$G = (N_Y + 1)/2$$
$$B = (N_Z + 1)/2$$

Normal mapping utilizes an image file (called a *normal map*) that contains normals corresponding to a desired surface appearance in the presence of lighting. In a normal map, the vectors are represented relative to an arbitrary plane X-Y, with their X and Y components representing deviations from "vertical" and their Z component set to 1. A vector strictly perpendicular to the X-Y plane (i.e., with no deviation) would be represented (0,0,1), whereas non-perpendicular vectors would have non-zero X and/or Y components. We use the above formulae to convert to RGB space; for example, (0,0,1) would be stored as (.5,.5,1), since actual offsets range [-1..+1], but RGB values range [0..1].

We can make use of such a normal map through yet another clever application of texture units: Instead of storing colors in the texture unit, we store the desired normal vectors. We can then use a sampler to look up the value in the normal map for a given fragment, and then rather than applying the returned value to the output pixel color (as we did in texture mapping), we instead use it as the normal vector.

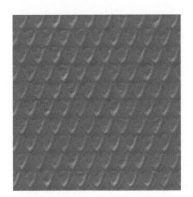

Figure 10.3
Normal mapping image file example [ME11].

One example of such a normal map image file is shown in Figure 10.3. It was generated by applying the GIMP normal mapping plugin [GI16] to a texture from Luna [LU16]. Normal mapping image files are not intended for viewing; we show this one to point out that such images end up being largely blue. This is because every entry in the image file has a B value of 1 (maximum blue), making the image appear "bluish" if viewed.

Figure 10.4 shows two different normal map image files (both are built out of textures

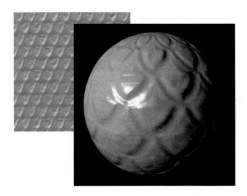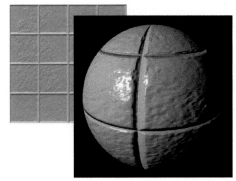

Figure 10.4
Normal mapping examples.

from Luna [LU16]) and the result of applying them to a sphere in the presence of Blinn-Phong lighting.

Normal vectors retrieved from a normal map cannot be utilized directly, because they are defined relative to an arbitrary X-Y plane as described above, without taking into account their position on the object and their orientation in camera space. Our strategy for addressing this will be to build a transformation matrix for converting the normals into camera space, as follows.

At each vertex on an object, we consider a plane that is tangent to the object. The object normal at that vertex is perpendicular to this plane. We define two mutually perpendicular vectors in that plane, also perpendicular to the normal, called the *tangent* and *bitangent* (sometimes called the *binormal*). Constructing our desired transformation matrix requires that our models include a tangent vector for each vertex (the bitangent can be built by computing the cross product of the tangent and the normal). If the model does not already have tangent vectors defined, they could be computed. In the case of a sphere they can be computed exactly, as shown in the following modifications to Program 6.1:

```
. . .
for (int i=0; i<=prec; i++)
{   for (int j=0; j<=prec; j++)
    {   float y = (float)cos(toRadians(180-i*180/prec));
        float x = -(float)cos(toRadians(j*360/prec)) * (float)abs(cos(asin(y)));
        float z = (float)sin(toRadians(j*360/prec)) * (float)abs(cos(asin(y)));
        vertices[i*(prec+1)+j].set(x,y,z));
```

```
// calculate tangent vector
if (((x==0) && (y==1) && (z==0)) || ((x==0) && (y==-1) && (z==0)))   // if north or south pole,
{   tangent[i*(prec+1)+j].set(0.0f, 0.0f, -1.0f);                    //   set tangent to -Z axis
}
else                                              // otherwise, calculate tangent
{   tangent[i*(prec+1)+j] = (new Vector3f(0,1,0)).cross(new Vector3f(x,y,z));
}
. . . // remaining computations are unchanged
}
}
```

For models that don't lend themselves to exact analytic derivation of surface tangents, the tangents can be approximated, for example by drawing vectors from each vertex to the next as they are constructed (or loaded). Note that such an approximation can lead to tangent vectors that are not strictly perpendicular to the corresponding vertex normals. Implementing normal mapping that works across a variety of models therefore needs to take this possibility into account (our solution will).

The tangent vectors are sent from a buffer (VBO) to a vertex attribute in the vertex shader, as is done for the vertices, texture coordinates, and normals. The vertex shader then processes them the same as is done for normal vectors, by applying the inverse transpose of the MV matrix and forwarding the result down the pipeline for interpolation by the rasterizer and ultimately into the fragment shader. The application of the inverse transpose converts the normal and tangent vectors into camera space, after which we construct the bitangent using the cross product.

Once we have the normal, tangent, and bitangent vectors in camera space, we can use them to construct a matrix (called the "TBN" matrix, after its components) which transforms the normals retrieved from the normal map into their corresponding orientation in camera space relative to the surface of the object.

In the fragment shader, the computing of the new normal is done in the calcNewNormal() function. The computation in the third line of the function (the one containing dot(tangent, normal)) ensures that the tangent vector is perpendicular to the normal vector. A cross product between the new tangent and the normal produces the bitangent.

We then create the TBN as a 3×3 mat3 matrix. The mat3 constructor takes three vectors and generates a matrix containing the first vector in the top row, the second vector in the middle row, and the third in the bottom row (similar to building a view matrix from a camera position—see Figure 3.13).

The shader uses the fragment's texture coordinates to extract the normal map entry corresponding to the current fragment. The sampler variable "normMap" is used for this, and in this case is bound to texture unit 0 (note the Java/JOGL application must therefore have attached the normal map image to texture unit 0). To convert the color component from the stored range [0..1] to its original range [-1..+1] we multiply by 2.0 and subtract 1.0.

The TBN matrix is then applied to the resulting normal to produce the final normal for the current pixel. The rest of the shader is identical to the fragment shader used for Phong lighting. The fragment shader is shown in Program 10.2 and is based on a version by Etay Meiri [ME11].

A variety of tools exist for developing normal map images. Some image editing tools, such as GIMP [GI16] and Photoshop [PH16], have such capabilities. Such tools analyze the edges in an image, inferring peaks and valleys and producing a corresponding normal map.

Figure 10.5 shows a texture map of the surface of the moon created by Hastings-Trew [HT16] based on NASA satellite data. The corresponding normal map was generated by applying the GIMP normal map plugin [GP16] to a black-and-white reduction also created by Hastings-Trew.

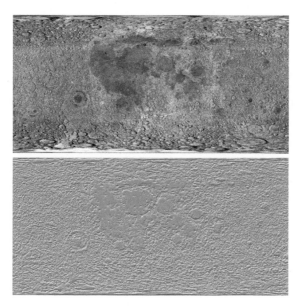

Figure 10.5
Moon, texture and normal map.

Program 10.2 Normal Mapping Fragment Shader

```
#version 430
in vec3 varyingLightDir;
in vec3 varyingVertPos;
in vec3 varyingNormal;
in vec3 varyingTangent;
in vec3 originalVertex;
in vec2 tc;
in vec3 varyingHalfVector;
out vec4 fragColor;

layout (binding=0) uniform sampler2D normMap;
// remaining uniforms same as before
. . .
vec3 calcNewNormal()
{   vec3 normal = normalize(varyingNormal);
    vec3 tangent = normalize(varyingTangent);
    tangent = normalize(tangent - dot(tangent, normal) * normal);   // tangent is perpendicular to normal
    vec3 bitangent = cross(tangent, normal);
    mat3 tbn = mat3(tangent, bitangent, normal);        // TBN matrix to convert to camera space
    vec3 retrievedNormal = texture(normMap,tc).xyz;
    retrievedNormal = retrievedNormal * 2.0 - 1.0;        // convert from RGB space
    vec3 newNormal = tbn * retrievedNormal;
    newNormal = normalize(newNormal);
    return newNormal;
}

void main(void)
{   // normalize the light, normal, and view vectors:
    vec3 L = normalize(varyingLightDir);
    vec3 V = normalize(-varyingVertPos);
    vec3 N = calcNewNormal();

    // get the angle between the light and surface normal:
    float cosTheta = dot(L,N);

    // compute half vector for Blinn optimization:
    vec3 H = normalize(varyingHalfVector);

    // angle between the view vector and reflected light:
    float cosPhi = dot(H,N);

    // compute ADS contributions (per pixel):
    fragColor = globalAmbient * material.ambient
    + light.ambient * material.ambient
    + light.diffuse * material.diffuse * max(cosTheta,0.0)
    + light.specular  * material.specular * pow(max(cosPhi,0.0), material.shininess*3.0);
}
```

 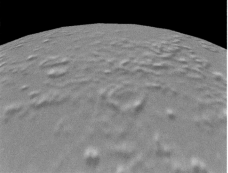

Figure 10.6
Sphere textured with moon texture (left) and normal map (right).

Figure 10.6 shows a sphere with the moon surface rendered in two different ways: on the left, simply textured with the original texture map; on the right, textured with the image normal map (for reference). Normal mapping has not been applied in either case. As realistic as the textured "moon" is, close examination reveals that the texture image was apparently taken when the moon was being lit from the left, because ridge shadows are cast to the right (most clearly evident in the crater at the bottom center). If we were to add lighting to this scene with Phong shading, and then animate the scene by moving the moon, the camera, or the light, those shadows would not change as we would expect them to.

Furthermore, as the light source moves (or as the camera moves), we would expect many specular highlights to appear on the ridges. But a plain textured sphere such as at the left of Figure 10.6 would produce only one specular highlight, corresponding to what would appear on a smooth sphere, which would look very unrealistic. Incorporation of the normal map can improve the realism of lighting on objects such as this considerably.

If we use normal mapping on the sphere (rather than applying the texture), we obtain the results shown in Figure 10.7. Although not as realistic (yet) as standard texturing, it now *does* respond to lighting changes. The first image is lit from the left, and the second is lit from the right. Note the blue and yellow arrows showing the change in diffuse lighting around ridges and the movement of specular highlights.

Figure 10.8 shows the effect of combining normal mapping with standard texturing, in the presence of Phong lighting. The image of the moon is enhanced with diffuse-lit regions and specular highlights that respond to the movement of the

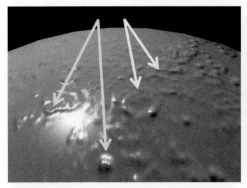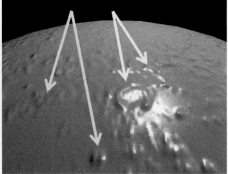

Figure 10.7
Normal map lighting effects on moon.

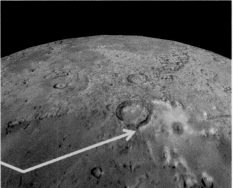

Figure 10.8
Texturing plus normal mapping, with lighting from the left and right.

light source (or camera or object movement). Lighting in the two images is from the left and right sides, respectively.

Our program now requires two textures—one for the moon surface image, and one for the normal map—and thus two samplers. The fragment shader blends the texture color with the color produced by the lighting computation as shown in Program 10.3, using the technique described previously in Section 7.6.

Program 10.3 Texturing plus Normal Map

```
//  variables and structs as in previous fragment shader, plus:
layout (binding=0) uniform sampler2D s0;        // normal map
layout (binding=1) uniform sampler2D s1;        // texture
```

```
void main(void)
{   // computations same as before, until:

    vec3 N = calcNewNormal();
    vec4 texel = texture(s1,tc);  // standard texture

    . . .

    // reflection computations as before, then blend results:
    fragColor = globalAmbient +
        texel * (light.ambient + light.diffuse * max(cosTheta,0.0)
        + light.specular * pow(max(cosPhi,0.0), material.shininess));
}
```

Interestingly, normal mapping can benefit from *mipmapping*, because the same "aliasing" artifacts that we saw in Chapter 5 for texturing also occur when using a texture image for normal mapping. Figure 10.9 shows a normal mapped moon, with and without mipmapping. Although not easily shown in a still image, the sphere at the left (*not* mipmapped) has shimmering artifacts around its perimeter.

Anisotropic filtering (AF) works even better, reducing sparkling artifacts while preserving detail, as illustrated in Figure 10.10 (compare the detail on the edge along the lower right). A version combining equal parts texture and lighting with normal mapping and AF is shown alongside, in Figure 10.11.

The results are imperfect. Shadows appearing in the original texture image will still show on the rendered result, regardless of lighting. Also, while normal

Figure 10.9
Normal mapping artifacts, corrected with mipmapping.

Figure 10.10
Normal mapping with AF.

Figure 10.11
Texturing plus normal mapping with AF.

mapping can affect diffuse and specular effects, it cannot cast shadows. Therefore, this method is best used when the surface features are small.

10.3 HEIGHT MAPPING

We now extend the concept of normal mapping—where a texture image is used to perturb normals—to instead *perturb the vertex locations themselves*. Actually modifying an object's geometry in this way has certain advantages, such as making the surface features visible along the object's edge and enabling the features to respond to shadow mapping. It can also facilitate building *terrain*, as we will see.

A practical approach is to use a texture image to store *height* values, which can then be used to raise (or lower) vertex locations. An image that contains height information is called a *height map*, and using a height map to alter an object's vertices is called *height mapping*. Height maps usually encode height information as grayscale colors: (0,0,0) (black) = *low* height and (1,1,1) (white) = *high* height. This makes it easy to create height maps algorithmically, or by using a "paint" program. The higher the image contrast, the greater the variation in height expressed by the map. These concepts are illustrated in Figure 10.12 (showing a randomly generated map) and Figure 10.13 (showing a map with an organized pattern).

The usefulness of altering vertex locations depends on the model being altered. Vertex manipulation is easily done in the vertex shader, and when there is a high level of detail in the model vertices (such as in a sphere with sufficiently high precision), this approach can work well. However, when the underlying number of vertices is small (such as the corners of a cube), rendering the object's surface relies on vertex interpolation in the rasterizer to fill in the detail. When there are very few vertices available in the vertex shader to perturb, the heights of many pixels would be interpolated rather than retrieved from the height map, leading to poor surface detail. Vertex manipulation in the fragment shader is, of course, impossible because by then the vertices have been rasterized into pixel locations.

Program 10.4 shows a vertex shader that moves the vertices "outward" (i.e., in the direction of the surface normal), by multiplying the vertex normal by the value retrieved from the height map and then adding that product to the vertex position.

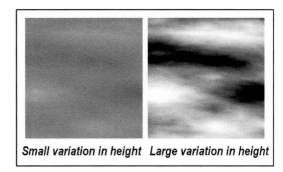

Small variation in height *Large variation in height*

Figure 10.12
Height map examples.

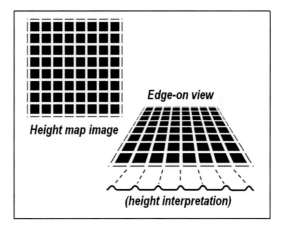

Edge-on view

Height map image

(height interpretation)

Figure 10.13
Height map interpretation.

Program 10.4 Height Mapping in Vertex Shader

```
#version 430

layout (location=0) in vec3 vertPos;
layout (location=1) in vec2 texCoord;
layout (location=2) in vec3 vertNormal;

out vec2 tc;

uniform mat4 mv_matrix;
uniform mat4 proj_matrix;
```

```
layout (binding=0) uniform sampler2D t;          // for texture
layout (binding=1) uniform sampler2D h;          // for heightmap

void main(void)
{   // "p" is the vertex position altered by the height map.
    // Since the height map is grayscale, any of the color components can be
    // used (we use "r"). Dividing by 5.0 is to adjust the height.
    vec4 p = vec4(vertPos,1.0) + vec4( (vertNormal * ((texture(h, texCoord).r) / 5.0f)),1.0f );
    tc = tex_coord;
    gl_Position = proj_matrix * mv_matrix * p;
}
```

Figure 10.14 shows a simple height map (top left) created by scribbling in a paint program. A white square is also drawn in the height map image. A green-tinted version of the height map (bottom left) is used as a texture. When the height map is applied to a rectangular 100×100 grid model using the shader shown in Program 10.4, it produces a sort of "terrain" (shown on the right). Note how the white square results in the precipice at the right.

Figure 10.15 shows another example of doing height mapping in a vertex shader. This time the height map is an outline of the continents of the world [HT16]. It is applied to a sphere textured with a blue-tinted version of the height map (see top left—note the original black and white version is not shown), and lit with Blinn-Phong shading using a normal map (shown at the lower left) built using the

Figure 10.14
Terrain, height mapped in the vertex shader.

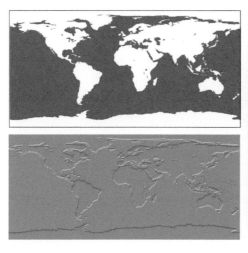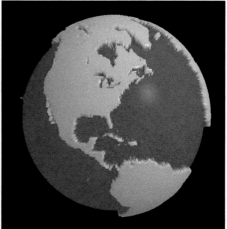

Figure 10.15
Vertex shader-based height mapping, applied to a sphere.

tool *SS_Bump_Generator* [SS16]. The sphere precision was increased to 500 to ensure enough vertices to render the detail. Note how the raised vertices affect not only the lighting, but also the silhouette edges.

The rendered examples shown in Figure 10.14 and Figure 10.15 work acceptably because the two models (grid and sphere) have a sufficient number of vertices to sample the height map values. That is, they each have a fairly large number of vertices, and the height map is relatively coarse and adequately sampled at a low resolution. However, close inspection still reveals the presence of resolution artifacts, such as along the bottom left edge of the raised box at the right of the terrain in Figure 10.14. The reason that the sides of the raised box don't appear perfectly square, and include gradations in color, is because the 100×100 resolution of the underlying grid cannot adequately align perfectly with the white box in the height map, and the resulting rasterization of texture coordinates produces artifacts along the sides.

The limitations of doing height mapping in the vertex shader are further exposed when trying to apply it with a more demanding height map. Consider the moon image shown back in Figure 10.5. Normal mapping did an excellent job of capturing the detail in the image (as shown previously in Figure 10.9 and Figure 10.11), and since it is grayscale, it would seem natural to try applying it as a height map. However, vertex-shader-based height mapping would be inadequate for this task, because the number of vertices sampled in the vertex shader (even for a sphere with precision = 500) is small compared to the fine level of detail in the image. By contrast, normal mapping *was* able to capture the detail impressively, because the normal map is sampled in the fragment shader, at the pixel level.

We will revisit height mapping later in Chapter 12 when we discuss methods for generating a greater number of vertices in a *tessellation shader.*

SUPPLEMENTAL NOTES

One of the fundamental limitations of bump or normal mapping is that, while they are capable of providing the appearance of surface detail in the interior of a rendered object, the silhouette (outer boundary) doesn't show any such detail (it remains smooth). Height mapping, if used to actually modify vertex locations, fixes this deficiency, but has its own limitations. As we will see later in this book, sometimes a geometry or tessellation shader can be used to increase the number of vertices, making height mapping more practical and more effective.

We have taken the liberty of simplifying some of the bump and normal mapping computations. More accurate and/or more efficient solutions are available for critical applications [BN12].

Exercises

10.1 Experiment with Program 10.1 by modifying the settings and/or computations in the fragment shader and observing the results.

10.2 Using a paint program, generate your own height map and use it in Program 10.4. See if you can identify locations where detail is missing as the result of the vertex shader being unable to adequately sample the height map. You will probably find it useful to also texture the terrain with your height map image file as shown in Figure 10.14 (or with some sort of pattern that exposes the surface structure, such as a grid), so that you can see the hills and valleys of the resulting terrain.

10.3 *(PROJECT)* Add lighting to Program 10.4, so that the surface structure of the height-mapped terrain is further exposed.

10.4 *(PROJECT)* Add shadow mapping to your code from Exercise 10.3 so that your height-mapped terrain casts shadows.

References

[BL78] J. Blinn, "Simulation of Wrinkled Surfaces," *Computer Graphics* 12, no. 3 (1978): 286–292.

[BN12] E. Bruneton and F. Neyret, "A Survey of Non-Linear Pre-Filtering Methods for Efficient and Accurate Surface Shading," *IEEE Transactions on Visualization and Computer Graphics* 18, no. 2 (2012), pp 242–260.

[GI16] GNU Image Manipulation Program, accessed July 2016, http://www.gimp.org

[GP16] GIMP Plugin Registry, *normalmap Plugin*, accessed July 2016, http://registry.gimp.org/node/69

[HT16] J. Hastings-Trew, *JHT's Planetary Pixel Emporium*, accessed July 2016, http://planetpixelemporium.com/

[LU16] F. Luna, *Introduction to 3D Game Programming with DirectX 12*, 2nd ed. (Mercury Learning, 2016).

[ME11] E. Meiri, *OGLdev Tutorial 26*, 2011, accessed July 2016, http://ogldev.atspace.co.uk/index.html

[PH16] Adobe Photoshop, accessed July 2016, http://www.photoshop.com

[SS16] SS Bump Generator, accessed July 2016, http://ssbump-generator.yolasite.com/

PARAMETRIC SURFACES

■ ■ ■ ■ ■

While working at the Renault corporation in the 1950s and 1960s, Pierre Bézier developed software systems for designing automobile bodies. His programs utilized mathematical systems of equations developed earlier by Paul de Casteljau, who was working for the competing Citroën automobile manufacturer [BE72, DC63]. The de Casteljau equations describe curves using just a few scalar parameters and are accompanied by a clever recursive algorithm dubbed "de Casteljau's algorithm" for generating the curves to arbitrary precision. Now known as "Bézier curves" and "Bézier surfaces," these methods are commonly used to efficiently model many kinds of curved 3D objects.

▰▰▰ 11.1 QUADRATIC BÉZIER CURVES

A *Quadratic Bézier curve* is defined by a set of parametric equations that specify a particular curved shape using three *control points*, each of which is a point in 2D space.[1] Consider, for example, the set of three points [p_0, p_1, p_2] shown in Figure 11.1.

Figure 11.1
Control points for a Bézier curve.

---

[1] Of course, a curve can exist in 3D space. However, a quadratic curve lies entirely within a 2D plane.

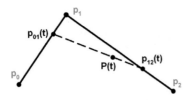

Figure 11.2
Points at parametric position t = 0.75.

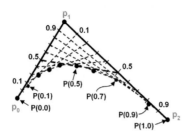

Figure 11.3
Building a quadratic Bézier curve.

By introducing a parameter **t**, we can build a system of parametric equations that define a curve. The t represents a fraction of the distance along the line segment connecting one control point to the next control point. Values for t are within the range [0..1] for points along the segment. Figure 11.2 shows one such value, t = 0.75, applied to the lines connecting p_0-p_1 and p_1-p_2, respectively. Doing this defines two new points $p_{01}(t)$ and $p_{12}(t)$ along the two original lines. We repeat this process for the line segment connecting the two new points $p_{01}(t)$ and $p_{12}(t)$ producing point P(t) where t = 0.75 along the line $p_{01}(t)$-$p_{12}(t)$. P(t) is one of the points on the resulting curve, and for this reason is denoted with a capital P.

Collecting many points P(t) for various values of t generates a curve, as shown in Figure 11.3. The more parameter values for t that are sampled, the more points P(t) are generated, and the smoother the resulting curve.

The analytic definition for a quadratic Bézier curve can now be derived. First, we note that an arbitrary point p on the line segment p_a-p_b connecting two points p_a and p_b can be represented in terms of the parameter t as follows:

$$p(t) = tp_a + (1-t)p_b$$

Using this, we find the points p_{01} and p_{12} (points on p_0-p_1 and p_1-p_2, respectively) as follows:

$$p_{01}(t) = tp_1 + (1-t)p_0$$
$$p_{12}(t) = tp_2 + (1-t)p_1$$

Similarly, a point on the connecting line segment between these points would be

$$P(t) = tp_{12}(t) + (1-t)p_{01}(t)$$

Substituting the definitions of p_{12} and p_{01} gives

$$P(t) = t[tp_2 + (1-t)p_1] + (1-t)[tp_1 + (1-t)p_0]$$

Factoring and combining terms then gives

$$P(t) = (1-t)^2 p_0 + (-2t^2 + 2t)p_1 + t^2 p_2$$

or

$$P(t) = \sum_{i=0}^{2} p_i B_i(t)$$

where

$$B_0(t) = (1-t)^2$$
$$B_1(t) = -2t^2 + 2t$$
$$B_2(t) = t^2$$

Thus, we find any point on the curve by a weighted sum of the control points. The weighting function B is often called a "blending function" (although the name B actually derives from Sergei Bernstein [BE16] who first characterized this family of polynomials). Note that the blending functions are all quadratic in form, which is why the resulting curve is called a quadratic Bézier curve.

11.2 CUBIC BÉZIER CURVES

We now extend our model to *four* control points, resulting in a *cubic* Bézier curve as shown in Figure 11.4. Cubic Bézier curves are capable of defining a much richer set of shapes than are quadratic curves, which are limited to concave shapes.

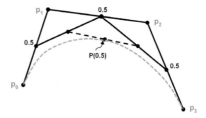

Figure 11.4
Building a cubic Bézier curve.

As for the quadratic case, we can derive an analytic definition for cubic Bézier curves:

$$p_{01}(t) = tp_1 + (1-t)p_0$$
$$p_{12}(t) = tp_2 + (1-t)p_1$$

$$p_{23}(t) = tp_3 + (1-t)p_2$$
$$p_{01-12}(t) = tp_{12}(t) + (1-t)p_{01}(t)$$
$$p_{12-23}(t) = tp_{23}(t) + (1-t)p_{12}(t)$$

A point on the curve would then be

$$P(t) = tp_{12-23}(t) + (1-t)p_{01-12}(t)$$

Substituting the definitions of p_{12-23} and p_{01-12} and collecting terms yields

$$P(t) = \sum_{i=0}^{3} p_i B_i(t)$$

where

$$B_0(t) = (1-t)^3$$
$$B_1(t) = 3t^3 - 6t^2 + 3t$$
$$B_2(t) = -3t^3 + 3t^2$$
$$B_3(t) = t^3$$

There are many different techniques for rendering Bézier curves. One approach is to iterate through successive values of t, starting at 0.0 and ending at 1.0, using a fixed increment. For instance, if the increment is 0.1, then we could use a loop with t values 0.0, 0.1, 0.2, 0.3, and so on. For each value of t, the corresponding point on the Bézier curve would be computed and a series of line segments connecting the successive points would be drawn, as described in the algorithm in Figure 11.5.

Another approach is to use de Casteljau's algorithm to *recursively subdivide* the curve in half, where $t = \frac{1}{2}$ at each recursive step. Figure 11.6 shows the left side subdivision into new cubic control points (q_0,q_1,q_2,q_3) shown in green, as derived by de Casteljau (a full derivation can be found in [AS14]).

The algorithm is shown in Figure 11.7. It subdivides the curve segments in half repeatedly, until each curve segment is sufficiently straight enough that further subdivision produces no tangible benefit. In the limiting case (as the control points are generated closer and closer together), the curve segment itself is effectively the same as a straight line between the first and last control points (q_0 and q_3). Determining whether a curve segment is "straight enough" can therefore be done

```
void drawBezierCurve (controlPointVector C)
{   currentPoint = C[0];   // curve starts at first control point
    t = 0.0;
    while (t <= 1.0)
    {   // compute next point as the sum of the Control Points,
        // weighted by the blending function evaluated at 't'.
        nextPoint = (0,0) ;
        for (int i=0; i<=3; i++)
            nextPoint = nextPoint + (blending(i,t) * C[i]);
        drawLine (currentPoint,nextPoint);
        currentPoint = nextPoint;
        t = t + increment;
}   }

double blending(int i, double t)
{   switch (i)
    {   case 0: return ((1-t)*(1-t)*(1-t));     // (1-t)³
        case 1: return (3*t*(1-t)*(1-t));       // 3t(1-t)²
        case 2: return (3*t*t*(1-t));           // 3t²(1-t)
        case 3: return (t*t*t);                 // t³
}   }
```

Figure 11.5
Iterative algorithm for rendering Bézier curves.

by comparing the distance from the first control point to the last control point, versus the sum of the lengths of the three lines connecting the four control points:

$$D_1 = |\, p_0\text{-}p_1 \,| + |\, p_1\text{-}p_2 \,| + |\, p_2\text{-}p_3 \,|$$

$$D_2 = |\, p_0\text{-}p_3 \,|$$

Then, if D_1-D_2 is less than a sufficiently small tolerance, there is no point in further subdivision.

An interesting property of the de Casteljau algorithm is that it is possible to generate all of the points on the curve without actually using the previously described blending

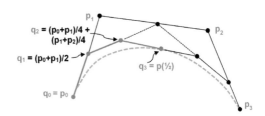

$q_2 = (p_0+p_1)/4 + (p_1+p_2)/4$

$q_1 = (p_0+p_1)/2$

$q_3 = p(\frac{1}{2})$

$q_0 = p_0$

Figure 11.6
Subdividing a cubic Bézier curve.

```
drawBezierCurve(ControlPointVector C)
{    if (C is "straight enough")
          draw line from first to last control point
     else
     {    subdivide(C, LeftC, RightC)
          drawBezierCurve(LeftC)
          drawBezierCurve(RightC)
}    }
subdivide(ControlPointVector p, q, r)
{    // compute left subdivision control points
     q(0) = p(0)
     q(1) = (p(0)+p(1)) / 2
     q(2) = (p(0)+p(1)) / 4 + (p(1)+p(2)) / 4
     // compute right subdivision control points
     r(1) = (p(1)+p(2)) / 4 + (p(2)+p(3)) / 4
     r(2) = (p(2)+p(3)) / 2
     r(3) = p(3)
     // compute "shared" center point at t=0.5
     q(3) = r(0) = (q(2)+r(1)) / 2
}
```

Figure 11.7
Recursive subdivision algorithm for Bézier curves.

functions. Also, note that the center point at $p(\frac{1}{2})$ is "shared"; that is, it is both the rightmost control point in the left subdivision and the leftmost control point in the right subdivision. It can be computed either using the blending functions at $t = \frac{1}{2}$ or by using the formula $(q_2 + r_1)/2$, as derived by de Casteljau.

As a side note, we point out that the subdivide() function shown in Figure 11.7 assumes that the incoming parameters p, q, and r are "reference" parameters (such as Java objects), and hence the computations in the function modify the actual parameters in the calls from the drawBezierCurve() function listed above it.

11.3 QUADRATIC BÉZIER SURFACES

Whereas Bézier curves define curved *lines* (in 2D or 3D space), Bézier *surfaces* define *curved surfaces* in *3D space*. Extending the concepts we saw in curves to surfaces requires extending our system of parametric equations from one parameter to two parameters. For Bézier curves, we called that parameter t. For Bézier surfaces, we will refer to the parameters as u and v. Whereas our curves were composed of points P(t), our surfaces will comprise points P(u,v), as shown in Figure 11.8.

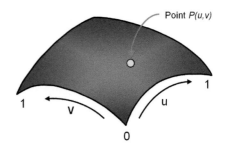

Point $P(u,v)$

Figure 11.8
Parametric surface.

For quadratic Bézier surfaces, there are three control points on each axis u and v, for a total of *nine* control points. Figure 11.9 shows an example of a set of nine control points (typically called a *control point "mesh"*) in blue, and the associated corresponding curved surface (in red).

The nine control points in the mesh are labeled p_{ij}, where i and j represent the indices in the u and v directions, respectively. Each set of three adjacent control points, such as (p_{00}, p_{01}, p_{02}), defines a Bézier curve. Points P(u,v) on the surface are then defined as a sum of two blending functions, one in the u direction and

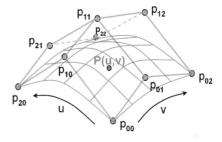

Figure 11.9
Quadratic Bézier control mesh and corresponding surface.

one in the v direction. The form of the two blending functions for building Bézier surfaces then follows from the methodology given previously for Bézier curves:

$$B_0(u) = (1-u)^2$$
$$B_1(u) = -2u^2 + 2u$$
$$B_2(u) = u^2$$
$$B_0(v) = (1-v)^2$$
$$B_1(v) = -2v^2 + 2v$$
$$B_2(v) = v^2$$

The points $P(u,v)$ comprising the Bézier surface are then generated by summing the product of each control point p_{ij} and the ith and jth blending functions evaluated at parametric values u and v, respectively:

$$P(u,v) = \sum_{i=0}^{2} \sum_{j=0}^{2} p_{ij} * B_i(u) * B_j(v)$$

The set of generated points that comprise a Bézier surface is sometimes called a *patch*. The term *patch* can sometimes be confusing, as we will see later when we study tessellation shaders (useful for actually implementing Bézier surfaces). There, it is the grid of control points that is typically called a "patch."

11.4 CUBIC BÉZIER SURFACES

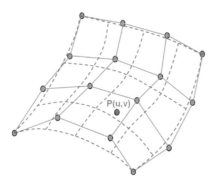

Moving from quadratic to cubic surfaces requires utilizing a larger mesh—4x4 rather than 3x3. Figure 11.10 shows an example of a 16-control-point mesh (in blue) and the corresponding curved surface (in red).

As before, we can derive the formula for points P(u,v) on the surface by combining the associated blending functions for cubic Bézier curves:

Figure 11.10
Cubic Bézier control mesh and corresponding surface.

$$P(u,v) = \sum_{i=0}^{3} \sum_{j=0}^{3} p_{ij} * B_i(u) * B_j(v)$$

where

$$B_0(u) = (1-u)^3 \qquad\qquad B_0(v) = (1-v)^3$$
$$B_1(u) = 3u^3 - 6u^2 + 3u \qquad B_1(v) = 3v^3 - 6v^2 + 3v$$
$$B_2(u) = -3u^3 + 3u^2 \qquad\quad B_2(v) = -3v^3 + 3v^2$$
$$B_3(u) = u^3 \qquad\qquad\qquad B_3(v) = v^3$$

Rendering Bézier surfaces can also be done with recursive subdivision [AS14], by alternately splitting the surface in half along each dimension, as shown in Figure 11.11. Each subdivision produces four new control point meshes, each containing 16 points, which define one quadrant of the surface.

When rendering Bézier *curves*, we stopped subdividing when the *curve* was "straight enough." For Bézier surfaces, we stop recursing when the *surface* is "flat enough." One way of doing this is to ensure that all of the recursively generated

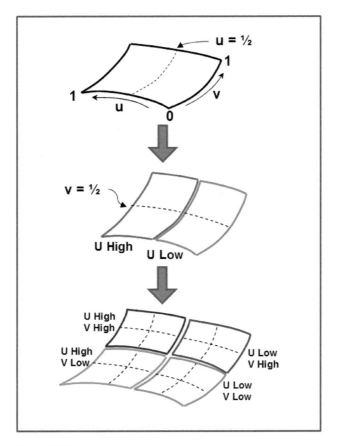

Figure 11.11
Recursive subdivision for Bézier surfaces.

points in a subquadrant control mesh are within some small allowable distance from a plane defined by three of the four corner points of that mesh. The distance d between a point (x,y,z) and a plane (A,B,C,D) is

$$d = abs\left(\frac{Ax + By + Cz + D}{\sqrt{A^2 + B^2 + C^2}} \right)$$

If d is less than some sufficiently small tolerance, then we stop subdividing, and simply use the four corner control points of the subquadrant mesh to draw two triangles.

The *tessellation* stage of the OpenGL pipeline offers an attractive alternative approach for rendering Bézier surfaces based on the iterative algorithm in Figure 11.5 for Bezier curves. The strategy is to have the tessellator generate a large grid of vertices, and then use the blending functions to reposition those vertices onto the Bézier surface as specified by the cubic Bézier control points. We implement this in Chapter 12.

SUPPLEMENTAL NOTES

This chapter focused on the mathematical fundamentals of parametric Bézier curves and surfaces. We have deferred presenting an implementation of any of them in OpenGL, because an appropriate vehicle for this is the tessellation stage, covered in the next chapter. We also skipped some of the derivations, such as for the recursive subdivision algorithm.

In 3D graphics, there are many advantages to using Bézier curves for modeling objects. First, those objects can, in theory, be scaled arbitrarily and still retain smooth surfaces without "pixelating." Second, many objects made up of complex curves can be stored much more efficiently as sets of Bézier control points rather than storing thousands of vertices.

Bézier curves have many real-world applications besides computer graphics and automobiles. They can also be found in the design of bridges, such as in the Chords Bridge in Jerusalem [CB16]. Similar techniques are used for building TrueType fonts, which as a result can be scaled to any arbitrary size, or zoomed in to any degree of closeness, while always retaining smooth edges.

Exercises

11.1 Quadratic Bézier curves are limited to defining curves that are wholly "concave" or "convex." Describe (or draw) an example of a curve that bends in a manner that is neither wholly concave nor convex, and thus could not possibly be approximated by a *quadratic* Bézier curve.

11.2 Using a pen or pencil, draw an arbitrary set of four points on a piece of paper, number them from 1 to 4 in any order, and then try to draw an approximation of the cubic Bézier curve defined by those four ordered control points. Then rearrange the numbering of the control points (i.e., their order, but without changing their positions) and redraw the new resulting cubic Bézier curve. There are numerous online tools for drawing Bézier curves you can use to check your approximation.

References

[AS14] E. Angel and D. Shreiner, *Interactive Computer Graphics: A Top-Down Approach with WebGL*, 7th ed. (Pearson, 2014).

[BE16] S. Bernstein, Wikipedia, accessed July 2016, https://en.wikipedia.org/wiki/Sergei_Natanovich_Bernstein

[BE72] P. Bézier, *Numerical Control: Mathematics and Applications* (John Wiley & Sons, 1972).

[CB16] Chords Bridge, Wikipedia, accessed July 2016, https://en.wikipedia.org/wiki/Chords_Bridge

[DC63] P. de Casteljau, *Courbes et surfaces à pôles*, technical report (A. Citroën, 1963).

TESSELLATION

■■■■■■

The English language term *tessellation* refers to a large class of design activities in which tiles of various geometric shapes are arranged adjacently to form patterns, generally on a flat surface. The purpose can be artistic or practical, with examples dating back thousands of years [TS16].

In 3D graphics, *tessellation* refers to something a little bit different, but no doubt inspired by its classical counterpart. Here tessellation refers to the generation and manipulation of large numbers of triangles for rendering complex shapes and surfaces, preferably in hardware. Tessellation is a rather recent addition to the OpenGL core, not appearing until 2010 with version 4.0.[1]

12.1 TESSELLATION IN OPENGL

OpenGL support for hardware tessellation is made available through three pipeline stages:

1. the *tessellation control shader*
2. the *tessellator*
3. the *tessellation evaluation shader*

---

[1] Although the GLU toolset previously included a utility for tessellation much earlier called *gluTess*. In 2001, Radeon released the first commercial graphics card with tessellation support, but there were few tools able to take advantage of it.

The first and third stages are programmable; the intervening second stage is not. In order to use tessellation, the programmer generally provides both a control shader and an evaluation shader.

The tessellator (its full name is *tessellation primitive generator,* or *TPG*) is a hardware-supported engine that produces fixed grids of triangles.[2] The control shader allows us to configure what sort of triangle mesh the tessellator is to build. The evaluation shader then lets us manipulate the grid in various ways. The manipulated triangle mesh is then the source of vertices that proceed through the pipeline. Recall from Figure 2.2 that tessellation sits in the pipeline between the vertex and geometry shader stages.

Let's start with an application that simply uses the tessellator to create a triangle mesh of vertices, and then displays it without any manipulation. For this, we will need the following modules:

1. *Java/JOGL application:*
   Creates a camera and associated mvp matrix. The view (v) and projection (p) matrices orient the camera; the model (m) matrix can be used to modify the location and orientation of the grid.

2. *Vertex Shader:*
   Essentially does nothing in this example; the vertices will be generated in the tessellator.

3. *Tessellation Control Shader (TCS):*
   Specifies the grid for the tessellator to build.

4. *Tessellation Evaluation Shader (TES):*
   Applies the mvp matrix to the vertices in the grid.

5. *Fragment Shader:*
   Simply outputs a fixed color for every pixel.

Program 12.1 shows the entire application code. Even a simple example such as this one is fairly complex, so many of the code elements will require explanation. Note that this is the first time we must build a GLSL rendering program with components beyond just vertex and fragment shaders. So a four-parameter overloaded version of createShaderProgram() is implemented.

---

[2] Or lines, but we will focus on triangles.

Program 12.1 Basic Tessellator Mesh

Java / JOGL application

```java
public int createShaderProgram(String vS, String tCS, String tES, String fS)
{   GL4 gl = (GL4) GLContext.getCurrentGL();

    String vshaderSource[ ] = Utils.readShaderSource(vS);
    String tcshaderSource[ ] = Utils.readShaderSource(tCS);
    String teshaderSource[ ] = Utils.readShaderSource(tES);
    String fshaderSource[ ] = Utils.readShaderSource(fS);

    int vShader  = gl.glCreateShader(GL_VERTEX_SHADER);
    int tcShader = gl.glCreateShader(GL_TESS_CONTROL_SHADER);
    int teShader = gl.glCreateShader(GL_TESS_EVALUATION_SHADER);
    int fShader  = gl.glCreateShader(GL_FRAGMENT_SHADER);

    gl.glShaderSource(vShader, vshaderSource.length, vshaderSource, null, 0);
    gl.glShaderSource(tcShader, tcshaderSource.length, tcshaderSource, null, 0);
    gl.glShaderSource(teShader, teshaderSource.length, teshaderSource, null, 0);
    gl.glShaderSource(fShader, fshaderSource.length, fshaderSource, null, 0);

    gl.glCompileShader(vShader);
    gl.glCompileShader(tcShader);
    gl.glCompileShader(teShader);
    gl.glCompileShader(fShader);

    int vtfprogram = gl.glCreateProgram();
    gl.glAttachShader(vtfprogram, vShader);
    gl.glAttachShader(vtfprogram, tcShader);
    gl.glAttachShader(vtfprogram, teShader);
    gl.glAttachShader(vtfprogram, fShader);
    gl.glLinkProgram(vtfprogram);
    return vtfprogram;
}

public void init(GLAutoDrawable drawable)
{   ...
    renderingProgram = createShaderProgram("vertShader.glsl",
        "tessCShader.glsl", "tessEShader.glsl", "fragShader.glsl");
}

public void display(GLAutoDrawable drawable)
{   ...
    gl.glUseProgram(renderingProgram);
    ...
```

```
    gl.glPatchParameteri(GL_PATCH_VERTICES, 1);
    gl.glPolygonMode(GL_FRONT_AND_BACK, GL_LINE);
    gl.glDrawArrays(GL_PATCHES, 0, 1);
}
```

Vertex Shader

```
#version 430
uniform mat4 mvp;
void main(void) { }
```

Tessellation Control Shader

```
#version 430
uniform mat4 mvp;
layout (vertices = 1) out;

void main(void)
{   gl_TessLevelOuter[0] = 6;
    gl_TessLevelOuter[1] = 6;
    gl_TessLevelOuter[2] = 6;
    gl_TessLevelOuter[3] = 6;
    gl_TessLevelInner[0] = 12;
    gl_TessLevelInner[1] = 12;
}
```

Tessellation Evaluation Shader

```
#version 430
uniform mat4 mvp;
layout (quads, equal_spacing, ccw) in;

void main (void)
{   float u = gl_TessCoord.x;
    float v = gl_TessCoord.y;
    gl_Position = mvp * vec4(u,0,v,1);
}
```

Fragment Shader

```
#version 430
out vec4 color;
uniform mat4 mvp;
void main(void)
{   color = vec4(1.0, 1.0, 0.0, 1.0);      // yellow
}
```

The resulting output mesh is shown in Figure 12.1.

The tessellator produces a mesh of vertices defined by two parameters: *inner level* and *outer level*. In this case, the inner level is 12 and the outer level is 6—the outer edges of the grid are divided into 6 segments, while the lines spanning the interior are divided into 12 segments.

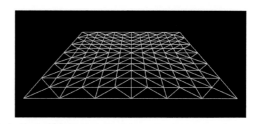

Figure 12.1
Tessellator triangle mesh output.

The specific relevant new constructs in Program 12.1 are highlighted. Let's start by discussing the first portion—the Java/JOGL code.

Compiling the two new shaders is done exactly the same as for the vertex and fragment shaders. They are then attached to the same rendering program, and the linking call is unchanged. The only new items are the constants for specifying the type of shader being instantiated—the new constants are named

```
GL_TESS_CONTROL_SHADER
GL_TESS_EVALUATION_SHADER
```

Note the new items in the display() function. The glDrawArrays() call now specifies GL_PATCHES. When using tessellation, vertices sent from the Java/JOGL application into the pipeline (i.e., in a VBO) *aren't rendered* but are usually *control points*, such as those we saw for Bézier curves. A set of control points is called a *patch*, and in those sections of the code using tessellation, GL_PATCHES is the only allowable primitive. The number of vertices in a patch is specified in the call to glPatchParameteri(). In this particular example, there aren't any control points being sent, but we are still required to specify at least one. Similarly, in the glDrawArrays() call we indicate a start value of 0 and a vertex count of 1, even though we aren't actually sending any vertices from the JOGL program.

The call to glPolygonMode() specifies how the mesh should be rasterized. The default is GL_FILL. Shown in the code is GL_LINE, which as we saw in Figure 12.1 caused only connecting lines to be rasterized (so we could see the grid itself that was produced by the tessellator). If we change that line of code to GL_FILL (or comment it out, resulting in the default behavior GL_FILL), we get the version shown in Figure 12.2.

Figure 12.2
Tessellated mesh rendered with GL_FILL.

Now let's work our way through the four shaders. As indicated earlier, the vertex shader has little to do, since the Java/JOGL application isn't providing any vertices. All it contains is a uniform declaration, to match the other shaders, and an empty main(). In any case, it is a requirement that all shader programs include a vertex shader.

The Tessellation Control Shader specifies the topology of the triangle mesh that the tessellator is to produce. Six "level" parameters are set—two "inner" and four "outer" levels—by assigning values to the reserved words named gl_TessLevel*xxx*. This is for tessellating a large *rectangular* grid of triangles, called a *quad*.[3] The levels tell the tessellator how to subdivide the grid when forming triangles, and are arranged as shown in Figure 12.3.

Note the line in the control shader that says

layout (vertices=1) out;

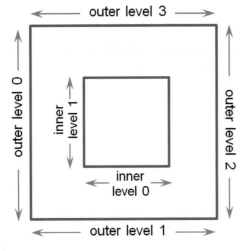

Figure 12.3
Tessellation levels.

This is related to the prior GL_PATCHES discussion and specifies the number of vertices per "patch" being passed from the vertex shader to the control shader (and "out" to the evaluation shader). In this particular program there are none, but we still must specify at least one, because it also affects how many times the control shader executes. Later this value will reflect the number of control points and must match the value in the glPatchParameteri() call in the Java/JOGL application.

---

[3] The tessellator is also capable of building a *triangular* grid of triangles, but that isn't covered in this textbook.

Next let's look at the tessellation evaluation shader. It starts with a line of code that says

```
layout (quads, equal_spacing, ccw) in;
```

This may at first appear to be related to the "out" layout statement in the control shader, but actually they are unrelated. Rather, this line is where we instruct the tessellator to generate vertices so they are arranged in a large rectangle (a "quad"). It also specifies the subdivisions (inner and outer) to be of equal length (later we will see a use for subdivisions of unequal length). The "ccw" parameter specifies the winding order in which the tessellated grid vertices are generated (in this case, counterclockwise).

The vertices generated by the tessellator are then sent to the evaluation shader. Thus, the evaluation shader *may* receive vertices *both* from the control shader (typically as control points) and from the tessellator (the tessellated grid). In Program 12.1, vertices are only received from the tessellator.

The evaluation shader executes once for each vertex produced by the tessellator. The vertex location is accessible using the built-in variable gl_TessCoord. The tessellated grid is oriented such that it lies in the X-Z plane, and therefore gl_TessCoord's X and Y components are applied at the grid's X and Z coordinates. The grid coordinates, and thus the values of gl_TessCoord, range from 0.0 to 1.0 (this will be handy later when computing texture coordinates). The evaluation shader then uses the mvp matrix to orient each vertex (this was done in the vertex shader in examples from earlier chapters).

Finally, the fragment shader simply outputs a constant color yellow for each pixel. We can, of course, also use it to apply a texture or lighting to our scene as we saw in previous chapters.

12.2 ■ TESSELLATION FOR BÉZIER SURFACES

Let's now extend our program so that it turns our simple rectangular grid into a Bézier surface. The tessellated grid should give us plenty of vertices for sampling the surface (and we can increase the inner/outer subdivision levels if we want more). What we now need is to send *control points* through the pipeline, and then use those control points to perform the computations to convert the tessellated grid into the desired Bézier surface.

Java/JOGL code

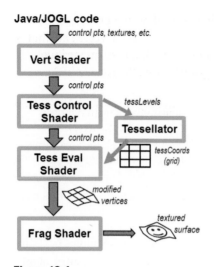

Figure 12.4
Overview of tessellation for Bézier surfaces.

Assuming that we wish to build a *cubic* Bézier surface, we will need 16 control points. We could send them from the Java side in a VBO, or we could hardcode them in the vertex shader. Figure 12.4 shows an overview of the process, with the control points coming from the Java side.

Now is a good time to explain a bit more precisely how the tessellation control shader (TCS) works. Similar to the vertex shader, the TCS executes *once per incoming vertex*. Also, recall from Chapter 2 that OpenGL provides a built-in variable called gl_VertexID which holds a counter that indicates which invocation of the vertex shader is currently executing. A similar built-in variable called gl_InvocationID exists for the tessellation control shader.

A powerful feature of tessellation is that the TCS (and also the TES) shader has access to *all* of the control point vertices simultaneously, in arrays. At first, it may seem confusing that the TCS executes once per vertex, when each invocation has access to all of the vertices. It is also counterintuitive that the tessellation levels are specified in assignment statements which are redundantly set at each TCS invocation. Although all of this may seem odd, it is done this way because the tessellation architecture is designed so that TCS invocations can run in parallel.

OpenGL provides several built-in variables for use in the TCS and TES shaders. Ones that we have already mentioned are gl_InvocationID and, of course, gl_TessLevelInner and gl_TessLevelOuter. Here are some more details and descriptions of some of the most useful built-in variables:

Tessellation Control Shader (TCS) built-in variables:

- **gl_in [ ]** – an array containing each of the incoming control point vertices—one array element per incoming vertex. Particular vertex attributes can be accessed as fields using the "." notation. One built-in attribute is gl_Position—thus, the position of incoming vertex "i" is accessed as gl_in[i].gl_Position.

- **gl_out [ ]** – an array for sending outgoing control point vertices to the TES—one array element per outgoing vertex. Particular vertex attributes can be accessed as fields using the "**.**" notation. One built-in attribute is gl_Position—thus, the position of outgoing vertex "i" is accessed as gl_out[i].gl_Position.

- **gl_InvocationID** – an integer ID counter indicating which invocation of the TCS is currently executing. One common use is for passing through vertex attributes; for example, passing the current invocation's vertex position from the TCS to the TES would be done as follows: gl_out[gl_InvocationID].gl_Position = gl_in[gl_InvocationID].gl_Position;

Tessellation Evaluation Shader (TES) built-in variables:

- **gl_in [ ]** – an array containing each of the incoming control point vertices—one element per incoming vertex. Particular vertex attributes can be accessed as fields using the "**.**" notation. One built-in attribute is gl_Position—thus, incoming vertex positions are accessed as gl_in[*xxx*].gl_Position.

- **gl_Position** – output position of a tessellated grid vertex, possibly modified in the TES. It is important to note that gl_Position and gl_in[*xxx*].gl_Position are different—gl_Position is the position of an output vertex that originated in the tessellator, while gl_in[*xxx*].gl_Position is a control point vertex position coming into the TES from the TCS.

It is important to note that input and output control point vertex attributes in the TCS are arrays. By contrast, input control point vertices and vertex attributes in the TES are arrays, but output vertices are scalars. Also, it is easy to become confused as to which vertices are for control points and which are tessellated and then moved to form the resulting surface. To summarize, all vertex inputs and outputs to the TCS are control points, whereas in the TES, gl_in[ ] holds incoming control points, gl_TessCoord holds incoming tessellated grid points, and gl_Position holds output surface vertices for rendering.

Our tessellation control shader now has two tasks: specifying the tessellation levels *and* passing the control points through from the vertex shader to the evaluation shader. The evaluation shader can then modify the locations of the grid points (the gl_TessCoords) based on the Bézier control points.

Program 12.2 shows all four shaders—vertex, TCS, TES, and fragment—for specifying a control point patch, generating a flat tessellated grid of vertices, repositioning those vertices on the curved surface specified by the control points, and painting the resulting surface with a texture image. It also shows the relevant portion of the Java/JOGL application, specifically in the display() function. In this example, the control points originate in the vertex shader (they are hardcoded there) rather than entering the OpenGL pipeline from the Java/JOGL application. Additional details follow after the code listing.

Program 12.2 Tessellation for Bézier Surface

Vertex Shader

```
#version 430
out vec2  texCoord;
uniform mat4 mvp;
layout (binding = 0) uniform sampler2D tex_color;

void main(void)
{  //  this time the vertex shader defines and sends out control points:
    const vec4 vertices[ ] =
    vec4[ ] ( vec4(-1.0, 0.5, -1.0, 1.0), vec4(-0.5, 0.5, -1.0, 1.0),
              vec4( 0.5, 0.5, -1.0, 1.0), vec4( 1.0, 0.5, -1.0, 1.0),

              vec4(-1.0, 0.0, -0.5, 1.0), vec4(-0.5, 0.0, -0.5, 1.0),
              vec4( 0.5, 0.0, -0.5, 1.0), vec4( 1.0, 0.0, -0.5, 1.0),

              vec4(-1.0, 0.0,  0.5, 1.0), vec4(-0.5, 0.0,  0.5, 1.0),
              vec4( 0.5, 0.0,  0.5, 1.0), vec4( 1.0, 0.0,  0.5, 1.0),

              vec4(-1.0, -0.5,  1.0, 1.0), vec4(-0.5, 0.3,  1.0, 1.0),
              vec4( 0.5, 0.3,  1.0, 1.0), vec4( 1.0, 0.3,  1.0, 1.0) );

    //  compute an appropriate texture coordinate for the current vertex, shifted from [-1..+1] to [0..1]
    texCoord = vec2((vertices[gl_VertexID].x + 1.0) / 2.0, (vertices[gl_VertexID].z + 1.0) / 2.0);

    gl_Position = vertices[gl_VertexID];
}
```

Tessellation Control Shader

```
#version 430

in vec2 texCoord[ ];            // The texture coords output from the vertex shader as scalars arrive
out vec2 texCoord_TCSout[ ];    // in an array and are then passed through to the evaluation shader

uniform mat4 mvp;
layout (binding = 0) uniform sampler2D tex_color;
layout (vertices = 16) out;     // there are 16 control points per patch
```

```
void main(void)
{   int TL = 32;        // tessellation levels are all set to this value
    if (gl_InvocationID == 0)
    {   gl_TessLevelOuter[0] = TL; gl_TessLevelOuter[2] = TL;
        gl_TessLevelOuter[1] = TL; gl_TessLevelOuter[3] = TL;
        gl_TessLevelInner[0] = TL; gl_TessLevelInner[1] = TL;
    }
    //  forward the texture and control points to the TES
    texCoord_TCSout[gl_InvocationID] = texCoord[gl_InvocationID];
    gl_out[gl_InvocationID].gl_Position = gl_in[gl_InvocationID].gl_Position;
}
```

Tessellation Evaluation Shader

```
#version 430
layout (quads, equal_spacing,ccw) in;
uniform mat4 mvp;
layout (binding = 0) uniform sampler2D tex_color;
in vec2 texCoord_TCSout[ ];          // texture coordinate array coming in
out vec2 texCoord_TESout;            // scalars going out one at a time

void main (void)
{   vec3 p00 = (gl_in[0].gl_Position).xyz;
    vec3 p10 = (gl_in[1].gl_Position).xyz;
    vec3 p20 = (gl_in[2].gl_Position).xyz;
    vec3 p30 = (gl_in[3].gl_Position).xyz;
    vec3 p01 = (gl_in[4].gl_Position).xyz;
    vec3 p11 = (gl_in[5].gl_Position).xyz;
    vec3 p21 = (gl_in[6].gl_Position).xyz;
    vec3 p31 = (gl_in[7].gl_Position).xyz;
    vec3 p02 = (gl_in[8].gl_Position).xyz;
    vec3 p12 = (gl_in[9].gl_Position).xyz;
    vec3 p22 = (gl_in[10].gl_Position).xyz;
    vec3 p32 = (gl_in[11].gl_Position).xyz;
    vec3 p03 = (gl_in[12].gl_Position).xyz;
    vec3 p13 = (gl_in[13].gl_Position).xyz;
    vec3 p23 = (gl_in[14].gl_Position).xyz;
    vec3 p33 = (gl_in[15].gl_Position).xyz;

    float u = gl_TessCoord.x;
    float v = gl_TessCoord.y;

    // cubic Bezier basis functions
    float bu0 = (1.0-u) * (1.0-u) * (1.0-u);      // (1-u)^3
    float bu1 = 3.0 * u * (1.0-u) * (1.0-u);      // 3u(1-u)^2
```

```
float bu2 = 3.0 * u * u * (1.0-u);          // 3u^2(1-u)
float bu3 = u * u * u;                        // u^3
float bv0 = (1.0-v) * (1.0-v) * (1.0-v);     // (1-v)^3
float bv1 = 3.0 * v * (1.0-v) * (1.0-v);     // 3v(1-v)^2
float bv2 = 3.0 * v * v * (1.0-v);           // 3v^2(1-v)
float bv3 = v * v * v;                        // v^3

// output the position of this vertex in the tessellated patch
vec3 outputPosition =
     bu0 * ( bv0*p00 + bv1*p01 + bv2*p02 + bv3*p03 )
   + bu1 * ( bv0*p10 + bv1*p11 + bv2*p12 + bv3*p13 )
   + bu2 * ( bv0*p20 + bv1*p21 + bv2*p22 + bv3*p23 )
   + bu3 * ( bv0*p30 + bv1*p31 + bv2*p32 + bv3*p33 );
gl_Position = mvp * vec4(outputPosition,1.0f);

// output the interpolated texture coordinates
vec2 tc1 = mix(texCoord_TCSout[0], texCoord_TCSout[3], gl_TessCoord.x);
vec2 tc2 = mix(texCoord_TCSout[12], texCoord_TCSout[15], gl_TessCoord.x);
vec2 tc = mix(tc2, tc1, gl_TessCoord.y);
texCoord_TESout = tc;
}
```

Fragment Shader

```
#version 430
in vec2 texCoord_TESout;
out vec4 color;
uniform mat4 mvp;
layout (binding = 0) uniform sampler2D tex_color;

void main(void)
{   color = texture(tex_color, texCoord_TESout);
}
```

Java / JOGL application

```
//  This time we also pass a texture to paint the surface.
//  Load the texture in init() as usual, then enable it in display()

public void display(GLAutoDrawable drawable)
{   ...
    gl.glActiveTexture(GL_TEXTURE0);
    gl.glBindTexture(GL_TEXTURE_2D, textureID);

    gl.glFrontFace(GL_CCW);
```

```
gl.glPatchParameteri(GL_PATCH_VERTICES, 16);      // number of vertices per patch = 16
gl.glPolygonMode(GL_FRONT_AND_BACK, GL_FILL);
gl.glDrawArrays(GL_PATCHES, 0, 16);      // total number of patch vertices: 16 x 1 patch = 16
}
```

The vertex shader now specifies 16 control points (the "patch" vertices) representing a particular Bézier surface. In this example they are all normalized to the range [-1..+1]. The vertex shader also uses the control points to determine texture coordinates appropriate for the tessellated grid, with values in the range [0..1]. It is important to reiterate that the vertices output from the vertex shader are *not* vertices that will be rasterized, but instead are Bézier control points. When using tessellation, patch vertices are *never* rasterized—only tessellated vertices proceed to rasterization.

The control shader still specifies the inner and outer tessellation levels. It now has the additional responsibility of forwarding the control points and texture coordinates to the evaluation shader. Note that the tessellation levels only need to be specified once, and therefore that step is done only during the 0th invocation (recall that the TCS runs once per vertex—thus there are 16 invocations in this example). For convenience, we have specified 32 subdivisions for each tessellation level.

Next, the evaluation shader performs all of the Bézier surface computations. The large block of assignment statements at the beginning of main() extract the control points from the incoming gl_Positions of each incoming gl_in (note that these correspond to the control shader's gl_out variable). The weights for the blending functions are then computed using the grid points coming in from the tessellator, resulting in a new outputPosition, to which the model-view-projection matrix is then applied, producing an output gl_Position for each grid point, forming the Bézier surface.

It is also necessary to create texture coordinates. The vertex shader only provided one for each control point location. But it isn't the control points that are being rendered—we ultimately need texture coordinates for the much larger number of tessellated grid points. There are various ways of doing this—here we linearly interpolate them using GLSL's handy *mix* function. The mix() function expects three parameters: (a) starting point, (b) ending point, and (c) interpolation value, which ranges from 0 to 1. It returns the value between the starting and ending point corresponding to the interpolation value. Since the tessellated grid coordinates also range from 0 to 1, they can be used directly for this purpose.

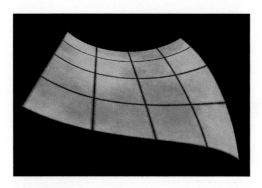

Figure 12.5
Tessellated Bézier surface.

This time in the fragment shader, rather than outputting a single color, standard texturing is applied. The texture coordinates, in the attribute texCoord_TESout, are those that were produced in the evaluation shader. The changes to the JOGL program are similarly straightforward—note that a patch size of 16 is now specified. The resulting output is shown in Figure 12.5 (a tile texture from [LU16] is applied).

12.3 TESSELLATION FOR TERRAIN/HEIGHT MAPS

Recall that performing height mapping in the vertex shader can suffer from an insufficient number of vertices to render the desired detail. Now that we have a way to generate lots of vertices, let's go back to Hastings-Trew's moon surface texture map (from [HT16]) and use it as a *height map* by raising *tessellated* vertices to produce moon surface detail. As we will see, this has the dual advantages of achieving vertex geometry that better matches the moon image along with producing improved silhouette (edge) detail.

Our strategy is to modify Program 12.1, placing a tessellated grid in the X-Z plane and using height mapping to set the Y coordinate of each tessellated grid point. To do this, a patch isn't needed, because we can hardcode the location of the tessellated grid, so we will specify the required minimum of 1 vertex per patch in glDrawArrays() and glPatchParameteri() as was done in Program 12.1. Hastings-Trew's moon texture image is used both for color and as the height map.

We generate vertex and texture coordinates in the evaluation shader by mapping the tessellated grid's gl_TessCoord values to appropriate ranges for vertices and textures.[4] The evaluation shader also is where the height mapping is performed by adding a fraction of the color component of the moon texture to the Y component of output vertex. The changes to the shaders are shown in Program 12.3.

---

4 In some applications the texture coordinates are produced externally, such as when tessellation is being used to provide additional vertices for an imported model. In such cases, the provided texture coordinates would need to be interpolated.

Program 12.3 Simple Tessellated Terrain

Vertex Shader

```
#version 430
uniform mat4 mvp;
layout (binding = 0) uniform sampler2D tex_color;
void main(void)  { }
```

Tessellation Control Shader

```
. . .
layout (vertices = 1) out;       // no control points are necessary for this application

void main(void)
{   int TL=32;
    if (gl_InvocationID == 0)
    {   gl_TessLevelOuter[0] = TL;  gl_TessLevelOuter[2] = TL;
        gl_TessLevelOuter[1] = TL;  gl_TessLevelOuter[3] = TL;
        gl_TessLevelInner[0] = TL;  gl_TessLevelInner[1] = TL;
    }
}
```

Tessellation Evaluation Shader

```
. . .
out vec2 tes_out;
uniform mat4 mvp;
layout (binding = 0) uniform sampler2D tex_color;

void main (void)
{   // map the tessellated grid vertices from [0..1] onto the desired vertices [-0.5..+0.5]
    vec4  tessellatedPoint = vec4(gl_TessCoord.x - 0.5, 0.0, gl_TessCoord.y - 0.5, 1.0);

    // map the tessellated grid vertices as texture coordinates by "flipping" the Y values vertically.
    // Vertex coordinates have (0,0) at upper left, texture coordinates have (0,0) at the lower left.
    vec2 tc = vec2(gl_TessCoord.x, 1.0 - gl_TessCoord.y);

    // The image is grayscale, so either component (R, G, or B) can serve as height offset.
    tessellatedPoint.y += (texture(tex_color, tc).r) / 40.0;       // Scale down color values.

    // convert the height-map raised point to eye space
    gl_Position = mvp * tessellatedPoint;
    tes_out = tc;
}
```

Fragment Shader

```
. . .
in vec2 tes_out;
out vec4 color;
layout (binding = 0) uniform sampler2D tex_color;

void main(void)
{   color = texture(tex_color, tes_out);
}
```

The fragment shader is similar to the one for Program 12.2 and simply outputs the color based on the texture image. The Java/JOGL application is essentially unchanged—it loads the texture (serving as both the texture and height map) and enables a sampler for it. Figure 12.6 shows the texture image (on the left) and the final output of this first attempt, which unfortunately does not yet achieve proper height mapping.

The first results are severely flawed. Although we can now see silhouette detail on the far horizon, the bumps there don't correspond to the actual detail in the texture map. Recall that in a height map, white is supposed to mean "high" and black is supposed to mean "low." The area at the upper right, in particular, shows large hills that bear no relation to the light and dark colors in the image.

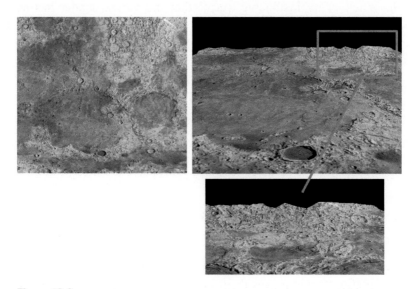

Figure 12.6
Tessellated terrain—failed first attempt, with insufficient number of vertices.

The cause of this problem is the resolution of the tessellated grid. The maximum number of vertices that can be generated by the tessellator is hardware dependent, and a maximum value of at least 64 for each tessellation level is all that is required for compliance with the OpenGL standard. Our program specified a single tessellated grid with inner and outer tessellation levels of 32, so we generated about 32*32, or just over 1000 vertices, which is insufficient to reflect the detail in the image accurately. This is especially apparent along the upper right (enlarged in the figure)—the edge detail is only sampled at 32 points along the horizon, producing large, random-looking hills. Even if we increased the tessellation values to 64, the total of 64*64 or just over 4000 vertices would still be woefully inadequate to do height mapping using the moon image.

A good way to increase the number of vertices is by using *instancing*, which we saw in Chapter 4. Our strategy will be to have the tessellator generate grids, and use instancing to repeat this many times. In the vertex shader we build a patch defined by four vertices, one for each corner of a tessellated grid. In our Java/JOGL application we change the glDrawArrays() call to glDrawArraysInstanced(). There we specify a grid of 64 by 64 patches, each of which contains a tessellated mesh with levels of size 32. This will give us a total of 64*64*32*32, or over four million vertices.

The vertex shader starts by specifying four texture coordinates (0,0), (0,1), (1,0), and (1,0). When using instancing, recall that the vertex shader has access to an integer variable gl_InstanceID, which holds a counter corresponding to the glDrawArraysInstanced() call that is currently being processed. We use this ID value to distribute the locations of the individual patches within the larger grid. The patches are positioned in rows and columns, the first patch at location (0,0), the second at (1,0), the next at (2,0), and so on, and the final patch in the first column at (63,0). The next column has patches at (0,1), (1,1), and so forth up to (63,1). The final column has patches at (0,63), (1,63), and so on up to (63,63). The X coordinate for a given patch is the instance ID modulo 64, and the Y coordinate is the instance ID divided by 64 (with integer division). The shader then scales the coordinates back down to the range [0..1].

The control shader is unchanged, except that it passes through the vertices and texture coordinates.

Next, the evaluation shader takes the incoming tessellated grid vertices (specified by gl_TessCoord) and moves them into the coordinate range specified by the incoming patch. It does the same for the texture coordinates. It also applies height mapping in the same way as was done in Program 12.3. The fragment shader is unchanged.

The changes to each of the components are shown in Program 12.4. The result is shown in Figure 12.7. Note that the highs and lows now correspond much more closely to light and dark sections of the image.

Program 12.4 Instanced Tessellated Terrain

Java / JOGL application

```
// same as for Bezier surface example, with these changes:
gl.glPatchParameteri(GL_PATCH_VERTICES, 4);
gl.glDrawArraysInstanced(GL_PATCHES, 0, 4, 64*64);
```

Vertex Shader

```
. . .
out vec2 tc;
. . .
void main(void)
{   vec2 patchTexCoords[ ] = vec2[ ] (vec2(0,0), vec2(1,0), vec2(0,1), vec2(1,1));

    // compute an offset for coordinates based on which instance this is
    int x = gl_InstanceID % 64;
    int y = gl_InstanceID / 64;

    // tex coords are distributed across 64 patches, normalized to [0..1].  Flip Y coordinates.
    tc = vec2( (x+patchTexCoords[gl_VertexID].x) / 64.0,  (63 - y+patchTexCoords[gl_VertexID].y) / 64.0);

    // vertex locations are the same as texture coordinates, except they range from -0.5 to +0.5.
    gl_Position = vec4(tc.x - 0.5, 0.0, (1.0 - tc.y) - 0.5, 1.0);   // Also un-flip the Y's
}
```

Tessellation Control Shader

```
. . .
layout (vertices = 4) out;
in vec2 tc[ ];
out vec2 tcs_out[ ];
. . .
void main(void)
{   // tessellation level specification the same as the previous example
    . . .
```

```
    tcs_out[gl_InvocationID] = tc[gl_InvocationID];
    gl_out[gl_InvocationID].gl_Position = gl_in[gl_InvocationID].gl_Position;
}
```

Tessellation Evaluation Shader

```
. . .
in vec2 tcs_out[ ];
out vec2 tes_out;
void main (void)
{   // map the texture coordinates onto the sub-grid specified by the incoming control points
    vec2 tc = vec2(tcs_out[0].x + (gl_TessCoord.x) / 64.0, tcs_out[0].y + (1.0 - gl_TessCoord.y) / 64.0);

    // map the tessellated grid onto the sub-grid specified by the incoming control points
    vec4 tessellatedPoint = vec4(gl_in[0].gl_Position.x + gl_TessCoord.x / 64.0, 0.0,
                                 gl_in[0].gl_Position.z + gl_TessCoord.y / 64.0, 1.0);

    // add the height from the height map to the vertex:
    tessellatedPoint.y += (texture(tex_height, tc).r) / 40.0;

    gl_Position = mvp * tessellatedPoint;
    tes_out = tc;
}
```

Now that we have achieved height mapping, we can work on improving it and incorporating lighting. One challenge is that our vertices do not yet have normal vectors associated with them. Another challenge is that simply using the texture image as a height map has produced an overly "jagged" result—in this case because not all grayscale variation in the texture image is due to height. For this particular texture map, it so happens that Hastings-Trew has already produced an improved height map that we can use [HT16]. It is shown in Figure 12.8 (on the left).

To create normals, we could compute them on the fly, by generating the heights of neighboring vertices (or neighboring texels in the height map), building vectors connecting them, and using a cross

Figure 12.7
Tessellated terrain—second attempt, with instancing.

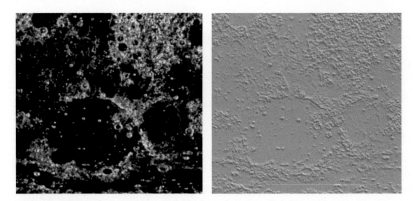

Figure 12.8
Moon surface: height map [HT16] and normal map.

product to find the normal. This requires some tuning, depending on the precision of the scene (and/or the height map image). Here we have instead used the GIMP "normalmap" plugin [GP16] to generate a normal map based on Hastings-Trew's height map, shown in Figure 12.8 (on the right).

Most of the changes to our code are now simply to implement the standard methods for Phong shading:

- *Java /JOGL application*

  We load and activate an additional texture to hold the normal map. We also add code to specify the lighting and materials as we have done in previous applications.

- *Vertex shader*

  The only additions are declarations for lighting uniforms and the sampler for the normal map. Lighting code customarily done in the vertex shader is moved to the tessellation evaluation shader, because the vertices aren't generated until the tessellation stage.

- *Tessellation control shader*

  The only additions are declarations for lighting uniforms and the sampler for the normal map.

- *Tessellation evaluation shader*

  The preparatory code for Phong lighting is now placed in the evaluation shader:

```
varyingVertPos = (mv_matrix * tessellatedPoint).xyz;
varyingLightDir = light.position - varyingVertPos;
```

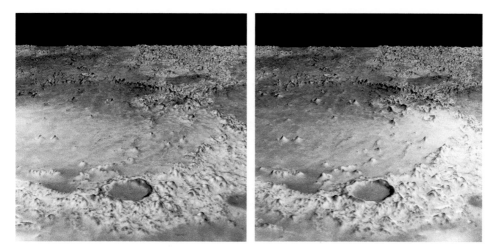

Figure 12.9
Tessellated terrain with normal map and lighting (light source positioned at left and at right, respectively).

- *Fragment shader*

  The typical code sections, described previously, for computing Phong (or Blinn-Phong) lighting are done here, as well as the code to extract normals from the normal map. The lighting result is then combined with the texture image with a weighted sum.

The final result, with height and normal mapping as well as Phong lighting, is shown in Figure 12.9. The terrain now responds to lighting. In this example, a positional light has been placed to the left of center in the image on the left, and to the right of center in the image on the right.

Although the response to the movement of the light is difficult to tell from a still picture, the reader should be able to discern the diffuse lighting changes and that specular highlights on the peaks are very different in the two images. This is of course more obvious when the camera or the light source is moving. The results are still imperfect, because the original texture that is incorporated in the output includes shadows that will appear on the rendered result, regardless of lighting.

12.4 CONTROLLING LEVEL OF DETAIL (LOD)

Using instancing to generate millions of vertices in real time, as in Program 12.4, is likely to place a load on even a well-equipped modern computer. Fortunately, the strategy of dividing the terrain into separate patches, as we have done to increase the number of generated grid vertices, also affords us a nice mechanism for reducing that load.

Of the millions of vertices being generated, many aren't necessary. Vertices in patches that are close to the camera *are* important because we expect to discern detail in nearby objects. However, the further the patches are from the camera, the less likely there will even be enough pixels in the rasterization to warrant the number of vertices we are generating!

Changing the number of vertices in a patch based on the distance from the camera is a technique called *level of detail*, or *LOD*. Sellers and colleagues describe a way of controlling LOD in instanced tessellation [SW15] by modifying the control shader. Program 12.5 shows a simplified version of this approach. The strategy is to use the patch's perceived size to determine the values of its tessellation levels. Since the tessellated grid for a patch will eventually be placed within the square defined by the four control points entering the control shader, we can use the locations of the control points relative to the camera to determine how many vertices should be generated for the patch. The steps are as follows:

1. Calculate the screen locations of the four control points by applying the MVP matrix to them.
2. Calculate the lengths of the sides of the square (i.e., the width and height) defined by the control points (in screen space). Note that even though the four control points form a square, these side lengths can differ because the perspective matrix has been applied.
3. Scale the lengths' values by a tunable constant, depending on the precision needed for the tessellation levels (based on the amount of detail in the height map).
4. Add 1 to the scaled length values, to avoid the possibility of specifying a tessellation level of 0 (which would result in no vertices being generated).
5. Set the tessellation levels to the corresponding calculated width and height values.

Recall that in our instanced example we are not creating just one grid, but 64*64 of them. So the five steps listed above are performed for each patch. Thus, the level of detail varies from patch to patch.

All of the changes are in the control shader and are shown in Program 12.5, with the generated output following in Figure 12.10. Note that the variable gl_InvocationID refers to which vertex in the patch is being processed (not which patch is being processed). Therefore, the LOD computation which tells the tessellator how many vertices to generate occurs during the processing of the 0th vertex in each patch.

Program 12.5 Tessellation Level of Detail (LOD)

Tessellation Control Shader

```
. . .
void main(void)
{   float subdivisions = 16.0;   // tunable constant based on density of detail in height map
    if (gl_InvocationID == 0)
    {   vec4 p0 = mvp * gl_in[0].gl_Position;   // control pt. positions in screen space
        vec4 p1 = mvp * gl_in[1].gl_Position;
        vec4 p2 = mvp * gl_in[2].gl_Position;
        p0 = p0 / p0.w;
        p1 = p1 / p1.w;
        p2 = p2 / p2.w;
        float width  = length(p2.xy - p0.xy) * subdivisions + 1.0;    // perceived "width" of tess grid
        float height = length(p1.xy - p0.xy) * subdivisions + 1.0;    // perceived "height" of tess grid
        gl_TessLevelOuter[0] = height;          // set tess levels based on perceived side lengths
        gl_TessLevelOuter[1] = width;
        gl_TessLevelOuter[2] = height;
        gl_TessLevelOuter[3] = width;
        gl_TessLevelInner[0] = width;
        gl_TessLevelInner[1] = height;
    }
    //  forward texture coordinates and control points to TES as before
    tcs_out[gl_InvocationID] = tc[gl_InvocationID];
    gl_out[gl_InvocationID].gl_Position = gl_in[gl_InvocationID].gl_Position;
}
```

Applying these control shader changes to the instanced (but not lighted) version of our scene from Figure 12.7 and replacing the height map with Hastings-Trew's more finely tuned version shown in Figure 12.8 produces the improved scene, with more realistic horizon detail, shown in Figure 12.10.

In this example it is also useful to change the layout specifier in the evaluation shader from

```
layout (quads, equal_spacing) in;
```

to

```
layout (quads, fractional_even_spacing) in;
```

Figure 12.10
Tessellated moon with controlled level of detail (LOD).

The reason for this modification is difficult to illustrate in still images. In an animated scene as a tessellated object moves through 3D space, it is sometimes possible, if LOD is used, to *see* the changes in tessellation levels on the surface of the object as wiggling artifacts called "popping." Changing from *equal spacing* to *fractional spacing* reduces this effect by making the grid geometry of adjacent patch instances more similar, even if they differ in level of detail. (See Exercises 12.2 and 12.3.)

Employing LOD can dramatically reduce the load on the system. For example, when animated, the scene might be less likely to appear jerky or to lag than would be the case without controlling LOD.

Applying this simple LOD technique to the version that includes Phong shading (i.e., Program 12.4) is a bit trickier. This is because the changes in LOD between adjacent patch instances can in turn cause sudden changes to the associated normal vectors, causing popping artifacts in the lighting! As always, there are tradeoffs and compromises to consider when constructing a complex 3D scene.

SUPPLEMENTAL NOTES

Combining tessellation with LOD is particularly useful in real-time virtual reality applications that require both complex detail for realism and frequent object movement and/or changes in camera position, such as in computer games. In this chapter we have illustrated the use of tessellation and LOD for real-time terrain generation, although it can also be applied in other areas such as in displacement mapping for 3D models (where tessellated vertices are added to the surface of a model and then moved so as to add detail). It is also useful in computer-aided design applications.

Sellers and colleagues extend the LOD technique (shown in Program 12.5) further than we have presented by also eliminating vertices in patches that are *behind the camera* (they do this by setting their inner and outer levels to zero) [SW15].

This is an example of a *culling* technique, and it is a very useful one because of the load that instanced tessellation can still place on the system.

The four-parameter version of createShaderProgram() described in Program 12.1 is added to the Utils.java file. Later, we will add additional versions to accomodate the geometry shader stage.

Exercises

12.1 Modify Program 12.1 to experiment with various values for inner and outer tessellation levels and observing the resulting rendered mesh.

12.2 Modify Program 12.1 by changing the layout specifier in the evaluation shader from equal_spacing to fractional_even_spacing, as shown in Section 12.4. Observe the effect on the generated mesh.

12.3 Test Program 12.5 with the layout specifier in the evaluation shader set to equal_spacing, and then to fractional_even_spacing, as described in Section 12.4. Observe the effects on the rendered surface as the camera moves. You should be able to observe popping artifacts in the first case, which are mostly alleviated in the second case.

12.4 *(PROJECT)* Modify Program 12.3 to utilize a height map of your own design (you could use the one you built previously in Exercise 10.2). Then add lighting and shadow mapping so that your tessellated terrain casts shadows. This is a complex exercise, because some of the code in the first and second shadow mapping passes will need to be moved to the evaluation shader.

References

[GP16] GIMP Plugin Registry, *normalmap plugin*, accessed July 2016, http://registry.gimp.org/node/69

[HT16] J. Hastings-Trew, *JHT's Planetary Pixel Emporium*, accessed July 2016, http://planetpixelemporium.com/

[LU16] F. Luna, *Introduction to 3D Game Programming with DirectX 12*, 2nd ed. (Mercury Learning, 2016).

[SW15] G. Sellers, R. Wright Jr., and N. Haemel, *OpenGL SuperBible: Comprehensive Tutorial and Reference*, 7th ed. (Addison-Wesley, 2015).

[TS16] Tessellation, Wikipedia, accessed July 2016, https://en.wikipedia.org/wiki/Tessellation

GEOMETRY SHADERS

■ ■ ■ ■ ■

Immediately following tessellation in the OpenGL pipeline is the *geometry* stage. Here the programmer has the option of including a *geometry shader*. This stage actually predates tessellation; it became part of the OpenGL core at version 3.2 (in 2009).

Like tessellation, geometry shaders enable the programmer to manipulate *groups* of vertices, in ways that are impossible to do in a vertex shader. In some cases, a task might be accomplished using either a tessellation shader or a geometry shader, as their capabilities overlap in some ways.

◼13.1◼ PER-PRIMITIVE PROCESSING IN OPENGL

The geometry shader stage is situated between tessellation and rasterization, within the segment of the pipeline devoted to *primitive processing* (refer back to Figure 2.2). Whereas vertex shaders enable the manipulation of one vertex at a time and fragment shaders enable the manipulation of one fragment (essentially one pixel) at a time, *geometry shaders enable manipulation of one <u>primitive</u> at a time.*

Recall that primitives are the basic building blocks in OpenGL for drawing objects. Only a few types of primitives are available; we will focus primarily on geometry shaders that manipulate triangles. Thus, when we say that a geometry shader can manipulate one primitive at a time, we usually mean that the shader has access to *all three vertices of a triangle* at a time. Geometry shaders allow you to

- access all vertices in a primitive at once, then
- output the same primitive unchanged, or
- output the same primitive with modified vertex locations, or
- output a different type of primitive, or
- output additional primitives, or
- delete the primitive (not output it at all).

Similar to the tessellation evaluation shader, incoming vertex attributes are accessible in a geometry shader as *arrays*. However, in a geometry shader, incoming attribute arrays are indexed only up to the primitive size. For example, if the primitives are triangles, then the available indices are 0, 1, and 2. Accessing the vertices themselves is done using the predefined array gl_in, as follows:

gl_in[2].gl_Position   *// position of the 3rd vertex*

Also similar to the tessellation evaluation shader, the geometry shader's output vertex attributes are all *scalars*. That is, the output is a stream of individual vertices (their positions and other attribute variables, if any) that form primitives.

There is a layout qualifier used to set the primitive input/output types and the output size.

The special GLSL command EmitVertex() specifies that a vertex is to be output. The special GLSL command EndPrimitive() indicates the completion of building a particular primitive.

The built-in variable gl_PrimitiveIDIn is available and holds the ID of the current primitive. The ID numbers start at 0 and count up to the number of primitives minus 1.

We will explore four common categories of operations:

- altering primitives
- deleting primitives
- adding primitives
- changing primitive types

▉13.2▉ ALTERING PRIMITIVES

Geometry shaders are convenient for changing the shape of an object when that change can be affected through isolated changes to the primitives (typically triangles).

Consider, for example, the torus we rendered previously in Figure 7.12. Suppose that torus represented an inner tube (such as for a tire), and we want to "inflate" it. Simply applying a scale factor in the Java/JOGL code won't accomplish this, because its fundamental shape wouldn't change. Giving it the appearance of being "inflated" requires also making the inner hole smaller as the torus stretches into the empty center space.

One way of doing this would be to add the surface normal vector to each vertex. While it is true that this could be done in the vertex shader, let's do it in the geometry shader, for practice. Program 13.1 shows the GLSL geometry shader code. The other modules are the same as for Program 7.3, with a few minor changes: The fragment shader input names now need to reflect the geometry shader outputs (for example, varyingNormal becomes varyingNormalG), and the Java/JOGL application needs to compile the geometry shader and attach it to the shader program prior to linking. The new shader is specified as being a geometry shader as follows:

```
int gShader = gl.glCreateShader(GL_GEOMETRY_SHADER);
```

Program 13.1 Geometry Shader: Altering Vertices

```
#version 430

layout (triangles) in;

in vec3 varyingNormal[ ];        // inputs from the vertex shader
in vec3 varyingLightDir[ ];
in vec3 varyingHalfVector[ ];

out vec3 varyingNormalG;         // outputs through the rasterizer to the fragment shader
out vec3 varyingLightDirG;
out vec3 varyingHalfVectorG;

layout (triangle_strip, max_vertices=3) out;

// matrices and lighting uniforms same as before
. . .
void main (void)
{   // move vertices along the normal, and pass through the other vertex attributes unchanged
```

```
for (int i=0; i<3; i++)
{   gl_Position = proj_matrix *
        gl_in[i].gl_Position + normalize(vec4(varyingNormal[i],1.0)) * 0.4;
    varyingNormalG = varyingNormal[i];
    varyingLightDirG = varyingLightDir[i];
    varyingHalfVectorG = varyingHalfVector[i];
    EmitVertex();
}
EndPrimitive();
}
```

Note in Program 13.1 that the input variables corresponding to the output variables from the vertex shader are declared as *arrays*. This provides the programmer a mechanism for accessing each of the vertices in the triangle primitive and their attributes using the indices 0, 1, and 2. We wish to move those vertices outward along their surface normals. Both the vertices and the normals have already been transformed to view space in the vertex shader. We add a fraction of the normal to each of the incoming vertex positions (gl_in[i].gl_Position), and then apply the projection matrix to the result, producing each output gl_Position.

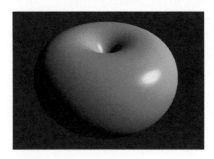

Figure 13.1
"Inflated" torus with vertices altered by geometry shader.

Note the use of the GLSL call EmitVertex() that specifies when we have finished computing the output gl_Position and its associated vertex attributes and are ready to output a vertex. The EndPrimitive() call specifies that we have completed the definition of a set of vertices comprising a primitive (in this case, a triangle). The result is shown in Figure 13.1.

The geometry shader includes two layout qualifiers. The first specifies the input primitive type and must be compatible with the primitive type in the Java-side glDrawArrays() or glDrawElements() call. The options are as follows:

geometry shader input primitive	compatible OpenGL primitives sent from glDrawArrays()	#vertices per invocation
points	GL_POINTS	1
lines	GL_LINES, GL_LINE_STRIP	2

lines_adjacency	GL_LINES_ADJACENCY, GL_LINE_STRIP_ADJACENCY	4
triangles	GL_TRIANGLES, GL_TRIANGLE_STRIP, GL_TRIANGLE_FAN	3
triangles_adjacency	GL_TRIANGLES_ADJACENCY, GL_TRIANGLE_STRIP_ADJACENCY	6

The various OpenGL primitive types (including "strip" and "fan" types) were described in Chapter 4. "Adjacency" types were introduced in OpenGL for use with geometry shaders and allow access to vertices adjacent to the primitive. We don't use them in this book, but they are listed for completeness.

The output primitive type must be *points*, *line_strip*, or *triangle_strip*. Note that the output layout qualifier also specifies the maximum number of vertices the shader outputs in each invocation.

This particular alteration to the torus could have been done more easily in the vertex shader. However, suppose that instead of moving each vertex outward along its own surface normal, we wished instead to move each *triangle* outward along its surface normal, in effect "exploding" the torus triangles outward. The vertex shader cannot do that, because computing a normal for the triangle requires averaging the vertex normals of all three triangle vertices, and the vertex shader only has access to the vertex attributes of one vertex in the triangle at a time. We can, however, do this in the geometry shader, because the geometry shader *does* have access to all three vertices in each triangle. We average their normals to compute a surface normal for the triangle, then add that averaged normal to each of the vertices in the triangle primitive. Figures 13.2, 13.3, and 13.4 show the averaging of the surface normals, the modified geometry shader main() code, and the resulting output, respectively.

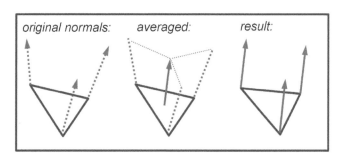

Figure 13.2
Applying averaged triangle surface normal to triangle vertices.

```
void main (void)
{    //  average the three triangle vertex normals, creating a single triangle surface normal
     vec4 triangleNormal =
          vec4(((varyingNormal[0] + varyingNormal[1] + varyingNormal[2]) / 3.0),1.0);

     //  move all three vertices outward along the same normal
     for (i=0; i<3; i++)
     {    gl_Position = proj_matrix * (gl_in[i].gl_Position + normalize(triangleNormal) * 0.4);
          varyingNormalG = varyingNormal[i];
          varyingLightDirG = varyingLightDir[i];
          varyingHalfVectorG = varyingHalfVector[i];
          EmitVertex();
     }
     EndPrimitive();
}
```

Figure 13.3
Modified geometry shader for "exploding" the torus.

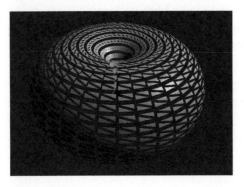

Figure 13.4
"Exploded" torus.

The appearance of the "exploded" torus can be improved by ensuring that the inside of the torus is also visible (normally those triangles are culled by OpenGL because they are "back-facing"). One way of doing this is to render the torus twice, once in the normal manner and once with winding order reversed (reversing the winding order effectively switches which faces are front-facing and which are back-facing). We also send a flag to the shaders (in a uniform) to disable diffuse and specular lighting on the back-facing triangles, to make them less prominent. The changes to the code are as follows:

changes to display() function:

```
. . .
//  draw front-facing triangles – enable lighting
gl.glUniform1i(enableLightingLoc, 1);
gl.glFrontFace(GL_CCW);
gl.glDrawElements(GL_TRIANGLES, numTorusIndices, GL_UNSIGNED_INT, 0);

//  draw back-facing triangles – disable lighting
gl.glUniform1i(enableLightingLoc, 0);
gl.glFrontFace(GL_CW);
gl.glDrawElements(GL_TRIANGLES, numTorusIndices, GL_UNSIGNED_INT, 0);
```

modification to fragment shader:

```
...
if (enableLighting == 1)
{   fragColor = ...    // when rendering front faces, use normal lighting computations
}
else                  // when rendering back faces, enable only the ambient lighting component
{   fragColor = globalAmbient * material.ambient +  light.ambient * material.ambient;
}
```

The resulting "exploded" torus, including back faces, is shown in Figure 13.5.

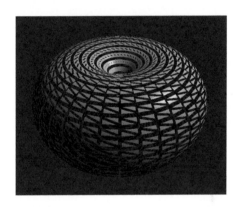

Figure 13.5
"Exploded" torus, including back faces.

13.3 ■ DELETING PRIMITIVES

A common use for geometry shaders is to build richly ornamental objects out of simple ones, by judiciously deleting some of the primitives. For example, removing some of the triangles from our torus can turn it into a sort of complex latticed structure that would be more difficult to model from scratch. A geometry shader that does this is shown in Program 13.2, and the output is shown in Figure 13.6.

Program 13.2 Geometry: Delete Primitives

```
//  inputs, outputs, and uniforms as before
...
void main (void)
{   if ( mod(gl_PrimitiveIDIn,3) != 0 )
    {   for (int i=0; i<3; i++)
        {   gl_Position = proj_matrix * gl_in[i].gl_Position;
            varyingNormalG = varyingNormal[i];
            varyingLightDirG = varyingLightDir[i];
            varyingHalfVectorG = varyingHalfVector[i];
            EmitVertex();
    }  }
    EndPrimitive();
}
```

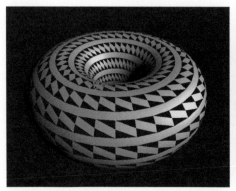

Figure 13.6
Geometry shader: primitive deletion.

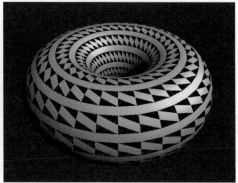

Figure 13.7
Primitive deletion showing back faces.

No other changes to the code are necessary. Note the use of the mod function—all vertices are passed through except those in the first of every three primitives, which are ignored. Here too, rendering the back-facing triangles can improve realism, as shown in Figure 13.7.

13.4 ADDING PRIMITIVES

Perhaps the most interesting and powerful use of geometry shaders is for adding additional vertices and/or primitives to a model being rendered. This makes it possible to do such things as increase the detail in an object to improve height mapping or to change the shape of an object completely.

Consider the following example, where we change each triangle in the torus to a tiny triangular pyramid.

Our strategy, similar to our previous "exploded" torus example, is illustrated in Figure 13.8. The vertices of an incoming triangle primitive are used to define the base of a pyramid. The walls of the pyramid are constructed of those vertices, and of a new point (called the "spike point") computed by averaging the normals of the original vertices. New normal vectors are then computed for each of the three "sides" of the pyramid by taking the cross product of two vectors from the spike point to the base.

The geometry shader in Program 13.3 does this for each triangle primitive in the torus. For each incoming triangle, it outputs three triangle primitives, for a total of nine vertices. Each new triangle is built in the function makeNewTriangle(), which

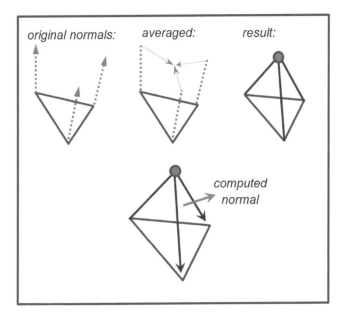

Figure 13.8
Converting triangles to pyramids.

is called three times. It computes the normal for the specified triangle, then calls the function setOutputValues() to assign the appropriate output vertex attributes for each vertex emitted. After emitting all three vertices, it calls EndPrimitive(). To ensure that the lighting is performed accurately, new values of the light direction vector are computed for each newly created vertex.

Program 13.3 Geometry: Add Primitives

```
. . .
vec3 newPoints[ ], lightDir[ ];
float sLen = 0.01;   // sLen is the "spike length", the height of the small pyramid

void setOutputValues(int p, vec3 norm)
{   varyingNormal = norm;
    varyingLightDir = lightDir[p];
    varyingVertPos = newPoints[p];
    gl_Position = proj_matrix * vec4(newPoints[p], 1.0);
}

void makeNewTriangle(int p1, int p2)
{   // generate surface normal for this triangle
    vec3 c1 = normalize(newPoints[p1] - newPoints[3]);
```

```
    vec3 c2 = normalize(newPoints[p2] - newPoints[3]);
    vec3 norm = cross(c1,c2);

    // generate and emit the three vertices
    setOutputValues(p1, norm); EmitVertex();
    setOutputValues(p2, norm); EmitVertex();
    setOutputValues(3, norm); EmitVertex();
    EndPrimitive();
}

void main(void)
{   // offset the three triangle vertices by the original surface normal
    vec3 sp0 = gl_in[0].gl_Position.xyz + varyingOriginalNormal[0]*sLen;
    vec3 sp1 = gl_in[1].gl_Position.xyz + varyingOriginalNormal[1]*sLen;
    vec3 sp2 = gl_in[2].gl_Position.xyz + varyingOriginalNormal[2]*sLen;

    // compute the new points comprising a small pyramid
    newPoints[0] = gl_in[0].gl_Position.xyz;
    newPoints[1] = gl_in[1].gl_Position.xyz;
    newPoints[2] = gl_in[2].gl_Position.xyz;
    newPoints[3] = (sp0 + sp1 + sp2)/3.0;          // spike point

    // compute the directions from the vertices to the light
    lightDir[0] = light.position - newPoints[0];
    lightDir[1] = light.position - newPoints[1];
    lightDir[2] = light.position - newPoints[2];
    lightDir[3] = light.position - newPoints[3];

    // build three new triangles to form a small pyramid on the surface
    makeNewTriangle(0,1);  // the third point is always the spike point
    makeNewTriangle(1,2);
    makeNewTriangle(2,0);
}
```

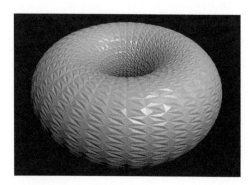

Figure 13.9
Geometry shader: primitive addition.

The resulting output is shown in Figure 13.9. If the spike length (sLen) variable is increased, the added surface "pyramids" would be taller. However, they could appear unrealistic in the absence of shadows. Adding shadow mapping to Program 13.3 is left as an exercise for the reader.

Careful application of this technique can enable the simulation of spikes, thorns, and other fine surface protrusions, as well as the reverse, such as indentations and craters ([DV14], [KS16], and [TR13]).

13.5 CHANGING PRIMITIVE TYPES

OpenGL allows for switching primitive types in a geometry shader. A common use for this feature is to convert input *triangles* into one or more output *line segments*, simulating fur or hair. Although hair remains one of the more difficult real-world items to generate convincingly, geometry shaders can help make real-time rendering achievable in many cases.

Program 13.4 shows a geometry shader that converts each incoming three-vertex triangle to an outward-facing two-vertex line segment. It starts by computing a starting point for the strand of hair by averaging the triangle vertex locations, thus generating the centroid of the triangle. It then uses the same "spike point" from Program 13.3 as the hair's ending point. The output primitive is specified as a line strip with two vertices, the first vertex being the start point and the second vertex being the end point. The result is shown in Figure 13.10 for a torus instantiated with a dimensionality of 72 slices.

Of course, this is merely the starting point for generating fully realistic hair. Making the hair bend or move would require several modifications, such as generating more vertices for the line strip and computing their positions along curves and/or incorporating randomness. Lighting is complicated by the lack of an obvious surface normal for a line segment; in this example, we simply assigned the normal to be the same as the original triangle's surface normal.

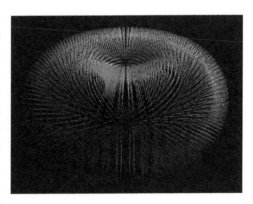

Figure 13.10
Changing triangle primitives to line primitives.

Program 13.4 Geometry: Changing Primitive Types

```
layout (line_strip, max_vertices=2) out;

. . .

void main(void)
{   vec3 op0 = gl_in[0].gl_Position.xyz;        // original triangle vertices
```

```
vec3 op1 = gl_in[1].gl_Position.xyz;
vec3 op2 = gl_in[2].gl_Position.xyz;
vec3 ep0 = gl_in[0].gl_Position.xyz + varyingNormal[0]*sLen;      // offset triangle vertices
vec3 ep1 = gl_in[1].gl_Position.xyz + varyingNormal[1]*sLen;
vec3 ep2 = gl_in[2].gl_Position.xyz + varyingNormal[2]*sLen;

// compute the new points comprising a small line segment
vec3 newPoint1 = (op0 + op1 + op2)/3.0;      // original (start) point
vec3 newPoint2 = (ep0 + ep1 + ep2)/3.0;      // end point

gl_Position = proj_matrix * vec4(newPoint1, 1.0);
varyingVertPosG = newPoint1;
varyingLightDirG = light.position - newPoint1;
varyingNormalG = varyingNormal[0];
EmitVertex();

gl_Position = proj_matrix * vec4(newPoint2, 1.0);
varyingVertPosG = newPoint2;
varyingLightDirG = light.position - newPoint2;
varyingNormalG = varyingNormal[1];
EmitVertex();

EndPrimitive();
}
```

SUPPLEMENTAL NOTES

One of the appeals of geometry shaders is that they are relatively easy to use. Although many applications for which geometry shaders are used *could* be achieved using tessellation, the mechanism of geometry shaders often makes them easier to implement and debug. Of course, the relative fit of geometry versus tessellation depends on the particular application.

Generating convincing hair or fur is challenging, and there is a wide range of techniques employed depending on the application. In some cases, simple texturing is adequate and/or the use of tessellation or geometry shaders such as the basic technique shown in this chapter. When greater realism is required, movement (animation) and lighting become tricky. Two dedicated tools for hair and fur generation are *HairWorks* which is part of the NVIDIA GameWorks suite [GW18] and *TressFX* which was developed by AMD [TR18]. The former works with both OpenGL and DirectX, whereas the latter works only with DirectX. Examples of using TressFX can be found in [GP14].

Exercises

13.1 Modify Program 13.1 so that it moves each vertex slightly toward the center of its primitive triangle. The result should look similar to the exploded torus in Figure 13.5, but without the overall change in torus size.

13.2 Modify Program 13.2 so that it deletes every other primitive, or every fourth primitive (rather than every third primitive), and observe the effect on the resulting rendered torus. Also, try changing the dimensionality of the instantiated torus to a value that is *not* a multiple of three (such as 40), while still deleting every third primitive. There are many possible effects.

13.3 *(PROJECT)* Modify Program 13.4 to additionally render the original torus. That is, render *both* a lighted torus (as previously done in Chapter 7) *and* the outgoing line segments (using a geometry shader) so that the "hair" looks like it is coming out of the torus.

13.4 *(PROJECT)* Modify Program 13.4 so that it produces outward-facing line segments with *more than two* vertices, arranged so as to make the line segments appear to bend slightly.

References

[DV14]   J. deVries, *LearnOpenGL*, 2014, accessed July 2016, http://www.learnopengl.com/

[GP14]   *GPU Pro 5: Advanced Rendering Techniques*, ed. W. Engel (CRC Press, 2014).

[GW18]   NVIDIA GameWorks Suite, 2018, accessed May 2018, https://developer.nvidia.com/gameworks

[KS16]   J. Kessenich, G. Sellers, and D. Shreiner, *OpenGL Programming Guide: The Official Guide to Learning OpenGL, Version 4.5 with SPIR-V*, 9th ed. (Addison-Wesley, 2016).

[TR13]   P. Trettner, *Prototype Grass* (blog), 2013, accessed July 2016, https://upvoid.com/devblog/2013/02/prototype-grass/

[TR18]   TressFX Hair, AMD, 2018, accessed May 2018, https://www.amd.com/en/technologies/tressfx

OTHER TECHNIQUES

In this chapter we explore a variety of techniques utilizing the tools we have learned about throughout the book. Some we will develop fully, while for others we will offer a more cursory description. Graphics programming is a huge field, and this chapter is by no means comprehensive, but rather an introduction to just a few of the creative effects that have been developed over the years.

14.1 FOG

Usually when people think of fog, they think of early misty mornings with low visibility. In truth, atmospheric haze (such as fog) is more common than most of us think. The majority of the time, there is some degree of haze in the air, and although we have become accustomed to seeing it, we don't usually realize it is there. So we can enhance the realism in our outdoor scenes by introducing fog—even if only a small amount.

Fog also can enhance the sense of depth. When close objects have better *clarity* than distant objects, it is one more visual cue that our brains can use to decipher the topography of a 3D scene.

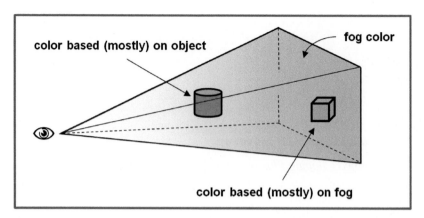

Figure 14.1
Fog: blending based on distance.

There are a variety of methods for simulating fog, from very simple ones to sophisticated models that include light scattering effects. However, even very simple approaches can be effective. One such method is to blend the actual pixel color with another color (the "fog" color, typically gray or bluish-gray—also used for the background color), based on the distance the object is from the eye.

Figure 14.1 illustrates the concept. The eye (camera) is shown at the left, and two red objects are placed in the view frustum. The cylinder is closer to the eye, so it is mostly its original color (red); the cube is further from the eye, so it is mostly fog color. For this simple implementation, virtually all of the computations can be performed in the fragment shader.

Program 14.1 shows the relevant code for a very simple fog algorithm that uses a linear blend from object color to fog color based on the distance from the camera to the pixel. Specifically, this example adds fog to the height mapping example from Program 10.4.

Program 14.1 Simple Fog Generation

Vertex (or Tessellation Control) shader

```
. . .
out vec3 vertEyeSpacePos;

. . .
// Compute vertex position in eye space, without perspective, and send it to the fragment shader.
// The variable "p" is the height-mapped vertex, as described earlier in Program 10-4.
vertEyeSpacePos = (mv_matrix * p).xyz;
```

Fragment shader

```
. . .
in vec3 vertEyeSpacePos;
out vec4 fragColor;
. . .
void main(void)
{   vec4 fogColor = vec4(0.7, 0.8, 0.9, 1.0);        // bluish gray
    float fogStart = 0.2;
    float fogEnd = 0.8;

    // the distance from the camera to the vertex in eye space is simply the length of a
    // vector to that vertex, because the camera is at (0,0,0) in eye space.
    float dist = length(vertEyeSpace.xyz);
    float fogFactor = clamp(((fogEnd - dist) / (fogEnd - fogStart)), 0.0, 1.0);
    fragColor = mix(fogColor, (texture(t,tc), fogFactor);
}
```

The variable fogColor specifies a color for the fog. The variables fogStart and fogEnd specify the range (in eye space) over which the output color transitions from object color to fog color, and can be tuned to meet the needs of the scene. The percentage of fog mixed with the object color is calculated in the variable fogFactor, which is the ratio of how close the vertex is to fogEnd to the total length of the transition region. The GLSL clamp() function is used to restrict this ratio to being between the values 0.0 and 1.0. The GLSL mix() function then returns a weighted average of fog color and object color, based on the value of fogFactor. Figure 14.2 shows the addition of fog to a scene with height-mapped terrain. (A rocky texture from [LU16] has also been applied.)

Figure 14.2
Fog example.

▇14.2▇ COMPOSITING/BLENDING/TRANSPARENCY

We have already seen a few examples of blending—in the supplementary notes for Chapter 7 and just above in our implementation of fog. However, we haven't yet seen how to utilize the blending (or *compositing*) capabilities that follow after the fragment shader, during pixel operations (recall the pipeline sequence shown in Figure 2.2). It is there that *transparency* is handled, which we look at now.

Throughout this book we have made frequent use of the vec4 data type, to represent 3D points and vectors in a homogenous coordinate system. You may have noticed that we also frequently use a vec4 to store *color* information, where the first three values consist of red, green, and blue, and the fourth element is—what?

The fourth element in a color is called the *alpha channel* and specifies the *opacity* of the color. Opacity is a measure of how *non*-transparent the pixel color is. An alpha value of 0 means "no opacity," or completely transparent. An alpha value of 1 means "fully opaque," not at all transparent. In a sense, the "transparency" of a color is 1-α, where α is the value of the alpha channel.

Recall from Chapter 2 that pixel operations utilize the *Z-buffer*, which achieves hidden surface removal by replacing an existing pixel color when another object's location at that pixel is found to be closer. We actually have more control over this process—we may choose to *blend* the two pixels.

When a pixel is being rendered, it is called the "source" pixel. The pixel already in the frame buffer (presumably rendered from a previous object) is called the "destination" pixel. OpenGL provides many options for deciding which of the two pixels, or what sort of combination of them, ultimately is placed in the frame buffer. Note that the pixel operations step is not a programmable stage—so the OpenGL tools for configuring the desired compositing are found in the Java/ JOGL application rather than in a shader.

The two OpenGL functions for controlling compositing are glBlendEquation(mode) and glBlendFunc(srcFactor, destFactor). Figure 14.3 shows an overview of the compositing process.

The compositing process works as follows:

1. The *source* and *destination* pixels are multiplied by *source factor* and *destination factor*, respectively. The source and destination factors are specified in the blendFunc() function call.

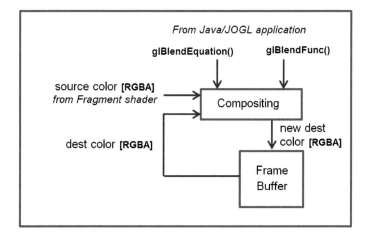

Figure 14.3
OpenGL compositing overview.

2. The specified *blendEquation* is then used to combine the modified source and destination pixels to produce a new destination color. The blend equation is specified in the glBlendEquation() call.

The most common options for glBlendFunc() parameters (i.e., srcFactor and destFactor) are shown in the following table:

glBlendFunc() parameter	resulting srcFactor or destFactor
GL_ZERO	(0,0,0,0)
GL_ONE	(1,1,1,1)
GL_SRC_COLOR	$(R_{src}, G_{src}, B_{src}, A_{src})$
GL_ONE_MINUS_SRC_COLOR	$(1,1,1,1) - (R_{src}, G_{src}, B_{src}, A_{src})$
GL_DST_COLOR	$(R_{dest}, G_{dest}, B_{dest}, A_{dest})$
GL_ONE_MINUS_DST_COLOR	$(1,1,1,1) - (R_{dest}, G_{dest}, B_{dest}, A_{dest})$
GL_SRC_ALPHA	$(A_{src}, A_{src}, A_{src}, A_{src})$
GL_ONE_MINUS_SRC_ALPHA	$(1,1,1,1) - (A_{src}, A_{src}, A_{src}, A_{src})$
GL_DST_ALPHA	$(A_{dest}, A_{dest}, A_{dest}, A_{dest})$
GL_ONE_MINUS_DST_ALPHA	$(1,1,1,1) - (A_{dest}, A_{dest}, A_{dest}, A_{dest})$
GL_CONSTANT_COLOR	$(R_{blendColor}, G_{blendColor}, B_{blendColor}, A_{blendColor})$
GL_ONE_MINUS_CONSTANT_ COLOR	$(1,1,1,1) - (R_{blendColor}, G_{blendColor}, B_{blendColor}, A_{blendColor})$

GL_CONSTANT_ALPHA	$(A_{blendColor}, A_{blendColor}, A_{blendColor}, A_{blendColor})$
GL_ONE_MINUS_CONSTANT_ALPHA	$(1,1,1,1) - (A_{blendColor}, A_{blendColor}, A_{blendColor}, A_{blendColor})$
GL_ALPHA_SATURATE	$(f, f, f, 1)$ where $f = min(A_{src}, 1)$

Those options that indicate a "blendColor" (GL_CONSTANT_COLOR, etc.) require an additional call to glBlendColor() to specify a constant color that will be used to compute the blend function result. There are a few additional blend functions that aren't listed above (not described here).

The possible options for the glBlendEquation() parameter (i.e., mode) are as follows:

mode	blended color
GL_FUNC_ADD	result = $source_{RGBA}$ + $destination_{RGBA}$
GL_FUNC_SUBTRACT	result = $source_{RGBA}$ − $destination_{RGBA}$
GL_FUNC_REVERSE_SUBTRACT	result = $destination_{RGBA}$ − $source_{RGBA}$
GL_MIN	result = $min(source_{RGBA}, destination_{RGBA})$
GL_MAX	result = $max(source_{RGBA}, destination_{RGBA})$

The glBlendFunc() defaults are GL_ONE (1.0) for srcFactor and GL_ZERO (0.0) for destFactor. The default for glBlendEquation() is GL_FUNC_ADD. Thus, by default, the source pixel is unchanged (multiplied by 1), the destination pixel is scaled to 0, and the two are added—meaning that the source pixel becomes the frame buffer color.

There are also the commands glEnable(GL_BLEND) and glDisable(GL_BLEND), which can be used to tell OpenGL to apply the specified blending or to ignore it.

We won't illustrate the effects of all of the options here, but will walk through some illustrative examples. Suppose we specify the following settings in the Java/JOGL application:

- glBlendFunc(GL_SRC_ALPHA, GL_ONE_MINUS_SRC_ALPHA)
- glBlendEquation(GL_FUNC_ADD)

Compositing would proceed as follows:

1. The source pixel is scaled by its alpha value.
2. The destination pixel is scaled by 1-srcAlpha (the *source transparency*).
3. The pixel values are added together.

For example, if the source pixel is red, with 75% opacity ([1, 0, 0, 0.75]) and the destination pixel contains completely opaque green ([0, 1, 0, 1]), then the result placed in the frame buffer would be

srcPixel * srcAlpha = [0.75, 0, 0, 0.5625]
destPixel * (1-srcAlpha) = [0, 0.25, 0, 0.25]
resulting pixel = [0.75, 0.25, 0, 0.8125]

That is, predominantly red, with some green, and mostly solid. The overall effect of the settings is to let the destination show through by an amount corresponding to the source pixel's transparency. In this example, the pixel in the frame buffer is green, and the incoming pixel is red with 25% transparency (75% opacity). So some green is allowed to show through the red.

It turns out that these settings for blend function and blend equation work well in many cases. Let's apply them to a practical example in a scene containing two 3D models: a torus and a pyramid in front of the torus. Figure 14.4 shows such a scene, on the left with an opaque pyramid and on the right with the pyramid's alpha value set to 0.8. Lighting has been added.

For many applications—such as creating a flat "window" as part of a model of a house—this simple implementation of transparency may be sufficient. However, in the example shown in Figure 14.4, there is a fairly obvious inadequacy. Although the pyramid model is now effectively transparent, an actual transparent pyramid should reveal not only the objects behind it but also *its own back surfaces*.

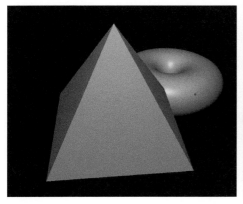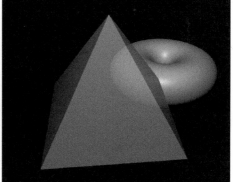

Figure 14.4
Pyramid with alpha=1.0 (left), and alpha=0.8 (right).

Actually, the reason that the back faces of the pyramid did not appear is because we enabled back-face culling. A reasonable idea might be to disable back-face culling while drawing the pyramid. However, this often produces other artifacts, as shown in Figure 14.5 (on the left). The problem with simply disabling back-face culling is that the effects of blending depend on the order that surfaces are rendered (because that determines the source and destination pixels) and we don't always have control over the rendering order. It is generally advantageous to render opaque objects first, as well as objects that are in the back (such as the torus), before any transparent objects. This also holds true for the surfaces of the pyramid, and in this case the reason that the two triangles comprising the base of the pyramid appear different is that one of them was rendered before the front of the pyramid and one was rendered after. Artifacts such as this are sometimes called "ordering" artifacts and can manifest in transparent models, because we cannot always predict the order that its triangles will be rendered.

We can solve the problem in our pyramid example by rendering the front and back faces separately, ourselves, starting with the back faces. Program 14.2 shows the code for doing this. We specify the alpha value for the pyramid by passing it to the shader program in a uniform variable, and then apply it in the fragment shader by substituting the specified alpha into the computed output color.

Note also that for lighting to work properly, we must flip the normal vector when rendering the back faces. We accomplish this by sending a flag to the vertex shader, where we then flip the normal vector.

Program 14.2 Two-Pass Blending for Transparency

JOGL/Java application - in display() for rendering pyramid:

```
. . .
gl.glEnable(GL_CULL_FACE);
. . .
gl.glEnable(GL_BLEND);                                    // configure blend settings
gl.glBlendFunc(GL_SRC_ALPHA, GL_ONE_MINUS_SRC_ALPHA);
gl.glBlendEquation(GL_FUNC_ADD);

gl.glCullFace(GL_FRONT);                                  // render pyramid back faces first
gl.glProgramUniform1f(renderingProgram, alphaLoc, 0.3f); // back faces very transparent
gl.glProgramUniform1f(renderingProgram, flipLoc, -1.0f); // flip normals on back faces
gl.glDrawArrays(GL_TRIANGLES, 0, numPyramidVertices);
```

```
gl.glCullFace(GL_BACK);                                       // then render pyramid front faces
gl.glProgramUniform1f(renderingProgram, alphaLoc, 0.7f);      // front faces slighlty transparent
gl.glProgramUniform1f(renderingProgram, flipLoc, 1.0f);       // don't flip normals on front faces
gl.glDrawArrays(GL_TRIANGLES, 0, numPyramidVertices);

gl.glDisable(GL_BLEND);
```

Vertex shader:

```
. . .
if (flipNormal < 0) varyingNormal = -varyingNormal;
. . .
```

Fragment shader:

```
. . .
fragColor = globalAmbient * material.ambient + ... etc.       // same as for Blinn-Phong lighting.
fragColor = vec4(fragColor.xyz, alpha);        // replace alpha value with one sent in uniform variable
```

The result of this "two-pass" solution is shown in Figure 14.5, on the right.

Although it works well here, the two-pass solution shown in Program 14.2 is not always adequate. For example, some more complex models may have hidden surfaces that are *front facing*, and if such an object were made transparent, our algorithm would fail to render those hidden front-facing portions of the model. Alec Jacobson describes a five-pass sequence that works in a large number of cases [JA12].

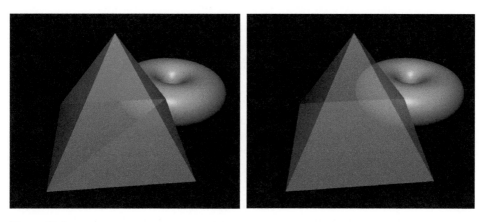

Figure 14.5
Transparency and back faces: ordering artifacts (left) and two-pass correction (right).

14.3 USER-DEFINED CLIPPING PLANES

OpenGL includes the capability to specify clipping planes beyond those defined by the view frustum. One use for a user-defined clipping plane is to slice a model. This makes it possible to create complex shapes by starting with a simple model and slicing sections off of it.

A clipping plane is defined according to the standard mathematical definition of a plane:

$$ax + by + cz + d = 0$$

where a, b, c, and d are parameters defining a particular plane in 3D space with X, Y, and Z axes. The parameters represent a vector (a,b,c) normal to the plane and a distance d from the origin to the plane. Such a plane can be specified in the vertex shader using a vec4, as follows:

```
vec4 clip_plane = vec4(0.0, 0.0, -1.0, 0.2);
```

This would correspond to the plane

$$(0.0) x + (0.0) y + (-1.0) z + 0.2 = 0$$

The clipping can then be achieved, also in the vertex shader, by using the built-in GLSL variable gl_ClipDistance[ ], as in the following example:

```
gl_ClipDistance[0] = dot(clip_plane.xyz, vertPos) + clip_plane.w;
```

In this example, vertPos refers to the vertex position coming into the vertex shader in a vertex attribute (such as from a VBO); clip_plane was defined above. We then compute the signed distance from the clipping plane to the incoming vertex (shown in Chapter 3), which is either 0 if the vertex is on the plane, or is negative or positive depending on which side of the plane the vertex lies. The subscript on the gl_ClipDistance array enables multiple clipping distances (i.e., multiple planes) to be defined. The maximum number of user clipping planes that can be defined depends on the graphics card's OpenGL implementation.

User-defined clipping must then be *enabled* in the Java/JOGL application. There are built-in OpenGL identifiers GL_CLIP_DISTANCE0, GL_CLIP_DISTANCE1, and so on, corresponding to each gl_ClipDistance[ ] array element. The 0th user-defined clipping plane can be enabled, for example, as follows:

```
gl.glEnable(GL_CLIP_DISTANCE0);
```

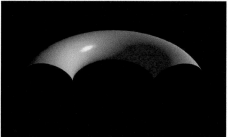

Figure 14.6
Clipping a torus.

Figure 14.7
Clipping with back faces.

Applying the above steps to our lighted torus results in the output shown in Figure 14.6, in which the front half of the torus has been clipped. (A rotation has also been applied to provide a clearer view.)

It may appear that the bottom portion of the torus has also been clipped, but that is because the inside faces of the torus were not rendered. When clipping reveals the inside surfaces of a shape, it is necessary to render them as well, or the model will appear incomplete (as it does in Figure 14.6).

Rendering the inner surfaces requires making a second call to gl_DrawArrays(), with the winding order reversed. Additionally, it is necessary to reverse the surface normal vector when rendering the back-facing triangles (as was done in the previous section). The relevant modifications to the Java application and the vertex shader are shown in Program 14.3, with the output shown in Figure 14.7.

Program 14.3 Clipping with Back Faces

Java/JOGL application:

```
public void display(GLAutoDrawable drawable)
{   ...
    flipLoc = gl.glGetUniformLocation(renderingProgram, "flipNormal");
    ...
    gl.glEnable(GL_CLIP_DISTANCE0);

    // normal drawing of external faces
    gl.glUniform1i(flipLoc, 0);
    gl.glFrontFace(GL_CCW);
    gl.glDrawElements(GL_TRIANGLES, numTorusIndices, GL_UNSIGNED_INT, 0);
```

```
// rendering of back faces with normals reversed
gl.glUniform1i(flipLoc, 1);
gl.glFrontFace(GL_CW);
gl.glDrawElements(GL_TRIANGLES, numTorusIndices, GL_UNSIGNED_INT, 0);
}
```

Vertex shader:

```
. . .
vec4 clip_plane = vec4(0.0, 0.0, -1.0, 0.5);
uniform int flipNormal;          // flag for inverting normal
. . .
void main(void)
{   . . .
    if (flipNormal==1) varyingNormal = -varyingNormal;
    . . .
    gl_ClipDistance[0] = dot(clip_plane.xyz, vertPos) - clip_plane.w;
    . . .
}
```

14.4 3D TEXTURES

Whereas 2D textures contain image data indexed by two variables, 3D textures contain the same type of image data, but in a 3D structure that is indexed by three variables. The first two dimensions still represent *width* and *height* in the texture map; the third dimension represents *depth*.

Because the data in a 3D texture is stored in a similar manner as for 2D textures, it is tempting to think of a 3D texture as a sort of 3D "image." However, we generally don't refer to 3D texture source data as a 3D image, because there are no commonly used image file formats for this sort of structure (i.e., there is nothing akin to a 3D JPEG, at least not one that is truly three-dimensional). Instead, we suggest thinking of a 3D texture as a sort of substance into which we will submerge (or "dip") the object being textured, resulting in the object's surface points obtaining their colors from the corresponding locations in the texture. Alternatively, it can be useful to imagine that the object is being "carved" out of the 3D texture "cube," much like a sculptor carves a figure out of a single solid block of marble.

OpenGL has support for 3D texture objects. In order to use them, we need to learn how to build the 3D texture and how to use it to texture an object.

Unlike 2D textures, which can be built from standard image files, 3D textures are usually generated *procedurally*. As was done previously for 2D textures, we decide on a resolution—that is, the number of texels in each dimension. Depending on the colors in the texture, we may build a three-dimensional array containing those colors. Alternatively, if the texture holds a "pattern" that could be utilized with various colors, we might instead build an array that holds the pattern, such as with 0s and 1s.

For example, we can build a 3D texture that represents horizontal stripes by filling an array with 0s and 1s corresponding to the desired stripe pattern. Suppose that the desired resolution of the texture is 200x200x200 texels and the texture comprises alternating stripes that are each 10 texels high. A simple function that builds such a structure by filling an array with appropriate 0s and 1s in a nested loop (assuming in this case that width, height, and depth variables are each set to 200), would be as follows:

```
void generate3Dpattern()
{   for (int x=0; x<texWidth; x++)
    {   for (int y=0; y<texHeight; y++)
        {   for (int z=0; z<texDepth; z++)
            {   if ((y/10) % 2 == 0)
                    tex3Dpattern[x][y][z] = 0.0;
                else
                    tex3Dpattern[x][y][z] = 1.0;
            }
        }
    }
}
```

The pattern stored in the **tex3Dpattern** array is illustrated in Figure 14.8, with the 0s rendered in blue and the 1s rendered in yellow.

Texturing an object with the above striped pattern requires the following steps:

1. Generating the pattern as already shown

2. Using the pattern to fill a byte array of desired colors

3. Loading the byte array into a texture object

Figure 14.8
Striped 3D texture pattern.

4. Deciding on appropriate 3D texture coordinates for the object vertices

5. Texturing the object in the fragment shader using an appropriate sampler

Texture coordinates for 3D textures range from 0 to 1, in the same manner as for 2D textures.

Interestingly, step 4 (determining 3D texture coordinates) is usually a lot simpler than one might initially suspect. In fact, it is usually simpler than for 2D textures! This is because (in the case of 2D textures), since a 3D object was being textured with a 2D image, we needed to decide how to "flatten" the 3D object's vertices (such as by UV mapping) to create texture coordinates. But when 3D texturing, both the object and the texture are of the same dimensionality (three). In most cases, we want the object to reflect the texture pattern, as if it were "carved" out of it (or dipped into it). So the vertex locations themselves serve as the texture coordinates! Usually all that is necessary is to apply some simple scaling to ensure that the object's vertices' location coordinates map to the 3D texture coordinates' range [0..1].

Since we are generating the 3D texture procedurally, we need a way of constructing an OpenGL texture map out of generated data. The process for loading data into a texture is similar to what we saw earlier in Section 5.12. In this case, we fill a 3D array with color values, and then copy them into a texture object.

Program 14.4 shows the various components for achieving all of the steps listed above, in order to texture an object with blue and yellow horizontal stripes from a procedurally built 3D texture. The desired pattern is built in the generate3Dpattern() function, which stores the pattern in an array named tex3Dpattern. The "image" data is then built in the function fillDataArray(), which fills a 3D array with byte data corresponding to the RGB colors R, G, B, and A, each in the range [0..255], according to the pattern. Those values are then copied into a texture object in the load3DTexture() function.

Program 14.4 3D Texturing: Striped Pattern

Java/JOGL application:

```
. . .
private int texHeight= 200;
private int texWidth = 200;
private int texDepth = 200;
private double[ ][ ][ ] tex3Dpattern = new double[texWidth][texHeight][texDepth];
. . .
```

```
// fill a byte array with RGB blue/yellow values corresponding to the pattern built by generate3Dpattern()
private void fillDataArray(byte data[ ])
{   for (int i=0; i<texWidth; i++)
    {   for (int j=0; j<texHeight; j++)
        {   for (int k=0; k<texDepth; k++)
            {   if (tex3Dpattern[i][j][k] == 1.0)
                {   // yellow color
                    data[i*(texWidth*texHeight*4) + j*(texHeight*4)+ k*4+0] = (byte) 255;      // red
                    data[i*(texWidth*texHeight*4) + j*(texHeight*4)+ k*4+1] = (byte) 255;      // green
                    data[i*(texWidth*texHeight*4) + j*(texHeight*4)+ k*4+2] = (byte) 0;        // blue
                    data[i*(texWidth*texHeight*4) + j*(texHeight*4)+ k*4+3] = (byte) 255;      // alpha
                }
                else
                {   // blue color
                    data[i*(texWidth*texHeight*4) + j*(texHeight*4)+ k*4+0] = (byte) 0;        // red
                    data[i*(texWidth*texHeight*4) + j*(texHeight*4)+ k*4+1] = (byte) 0;        // green
                    data[i*(texWidth*texHeight*4) + j*(texHeight*4)+ k*4+2] = (byte) 255;      // blue
                    data[i*(texWidth*texHeight*4) + j*(texHeight*4)+ k*4+3] = (byte) 255;      // alpha
                }
}   }   }   }   }

// build 3D pattern of stripes
void generate3Dpattern()
{   for (int x=0; x<texWidth; x++)
    {   for (int y=0; y<texHeight; y++)
        {   for (int z=0; z<texDepth; z++)
            {   if ((y/10)%2 == 0)
                    tex3Dpattern[x][y][z] = 0.0;
                else
                    tex3Dpattern[x][y][z] = 1.0;
}   }   }   }

// load the sequential byte data array into a texture object
private int load3DTexture()
{   GL4 gl = (GL4) GLContext.getCurrentGL();

    byte[ ] data = new byte[texWidth * texHeight * texDepth * 4];
    fillDataArray(data);
    ByteBuffer bb = Buffers.newDirectByteBuffer(data);

    int[ ] textureIDs = new int[1];
    gl.glGenTextures(1, textureIDs, 0);
    int textureID = textureIDs[0];

    gl.glBindTexture(GL_TEXTURE_3D, textureID);
    gl.glTexStorage3D(GL_TEXTURE_3D, 1, GL_RGBA8, texWidth, texHeight, texDepth);
    gl.glTexSubImage3D(GL_TEXTURE_3D, 0, 0, 0, 0,
```

```
            texWidth, texHeight, texDepth, GL_RGBA, GL_UNSIGNED_INT_8_8_8_8_REV, bb);
    gl.glTexParameteri(GL_TEXTURE_3D, GL_TEXTURE_MIN_FILTER, GL_LINEAR);
    return textureID;
}

public void init(GLAutoDrawable drawable)
{  . . .
    generate3Dpattern();                 // 3D pattern and texture only loaded once, so done from init()
    stripeTexture = load3DTexture();     // holds the integer texture ID for the 3D texture
}

public void display(GLAutoDrawable drawable)
{  . . .
    gl.glActiveTexture(GL_TEXTURE0);
    gl.glBindTexture(GL_TEXTURE_3D, stripeTexture);
    gl.glDrawArrays(GL_TRIANGLES, 0, numObjVertices);
}
```

Vertex Shader:

```
. . .
out vec3 originalPosition;        // the original model vertices will be used for texture coordinates
. . .
layout (binding=0) uniform sampler3D s;

void main(void)
{   originalPosition = position;   // pass original model coordinates for use as 3D texture coordinates
    gl_Position = proj_matrix * mv_matrix * vec4(position,1.0);
}
```

Fragment Shader:

```
. . .
in vec3 originalPosition;        // receive original model coordinates for use as 3D texture coordinates
out vec4 fragColor;
. . .
layout (binding=0) uniform sampler3D s;

void main(void)
{
    fragColor = texture(s, originalPosition/2.0 + 0.5);   // vertices are [-1..+1], tex coords are [0..1]
}
```

In the Java/JOGL application, the load3Dtexture() function is similar to the Java AWT loadTexture() function shown earlier in Program 5.2. As before, it expects the image data to be formatted as a sequence of bytes corresponding to RGBA color components. The function fillDataArray() does this, applying the RGB values for yellow and blue corresponding to the striped pattern built by the generate3Dpattern() function and held in the tex3Dpattern array. Note also the specification of texture type GL_TEXTURE_3D in the display() function.

Figure 14.9
Dragon object with 3D striped texture.

Since we wish to use the object's vertex locations as texture coordinates, we pass them through from the vertex shader to the fragment shader. The fragment shader then scales them so that they are mapped into the range [0..1] as is standard for texture coordinates. Finally, 3D textures are accessed via a sampler3D uniform, which takes three parameters instead of two. We use the vertex's original X, Y, and Z coordinates, scaled to the correct range, to access the texture. The result is shown in Figure 14.9.

More complex patterns can be generated by modifying generate3Dpattern(). Figure 14.10 shows a simple change that converts the striped pattern to a 3D

```
void generate3Dpattern()
{  int xStep, yStep, zStep, sumSteps;
   for (int x=0; x<texWidth; x++)
   {  for (int y=0; y<texHeight; y++)
      {  for (int z=0; z<texDepth; z++)
         {  xStep = (x / 10) % 2;
            yStep = (y / 10) % 2;
            zStep = (z / 10) % 2;
            sumSteps = xStep + yStep + zStep;
            if ((sumSteps % 2) == 0)
               tex3Dpattern[x][y][z] = 0.0;
            else
               tex3Dpattern[x][y][z] = 1.0;
} } } }
```

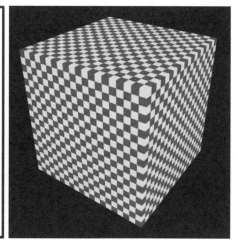

Figure 14.10
Generating a checkerboard 3D texture pattern.

Figure 14.11
Dragon with 3D checkerboard texture.

checkerboard. The resulting effect is then shown in Figure 14.11. It is worth noting that the effect is very different than would be the case if the dragon's surface had been textured with a 2D checkerboard texture pattern. (See Exercise 14.3)

14.5 NOISE

Many natural phenomena can be simulated using randomness, or *noise*. One common technique, *Perlin Noise* [PE85], is named after Ken Perlin, who in 1997 received an Academy Award[1] for developing a practical way to generate and use 2D and 3D noise. The procedure described here is based on Perlin's method.

There are many applications of noise in graphics scenes. A few common examples are clouds, terrain, wood grain, minerals (such as veins in marble), smoke, fire, flames, planetary surfaces, and random movements. In this section, we focus on generating 3D textures containing noise, and then subsequent sections illustrate using the noise data to generate complex materials such as marble and wood and to simulate animated cloud textures for use with a cube map or sky-dome. A collection of spatial data (e.g., 2D or 3D) that contains noise is sometimes referred to as a *noise map*.

We start by constructing a 3D texture map out of random data. This can be done using the functions shown in the previous section, with a few modifications. First, we replace the generate3Dpattern() function from Program 14.4 with the following simpler generateNoise() function:

```
double[ ][ ][ ] noise = new double[noiseWidth][noiseHeight][noiseDepth];
java.util.Random random = new java.util.Random();
. . .
void generateNoise()
{   for (int x=0; x<noiseWidth; x++)
    {   for (int y=0; y<noiseHeight; y++)
```

---

[1]   The Technical Achievement Award, given by the Academy of Motion Picture Arts and Sciences.

```
    {   for (int z=0; z<noiseDepth; z++)
        {   noise[x][y][z] = random.nextDouble();          // returns a double in the range [0..1]
} } } }
```

Next, the fillDataArray() function from Program 14.4 is modified so that it copies the noise data into the byte array in preparation for loading into a texture object, as follows:

```
private void fillDataArray(byte data[ ])
{   for (int i=0; i<noiseWidth; i++)
    {   for (int j=0; j<noiseHeight; j++)
        {   for (int k=0; k<noiseDepth; k++)
            {   data[i*(noiseWidth*noiseHeight*4)+j*(noiseHeight*4)+k*4+0] = (byte) (noise[i][j][k] * 255);
                data[i*(noiseWidth*noiseHeight*4)+j*(noiseHeight*4)+k*4+1] = (byte) (noise[i][j][k] * 255);
                data[i*(noiseWidth*noiseHeight*4)+j*(noiseHeight*4)+k*4+2] = (byte) (noise[i][j][k] * 255);
                data[i*(noiseWidth*noiseHeight*4)+j*(noiseHeight*4)+k*4+3] = (byte) 255;
} } } }
```

The rest of Program 14.4 for loading data into a texture object and applying it to a model is unchanged. We can view this 3D noise map by applying it to our simple cube model, as shown in Figure 14.12. In this example, noiseHeight = noiseWidth = noiseDepth = 256.

This is a 3D noise map, although it isn't a very useful one. As is, it is just *too* noisy to have very many practical applications. To make more practical, tunable noise patterns, we will replace the fillData-Array() function with different noise-producing procedures.

Suppose that we fill the data array by "zooming in" to a small subsection of the noise map illustrated in Figure 14.12, using indexes made smaller by integer division. The modification to the fillDataArray() function is shown below. The resulting 3D texture can be made more or less "blocky" depending on the "zooming" factor used to divide the index. In Figure 14.13, the textures show

Figure 14.12
Cube textured with 3D noise data.

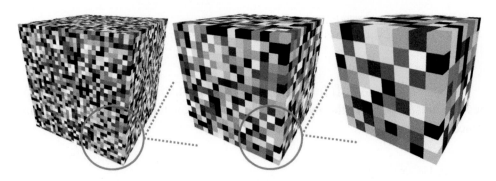

Figure 14.13
"Blocky" 3D noise maps with various "zooming-in" factors.

the result of zooming in by dividing the indices by zoom factors 8, 16, and 32 (left to right, respectively).

```
private void fillDataArray(byte data[ ])
{   int zoom = 8;    // zoom factor
    for (int i=0; i<noiseWidth; i++)
    {   for (int j=0; j<noiseHeight; j++)
        {   for (int k=0; k<noiseDepth; k++)
            {   data[i*(noiseWidth*noiseHeight*4)+j*(noiseHeight*4)+k*4+0] =
                    (byte) (noise [i/zoom] [j/zoom] [k/zoom] * 255);
                data[i*(noiseWidth*noiseHeight*4)+j*(noiseHeight*4)+k*4+1] =
                    (byte) (noise [i/zoom] [j/zoom] [k/zoom] * 255);
                data[i*(noiseWidth*noiseHeight*4)+j*(noiseHeight*4)+k*4+2] =
                    (byte) (noise [i/zoom] [j/zoom] [k/zoom] * 255);
                data[i*(noiseWidth*noiseHeight*4)+j*(noiseHeight*4)+k*4+3] = (byte) 255;
} } } }
```

The "blockiness" within a given noise map can be *smoothed* by interpolating from each discrete grayscale color value to the next one. That is, for each small "block" within a given 3D texture, we set each texel color within the block by interpolating from its color to its neighboring blocks' colors. The interpolation code is shown below in the function smoothNoise(), along with the modified fillDataArray() function. The resulting "smoothed" textures (for zooming factors 2, 4, 8, 16, 32, and 64—left to right, top to bottom) then follow in Figure 14.14. Note that the zoom factor is now a double, because we need the fractional component to determine the interpolated grayscale values for each texel.

```
private void fillDataArray(byte data[ ])
{   double zoom = 32.0;
    for (int i=0; i<noiseWidth; i++)
    {   for (int j=0; j<noiseHeight; j++)
        {   for (int k=0; k<noiseDepth; k++)
            {   data[i*(noiseWidth*noiseHeight*4) + j*(noiseHeight*4) + k*4 +0] =
                        (byte) (smoothNoise(i/zoom, j/zoom, k/zoom) * 255);
                data[i*(noiseWidth*noiseHeight*4) + j*(noiseHeight*4) + k*4 +1] =
                        (byte) (smoothNoise(i/zoom, j/zoom, k/zoom) * 255);
                data[i*(noiseWidth*noiseHeight*4) + j*(noiseHeight*4) + k*4 +2] =
                        (byte) (smoothNoise(i/zoom, j/zoom, k/zoom) * 255);
                data[i*(noiseWidth*noiseHeight*4) + j*(noiseHeight*4) + k*4 +3] = (byte) 255;
} } } }

double smoothNoise(double x1, double y1, double z1)
{   // fraction of x1, y1, and z1 (percentage from  current block to next block, for this texel)
    double fractX = x1 - (int) x1;
    double fractY = y1 - (int) y1;
    double fractZ = z1 - (int) z1;

    // the indices for neighboring pixels in the X, Y, and Z directions
    int x2 = ((int)x1 + noiseWidth + 1) % noiseWidth;
    int y2 = ((int)y1 + noiseHeight + 1) % noiseHeight;
    int z2 = ((int)z1 + noiseDepth + 1) % noiseDepth;

    // smooth the noise by interpolating the greyscale intensity along all three axes
    double value = 0.0;
    value += (1-fractX)   * (1-fractY)   * (1-fractZ)   * noise[(int)x1][(int)y1][(int)z1];
    value += (1-fractX)   * fractY       * (1-fractZ)   * noise[(int)x1][(int)y2][(int)z1];
    value += fractX       * (1-fractY)   * (1-fractZ)   * noise[(int)x2][(int)y1][(int)z1];
    value += fractX       * fractY       * (1-fractZ)   * noise[(int)x2][(int)y2][(int)z1];

    value += (1-fractX)   * (1-fractY)   * fractZ       * noise[(int)x1][(int)y1][(int)z2];
    value += (1-fractX)   * fractY       * fractZ       * noise[(int)x1][(int)y2][(int)z2];
    value += fractX       * (1-fractY)   * fractZ       * noise[(int)x2][(int)y1][(int)z2];
    value += fractX       * fractY       * fractZ       * noise[(int)x2][(int)y2][(int)z2];
    return value;
}
```

The smoothNoise() function computes a grayscale value for each texel in the smoothed version of a given noise map by computing a weighted average of the eight grayscale values surrounding the texel in the corresponding original "blocky" noise map. That is, it averages the color values at the eight vertices of the small "block" the texel is in. The weights for each of these "neighbor" colors are based on the texel's distance to each of its neighbors, normalized to the range [0..1].

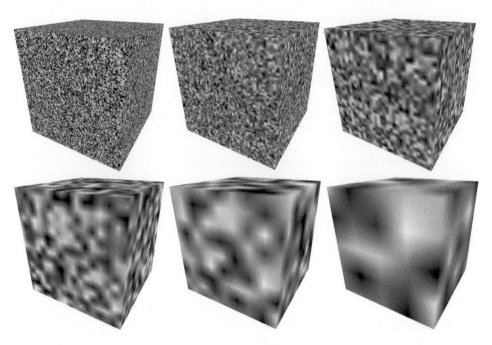

Figure 14.14
Smoothing of 3D textures, at various zooming levels.

Next, smoothed noise maps of various zooming factors are *combined*. A new noise map is created in which each of its texels is formed by another weighted average, this time based on the sum of the texels at the same location in each of the "smoothed" noise maps, with the zoom factor serving as the weight. The effect was dubbed "turbulence" by Perlin [PE85], although it is really more closely related to the harmonics produced by summing various waveforms. A new turbulence() function and a modified version of fillDataArray() that specifies a noise map that sums zoom levels 1 through 32 (the ones that are powers of two) are shown below, followed by an image of a cube textured with the resulting noise map.

```
private double turbulence(double x, double y, double z, double maxZoom)
{   double sum = 0.0, zoom = maxZoom;
    while (zoom >= 1.0)                  // the last pass is when zoom=1.
    {   // compute weighted sum of smoothed noise maps
        sum = sum + smoothNoise(x / zoom, y / zoom, z / zoom) * zoom;
        zoom = zoom / 2.0;              // for each zoom factor that is a power of two.
    }
```

```
    sum = 128.0 * sum / maxZoom;    // guarantees RGB < 256 for maxZoom values up to 64
    return sum;
}

private void fillDataArray(byte data[ ] )
{   double maxZoom = 32.0;
    for (int i=0; i<noiseWidth; i++)
    {   for (int j=0; j<noiseHeight; j++)
        {   for (int k=0; k<noiseDepth; k++)
            {   data[i*(noiseWidth*noiseHeight*4)+j*(noiseHeight*4)+k*4+0] =
                    (byte) turbulence(i, j, k, maxZoom);
                data[i*(noiseWidth*noiseHeight*4)+j*(noiseHeight*4)+k*4+1] =
                    (byte) turbulence(i, j, k, maxZoom);
                data[i*(noiseWidth*noiseHeight*4)+j*(noiseHeight*4)+k*4+2] =
                    (byte) turbulence(i, j, k, maxZoom);
                data[i*(noiseWidth*noiseHeight*4)+j*(noiseHeight*4)+k*4+3] =
                    (byte) 255;
} } } }
```

3D noise maps, such as the one shown in Figure 14.15, can be used for a wide variety of imaginative applications. In the next sections, we will use it to generate marble, wood, and clouds. The distribution of the noise can be adjusted by various combinations of zoom-in levels.

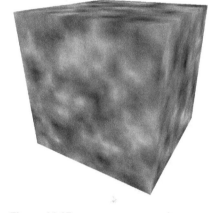

14.6 NOISE APPLICATION— MARBLE

Figure 14.15
3D texture map with combined "turbulence" noise.

By modifying the noise map and adding Phong lighting with an appropriate ADS material as described previously in Figure 7.3, we can make the dragon model appear to be made of a marble-like stone.

We start by generating a striped pattern somewhat similar to the "stripes" example from earlier in this chapter; however, the new stripes differ from the previous ones—first because they are diagonal and also because they are produced by a sine wave and therefore have blurry edges. We then use the noise map to perturb those lines, storing them as grayscale values. The changes to the fillDataArray() function are as follows:

```
private void fillDataArray(byte data[ ])
{   double veinFrequency = 2.0;
    double turbPower = 1.5;
    double maxZoom = 64.0;
    for (int i=0; i<noiseWidth; i++)
    {   for (int j=0; j<noiseHeight; j++)
        {   for (int k=0; k<noiseDepth; k++)
            {   double xyzValue = i / noiseWidth + j / noiseHeight + k / noiseDepth
                                + turbPower * turbulence(i,j,k,maxZoom) / 256.0;
                double sineValue = Math.abs(Math.sin(xyzValue * 3.14159 * veinFrequency));
                Color c = new Color((float)sineValue, (float)sineValue, (float)sineValue);
                data[i*(noiseWidth*noiseHeight*4) + j*(noiseHeight*4)+ k*4 + 0] = (byte) c.getRed();
                data[i*(noiseWidth*noiseHeight*4) + j*(noiseHeight*4)+ k*4 + 1] = (byte) c.getGreen();
                data[i*(noiseWidth*noiseHeight*4) + j*(noiseHeight*4)+ k*4 + 2] = (byte) c.getBlue();
                data[i*(noiseWidth*noiseHeight*4) + j*(noiseHeight*4)+ k*4 + 3] = (byte) 255;
} } } }
```

The variable veinFrequency is used to adjust the number of stripes, turbSize adjusts the zoom factor used when generating the turbulence, and turbPower adjusts the amount of perturbation in the stripes (setting it to zero leaves the stripes unperturbed). Since the same sine wave value is used for all three (RGB) color components, the final color stored in the image data array is grayscale. Figure 14.16 shows the resulting texture map for various values of turbPower (0.0, 0.5, 1.0, and 1.5, left to right).

Since we expect marble to have a shiny appearance, we incorporate Phong shading to make a "marble" textured object look convincing. Program 14.5

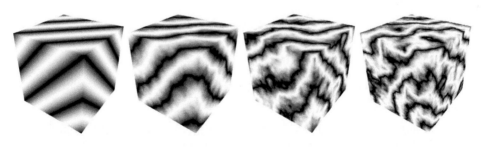

Figure 14.16
Building 3D "marble" noise maps.

summarizes the code for generating a marble dragon. The vertex and fragment shaders are the same as used for Phong shading, except that we also pass through the original vertex coordinates for use as 3D texture coordinates (as described earlier). The fragment shader combines the noise result with the lighting result using the technique described previously in Section 7.6.

Program 14.5 Building a Marble Dragon

Java/JOGL application:

```
. . .
public void init(GLAutoDrawable drawable)
{   . . .
    // white light ADS settings for use in Phong Shading
    float[ ] globalAmbient = new float[ ] {0.5f, 0.5f, 0.5f, 1.0f};
    float[ ] lightAmbient = new float[ ] {0.0f, 0.0f, 0.0f, 1.0f};
    float[ ] lightDiffuse = new float[ ] {1.0f, 1.0f, 1.0f, 1.0f};
    float[ ] lightSpecular = new float[ ] {1.0f, 1.0f, 1.0f, 1.0f};

    float matShi = 75.0f;
}
private void fillDataArray(byte data[ ])
{   double veinFrequency = 1.75;
    double turbPower = 3.0;
    double turbSize = 32.0;
    // remainder is as shown above for building the marble noise map
    . . .
}
```

Vertex Shader:

```
// unchanged from program 14-4
```

Fragment Shader:

```
. . .
void main(void)
{   . . .
    // model vertices are [-1.5..+1.5], texture coordinates are [0..1]
    vec4 texColor = texture(s, originalPosition / 3.0 + 0.5);

    fragColor =
        0.7 * texColor * (globalAmbient + light.ambient + light.diffuse * max(cosTheta,0.0))
        + 0.5 * light.specular * pow(max(cosPhi, 0.0), material.shininess);
}
```

There are various ways of simulating different colors of marble (or other stones). One approach for changing the colors of the "veins" in the marble is by modifying the definition of the Color variable in the fillDataArray() function—for example, by increasing the green component:

```
Color c = new Color((float) sineValue,
                    (float)Math.min(sineValue*1.5-0.25, 1.0),
                    (float) sineValue);
```

We can also introduce ADS material values (i.e., specified in init()) to simulate completely different types of stone, such as "jade."

Figure 14.17 shows four examples, the first three using the settings shown in Program 14.5 and the fourth incorporating the "jade" ADS material values shown earlier in Figure 7.3.

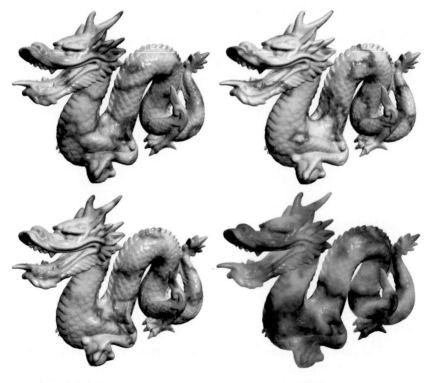

Figure 14.17
Dragon textured with 3D noise map—three marble and one jade.

14.7 NOISE APPLICATION—WOOD

Creating a "wood" texture can be done in a similar way as was done in the previous "marble" example. Trees grow in *rings*, and it is these rings that produce the "grain" we see in objects made of wood. As trees grow, environmental stresses create variations in the rings, which we also see in the grain.

We start by building a procedural "rings" 3D texture map, similar to the "checkerboard" from earlier in this chapter. We then use a noise map to perturb those rings, inserting dark and light brown colors into the ring texture map. By adjusting the number of rings and the degree to which we perturb the rings, we can simulate wood with various types of grain. Shades of brown can be made by combining similar amounts of red and green, with less blue. We then apply Phong shading with a low level of "shininess."

We can generate rings encircling the Z axis in our 3D texture map by modifying the fillDataArray() function, using trigonometry to specify values for X and Y that are equidistant from the Z axis. We use a sine wave to repeat this process cyclically, raising and lowering the red and green components equally based on this sine wave, to produce the varying shades of brown. The variable sineValue holds the exact shade, which can be adjusted by slightly offsetting one or the other (in this case increasing the red by 80 and the green by 30). We can create more (or fewer) rings by adjusting the value of xyPeriod. The resulting texture is shown in Figure 14.18.

```
private void fillDataArray(byte data[ ])
{   double xyPeriod = 40.0;
    for (int i=0; i<noiseWidth; i++)
    {   for (int j=0; j<noiseHeight; j++)
        {   for (int k=0; k<noiseDepth; k++)
            {   double xValue = (i - (double)noiseWidth/2.0) / (double)noiseWidth;
                double yValue = (j - (double)noiseHeight/2.0) / (double)noiseHeight;
                double distanceFromZ = Math.sqrt(xValue * xValue + yValue * yValue)
                double sineValue = 128.0 * Math.abs(Math.sin(2.0 * xyPeriod * distanceFromZ * 3.14159));
                Color c = new Color((int)(80+(int)sineValue), (int)(30+(int)sineValue), 0);
                data[i*(noiseWidth*noiseHeight*4) + j*(noiseHeight*4) + k*4+0] = (byte) c.getRed();
                data[i*(noiseWidth*noiseHeight*4) + j*(noiseHeight*4) + k*4+1] = (byte) c.getGreen();
                data[i*(noiseWidth*noiseHeight*4) + j*(noiseHeight*4) + k*4+2] = (byte) c.getBlue();
                data[i*(noiseWidth*noiseHeight*4) + j*(noiseHeight*4) + k*4+3] = (byte) 255;
} } } }
```

The wood rings in Figure 14.18 are a good start, but they don't look very realistic—they are too perfect. To improve this, we use the noise map (more specifically, turbulence) to perturb the distanceFromZ variable so that the rings have slight variations. The computation is modified as follows:

```
double distanceFromZ = Math.sqrt(xValue * xValue + yValue * yValue)
                       + turbPower * turbulence(i, j, k, maxZoom) / 256.0;
```

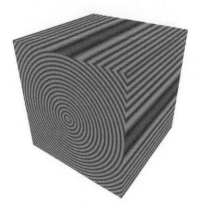

Again, the variable turbPower adjusts how much turbulence is applied (setting it to 0.0 results in the unperturbed version shown in Figure 14.18), and maxZoom specifies the zoom value (32 in this example). Figure 14.19 shows the resulting wood textures for turbPower values 0.05, 1.0, and 2.0 (left to right).

We can now apply the 3D wood texture map to a model. The realism of the texture can be further enhanced by applying a rotation to the originalPosition vertex locations used for texture coordinates; this is because most items carved out of wood don't perfectly align with

Figure 14.18
Creating rings for 3D wood texture.

the orientation of the rings. To accomplish this, we send an additional rotation matrix to the shaders for rotating the texture coordinates. We also add Phong shading, with appropriate wood-color ADS values, and a modest level of shininess. The complete additions and changes for creating a "wood dolphin" are shown in Program 14.6.

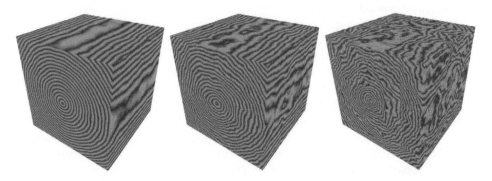

Figure 14.19
"Wood" 3D texture maps with rings perturbed by noise map.

Program 14.6 Creating a Wood Dolphin

Java/JOGL application:

```
private Matrix4f texRotMat = new Matrix4f();

// wood material (brown)
float[ ] matAmbient = new float[ ] {0.5f, 0.35f, 0.15f, 1.0f};
float[ ] matDiffuse = new float[ ] {0.5f, 0.35f, 0.15f, 1.0f};
float[ ] matSpecular = new float[ ] {0.5f, 0.35f, 0.15f, 1.0f};
float matShi = 15.0f;

public void init(GLAutoDrawable drawable)
{   ...
    // rotation to be applied to texture coordinates – adds additional grain variation
    texRotMat.rotateY((float)Math.toRadians(50.0f));
    texRotMat.rotateX((float)Math.toRadians(10.0f));
    texRotMat.rotateZ((float)Math.toRadians(10.0f));
}


private void fillDataArray(byte data[ ])
{   double xyPeriod = 40.0;
    double turbPower = 0.1;
    double maxZoom = 32.0;
    for (int i=0; i<noiseWidth; i++)
    {   for (int j=0; j<noiseHeight; j++)
        {   for (int k=0; k<noiseDepth; k++)
            {   double xValue = (i - (double)noiseWidth/2.0) / (double)noiseWidth;
                double yValue = (j - (double)noiseHeight/2.0) / (double)noiseHeight;
                double distanceFromZ = Math.sqrt(xValue * xValue + yValue * yValue)
                            + turbPower * turbulence(i, j, k, maxZoom) / 256.0;
                double sineValue = 128.0 * Math.abs(Math.sin(2.0 * xyPeriod * distanceFromZ * Math.PI));
                Color c = new Color((int)(80+(int)sineValue), (int)(30+(int)sineValue), 0);
                data[i*(noiseWidth*noiseHeight*4)+j*(noiseHeight*4)+k*4+0] = (byte) c.getRed();
                data[i*(noiseWidth*noiseHeight*4)+j*(noiseHeight*4)+k*4+1] = (byte) c.getGreen();
                data[i*(noiseWidth*noiseHeight*4)+j*(noiseHeight*4)+k*4+2] = (byte) c.getBlue();
                data[i*(noiseWidth*noiseHeight*4)+j*(noiseHeight*4)+k*4+3] = (byte) 255;
} } } }

private void display(GLAutoDrawable drawable)
{   ...
    texRotLoc = gl.glGetUniformLocation(renderingProgram, "texRot_matrix");
    gl.glUniformMatrix4fv(texRotLoc, 1, false, texRotMat.get(vals));

    ...
}
```

Vertex shader:

```
. . .
uniform mat4 texRot_matrix;

void main(void)
{  . . .
   originalPosition = vec3(texRot_matrix * vec4(position,1.0)).xyz;
   . . . .
}
```

Fragment shader:

```
. . .
void main(void)
{  . . .
   uniform mat4 texRot_matrix;
   . . .
   //  combine lighting with 3D texturing
   fragColor =
       0.5 * ( . . .)
           +
       0.5 * texture(s,originalPosition / 2.0 + 0.5);
}
```

Figure 14.20
Dolphin textured with "wood" 3D noise map.

The resulting 3D textured wood dolphin is shown in Figure 14.20.

There is one additional detail in the fragment shader worth noting. Since we are rotating the model within the 3D texture, it is sometimes possible for this to cause the vertex positions to move beyond the required [0..1] range of texture coordinates as a result of the rotation. If this were to happen, we could adjust for this possibility by dividing the original vertex positions by a larger number (such as 4.0 rather than 2.0), and then adding a slightly larger number (such as 0.6) to center it in the texture space.

14.8 ■ NOISE APPLICATION—CLOUDS

The "turbulence" noise map built earlier in Figure 14.15 already looks a bit like clouds. Of course, it isn't the right color, so we start by changing it from grayscale to an appropriate mix of light blue and white. A straightforward way of doing this is to assign a color with a maximum value of 1.0 for the blue component and varying (but equal) values between 0.0 and 1.0 for the red and green components, depending on the values in the noise map. The new fillDataArray() function follows:

```
private void fillDataArray(byte data[ ])
{   for (int i=0; i<noiseWidth; i++)
    {   for (int j=0; j<noiseHeight; j++)
        {   for (int k=0; k<noiseDepth; k++)
            {   float brightness = 1.0f - (float) turbulence(i,j,k,32) / 256.0f;
                Color c = new Color(brightness, brightness, 1.0f, 1.0f);
                data[i*(noiseWidth*noiseHeight*4)+j*(noiseHeight*4)+k*4+0] = (byte) c.getRed();
                data[i*(noiseWidth*noiseHeight*4)+j*(noiseHeight*4)+k*4+1] = (byte) c.getGreen();
                data[i*(noiseWidth*noiseHeight*4)+j*(noiseHeight*4)+k*4+2] = (byte) c.getBlue();
                data[i*(noiseWidth*noiseHeight*4)+j*(noiseHeight*4)+k*4+3] = (byte) 255;
}   }   }   }
```

The resulting blue version of the noise map can now be used to texture a skydome. Recall that a skydome is a sphere or half-sphere that is textured, rendered with depth testing disabled, and placed so that it surrounds the camera (similar to a skybox).

One way of building the skydome would be to texture it in the same way as we have for other 3D textures, using the vertex coordinates as texture coordinates. However, in this case, it turns out that using the skydome's 2D texture coordinates instead produces patterns that look more like clouds, because the spherical distortion slightly stretches the texture map horizontally. We can grab a 2D slice from the noise map by setting the third dimension in the GLSL texture() call to a constant value. Assuming that the skydome's texture coordinates have been sent to the OpenGL pipeline in a vertex attribute, in the standard way, the following fragment shader textures it with a 2D slice of the noise map:

```
#version 430
in vec2 tc;
out vec4 fragColor;
uniform mat4 mv_matrix;
uniform mat4 proj_matrix;
layout (binding=0) uniform sampler3D s;

void main(void)
{   fragColor = texture(s,vec3(tc.x, tc.y, 0.5));       // constant value in place of tc.z
}
```

Figure 14.21
Skydome textured with misty clouds.

The resulting textured skydome is shown in Figure 14.21. Although the camera is usually placed inside the skydome, we have rendered it here with the camera outside, so that the effect on the dome itself can be seen. The current noise map leads to "misty-looking" clouds.

Although our misty clouds look nice, we would like to be able to shape them—that is, make them more or less hazy. One way of doing this is to modify the turbulence() function so that it uses an exponential, such as a logistic function,[2] to make the clouds look more "distinct." The modified turbulence() function is shown in Program 14.7, along with an associated logistic() function. The complete Program 14.7 also incorporates the smooth(), fillDataArray(), and generateNoise() functions described earlier.

Program 14.7 Cloud Texture Generation

Java/JOGL application:

```
private double turbulence(double x, double y, double z, double size)
{   double value = 0.0, initialSize = size, cloudQuant;
    while(size >= 0.9)
    {   value = value + smoothNoise(x/size, y/size, z/size) * size;
        size = size / 2.0;
    }
    cloudQuant = 110.0;   // tunable quantity of clouds
    value = value / initialSize;
    value = 256.0 * logistic(value * 128.0 - cloudQuant);
    return value;
}

private double logistic(double x)
{   double k = 0.2;        // tunable haziness of clouds, produces more or less distinct cloud boundaries
    return (1.0 / (1.0+Math.pow(2.718, -k*x)));
}
```

---

[2] A "logistic" (or "sigmoid") function has an S-shaped curve with asymptotes on both ends. Common examples are hyperbolic tangent and $f(x) = 1/(1+e^{-x})$. They are also sometimes called "squashing" functions.

The logistic function causes the colors to tend more toward white or blue, rather than values in-between, producing the visual effect of more distinct cloud boundaries. The variable cloudQuant adjusts the relative amount of white (versus blue) in the noise map, which in turn leads to more (or fewer) generated white regions (i.e., distinct clouds) when the logistic function is applied. The resulting skydome, now with more distinct cloud formations, is shown in Figure 14.22.

Figure 14.22
Skydome with exponential cloud texture.

Finally, real clouds aren't static. To enhance the realism of our clouds, we should animate them by (a) making them move or "drift' over time and (b) gradually changing their form as they drift.

One simple way of making the clouds "drift" is to slowly rotate the skydome. This isn't a perfect solution, as real clouds tend to drift in a straight direction rather than rotating around the observer. However, if the rotation is slow and the clouds are simply for decorating a scene, the effect is likely to be adequate.

Having the clouds gradually change form as they drift may at first seem tricky. However, given the 3D noise map we have used to texture the clouds, there is actually a very simple and clever way of achieving the effect. Recall that although we constructed a 3D texture noise map for clouds, we have so far only used one "slice" of it, in conjunction with the skydome's 2D texture coordinates (we set the "Z" coordinate of the texture lookup to a constant value). The rest of the 3D texture has so far gone unused.

Our trick will be to replace the texture lookup's constant "Z" coordinate with a variable that changes gradually over time. That is, as we rotate the skydome, we gradually increment the depth variable, causing the texture lookup to use a different slice. Recall that when we built the 3D texture map, we applied smoothing to the color changes along all three axes. So neighboring slices from the texture map are very similar, but slightly different. Thus, by gradually changing the "Z" value in the texture() call, the appearance of the clouds will gradually change.

The code changes to cause the clouds to slowly move and change over time are shown in Program 14.8.

Program 14.8 Animating the Cloud Texture

Java/JOGL application:

```java
private double rotAmt = 0.0;   // Y-axis rotation amount to make clouds appear to drift
private float depth = 0.01f;   // depth lookup for 3D noise map, to make clouds gradually change
private int dOffsetLoc;        // location of depth uniform variable
. . .
public void display(GLAutoDrawable drawable)
{  . . .
    // gradually rotate the skydome
    m_matrix.identity();
    m_matrix.translate(objLocX, objLocY, objLocZ);
    rotAmt = rotAmt + 0.002;
    m_matrix.rotateY(rotAmt);

    // gradually alter the third texture coordinate to make clouds change
    dOffsetLoc = gl.glGetUniformLocation(renderingProgram, "d");
    depth = depth + 0.00005f;
    if (depth >= 0.99f) depth = 0.01f;       // wrap-around when we get to the end of the texture map
    gl.glUniform1f(dOffsetLoc, depth);
    . . .
}
```

Fragment Shader:

```glsl
#version 430

in vec2 tc;
out vec4 fragColor;

uniform mat4 mv_matrix;
uniform mat4 proj_matrix;
uniform float d;

layout (binding=0) uniform sampler3D s;

void main(void)
{   fragColor = texture(s, vec3(tc.x, tc.y, d));      // gradually-changing "d" replaces previous constant
}
```

While we cannot show the effect of gradually changing drifting and animated clouds in a single still image, Figure 14.23 shows such changes in a series of snapshots of the 3D generated clouds as they drift across the skydome from right to left and slowly change shape while drifting.

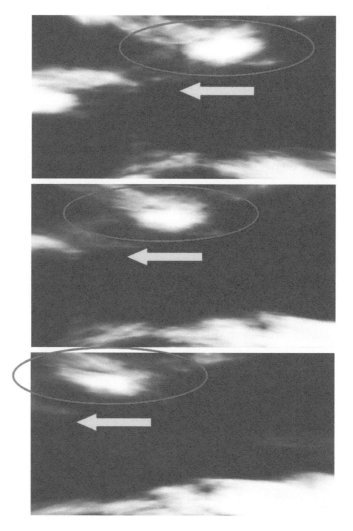

Figure 14.23
3D clouds changing while drifting.

14.9 ■ NOISE APPLICATION—SPECIAL EFFECTS

Noise textures can be used for a variety of special effects. In fact, there are so many possible uses that its applicability is limited only by one's imagination.

One very simple special effect that we will demonstrate here is a *dissolve effect*. This is where we make an object appear to gradually dissolve into small particles, until it eventually disappears. Given a 3D noise texture, this effect can be achieved with very little additional code. Note that this example only works if animation is incorporated, such as with the use of Animator.

To facilitate the dissolve effect, we introduce the GLSL discard command. This command is only legal in the fragment shader, and when executed, it causes the fragment shader to discard the current fragment (meaning not render it).

Our strategy is a simple one. In the Java/JOGL application, we create a fine-grained noise texture map identical to the one shown back in Figure 14.12, and also a float variable counter that gradually increases over time. This variable is then sent down the shader pipeline in a uniform variable, and the noise map is also placed in a texture map with an associated sampler. The fragment shader then accesses the noise texture using the sampler—in this case, we use the returned noise value to determine whether or not to discard the fragment. We do this by comparing the grayscale noise value against the counter, which serves as a sort of "threshold" value. Because the threshold is gradually changing over time, we can set it up so that gradually more and more fragments are discarded. The result is that the object appears to gradually dissolve. Program 14.9 shows the relevant code sections, which are added to the earth-rendered sphere from Program 6.1. The generated output is shown in Figure 14.24.

Program 14.9 Dissolve Effect Using discard Command

Java/JOGL application:

```
private float thresholdInc = 0.0f;     // gradually-increasing threshold for retaining/discarding fragment
. . .
```

in Display:

```
. . .
thresholdLoc = gl.glGetUniformLocation(renderingProgram, "threshold");
thresholdInc = thresholdInc + .002f;
gl.glUniform1f(thresholdLoc, thresholdInc);
. . .
gl.glActiveTexture(GL_TEXTURE0);
gl.glBindTexture(GL_TEXTURE_3D, noiseTexture);

gl.glActiveTexture(GL_TEXTURE1);
gl.glBindTexture(GL_TEXTURE_2D, earthTexture);
. . .
gl.glDrawArrays(GL_TRIANGLES, 0, numSphereVertices);
```

Fragment Shader:

```
#version 430
in vec2 tc;              // texture coordinates for this fragment
in vec3 origPos;         // original vertex positions in the model, for accessing 3D texture
. . .
layout (binding=0) uniform sampler3D n;   // sampler for noise texture
layout (binding=1) uniform sampler2D e;   // sampler for earth texture
. . .
uniform float thresold;                   // threshold for retaining or discarding fragment

void main(void)
{   float noise = texture(n, origPos).x;  // retrieve noise value for this fragment.
    if (noise > threshold)                // if the noise value > current threshold value,
    {   fragColor = texture(e, tc);       // render the fragment using the earth texture.
    }
    else
    {   discard;                          // otherwise, discard the fragment (do not render it)
    }
}
```

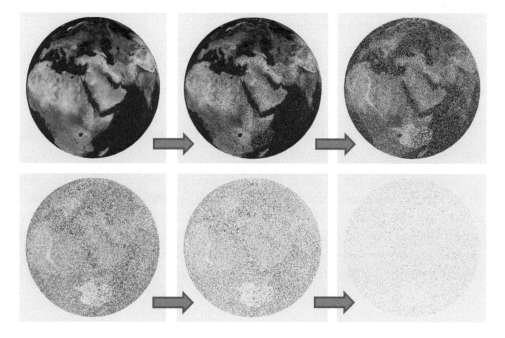

Figure 14.24
Dissolve effect with discard shader.

The discard command should, if possible, be used sparingly, because it can incur a performance penalty. This is because its presence makes it more difficult for OpenGL to optimize Z-buffer depth testing.

SUPPLEMENTAL NOTES

In this chapter, we used noise to generate clouds and to simulate both wood and a marble-like stone from which we rendered a dragon. People have found many other uses for noise. For example, it can be used to create fire and smoke [KE16, AF14], build realistic bump maps [GR05], and generate terrain, as in the videogame Minecraft [PE11].

The noise maps produced in this chapter are based on procedures outlined by Lode Vandevenne [VA04]. There remain some deficiencies in our 3D cloud generation. The texture is not seamless, so at the 360° point there is a noticeable vertical line. (This is also why we started the depth variable in Program 14.8 at 0.01 rather than at 0.0—to avoid encountering the seam in the Z dimension of the noise map.) Simple methods exist for removing the seams [AS04], if needed. Another issue is at the northern peak of the skydome where the spherical distortion in the skydome causes a pincushion effect.

The clouds we implemented in this chapter also fail to model some important aspects of real clouds, such as the way that they scatter the sun's light. Real clouds also tend to be more white on the top and grayer at the bottom. Our clouds also don't achieve a 3D "fluffy" look that many actual clouds have.

Similarly, more comprehensive models exist for generating fog, such as the one described by Kilgard and Fernando [KF03].

While perusing the OpenGL documentation, the reader might notice that GLSL includes some noise functions named noise1(), noise2(), noise3(), and noise4(), that are described as taking an input seed and producing Gaussian-like stochastic output. We didn't use these functions in this chapter because as of this writing, most vendors have not implemented them. For example, many NVIDIA cards currently return 0 for these functions, regardless of the input seed.

Exercises

14.1 Modify Program 14.2 to gradually increase the alpha value of an object, causing it to progressively fade out and eventually disappear.

14.2 Modify Program 14.3 to clip the torus along the horizontal, creating a circular "trough."

14.3 Modify Program 14.4 (the version including the modification in Figure 14.10 that produces a 3D cubed texture) so that it instead textures the Studio 522 dolphin. Then observe the results. Many people when first observing the result—such as that shown on the dragon, but also even on simpler objects—believe that there is some error in the program. Unexpected surface patterns can result from "carving" an object out of 3D textures, even in simple cases.

14.4 The simple sine wave used to define the wood "rings" (shown in Figure 14.18) generate rings in which the light and dark areas are of equal width. Experiment with modifications to the associated fillDataArray() function with the goal of making the dark rings narrower in width than the light rings. Then observe the effects on the resulting wood-textured object.

14.5 *(PROJECT)* Incorporate the logistic function (from Program 14.7) into the marble dragon from Program 14.5 and experiment with the settings to create more distinct veins.

14.6 Modify Program 14.9 to incorporate the zooming, smoothing, turbulence, and logistic steps described in the prior sections. Observe the changes in the resulting dissolve effect.

References

[AF14] S. Abraham and D. Fussell, "Smoke Brush," *Proceedings of the Workshop on Non-Photorealistic Animation and Rendering (NPAR'14)*, 2014, accessed July 2016, https://www.cs.utexas.edu/~theshark/smokebrush.pdf

[AS04] D. Astle, "Simple Clouds Part 1," gamedev.net, 2004, accessed July 2016, http://www.gamedev.net/page/resources/_/technical/game-programming/simple-clouds-part-1-r2085

[GR05] S. Green, "Implementing Improved Perlin Noise," *GPU Gems 2*, NVIDIA, 2005, accessed July 2016, http://http.developer.nvidia.com/GPUGems2/gpugems2_chapter26.html

[JA12] A. Jacobson, "Cheap Tricks for OpenGL Transparency," 2012, accessed July 2016, http://www.alecjacobson.com/weblog/?p=2750

[KE16] B. Kaskosz, D. Ensley, and D. Gries, "Billowing Fire with Perlin Noise and Filters—Flash AS3 Effect," *Flash & Math*, accessed July 2016, http://www.flashandmath.com/about/

[KF03] M. Kilgard and R. Fernando, "Advanced Topics," *The Cg Tutorial* (Addison-Wesley, 2003), accessed July 2016, http://http.developer.nvidia.com/CgTutorial/cg_tutorial_chapter09.html

[LU16] F. Luna, *Introduction to 3D Game Programming with DirectX 12*, 2nd ed. (Mercury Learning, 2016).

[PE11] M. Persson, "Terrain Generation, Part 1," *The Word of Notch* (blog), March 9, 2011, accessed July 2016, http://notch.tumblr.com/post/3746989361/terrain-generation-part-1

[PE85] K. Perlin, "An Image Synthesizer," SIGGRAPH '85 Proceedings of the 12th annual conference on computer graphics and interactive techniques (1985).

[VA04] L. Vandevenne, "Texture Generation Using Random Noise," *Lode's Computer Graphics Tutorial*, 2004, accessed July 2016, http://lodev.org/cgtutor/randomnoise.html

INSTALLATION AND SETUP
FOR PC (WINDOWS)

As described in Chapter 1, there are a number of installation and setup steps that must be accomplished in order to use OpenGL and Java on your machine. These steps vary depending on which platform you wish to use. The code samples in this book are designed to be run as given on a PC (Windows); this appendix provides step-by-step detailed setup instructions for the Windows platform. For information on setting up and running the code samples in the book on a Mac see "Appendix B: Installation and Setup for Macintosh."

A.1 INSTALLING THE LIBRARIES AND DEVELOPMENT ENVIRONMENT

A.1.1 Installing Java

To use Java for the examples in this book, you will need both the JRE (Java Runtime Environment) and the JDK (Java Development Kit). To install them, use Oracle's download site, http://www.oracle.com/technetwork/java, and click the "Java SE" (Standard Edition) link under Software Downloads. From there you can find instructions for downloading the latest JDK, which includes both the Java compiler and the JRE. We assume that the reader is experienced with programming in Java and is using at least version 8.

A.1.2 Installing OpenGL/GLSL

It is not necessary to "install" OpenGL or GLSL, but it is necessary to ensure that your graphics card supports at least version 4.3 of OpenGL. If you do not know what version of OpenGL your machine supports, you can use one of the various free applications (such as GLView [GV16]) to find out.

A.1.3 Installing JOGL

To install JOGL, visit the JogAmp website [JO16], http://jogamp.org. There, as of this writing (September 2018), the current version of JOGL is found in the Builds/Downloads section—look under Current and click on [zip]. The latest stable JOGL files are then displayed in a folder named /deployment/jogamp-current/archive. Download the following:

```
jogamp-all-platforms.7z
jogl-javadoc.7z
```

Unzip these files into the folder on your machine where you would like to store the JOGL system. A typical location in Windows could be, for example, in a folder named "JOGL" at the root of the C: drive.

The unzipped jogamp-all-platforms file contains a folder named jar which contains two important files that will be used by your applications:

```
jogl-all.jar
gluegen-rt.jar
```

Add the full path name of each of these two files to your CLASSPATH environment variable.

After you have copied the above files onto your machine, go into the jogl-javadoc folder and double-click the file named index.html. This opens the JOGL javadocs in a browser, which you should then bookmark for future reference.

A.1.4 Installing JOML

To install JOML, visit the JOML GitHub page and click on "Releases," or navigate directly to the Releases page [JR17]. You will probably want to download the latest version (1.9.11 at the time of this writing), specifically the .jar file named joml-1.9.11.jar. This file is also available on the companion CD distributed with this book.

After downloading the .jar file, move it to wherever you would like to store JOML—a typical location in Windows could be, for example, in a folder named "JOML" at the root of the C: drive. Then add the full path name of the .jar file to your CLASSPATH environment variable.

There is a lot of helpful reference material on JOML and how to most effectively use it. Note especially two pages definitely worth bookmarking:

- the readme for using JOML with JOGL [JJ17]
- the JOML Wiki [JW17]

References

[GV16] GLView, realtech-vr, accessed July 2016, http://www.realtech-vr.com/glview/

[JJ17] JOML, "Using with JOGL," accessed December 2017, https://github.com/JOML-CI/JOML#using-with-jogl

[JO16] JogAmp, accessed July 2016, http://jogamp.org/

[JR17] JOML, Releases, accessed December 2017, https://github.com/JOML-CI/JOML/releases

[JW17] JOML, wiki, accessed December 2017, https://github.com/JOML-CI/JOML/wiki

INSTALLATION AND SETUP
FOR MACINTOSH

■ ■ ■ ■ ■

As described in Chapter 1, there are a number of installation and setup steps that must be accomplished in order to use OpenGL and Java on your machine. These steps vary depending on which platform you wish to use. This appendix provides step-by-step detailed setup instructions for the Macintosh platform. For information on setting up and running the code samples in the book on a PC with Windows, see "Appendix A: Installation and Setup for PC (Windows)."

Apple support for OpenGL on the Macintosh has languished in the past few years. For example, modern Macs as of this writing still only support up to OpenGL version 4.1. Still, it is possible to run the examples in this book with minor modifications. As for preparing the necessary libraries, all of the libraries described in Chapter 1 are cross-platform and available for the Apple Macintosh. We first describe how to install these libraries.

In addition, since the code samples in this book are designed to be run (as given) *on a Windows platform*, this appendix provides details on converting the code samples so that they run correctly on the Macintosh.

B.1   INSTALLING THE LIBRARIES

B.1.1   Installing Java

To use Java for the examples in this book, you will need both the JRE (Java Runtime Environment) and the JDK (Java Development Kit). To install them, use Oracle's download site, http://www.oracle.com/technetwork/java, and click the "Java SE"

(Standard Edition) link under Software Downloads. From there you can find instructions for downloading the latest JDK, which includes both the Java compiler and the JRE. We assume that the reader is experienced with programming in Java and is using at least version 8.

B.1.2 Installing OpenGL/GLSL

It is not necessary to "install" OpenGL or GLSL, but it is necessary to ensure that your machine supports at least version 4.1 of OpenGL. If you do not know what version of OpenGL your machine supports, a list is available on the Apple website [AP18].

B.1.3 Installing JOGL

To install JOGL, visit the JogAmp website [JO16], http://jogamp.org. There, as of this writing (September 2018), the current version of JOGL is found in the Builds/Downloads section—look under Current and click on [zip]. The latest stable JOGL files are then displayed in a folder named /deployment/jogamp-current/archive. Download the following:

```
jogamp-all-platforms.7z
jogl-javadoc.7z
```

Unzip these files into the folder on your machine where you would like to store the JOGL system.

The unzipped jogamp-all-platforms file contains a folder named jar which contains several important files that will be used by your applications:

```
jogl-all.jar
jogl-all-natives-macosc-universal.jar
gluegen-rt.jar
gluegen-rt-natives-macosc-universal.jar
```

Traditionally these files would be placed in the /System/Library/Java/ Extensions folder. However, this Extensions mechanism has been deprecated [OR18]. So a better strategy going forward is to add paths to these files to your CLASSPATH environment variable.

After you have copied the above files onto your machine, go into the jogl-javadoc folder and double-click the file named index.html. This opens the JOGL javadocs in a browser, which you should then bookmark for future reference.

B.1.4 Installing JOML

To install JOML, visit the JOML GitHub page and click on "Releases," or navigate directly to the Releases page [J17]. You'll probably want to download the latest version (1.9.11 at the time of this writing), specifically the .jar file named joml-1.9.11.jar.

After downloading the .jar file, move it to wherever you would like to store JOML on your machine Then add the full path name of the .jar file to your CLASSPATH environment variable.

There is a lot of helpful reference material on JOML and how to most effectively use it. Note especially two pages definitely worth bookmarking:

- the readme for using JOML with JOGL [JJ17]
- the JOML Wiki [JW17]

B.2 MODIFYING THE JAVA/OPENGL/GLSL APPLICATION CODE FOR THE MAC

For the most part, the Java programs themselves, as described in this textbook, will run as-is. There are, however, a small number of changes that must be made. Some of these changes won't make much sense until one has studied the corresponding programming sections in the text. The reader may choose to skip parts of this section and return to it later while learning the material in question. Despite the possible risk of introducing confusion, we have decided to place all of the code changes for the Macintosh here, so that they are assembled in one place.

B.2.1 Modifying the Java Code

Many Macs default to much earlier versions of OpenGL. To force use of the latest version of OpenGL on the hardware, in each of the code examples in this book replace the line of code

```
myCanvas = new GLCanvas();
```

with the following lines:

```
GLProfile glp = GLProfile.getMaxProgrammableCore(true);
GLCapabilities caps = new GLCapabilities(glp);
myCanvas = new GLCanvas(caps);
```

B.2.2 Modifying the GLSL Code

Some changes will need to be made at various locations in our GLSL shader code (and some of the associated Java/OpenGL code) because of the slightly earlier version of OpenGL (specifically, 4.1) present in Macs:

- The specified version number in the shaders must be changed. Presuming that your Mac supports version 4.1, at the top of each shader locate the line that says

    #version 430

    and change it to

    #version 410

- Version 4.1 doesn't support layout binding qualifiers for texture sampler variables. This affects material starting from Chapter 5. You'll need to remove the layout binding qualifiers and replace them with another command that accomplishes the same thing. Specifically, look for lines in the shaders that have the following format:

    layout (binding=0) uniform sampler2D samp;

    The texture unit number specified in the binding clause might be different (it is "0" here), and the name of the sampler variable might be different (it is "samp" here). In any case, you'll need to remove the layout clause and simplify the command so that it just says

    uniform sampler2D samp;

    Then you'll need to add the following command to the Java program, for each texture enabled:

    glUniform1i(gl.glGetUniformLocation(renderingProgram, "samp"), 0);

    immediately after the glBindTexture() command in the Java display() function, where samp is the name of the uniform sampler variable and the 0 in the above example is the texture unit specified in the binding command that was removed earlier.

B.2.3 Compiling and Running a Program

To compile a program, open a terminal window, navigate to the parent folder of the .java files (if using the code on the accompanying CD, you can recognize this parent folder because it contains the compile.bat and run.bat files intended for use with a PC) and type

```
javac code/*.java
```

To run your compiled program, type

```
java code.Code
```

B.2.4 Additional Notes

- Pathname separators are sometimes listed as "\" in the textbook. These may need to be changed to "/" for the Mac.

References

[AP18] "Mac computers that use OpenCL and OpenGL graphics," accessed September 2018, https://support.apple.com/en-us/HT202823

[J17] JOML, Releases, accessed December 2017, https://github.com/JOML-CI/JOML/releases

[JJ17] JOML, "Using with JOGL," accessed December 2017, https://github.com/JOML-CI/JOML#using-with-jogl

[JO16] JogAmp, accessed July 2016, http://jogamp.org/

[JW17] JOML, wiki, accessed December 2017, https://github.com/JOML-CI/JOML/wiki

[OR18] "The Extension Mechanism for Support of Optional Packages" (Oracle), accessed September 2018, https://docs.oracle.com/javase/8/docs/technotes/guides/extensions/index.html

USING THE NSIGHT GRAPHICS
DEBUGGER

Debugging GLSL shader code is notoriously difficult. Unlike programming in typical languages such as Java or C++, it is often unclear exactly where a shader program failed. Often, a shader error manifests as a blank screen, offering no clues as to the nature of the error. Even more frustrating is that there is no way to print out the values of shader variables during run time, as one would commonly do when tracking down an elusive bug.

We listed some techniques for detecting OpenGL and GLSL errors in Section 2.2. Despite the help that these techniques provide, the lack of a simple ability to display shader variables is a serious handicap.

For this reason, graphics card manufacturers have sometimes provided capabilities in hardware for extracting information from shaders at run time, and then built tools for accessing the information in the form of a *graphics debugger*. Each manufacturer's debugging tool(s) work only in the presence of that manufacturer's graphics card. NVIDIA's graphics debugger is part of a larger suite of tools called *Nsight*, and AMD has a similar suite of tools called *CodeXL*. This appendix describes how to get started using Nsight with Java/JOGL on a PC (Windows) machine.

C.1 ABOUT NVIDIA NSIGHT

Nsight is an NVIDIA suite of tools that includes a graphics debugger, which makes it possible to look inside the stages of the OpenGL graphics pipeline, including shaders, while a program is running. It isn't necessary to change the code at all, or to add any code. Simply run an existing program with Nsight enabled. Nsight allows examining shaders at runtime, such as seeing the current contents of a shader's uniform variables. It also enables seeing the C calls being made by a JOGL-wrapped program.

There are versions of Nsight for Windows and for Linux/MacOS, including versions that run under Microsoft's Visual Studio and under the Eclipse IDE. As of this writing the Eclipse version of Nsight does not appear to provide graphics debugging support for Java-based programs, so we restrict our discussion to the Windows Visual Studio–based version, which can be made to work with Java/JOGL.

The Visual Studio (VS) version of Nsight was originally developed for debugging shader programs under control of application code written in C++. However, it is possible to get it to work with Java programs as well. To do this, the C++ plugin must first be installed in VS. This plugin among other things allows invoking an "external program" written in a different language—e.g., Java. So the approach we take is to set up VS as if it was going to run C++ code, then instead have it invoke our Java/JOGL application as an "external program."

Nsight works only with compatible NVIDIA graphics cards; it won't work with Intel or AMD graphics cards. A complete list of supported cards is available on the NVIDIA website [NS18].

■C.2■ SETTING UP NSIGHT FOR JOGL

Setting up Nsight for JOGL is suprisingly easy. Our instructions are based on version 5.3 of Nsight.

1. If you haven't already done so, install Visual Studio (VS), such as *Visual Studio 2017 Community*. Be sure to include the C++ core compiler. Note that Visual Studio installation can be notoriously slow. Visual Studio 2017 is available at https://www.visualstudio.com/downloads.

2. Install NVIDIA Nsight, Visual Studio Edition. This should be quicker than the installation of Visual Studio in step 1. While installing, the CUDA elements aren't necessary (unless you want them for other reasons). Nsight is available at https://developer.nvidia.com/nsight-visual-studio-edition.

3. Run Visual Studio, and make sure that the Nsight menu appears at the top of the menu bar.

4. Under the File menu, choose "New Project." A large selection box appears. On the left pane, click on "Visual C++" (so that it highlights), then in the

center box, choose "Windows Console Application"; then, in the lower right, click OK. After a few seconds, a short C++ program main should appear. We will not be using this C++ program, but it must be present.

Note: We are NOT going to enter our Java source code into Visual Studio. Instead, we are going to run our already-compiled Java/JOGL program as an "external application."

C.3 RUNNING A JAVA/JOGL APPLICATION IN NSIGHT

We continue our step-by-step instructions here with step 5.

5. In the right pane (called the "Solution Explorer"), the second line immediately under "Solution 'Console Application'" should show the name of the project, which is probably something like ConsoleApplication1. Right-click on that project name. A large menu should appear. Near the bottom is "Nsight User Properties." Click on that, as shown here:

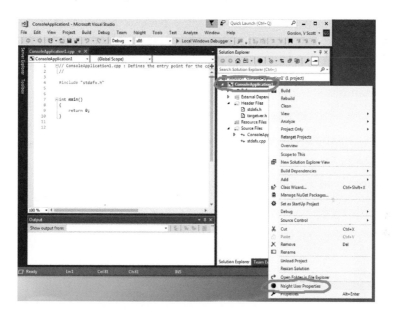

Note that VS has inserted a short default C++ program in the large left page. We will ignore this code—the steps that follow show how to launch our Java/JOGL program instead.

6. The Launch Action pane should appear (as shown in the image that follows). There are three things that need to be changed on this pane.

First, click the button to select "Launch external program": The box to the right of that probably contains something like $(LocalDebuggerCommand). Change that entry to instead contain the path to the Java SDK executable. On most Windows machines, this will be something like C:\Program Files\ Java\jdk1.8.0_101\bin\java.exe

Second, further down on the same pane, under Launch Options, there is a line that says "Command line arguments." In the box to the right of that, replace whatever is there with the command line arguments needed to run your Java/JOGL application. Each argument must be in its own set of quotations. For example, if you usually run your program with a command such as

> java –Dsun.java2d.d3d=false code.Code

then the entry in the argument box would need to be

> "-Dsun.java2d.d3d=false" "code.Code"

Note the sets of double quotes around EACH parameter, separately, with the last item being the Java/JOGL executable application.

Third, further down on the same pane is a line that says "Working directory:"; in the box to the right of that, replace whatever is there with the path to the directory from which you would execute the command to run your program (i.e., the call to "java" shown immediately above). For example, something like

> C:\Users\gordonvs\Documents\graphics\cubes

Note the box to the right of "Connection name:" probably says localhost; don't change that. Leave that entry as it is.

Here is an example screenshot showing all three changes:

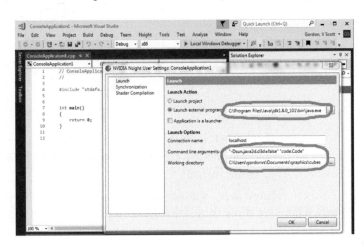

7. Click "OK" in the lower right. The NVIDIA Nsight User Settings box should close.

8. Under the File menu, save the project.

9. Under the Nsight menu (along the top menu bar), choose "Start Graphics Debugging" as shown here:

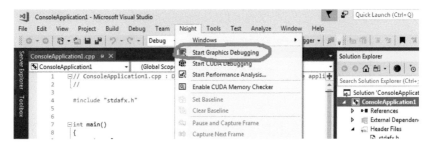

10. A window will pop up asking if you want to "connect without security?" Click on "Connect unsecurely." This should cause your external Java/JOGL graphics program to execute. You should see both a terminal window and your running program appear. Nsight may superimpose some information over your running program. Here is an example:

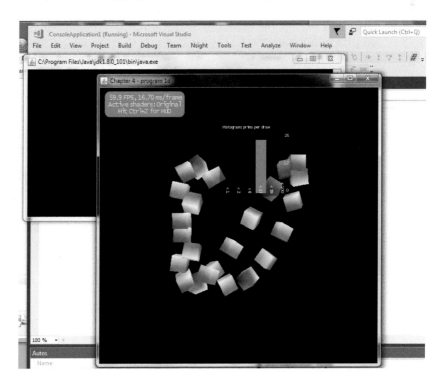

11. Once your program is running, interact with it in whatever area you wish to examine; then, from the Nsight menu, select "Pause and Capture Frame" as shown here:

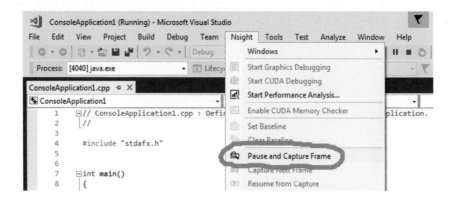

12. The Frame Debugger screen should appear, along with a HUD toolbar and a horizontal selection tool called a "scrubber." Your program will likely freeze at this point. In the center of the debugger screen is a left bar with buttons for each shader stage. For example, you can highlight "VS" for "Vertex Shader," and in the larger center box to its right, you can scroll down and look at the contents of the uniform variables (presuming you have "API inspector" selected above it). In the following figure, the small box to the right of "mv_matrix" has been opened, revealing the contents of the 4×4 MV matrix.

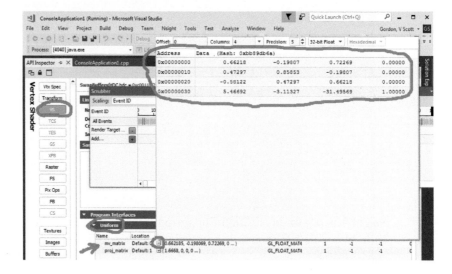

13. Another interesting window that appears is one that looks similar to your running program. This window has a timeline along the bottom, which allows you to click and see the sequence of items drawn on the frame. Following is an example—note the cursor has been clicked on the left area of the timeline and it shows those items that have been drawn up to that point:

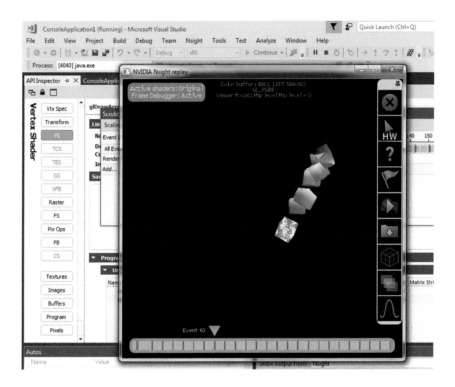

Consult Nsight documentation for details on how to get the most out of the Nsight tool.

References

[NS18] Nsight Visual Studio Edition Supported GPUs (Full List), accessed May 2018, https://developer.nvidia.com/nsight-visual-studio-edition-supported-gpus-full-list

Index